Student Study Gu

# CORRECTIONS
## The Fundamentals

# Burk Foster

PEARSON

Prentice
Hall

Upper Saddle River, New Jersey 07458

10  9  8  7  6  5  4  3
ISBN 0-13-170304-8

# Contents

**Part I. Corrections: History**

      **Chapter 1**     **Early Punishments**  1

      **Chapter 2**     **The Penitentiary and the 1800s**  9

      **Chapter 3**     **Twentieth Century Corrections Systems**  18

      **Chapter 4**     **Ideologies and Sentencing**  28

**Part II. Corrections: Systems**

      **Chapter 5**     **Jails**  39

      **Chapter 6**     **State and Federal Prisons**  50

      **Chapter 7**     **Management and Custody**  62

      **Chapter 8**     **Corrections Policies and Issues**  72

**Part III. Corrections: Prisoners**

      **Chapter 9**     **Male and Female Prisoners**  83

      **Chapter 10**    **Prison Life**  94

      **Chapter 11**    **Special Needs Prisoners**  108

      **Chapter 12**    **Prisoners' Rights**  122

**Part IV. Corrections: Alternatives**

      **Chapter 13**    **Rehabilitation**  137

      **Chapter 14**    **Parole and Release from Prison**  149

      **Chapter 15**    **Probation and Community Corrections**  162

      **Chapter 16**    **Contrasting Philosophies: American and International Corrections Today**  176

      **Answers to Chapter Self Tests**  194

# Preface

This study guide accompanies *Corrections: The Fundamentals,* a new text for introductory college courses in corrections. Being given the opportunity to prepare the study guide for my own text, I have taken the same approach that I have used in similar supplements over the years. The study guide follows the chapter structure of the text. Within each chapter, the format is the same:

    1. Chapter objectives introduce and outline the material in each chapter.

    2. Key terms featured in the text are also highlighted in the study guide.

    3. A narrative summary condenses the contents of each chapter.

    4. A self-test section provides three types of sample objective questions–multiple choice, true/false, and fill in the blanks–and several discussion questions. Answers to the objective questions are listed in an answer key arranged by chapters in the back of the study guide. Each answer is referenced to a page number in the text.

Because I wrote both the text and the study guide to it, I can only point to myself for any errors of style or substance that may be discovered. I hope such errors are few, and that this study guide serves its basic purposes as I see them: providing a brief review of the longer text, and giving students examples of the types of questions that might be posed about the material it contains.

## Acknowledgments

If you notice that many of the examples I use in my own writing make use of Louisiana, my adopted state, it is plainly because I have conducted research and worked inside jails and prisons--with both prisoners and staff--around the state for 30 years. Most of what I know about corrections is directly related to my work teaching corrections courses at the University of Louisiana-Lafayette. I wish to acknowledge the contribution of several of my colleagues here, particularly Dr. Clifford Dorne, Ken Jaccuzzo, and the late Sally McKissack, for sharing their perspectives on corrections with me. I am also most grateful to the staff and inmates of the Louisiana State Penitentiary at Angola--in particular Wilbert Rideau (now among the ex-prisoner population), Douglas Dennis, Lane Nelson, and the late Ron Wikberg--and to Warden C. M. Lensing, Jr., of Hunt Correctional Center for showing me the real world of prisons. Among the people at Prentice Hall who worked with me on *Corrections: The Fundamentals*, I would like to thank Mayda Bosco, Barbara Cappuccio, and Frank Mortimer; I also enjoyed the assistance of former Prentice Hall staff member Korrine Dorsey. They have all been great people to work with over the years.

## About the Author

Burk Foster is associate professor of criminal justice at the University of Louisiana-Lafayette, where he has been a faculty member since 1974. A former civilian police officer in Oklahoma, where he completed undergraduate and graduate degrees at the University of Oklahoma, he served as a lieutenant in the U.S. Air Force Security Police. After his move to Louisiana, his academic interests turned toward sentencing and corrections. He has testified as an expert witness in state and federal courts on issues related to corrections and the death penalty. Although he is not a convict and has never aspired to be one, he was a writer and contributing editor of *The Angolite*, the magazine of the Louisiana State Penitentiary, for 16 years. Professor Foster and Angola inmate Lane Nelson are co-authors of *Death Watch: A Death Penalty Anthology* (2001). His primary research interests at present focus on the history of prisons and the death penalty. He is a long-time member of the Academy of Criminal Justice Sciences and the American Correctional Association. In addition to the criminal justice courses he teaches at UL-Lafayette, he also teaches and directs seminars in the University's Honors Program.

CHAPTER ONE

# Early Punishments

Cesare Beccaria, who wrote the influential collection of essays *On Crimes and Punishments* in 1764, was an advocate of rational punishments to prevent and deter crime. He wrote, "The end of punishment, therefore, is no other than to prevent the criminal from doing further injury to society, and to prevent others from committing the like offense." This chapter considers the punishments early societies imposed on criminals before the development of modern prisons. The social and legal contexts of society before the 1700s were very different from what they are in most of the world today, and the types of punishments used on criminals were also very different from what we would expect today. After reading this chapter, you should be familiar with:

1. The forms of punishment most often used in societies through the 1700s.
2. The social and legal contexts within which punishments were applied.
3. Early and modern legal codes.
4. The impact of the Age of Enlightenment on eighteenth century Europe.
5. The views of several important correctional scholars and reformers of this period.
6. The institutions early societies used to hold criminals and social misfits.

## Key Terms

corporal punishment
whipping
branding
capital punishment
exile
banishment
outlawry
transportation
indentured servitude
slavery
economic sanctions
public humiliation
pillory
stocks
ducking stool
folkways
mores
Code of Hammurabi
Justinian Code
canon law
civil law
socialist law
common law
Islamic law
Shari'a

Age of Enlightenment
Cesare Beccaria
Jeremy Bentham
utilitarianism
hedonic calculus
Panopticon
John Howard
typhus
gaol fever
John Howard Society
William Penn
Quakers
Great Law
gaol
jail
detention
fee system
Bridewell
Houses of Correction
monastery
asylum
Mamertine Prison
Hospice of San Michele
Maison de Force
hulks

## Punishing Criminals: Corporal Punishments

In contemporary society we typically imagine a crime as being worth so much time in custody--three months, two years, ten years, in rare cases the rest of the criminal's natural life. But this notion of punishment as time in custody is of recent vintage in humankind's history. The use of the modern prison to lock up convicted criminals is only about 200 years old. What did early societies do with criminals before they started locking them up?

We know that early societies made frequent use of physical punishments, particularly corporal punishments and capital punishment. **Corporal punishment** is defined as any punishment that involves infliction of pain on the human body. A variety of such punishments come to mind--whipping, beating, branding, mutilation, and burning among the most common forms. Over time **whipping** emerged as the most prevalent method of physically

1

punishing criminals in early Western societies. A painful yet measured punishment, whipping was usually neither fatal nor incapacitating for life. The criminal would bear scars, but he would also be capable of resuming life as a productive citizen.

Other corporal punishments had their place. **Branding** of criminals with a hot iron became a more common practice by the sixteenth and seventeenth century. Not only did it cause pain, but it was also a useful method of marking criminals--an early form of criminal identification.

## Punishing Criminals: Death

**Capital punishment** in many forms was also common in early societies. Before the 1800s, the death penalty was generally available not only as a punishment for the most serious degree of homicide (as it is in the U.S. today) but for any serious crime, if the judge believed the offender deserved it. Torture before death was also commonplace.

Most felony offenses under English common law eventually became capital crimes. The prevalent methods of executing criminals changed over time. Early societies settled on simple methods, such as stoning, which was commonly used in Biblical times. Hanging and beheading were most common in the early modern era in Europe. In the first decade of the twenty-first century, shooting, beheading, hanging, and, in the United States, lethal injection are the principal methods employed by those nations still carrying out death sentences.

## Punishing Criminals: Exile

Many early societies, and a few more recent ones, avoided executing some deserving criminals by casting them out of society--sending them to some distant place and forbidding them to return home. This practice was called **exile** or **banishment** in its origins. In his historical writings, Robert Johnson has called the wilderness "the first penal colony," meaning a place to which criminals were sent. The British used the term **outlawry** to indicate a status outside the law.

From the 1600s through the mid-1800s, England practiced **transportation** of convicted felons to its colonies-- first to America, and later to Australia. The status of these convicts was closely akin to the British practice of **indentured servitude** existing at the same time. Private persons (usually poor people in extreme financial difficulty) sold their labor to an entrepreneur; they were bound by contract for the duration. At the end of the term, the servants went free. Convicts were also bound, but they were not volunteers and signed no contracts. Their status was more like that of persons held under **slavery**, except that slavery was for a lifetime (and into subsequent generations) while indentured servitude was for a specific period of years. This concept of penal servitude as being essentially equivalent to slave status would be very important to the evolution of the American prison after the founding of the penitentiary.

## Punishing Criminals: Other Sanctions

Early societies were not completely reliant on penalties imposing death, physical pain, banishment, or forced labor. From what we know of early legal systems, **economic sanctions** were commonly available for imposition on both property and violent criminals, at the court's discretion. Today we think of economic sanctions as being of two types--fines and restitution. In earlier societies, the compensation went directly to the victim or the victim's family, and not to the government. If the criminals were too poor or too deeply in debt to pay compensation, indentured servitude and slavery were options.

In the American colonies, **public humiliation** of criminals was used more often than it was in Europe, and the European physical punishments were used less. Public humiliation took many forms. Minor offenders, such as drunks, lazy workers, or people who had violated religious laws, might be displayed on the town square in a **pillory**, standing up with head and hands locked in a wooden frame, or the **stocks**, where a seated criminal would have both feet and hands locked in a frame. Women who nagged their spouses or gossiped might find themselves in a **ducking stool**, which was a chair on the end of a rope or the end of a see-saw in which they would be dunked in a creek to near drowning and warned about their behavior.

## The Social and Legal Context of Punishment

In the earliest historical societies, behavior was directed by social customs, called **folkways** and **mores**, more than by laws or formal rules. When someone violated these customs by an act of illicit sex, violence, or sorcery, it was up to a community leader, typically a tribal or later a village elder, to decide the appropriate penalty, perhaps in consultation with other advisors. No reference book of sanctions existed. Even after some of the larger and more complex cultures began to write down their laws and try to apply some kind of uniformity to the process by which members were judged and punished, most other people on earth continued to live in cultures where justice was much more informal, personal, and spontaneous.

## Early Legal Codes

Over time the more literate societies did develop written codes of laws. The Babylonian **Code of Hammurabi**--from about 2,000 B.C.--is the oldest extant legal code. Other well-known ancient codes includes the Hebrew law of Moses and various codes of the Greeks, particularly those of Draco and Solon. None of these ancient codes served as the direct basis of modern legal codes.

The thousand year history of Roman law, from the Twelve Tables of about 450 B.C. to the *Corpus Juris Civilis* of the Byzantine Emperor Justinian in the sixth century, was much more influential. The **Justinian Code**, published in two successive editions in 529 and 533 A.D., was a compilation of earlier Roman codes going back several hundred years. In the Middle Ages, when scholars began teaching the law in early law schools, they taught from this code and from the **canon law** of the Roman Catholic Church. The Justinian Code was the main secular, or worldly, law of the medieval period; canon law was ecclesiastical, or church, law. Canon law eventually diminished in importance as the influence of the medieval Church declined, but many of its principles were combined with Roman law to make up early continental or civil law.

## Modern Legal Codes

Legal scholars of today define four major families of law--civil law, common law, Islamic law, and socialist law. Two of these, civil law and socialist law, are directly descended from Roman law. Common law developed in Britain between the time of the Norman Conquest (1066) and the seventeenth century. Islamic law is based on the Qu'ran, written down in the seventh century by disciples of the Prophet Muhammad, who had recited its verses to his listeners as he said they had been told to him by the angel Gabriel.

**Civil law** became the predominant legal family on the continent of Europe. Based on the Roman law tradition, its two most important codifications in the modern era were the Napoleonic Code of early nineteenth century France and the Germanic Law of the People of the late nineteenth century. Civil law emphasizes the authority of the judge in getting at the truth of the matter at issue.

**Socialist law** prevails in those countries that have adopted communism as an economic system. The two most important examples of socialist law are the Soviet Union and China. Socialist law tended to be civil law but recast into a classless society in which the means of production were owned and managed by the state. The law is used to serve the interests of the communist party, and direct public participation at all levels is emphasized.

**Common law** is English law found today in various forms among English-speaking countries. Common law was made by English judges over a long period of time. The law was based on precedent, or previous decisions, and it was applied in practice for several centuries before it was written down in code form. It proceeds through an adversarial system emphasizing the opposing roles of prosecutor and defense counsel battling before a (supposedly) impartial judge. It is concerned with the due process rights of criminal defendants.

**Islamic law** is important in Muslim countries. It is different from the other legal systems because in its pure form it is religious law, God's law as revealed to Muhammad and recorded in the Qu'ran, the Muslin holy book. Islamic law, known as **Shari'a** ("the way"), combines religious expertise and legal expertise, and the interpretation of the law is left more to religious scholars than to legal functionaries. Crimes against God--including apostasy, rebellion, theft, adultery, and drug offenses--are the most serious criminal offenses.

## The Age of Enlightenment

The eighteenth century was a time of important change in the West, a time of intellectual inquiry articulating new perspectives on government, law, and society. During this **Age of Enlightenment**, the traditional methods of punishing criminals would be among many social institutions undergoing dramatic transformation. More and more, rational scholars rejected the absolute authority of church and state and advocated improving the lot of humanity by promoting tolerance and overcoming ignorance. New ideas and approaches were needed to eliminate the thriving criminal habits that were accompanying the growth of modern urban society.

## Scholars and Reformers

Many philosophers and practitioners influenced the changing views of law and crime that prevailed by the end of the 1700s. The most influential thinker of this era, in terms of his impact on the legal system, was the Italian nobleman, **Cesare Beccaria**. In 1764, this 26-year-old Milanese aristocrat published *On Crimes and Punishments*, a small volume of essays on the legal process and criminal punishments. As one of the founders of the Classical School of Criminology, Beccaria emphasized the need for law to be in conformity with the rationality and free will of humanity. He argued that the law ought to provide "the greatest happiness of the greatest number," which became the central concept of Utilitarian philosophy.

Following a few years behind Beccaria was the British political activist, legal scholar, and social philosopher **Jeremy Bentham**, who is known as the founder of British **utilitarianism**. Bentham claimed that all laws, ancient or modern, should be evaluated according to the single ethical principle of utility. A law is good or bad depending upon whether or not it increased general happiness of the population. Bentham was known as the originator of the **hedonic calculus** (or hedonistic calculus). His argument was that human action is based on our desire to maximize pleasure while minimizing pain.

Bentham designed a model prison called the **Panopticon**, or Inspection-House, a circular prison in which large square cells with glass front and rear walls faced a central guard tower. He proposed it as a model of prison discipline in which the intent was to create the perception of perpetual observation--to make the criminal think he was constantly under surveillance, and to make the watchers think that someone was always watching them as well.

One of Bentham's contemporaries was the English sheriff and reformer **John Howard**. Howard's work after his appointment as High Sheriff of Bedforshire in 1773 earned him historical recognition as the "father of prison reform." In 1777 he published *The State of Prisons in England and Wales, with Preliminary Observations and an Account of Some Foreign Prisons*, a 489-page book based on conditions he had observed in his travels in Britain and on the continent.

Howard introduced the word "penitentiary," to describe the ideal place to accomplish his reforms and induce penitence in the prisoner. The English Parliament, strongly influenced by his writing and advocacy, passed the Penitentiary Act of 1779, which provided for four major reforms--secure and sanitary structures, systematic inspections, abolition of fees for basic services, and a reformatory regime. These principles resulted in no immediate changes.

In 1790, while visiting Russian military hospitals, Howard contracted the infectious disease **typhus**, also known as **gaol fever**, which was spread by fleas and body lice. He contrtacted a fever and died. His legacy lives on more than two centuries later through the work of the **John Howard Society**, the international correctional reform organization.

In America the earliest correctional reformer of a stature comparable to Howard was the Quaker **William Penn**. Penn had been locked up several times as a young man in England, when the government was trying to stifle the **Quakers** as a dissident religious sect. When he founded the colony of Pennsylvania in 1682, as a land grant from Charles II, Penn adopted a legal code, referred to as the **Great Law**, that was very different from other legal codes of its time. It substituted imprisonment at hard labor for physical punishments. It first abolished the death penalty entirely, then reinstated it only for premeditated murder (similar to the capital offense of first degree murder today). Caring for prisoners became a public responsibility, and prisons were required to provide free food and lodging, rather than charging inmates fees, as was then common in England.

## Early Correctional Institutions: Gaols

From medieval times to the modern era, the basic English correctional institution was the **gaol**, Americanized as **jail** but pronounced the same way. The jail was a small town facility (or in a large city, such as London, a neighborhood facility) whose purpose was **detention**, or holding people for court. Gaols could range in size from one room to something the size of an old castle. Most colonial American jails were simply one-room wooden or stone structures that could be locked up.

Gaol populations were diverse--debtors; pre-trial inmates; sentenced inmates awaiting imposition of sentence; the poor and vagrants; the mentally ill; political dissidents and religious heretics (who were often confined in significant numbers in times of more rigid orthodoxy); runaway servants. Everyone was mixed up together--men and women; boys and girls; the insane and the sane; civil and criminal commitments--typically in conditions of vice, idleness, filth, malnourishment, disease, and despair. Gaols operated on the **fee system**, which charged prisoners daily fees to make money for the sheriffs and businessmen who operated the institutions.

## Early Correctional Institutions: Workhouses

From the 1500s through the 1800s, England developed a system of local workhouses to keep transient laborers (and the women and children who followed after them) from disrupting city life. In sixteenth century London, the **Bridewell**, formerly the king's palace, was turned into a refuge and workhouse for the displaced rural poor flooding into London from the countryside. **Houses of Correction** were created by statute in England in 1574 to house "rogues, vagabonds, and sturdy beggars." As time went on they came to house prisoners of all sorts, including political and religious dissenters.

Across Europe **the monastery** long played an important dual social role quite apart from its role as the center of religious teaching and learning. Church officials guilty of criminal or grossly inappropriate conduct were rarely punished in the secular courts; if they needed to be removed from their positions, many were sent to monasteries where they could be isolated and punished--doing the same kind of penance later associated with the penitentiary. The other purpose of the monastery was to help the poor. Poor wanderers in need of a handout or a place to stay could always seek refuge in a monastery.

The mentally ill were another problem for society in transition from medieval to modern times. From Roman times persons suffering from mental disorders had been viewed as possessed by evil spirits. They were generally subjected to torture and confinement, right along with criminals, and later were placed in an institution, the **asylum**, which grew very large in size long before the modern prison.

## Early Correctional Institutions: Prisons

Prisons in their early days were often no more than caves or holes that could be secured in some fashion. The **Mamertine Prison**, which was a dungeon under the sewers of Rome, is often identified as the first known ancient prison. The early Christians were kept there along with other political and religious criminals, until they were killed in the arena, sold into slavery, or otherwise eliminated.

Two continental European prisons were much admired as institutional models in the late eighteenth century. The **Hospice of San Michele** was built in Rome in 1704. It held delinquent youths and young men, like a modern reformatory. The inscription over the entrance to the hospice read: "It is insufficient to restrain the wicked by punishment unless you render them virtuous by corrective discipline."

The other model institution was the **Maison de Force** in Ghent, Belgium. Opening as a workhouse in 1773, this institution for beggars and vagrants was widely admired for its humane, reformative approach. The administrator, Jean-Jacques Vilain, maintained a system of strict discipline but avoided the excessive cruelty to prisoners that was commonplace in this era.

At the other end of the scale, probably the very worst institutions of this time were not proper prisons at all; they were ships, old ships at anchor in the harbor. They were called prison ships, or **hulks**, unseaworthy and sometimes sinking. The mortality rates on the hulks were the highest of any prisons of their era. The HMS Jersey and her dozen or so sister ships anchored in New York Harbor were responsible for more American deaths in the Revolutionary War--an estimated 11,500 sailors and soldiers dying in captivity--than all the deaths resulting from battle. Although prison ships were considered a temporary solution to jail and prison overcrowding on dry land, they were in use in Britain for over a hundred years, until about 1875, when prison building finally caught up with the population in confinement.

# SELF TEST

## Multiple Choice

1. This legal family is based most directly on religious principles:
   - a. civil law
   - b. Islamic law
   - c. socialist
   - d. common law
   - e. none of these

2. An offender sentenced to penal servitude was in essence being sentenced to a life of:
   - a. solitary confinement
   - b. banishment
   - c. slavery
   - d. military service
   - e. torture and mutilation

3. Which of the following would have been least likely to be found locked up in a jail several hundred years ago?
   - a. a dangerous inmate awaiting trial
   - b. a political dissident
   - c. a felon serving a sentence of ten years in prison
   - d. a debtor
   - e. a religious heretic

4. The basic purpose of the Bridewell was:
   - a. a floating jail
   - b. an insane asylum
   - c. to hold runaway husbands
   - d. a workhouse
   - e. to hold those awaiting hanging

5. The Italian legal scholar whose work, *On Crimes and Punishment*, promoted sweeping legal reforms, including the development of the penitentiary, was:
   - a. Cesare Beccaria
   - b. Guido Sarducci
   - c. Vito Corleone
   - d. Enrico Fermi
   - e. Benito Mussolini

6. The English practice of transportation was most closely related to the earlier practice of:
   - a. mutilation
   - b. public humiliation
   - c. property forfeiture
   - d. banishment
   - e. hanging

7. This infectious disease, carried by body lice, was so prevalent in English jails that it was called gaol fever:
   - a. malaria
   - b. typhus
   - c. diphtheria
   - d. mumps
   - e. rheumatic fever

8. What were prison hulks in England?
   - a. a type of cell
   - b. big, mean, sometimes greenish guards
   - c. old ships
   - d. a torture device
   - e. inmates who had been locked up a long time

9. Who made up the clientele of the Hospice of San Michele?
   - a. terminally ill inmates
   - b. women inmates training to be nuns
   - c. boys and young men
   - d. political criminals
   - e. drug addicts

10. Four of the following were provisions included in the Penitentiary Act of 1779 in England. Which one was NOT?

    a. secure and sanitary prison facilities         d. abolition of fees charged inmates
    b. a reformatory regime                    e. early parole of reformed inmates
    c. regular inspection

## True or False

_____ 11. The Great Law of the Quakers was unusual for colonial times in that it provided for the death penalty only in cases of premeditated murder.

_____ 12. Most of the rationalist scholars of the Age of Enlightenment agreed that the courts were too soft on crime; they wanted to see more severe punishment of criminals, including public executions.

_____ 13. Outlawry was an early practice which expelled the offender from the tribe or community.

_____ 14. Branding with a hot iron was used not only as a punishment but also as a form of criminal identification.

_____ 15. The legal codes of the Middle Ages on the continent of Europe rejected any influence of the Catholic Church, recognizing that the Church should not influence matters of state.

_____ 16. Although early courts made frequent use of physical punishments, they also applied economic sanctions such as fines and forfeiture of property to many offenders.

_____ 17. Small towns in colonial America rejected the practice of public humiliation of offenders, holding that it was degrading and barbaric.

_____ 18. Historians agree that the jails of the Middle Ages were generally pleasant, comfortable environments for the offenders confined there.

_____ 19. The Panopticon was a model prison designed to practice continuous surveillance of convicts.

_____ 20. English common law is said to be based directly on the old Hebrew law of Moses.

## Fill In the Blanks

21. The Belgian stronghouse whose regime of work and silence would prove very influential in the development of later prisons was the _____.

22. The English practice of sending criminals to the American colonies and Australia was called _____.

23. The English sheriff recognized as the most influential correctional practitioner of his time was _____.

24. This philosophy, important to development of the penitentiary, viewed the aim of society as being to provide the greatest good for the largest number of citizens; it was known as _____.

25. The Age of _____ was a time of great intellectual and political activity, from which many ideas critical to modern government emerged.

26. Islamic law is known by the term _____, meaning "the way."

27. Two forms of public humiliation frequently used in colonial America involved the offender being locked in wooden frames on public display; these were called _____ and _____.

28. Torture, mutilation, branding, and whipping are all examples of the class of _____ punishments.

29. The legal family associated with such communist countries as the Soviet Union and China is known as _____ law.

30. The principal piece of prison reform legislation accomplished through the efforts of Sheriff John Howard was the _____.

## Discussion

31. What punishments were most commonly used in pre-modern societies?

32. What kinds of offenders were kept in secure confinement?

33. What legal principles are associated with Cesare Beccaria's Classical School of Criminology?

34. What was John Howard's impact on English corrections?

35. What principal institutions made up the basic correctional alternatives of eighteenth century England?

36. Describe the practice of transportation.

37. What features of the Maison de Force and the Hospice of San Michele attracted so much favorable attention among correctional reformers of the 1700s?

# CHAPTER TWO

# The Penitentiary and the 1800s

This chapter considers the growth of the American penitentiary in the 1800s, and the development of other alternatives as reformers and public officials saw what was happening to the "ideal" social institution they had created. The corrections system of today is the direct descendant of the institutions and alternatives devised in the nineteenth century. After reading this chapter, you should be familiar with:

1. The penitentiary ideal.
2. The two contrasting models of American prisons.
3. Disciplinary practices in early penitentiaries.
4. Origins of probation and parole.
5. Separate prisons for women and juveniles.
6. Southern prisons and convict leasing.
7. Post-Civil War reforms and the reformatory movement.
8. The industrial prison model.

## Key Terms

penitentiary
penance
Thomas Eddy
Pennsylvania Prison Society
Benjamin Rush
Walnut Street Jail
Wymondham Gaol
John Haviland
Eastern State Penitentiary
Pennsylvania system
separate system
isolate system
Auburn
Sing Sing
Auburn system
congregate system
silent system
rule of silence
Elam Lynds
prison stripes
lockstep
cat-o'-nine-tails
suspended sentence
right of sanctuary
benefit of clergy
neck verse
filing of cases
recognizance
surcease
probation
John Augustus
parole
pardon

clemency
Alexander Maconochie
Norfolk Island
marks system
ticket-of-leave
indeterminate sentence
Walter Crofton
conditional liberty
good-time
Elizabeth Gurney Fry
Eliza W. B. Farnham
Indiana State Reformatory
Katherine B. Davis
Mabel Walker Willebrandt
Federal Women's Reformatory
Mary Belle Harris
Alderson
houses of refuge
training schools
Charles Loring Brace
orphan trains
child saving movement
juvenile court
convict lease system
Enoch Cobb Wines
National Prison Association
Rutherford B. Hayes
American Correctional Association
Zebulon Brockway
Elmira Reformatory
Elmira system
hard labor
the hole

## The Penitentiary Ideal

At the end of the 1700s, the word **penitentiary** had been in use for more than 20 years among scholarly intellectuals and reformers but no modern penitentiaries had been built. The penitentiary was more of an idea, or a set of principles, than a physical institution with shape and form. It was a concept rather than a building.

What was the penitentiary supposed to be? Its purposes were both secular and spiritual. It was supposed to be a place of humane punishment, as opposed to the physical punishments still prevalent in Western societies. It was supposed to be clean and healthy, in contrast to the jail, and to avoid the kind of contamination, both of body and of spirit, that took place in the existing lock-ups. Finally, and perhaps foremost as a social purpose, it was supposed to practice corrective discipline--to create habits of industry through the application of strictly enforced rules. Prisoners ought to work steadily at productive labor, not sit around idle as they often did in old jails and prisons. In the spiritual province, the penitentiary was to be a place of penitence, or **penance**, meaning to express regret for the wrongdoing one has done. The principal goal of the penitentiary was to achieve the kind of spiritual transformation in a criminal being that was associated with the religious beings of the medieval monastery.

Many early advocates of the penitentiary were highly religious. **Thomas Eddy**, who secured passage of a humane penal code in New York in 1796, was a Philadelphia Quaker by way of Virginia and the New York insurance business. Eddy made a fortune quickly and turned to social and legal reforms. He lobbied for, built, and opened New York's first state prison, Newgate, in New York City in 1797.

The most influential prison reformers of the new United States of America were Pennsylvania Quakers. Following the lead of William Penn, the acknowledged father of prison reform in the colonies, the Quakers combined social reforms within religious principles. When the civic-minded Quakers of Philadelphia met at Benjamin Franklin's house in 1787, they organized the Philadelphia Society for Alleviating the Miseries of Public Prisons, known today as the **Pennsylvania Prison Society**. Under the leadership of Dr. **Benjamin Rush**, who is also cited for his contribution to early psychiatry, the society's immediate objective was to improve conditions in the decade-old **Walnut Street Jail** at Sixth and Walnut in downtown Philadelphia.

In 1789 and 1790, the Pennsylvania legislature passed laws to accomplish several reforms. Historian John Roberts calls the redesigned Walnut Street Jail the world's first penitentiary, because it carried out incarceration as punishment, implemented a rudimentary classification system, featured individual cells, and was intended to provide a place for offenders to do penance.

The British had opened **Wymondham Gaol** at Norfolk, England, in 1785, applying John Howard's penitentiary principles. But Walnut Street, with the construction of a new, three-story wing that opened in 1790, became the prototype of the modern penitentiary. Convicted felons were housed in that wing--some in individual cells-- separated from the rest of the inmate population.

## Contrasting Models: Eastern State

In the 1820s, architect **John Haviland** designed and built **Eastern State Penitentiary** on the outskirts of Philadelphia. Featuring seven long cellblocks radiating like spokes from a central rotunda, Haviland's prison incorporated the principles of Quaker reformative imprisonment--complete isolation of inmates, fair treatment, and opportunity for work, reflection, and reformation. The cells were large with high ceilings and each had a skylight--"the eye of God"--and a walled exterior exercise yard, like an enclosed prison patio.

The prisoner was held in total solitary confinement. The **Pennsylvania system** thus came to be known as the **separate system** or **isolate system**. Prisoners were required to work in their cells at manual trades--weaving, leather-working, carpentry, and shoe-making. Keepers brought meals to the cells, and no visitors were allowed. Guards in the central rotunda could keep the entire prison under observation from this one vantage point. This was the model of self-containment in which reformation was intended to take place.

When Charles Dickens visited Eastern State in 1842, he called it a place of "solitary horrors." But his doubts about the effects of solitary confinement did not stem the worldwide tide of enthusiasm for Eastern State's model of reform. Of all nineteenth century prisons built in America, Eastern State came closest to the penitentiary ideal. At least 300 prisons around the world were designed to incorporate its architectural and reformation model--both built on the idea of inmate labor under complete solitary confinement.

## Contrasting Models: Auburn

Even before Eastern State was open for business, a contrasting prison model was being developed in New York. At Auburn in western New York and at Sing Sing 30 miles north of New York City two new prisons, **Auburn and Sing Sing**, were built to replace New York City's Newgate Prison. Auburn and Sing Sing were called prisons, not penitentiaries, when they opened; "penitentiary" was a term that originally meant a particular style of imprisonment neither of these institutions used.

The first convicts were moved into Auburn in 1817. They were housed in small cells--seven feet long by three-and-a-half feet wide by seven feet tall. The cells were stacked atop each other in tiers, and they had no outside exercise yards. Convicts were divided into three levels of control--from complete solitary to group work in the daytime and sleeping in single-person cells at night. The **Auburn system** of inmate management became known as the **congregate system**. It featured inmates living alone in their cells (at least until overcrowding became a persistent problem) while they spent most of their out-of-cell time in the company of other inmates--working, eating, chapel, maintenance and cleaning chores. The system was also called the **silent system**. When the prisoners were in contact with other prisoners, a rule of silence prevailed: no inmate was allowed to speak to another.

## Contrasting Models: And the Winner Is?

Reformers and government officials trekked to Pennsylvania and New York to take a look at the two contrasting prison models. Which system was better: Eastern State or Auburn? While the purists agreed that the Pennsylvania model was closer to ideal, the Auburn model was cheaper to build and operate, requiring fewer guards to service and control the prisoners, and used the space within the walls more intensively. Most important, group labor made it economically more productive. Auburn became the model for the maximum security prison, and solitary confinement came to be seen not as the norm but as punishment for violating prison rules.

## Prison Rules and Discipline

Nineteenth-century prisons employed strict controls and severe disciplinary practices, commonly based on physical punishment. The most important restriction was the **rule of silence** that was applied in Auburn-style prisons. The warden of Auburn and later Sing Sing was Captain **Elam Lynds**, who invented two of the control devices associated with early prisons--**prison stripes** and the **lockstep**. He put inmates in striped uniforms to make them more visible and also to humiliate them. The lockstep was a method of moving convicts around inside prison; prisoners marched--shuffled their feet, actually--with a hand on the shoulder of the man in front of them.

Lynds carried a bullwhip with him when he walked about the prison. He gave each of his guards a **cat-o'-nine-tails**, a whip with several knotted lines or cords attached to its handle. Guards were instructed to flog prisoners for any misconduct. In an early prison expose, *A Voice from Sing-Sing*, written in 1833 by inmate Levi Burr, Sing Sing was described as a "catocracy" for its extensive use of the cat-o'-nine-tails.

In a decade at Auburn and Sing Sing, Elam Lynds practiced what came to be called the Auburn system of prison management. Based on its view of the prisoner as a weak, very inferior being, it established a prison regimen of several key elements--silence, hard labor, regimentation, subservience, and immediate physical punishment. Lynds wanted to break the convict's spirit and remold his character.

This model of prison management became pervasive throughout American prisons in the nineteenth century. Prisoners in custody had no legal rights and no access to courts. What prisoners were allowed and how they were treated depended entirely on the administrators of their prison--in particular the personality and beliefs of the warden, who created the custodial atmosphere. At its heart, the prison relied on physical punishment to maintain discipline by instilling fear in convicts.

## Probation

Modern probation has its roots in earlier practices under English and continental law. In these early systems, it was common to withhold punishment--what today we would call a **suspended sentence**. **Right of sanctuary** under church doctrine set aside holy places for criminals to seek protection from secular laws. In the Middle

Ages, **benefit of clergy** allowed religious officials to avoid punishment in the criminal courts; their cases were referred to high church officials (which is how many of them came to be sent to monasteries for penance). Under English common law, persons who could recite Psalm 51 were presumed to be church officials who would not be punished criminally. So many criminals memorized this chapter of the Bible and used it to "save their necks" that it became known as the **neck verse**.

Other predecessors of probation in use in English and early American courts, such as **filing of cases** and **recognizance**, allowed judges to release deserving offenders without punishment. The suspended sentences these offenders received were less restrictive than contemporary probation; they did not require supervision or impose conditions of compliance on the criminal, as probation does. The European model of **surcease** withheld punishment if the offender committed no new crime during the period of suspension. The suspended sentence is still used for many traffic and petty offenses in American courts.

The origins of modern **probation** in America are often traced to the work of **John Augustus**, a Boston shoe manufacturer and civic leader of the 1840s and 1850s. Although probation was not then a legal sentence (all serious criminals were supposed to go straight to prison, like today's mandatory sentences), Augustus used his influence to persuade judges in Boston courts to assign criminals to his care. Augustus would clean up the criminal, get him a job using his business connections, and help him find a place to live. Later Augustus would take the criminal back to court, where the judge would terminate the sentence.

Civic reformers in Massachusetts were greatly encouraged by Augustus's example. They got the state to pass the first probation statute in 1878, legally allowing the judge to suspend imprisonment. This was to be done only for the selected few who truly deserved it. Probation was initially an informal practice found mostly in urban courts and relying heavily on volunteers, rather than paid probation officers. Over time it became more formalized, under the control of state or county governments. The rise of the juvenile court in the early twentieth century promoted the continued expansion of formal probation services.

## Parole

Today we say that probation is what you get instead of imprisonment; **parole** is what you get at the end of imprisonment. Early release from prison developed in the 1800s after prisons came into common usage, though for antecedents we can look to the king's **pardon** power or **clemency** power through which criminals in the past had been set free from imprisonment or had death sentences cancelled. Parole comes from the Old French *parole d'honneur*, meaning "word of honor." The practice of parole is said to have originated in two British prison systems half a world apart--in Australia and Ireland in the 1840s and 1850s.

**Alexander Maconochie** was a British naval officer and prison critic who in 1840 was made superintendent of Australia's "Devil's Island"--the penal colony of **Norfolk Island** located east of Brisbane. His basic premise was that convicts should be able to earn their way back to the main island through good behavior and hard labor. He set up the **marks system**, using a system of levels through which convicts would pass over time as they earned credits--"marks," he called them--toward their discharge. When they had earned enough marks, they were allowed to leave Norfolk Island on a **ticket-of-leave**. This is called the first example of the modern **indeterminate sentence**, which in effect allowed the prison system to determine when the convict would be released.

In the 1850s, under pressure from severe overcrowding, the Irish prison system under the direction of **Walter Crofton** set up a process in which the inmate moved through several stages toward early release. The sentence was indeterminate, and the release decision was made by the prison superintendent. When the prisoner was discharged, he was granted a ticket-of-leave to return home. His status was that of **conditional liberty**, in that he was still serving his original sentence and could be returned to prison for violating the law. A police officer was assigned to maintain general surveillance of the former prisoner in the community, and to recommend that he be put back in prison if he failed to follow the conditions of his release.

Parole began to be used in the United States in the late 1800s. Many prisoners were already leaving prison early through the use of **good-time** provisions that reduced time served for good behavior and many prisoners benefitted from the generous use of executive clemency by governors; pardons and commutations were frequent. Parole itself was identified specifically with the reformatory, which housed only a small percentage of prisoners in custody. Over time, its usage spread to all prisons. By the mid-1900s, virtually all inmates in American prisons were subject to parole review and conditional release.

## Women's Prisons

Women confined in jails and early prisons were generally mixed with male prisoners and supervised by male jailers, which made the women doubly subject to abuse and exploitation. This began to change in the early 1800s. **Elizabeth Gurney Fry** was an English Quaker and mother of 11 children. After a visit to Newgate prison in 1813, Fry began a ministry for the women of Newgate and eventually other London jails and prisons. She argued for separate prison facilities for women, run by women, and shaped toward the needs of women prisoners as a group different from men.

In the United States, other reformers took up the separatist cause. **Eliza W. B. Farnham** was the head matron of the women's wing at Sing Sing Prison in New York from 1844 to 1848. Like many early reformers, Farnham was often in trouble with her superiors for being too nice to convicts. She was fired after starting an education program for the women inmates that included reading works of fiction.

The **Indiana State Reformatory** was established in 1873 as the first separate prison for women in America. Several of the more progressive states, including Massachusetts and New York, opened separate women's prisons over the next few years. The Bedford Hills Reformatory for Women opened in New York in 1901. Its superintendent, **Katherine B. Davis**, brought in physicians and behavioral scientists to classify and study women prisoners and develop treatment programs.

As assistant attorney general of the United States in the 1920s, **Mabel Walker Willebrandt** was instrumental in the creation of the Federal Bureau of Prisons in 1930. Willebrandt was a Quaker who strongly advocated improving federal prison operations, particularly as they affected young people and women. It was under her direction that the **Federal Women's Reformatory** (initially named the Federal Industrial Institution for Women) at Alderson, West Virginia, opened in 1927. **Dr. Mary Belle Harris**, a Ph.D. in Sanskrit and a concert pianist, was the first warden of this prison, commonly known as **Alderson**. Located in the rolling hills of northern West Virginia, Alderson's cottage plan and absence of fences gave the prison the look of a weekend resort, though its prisoners called it "the farm."

While women prisoners in reformatories may have been expected to "act like ladies," the female inmates remaining in state prisons and local jails were more often treated like household servants and prostitutes. They worked as hard as the men, doing "women's work"--laundry, sewing, cleaning, and cooking. They were under the domination of men, both staff and the male trusties who were prominent in the day-to-day operation of the twentieth-century prison.

## Juvenile Prisons

Many early reformers wanted to separate juveniles from the adult prison system. These efforts were centered in America's large cities, where problems of juvenile criminal and anti-social behavior were most concentrated and most noticeable. In the 1820s and 1830s, New York, Boston, and Philadelphia set up **houses of refuge** to keep juveniles out of jail. The first of these, opened in New York City in 1825, was like a combination shelter and detention center, accepting juveniles convicted of crimes or sentenced as vagrants, a catch-all term for street youths.

By the 1850s, Massachusetts had opened separate **training schools** for boys and girls. Although juveniles were at this time still passing through the same legal system as adults, judges could send boys and girls deserving leniency to these training schools, where they would get the discipline, vocational training, and basic education to prepare them for a law-abiding, productive adult life.

Urban courts of the Northeast and Midwest moved toward de-facto age-based processing of criminals in the later 1800s. Juveniles often received more lenient treatment than adults, with a greater diversity of dispositional options. **Charles Loring Brace** was an early social worker who focused his attention on the poor children of New York City. In 1853, he led a group that founded the Children's Aid Society, which emphasized non-institutional assistance to poor and homeless children and their families. Brace theorized that institutional care "stunted and destroyed children," so his mission was to help their families, or failing this, to place them with new families. He was nationally known for organizing the **orphan trains** that sent many thousands (over 150,000 in 75 years, according to Children's Aid Society statistics) of abandoned, abused, and orphaned children out of New York City to small town and farm families across America. This theme of removing children from the pernicious city environment to the good life of the country became known as the **child-saving movement**.

A century of efforts by reformers to not only separate juveniles from adults but also adopt a less punitive legal approach resulted in the establishment of the first **juvenile court** in Chicago in 1899. Operating on principles of informality, confidentiality, leniency, and paternalism (in the form of the judge taking parental control over the child), this court assumed jurisdiction over its clientele based on age. Its goal, variously expressed in the statutes of the time, was to save, help, or reform (later rehabilitate) youngsters from wasted and sometimes criminal lives. Over the next two decades, other states set up similar courts based on age and emphasizing probation and non-custodial alternatives.

## Southern Prisons and Convict Leasing

Southern states--influenced by rural life, race, and lack of interest in reform--followed a different path in establishing their prison systems in the 1800s. The Civil War was an important influence. Louisiana historian Mark T. Carleton called the Civil War "the most decisive event in the history of the Southern penology," in that it freed the slaves and made them subject to equal punishment under law.

After the Civil War, the **convict lease system** flourished in the South. Several Southern states developed the predecessors of twentieth-century prison farms, following an obvious line of reasoning. Most new black convicts were accustomed to agricultural labor, so it made good business sense to keep them at it, whether on a public farm or one operated by a private owner. The last third of the nineteenth century was slavery rewritten as prison policy. Convicts were worked hard, with little thought for their health, safety, or improvement. Mortality rates were very high, compared to Northern prisons. Convicts privately leased had it the worst, laboring under deplorable conditions in the most primitive settings.

Reforms would eventually come to Southern prisons in the 1900s. But the legacy of local control over prisoners, the emphasis on economy, the lack of attention to rehabilitation, and a racist culture in which white keepers controlled majority black prison populations would continue to make living conditions in Southern prisons much worse than prisons elsewhere.

## The Reform Movement

The penitentiary was created as a reform; by the time of the Civil War, many penologists and social activists saw it as an evil--an institution badly in need of reform itself. In 1870, a well-known New York prison reformer, Dr. **Enoch Cobb Wines**, worked with other corrections critics to found the **National Prison Association**. This organization met in Cincinnati, Ohio, in October 1870. This first Congress, as it was called, was attended by delegates from 24 states and several foreign countries. Its most prominent American member was the Civil War general, **Rutherford B. Hayes**, then governor of Ohio, soon to be president of the United States, and later to serve ten years as president of the association. Delegates met for several days, discussing prison reform ideals and penitentiary shortcomings and, in the end, they adopted a "Declaration of Principles." First on their list was "Reformation, not vindictive suffering, as the purpose of penal treatment."

The Declaration of Principles also called for indeterminate sentencing, separate facilities for women and for juveniles, classification, centralized prison management in each state, and the Irish system of management and parole. It supported abolition of convict leasing, improvement of prison architecture, establishment of prison schools and hospitals, job training for staff, and rewards for good conduct by inmates.

The National Prison Association later changed its name to the American Prison Association and in the 1950s to the **American Correctional Association**. Today it is the largest professional organization of its type in the world. It remains the most important national forum for professional development and for addressing present and future policies in corrections.

## The Reformatory

One of the speakers at the Cincinnati National Prison Congress was an up-and-coming young prison warden, **Zebulon Brockway**. His paper was titled "Ideal for a True Prison System for a State." Six years later, Brockway got the chance to translate his ideals into reality--with the opening of the **Elmira Reformatory** in New York. Receiving its first inmates on July 24, 1876, Elmira was intended as a radical departure from other prisons of its time. It was supposed to work with young men, 18 to 30, who were first offenders and "redeemable."

Influenced by the practices of Maconochie and Crofton, Brockway's **Elmira system** stood in sharp contrast to the penitentiary in several respects. It treated prisoners better (at least officially). The prison did not employ the silent system or the most degrading aspects of the Auburn system then still apparent in American penitentiaries. Prisoners were motivated with rewards, not fear. They earned marks according to their work and behavior. Typically, those starting with a five-year indeterminate sentence could earn release in a year if all went well. When approved for discharge (as being "reformed") by the board of managers, they were released on parole and required to remain in contact with the superintendent.

Brockway's model was very influential in late-1800s prison circles. The penitentiary stood for regimentation and uniformity, while the reformatory promoted individualized treatment based on classification. The penitentiary, following the ideas of Beccaria and the classical school, sought to make the punishment fit the crime; the reformatory used the indeterminate sentence to make the punishment fit the criminal.

Between 1876 and 1913, most larger states of the Northeast and Midwest established reformatories as alternatives to their penitentiaries. While Elmira actually looked like a penitentiary, with its maximum security cellblocks and high walls, later reformatories adopted other architectural models. They incorporated dormitory and cottage housing, and replaced walls with perimeter fences, a feature of most prisons built after World War II. Still, only a small percentage of convicts were referred to reformatories. Those who were repeat offenders or viewed as unsuitable candidates for rehabilitation (which apparently included most blacks, Indians, and other minorities) went to ordinary prisons to do hard labor.

## The Prison as Factory

To most convicted felons of the late 1800s, these fancy sounding terms--probation, parole, reformatory--meant nothing. You were a felon; you went to prison; you worked; you went home. **Hard labor** really meant hard labor, and the reformative possibilities of imprisonment were generally forgotten about--a naively outmoded notion. The reform model changed to the labor model, and the penitentiary changed from a monastery to a factory. Rehabilitation activities did not yet exist in most prisons, and the only people who were idle were those who were too sick to work and those who were locked in solitary confinement--**"the hole"**--on a bread and water diet as punishment. Everyone else was hard at work in the Big House.

## SELF TEST

## Multiple Choice

1. In Walter Crofton's Irish system, what did it mean to the convict when he got a ticket-of-leave?
    a. He got a full pardon for all crimes.
    b. He was about to be executed.
    c. He got a Christmas furlough to go home.
    d. He was released on conditional liberty under supervision.
    e. He was shipped overseas.

2. Which type of prison system was associated with total isolation of inmates, craft work, and outside cells?
    a. Pennsylvania           d. California
    b. Auburn                e. Michigan
    c. Virginia

3. The American Prison Congress meeting of 1870 is considered the start of which era in corrections?
   - a. reformatory
   - b. work release
   - c. corporal punishment
   - d. convict leasing
   - e. deterrence

4. Alexander Maconochie's "mark system" is considered an early predecessor of:
   - a. capital punishment
   - b. psychotherapy
   - c. the indeterminate sentence
   - d. prison uniforms
   - e. solitary confinement

5. Which type of prison system was associated with congregate labor in shops, the rule of silence, and inside cells?
   - a. Attica
   - b. Atlanta
   - c. Auburn
   - d. Australian
   - e. Arkansas

6. Four of the following are associated with Elam Lynds's system of prison discipline; which one is NOT?
   - a. strict rules
   - b. group therapy
   - c. lockstep
   - d. flogging
   - e. prison stripes

7. The Walnut Street Jail in Philadelphia is often identified as the first:
   - a. juvenile group home
   - b. penitentiary
   - c. counseling center
   - d. insane asylum
   - e. reformatory

8. This English Quaker was one of the first advocates of separate prisons for women:
   - a. Mary Baker Eddy
   - b. Sister Helen Prejean
   - c. Hannah Alderson
   - d. Paris Faith Hilton
   - e. Elizabeth Gurney Fry

9. What do scholars think was probably the most important reason that Pennsylvania was the leader in prison reform in early America?
   - a. It had the highest crime rate.
   - b. Because of the Quaker influences.
   - c. No one has any idea.
   - d. All the universities were there.
   - e. The government funded research there.

10. Right of sanctuary and benefit of clergy are both identified as historical antecedents of:
   - a. capital punishment
   - b. the juvenile court
   - c. probation
   - d. psychotherapy
   - e. hard labor

## True or False

_____ 11. Crofton's Irish system was considered too punitive in its treatment of inmates and was finally prohibited by the British government.

_____ 12. The Eastern Penitentiary was considered the model of the Pennsylvania-style prison.

_____ 13. The lockstep was a metal device which was attached to the legs of prisoners who tried to escape from the old penitentiaries.

_____ 14. One of the principal reasons the Auburn prison model won out over the Pennsylvania model was that the Auburn model was economically more productive.

_____ 15. In the penitentiary by the end of the 1800s, solitary confinement was generally used to reward convicts for good behavior.

_____ 16. The National Prison Congress was called to lead the fight to "get tough on crime and criminals."

_____ 17. Houses of refuge were originally opened to hold homeless adults and transient laborers.

_____ 18. Women prisoners were always housed in facilities separate from men.

_____ 19. The orphan trains were set up to move country children into the cities for placement in state-operated orphanages and factories.

_____ 20. By the late 1800s, felons in prisons were not allowed to do work of any kind.

## Fill In the Blanks

21. The practice of _____ was used to prevent contamination among inmates working together in the congregate system.

22. The model of the penitentiary that was considered more reformative was the _____ system.

23. The model of the penitentiary that was considered more economical and efficient was the _____ system.

24. The mark system and the ticket-of-leave are both associated with the idea of the indeterminate sentence and the present day practice of _____.

25. The first federal prison for women was commonly known as _____, from its location in West Virginia.

26. Charles Loring Brace became closely identified with a movement known as _____.

27. The major institutional alternative to the penitentiary that had developed by the late 1800s was the _____.

28. The origin of the term "penitentiary" was in the idea of _____, or feeling sorry for your sins or offenses.

29. In contrast to Northern industrial prisons, post-Civil War Southern prisons first emphasized convict leasing, then later the operation of _____ to house and work their convicts.

30. The National Prison Congress identified _____, not "vindictive suffering," as the purpose of penal treatment.

## Discussion

31. Tell how an inmate's life would differ according to his placement in a Pennsylvania or Auburn prison.

32. What rules of prison discipline were devised to make it easier to control men in confinement?

33. What ideas and practices are associated with the reformatory era in American corrections?

34. What were the reformer's arguments about separate institutions for juveniles and women?

35. If you were a convict about to be placed in an Auburn- or Pennsylvania-style prison, which type would you choose, and why?

36. Although Elam Lynds's physical methods have mostly been abandoned, some suggest that his viewpoint or philosophy of imprisonment remains important. Which of his views do you think support this argument?

# CHAPTER THREE

# Twentieth Century Corrections Systems

This chapter considers the growth of the prison system in the twentieth century. What began in the 1800s as a small, single-purpose institution to which all criminals were sent became by the end of the 1900s a diverse bureaucratic system using dual methods of control--specialized secure-custody institutions and various non-secure alternatives to imprisonment. What started as "imprisonment" in the early 1800s was bureaucratically euphemized into "corrections" by the mid-1950s, as punishing and treating criminals became an industry involving local, state, and federal governments, with a subsidiary network of private organizations. After reading this chapter, you should be familiar with:

1. The "Big House" model of imprisonment of the early 1900s.
2. The rise and fall of labor in prison.
3. Prisons during and after World War II.
4. Contrasting models of rehabilitation and reintegration.
5. The prison population boom of the late 1900s.
6. Specialized prisons that developed in the 1900s.
7. The growth of state corrections departments.
8. An overview of the American penal system at the beginning of the twenty-first century.

## Key Terms

Big House
scientific management
hard labor
public account
state account
convict lease
contract
piece price
state use
public works and ways
Sanford Bates
Hawes-Cooper Act
Ashurst-Sumners Act
Sumners-Ashurst Act
Prison Industries Branch
Richard A. McGee
reform
rehabilitation
classification
treatment

James V. Bennett
medical model
Robert Martinson
"nothing works"
recidivism
Norval Morris
reintegration era
War on Crime
war on criminals
War on Drugs
warehousing
balanced model
icebox model
houses of refuge
training school
Indiana Reformatory Institute
open institutions
camps
department of corrections

## The Big House

At the end of the 1800s, the small penitentiaries that had originated in the Mid-Atlantic and New England states had spread across America and grow into much larger industrial prisons--factories behind walls. Several older prisons already held a thousand or more inmates. New prisons were designed according to the architectural model that came to be known as the **Big House**. Built on a larger scale and incorporating industrial buildings, dining halls, chapels, and other functional buildings not considered in early penitentiaries, the Big House looked like a fortress--a self-contained medieval town with high stone walls, guard towers, heavy gates, and concrete and steel construction. The Big House was intended to be a model of **scientific management**, with a proficient guard force under centralized administration, maintaining custody of an ever-increasing number of prisoners within an efficient, secure environment.

## Prison Labor: For and Against

The essence of the Big House was **hard labor**. Some early proponents of the penitentiary argued that confinement without labor was more reformative but, by the 1830s, every American prison required labor from its convicts. In some, it was craft work that men and women could do alone in their cells. With the rise of the Auburn model, congregate labor in prison workshops prevailed.

In early prisons, convicts commonly produced goods the penitentiary sold directly to the public on the open market. This was called the **public account** or **state account** system, meaning the prison was the merchant with no middle-man. Over time, except for the sale of agricultural commodities, such as truck vegetables and, occasionally, inmate-made crafts, this practice declined as other forms of prison labor developed.

Fred Haynes, surveying prison labor systems in *The American Prison System* (1939), identified four separate systems of importance in the penitentiary's first century--public account, convict lease, contract or piece price, and state use or public works and ways. Public account was the original model. Under the **convict lease**, a private contractor rented prisoners from the state, assuming responsibility for their care and control in return. This model prevailed in the post-Civil War South. The **contract** model and its variant, the **piece price**, allowed private businesses to contract with the prison, either for a certain number of workers or for the number of items the workers could produce. Businesses typically set up workshops on prison grounds and paid prisoners a wage much lower than free-world workers would have been paid. The **state use** model and its variant, the **public works and ways** system, had prisoners producing goods bought by government agencies or working on public projects, such as constructing roads and buildings.

Prisons made money and convicts were kept busy, but all was never entirely at ease on the prison-labor front. Opposition came from three sources. Many private businesses were in direct competition with the contract and public-account systems and strongly opposed prison-made goods being sold on the open market; it was bad for their business. Second, laborers and, after the Civil War, labor unions argued that prisoners took jobs away from free people who were more deserving of employment. Third, prison reformers deplored the way prisoners were worked, particularly under leasing in the South, where prisoners were underclothed, underfed, and overworked, often to death. Reformers wanted prisoners treated more like human beings even if profits suffered.

## The Demise of the Industrial Prison

Political debate over prison labor intensified in the 1920s and 1930s. The prison population had almost doubled during the 1920s to about 150,000 by 1930, while the number of inmates productively employed declined steadily--from 75 percent in 1885 to 61 percent in 1923 to 52 percent in 1932. **Sanford Bates**, director of the new Federal Bureau of Prisons, warned of the increased danger of prison riots if inmate idleness persisted.

By the 1930s, opponents of prison labor had an important new ally--the Great Depression. When national unemployment reached 25 percent at the peak of the depression in 1933, getting people back to work became a national priority. The old argument about prison labor depriving free people of jobs took on new force. From 1929 on, the U.S. Congress enacted a series of federal laws limiting shipment of prison-made goods and making it increasingly difficult to provide productive employment for prisoners. The **Hawes-Cooper Act** (1929) mandated that prison-made goods transported from one state to another be subject to the laws of the destination state. Hawes-Cooper went into effect in 1934 and affected only states that banned the sale of prisoner-made goods. The **Ashurst-Sumners Act** (1935) made shipping prisoner-made goods to a state where state law prohibited the receipt, possession, sale or use of such goods a federal offense. The **Sumners-Ashurst Act** (1940) made it a federal crime to knowingly transport convict-made goods in interstate commerce for private use, regardless of laws in the states.

Agricultural products were left out of this series of federal laws, leaving states with prison farms (particularly the belt of big plantation prisons from Texas across the South to the Atlantic coast) still able to sell their crops at home and abroad. The Big House, on the other hand, was devastated. These massive institutions, each on average holding 1,500 to 2,000 men behind their high walls, had been designed and built (or redesigned and rebuilt) as maximum-security factories. Suddenly cut off from the market, they had no use for prisoner labor, the center of their existence for a century.

19

What were prisoners to do with their time? Some could be assigned to maintenance and internal chores--food service, laundry, cleaning, groundskeeping, records, and janitorial work. But how many prisoners can be assigned to mop a hall or mow a square of grass? When we think of prisons as places of idleness, where prisoners sit around doing nothing or hang out in the yard socializing, working out, and playing games, it is important to note that this was not the intention of penitentiary founders. They viewed labor as positive, even necessary to the prison's mission. Persistent opposition from outside undercut this philosophy and killed productive prison labor in the 1930s.

## Prisons in World War II

When World War II was declared in December 1941, the new rules against prison labor were relaxed to put prisoners to work in the war effort. The **Prison Industries Branch** of the War Production Board was established in December 1941 to manage the industrial and agricultural output of state and federal prisons. The chairman of the War Production Board said in late 1942 that only about 10 percent of convicts were working in prison industries, which were producing at about a third of their estimated potential.

Federal prisons led the penal war effort. Inmates at McNeil Island Federal Penitentiary built Army patrol boats. Women at Alderson Reformatory sewed flags and bandoleers by day (working 48 hours a week) and volunteered to prepare Red Cross surgical dressings at night. Lewisburg Federal Penitentiary in Pennsylvania turned out thousands of bomb fins and steel mess trays. Atlanta Federal Penitentiary produced four million dollars worth of defense materials annually by the middle of the war period. Prisons in several states were also recognized for their productivity.

World War II was good for prison labor. The industrial and agricultural output of prisons increased steadily. Prisoners got the opportunity to show the public that they, too, wanted to help in the war effort, and prison morale was high. Many barriers that had separated prisoners from free people were relaxed during wartime, only to be put back in place once the war ended in 1945. For American prisons, World War II would prove to be only a rest stop on the road they had been traveling for a hundred years.

## Prisons in Crisis

After the war, prisons faded from public view. Their populations went up again, industrial and agricultural production declined, and restrictions on interstate shipment of prison-made goods were restored. Prisons became institutions of idleness, where growing numbers of prisoners were confined by penal officials who had nothing for them to do.

Inside prisons, tensions built up that prison officials had no way of relieving. Although prison violence, in the form of attacks on guards and other inmates, and escape attempts (many of them successful), was commonplace in American history, prison riots were infrequent until after World War II, when several circumstances--relaxed controls over prisoners, idleness, inattention to grievances, and deteriorating buildings--combined to create an atmosphere ripe for explosion. Scores of riots flared up in the 1950s. The spring of 1952 was especially violent with destructive riots at state prisons in Trenton, New Jersey; Bordentown, New Jersey; Rahway, New Jersey; Jackson, Michigan; Concord, Massachusetts; Soledad, California; and elsewhere. The New Jersey State Prison at Trenton suffered three riots in 1952. In another shocking incident that generated national attention, 37 convicts of the Louisiana State Penitentiary at Angola slashed their Achilles tendons to protest conditions of brutality and corruption that prevailed within their prison.

What was different about these prison uprisings in the 1950s was their explicitly political nature. They were not escape attempts or random assaults and vandalism. They were for the most part staged to draw outside attention to prison problems. Rioting often followed a pattern--seizing a building, taking hostages, presenting grievances, negotiating with the prison administration and political officials, and finally surrendering when faced with the use of overwhelming force. Most riots were resolved without serious injury or death.

When an investigative commission, appointed by the American Prison Association and headed by California Commissioner of Corrections **Richard A. McGee**, looked into the prison riots sweeping the country, it identified several major causes--idleness, severe overcrowding, political neglect, lack of public interest, lack of educational and vocational programs, poorly trained officers, difficulty in managing huge prisons, political interference in prison management, and anti-crime crusades that promoted overcrowding. To this list could be added chronic unresponsiveness of prison officials to convict grievances, though officials usually defended their inaction by blaming their political superiors.

## Rehabilitation and the Medical Model

In 1954 the American Prison Association voted to change its name to the American Correctional Association. The name change reflected the growing role of probation, parole, and other non-institutional methods of supervising and helping criminals. But symbolically it gave prisons a new mission--rehabilitation. Over the next 20 years, prisons would offer an unprecedented number of programs designed to change the behavior of men and women in prison--to turn law-breaking behavior into law-abiding behavior.

Today we use **reform** and **rehabilitation** as synonyms in their penal application. Both mean to change behavior. Early penitentiaries talked a lot about reformation, but not at all about rehabilitation, a term that came along at the end of the nineteenth century as part of the social-work movement. The birth of rehabilitation in corrections is usually tied to the creation of reformatories and juvenile training schools in the late 1800s.

While reformation was up to the individual--like changing your mind from criminal to non-criminal--rehabilitation put the burden of change on the prison. Its mission was to carry to the prisoner the programs needed to promote change. Matching of programs to individuals could be enhanced through **classification**, which took place upon the prisoner's entry into the system. Classification was critical to determining the background, capabilities, and needs of the criminal, which could then be met by assignment to particular prison programs.

In the aftermath of the 1950s prison riots, rehabilitation moved front-and-center. Many states vastly expanded the programs their prisons offered. Education, job training, counseling and therapy, drug and alcohol treatment, religious services, recreation, and self-help organizations proliferated. Professional staff--teachers, social workers, psychologists, counselors, and case managers--entered the prison. New prisoners were processed through reception or classification centers to determine their needs. Convicts served indeterminate sentences, which meant they could be paroled when the prison determined they had reached the state known as rehabilitation.

Rehabilitation, or **treatment**, as it is often called, was always secondary to secure custody; it never dominated prison operations. But the era from the mid-1950s through the mid-1970s did offer the hope of change through prison programming. It also gave inmates something to do with time they would otherwise have spent idle.

Federal prisons took rehabilitation a step further. **James V. Bennett**, director of the Bureau of Prisons from 1937 to 1964, believed that rehabilitation programs should be available to all inmates and that the programs should be matched to the individual's needs. The term for this individualized rehabilitation concept was the **medical model**. In the analogy, criminal behavior was a sickness, and prison was the hospital that treated it. The criminal was the patient who would be cured with treatment programs.

In the 1970s, rehabilitation came under simultaneous attack from two different directions. **Robert Martinson** studied national research on rehabilitation and wrote a summary article, "What Works? Questions and Answers about Prison Reform," in 1974. Martinson's answer to his question was, "**Nothing works**," or as he put it, "With few and isolated exceptions, the rehabilitative efforts that have been reported so far have had no appreciable effect on recidivism." He meant that no prison programs had been shown to achieve substantial, predictable reductions in **recidivism** (return to prison).

**Norval Morris**, an attorney and criminologist who was then dean of the University of Chicago School of Law, criticized rehabilitation for a different reason. Treatment, as Morris saw it, was a coercive game. Because it was tied to release on parole, prisoners had to admit that they needed treatment, complete a program successfully, and adopt the properly respectful attitude of the healed patient to get out of prison. Rehabilitation was unrelated to long-term failure and success, which were tied more to age, values, prior criminal history, family lifestyles, and other variables that had nothing to do with prison treatment programs.

The argument that rehabilitation was a waste of time and money or a mean-spirited, unpredictable charade had important effects. Rehabilitation's opponents and skeptics urged prisons to concentrate on locking criminals up and stop trying to change--or "help"--them. In 1975, the Federal Bureau of Prisons officially abandoned the medical model. Many state systems did the same with rehabilitation, cutting back on rehabilitation programming and reducing its ties to parole and release from prison. Participation became more voluntary than mandatory. Once again rehabilitation or reform became an individual proposition.

## The Reintegration Era

One persistent criticism of rehabilitation was that it took place in *prison*, which is after all a completely artificial environment. Security dominated the prison, and many (or most) convicts resisted rehabilitation. So if rehabilitation in prison was a bust, what could be done? Instead of bringing treatment programs into the prison, two alternatives were emphasized:

      1. Keep as many criminals as possible under supervision in the community to avoid the negative effects of imprisonment.

      2. Send as many prisoners as possible out into the community to take part in real-world programs, as opposed to inadequate prison programs.

These ideas were influential during the 1970s, which is often called the **reintegration era** in penology. This decade saw the expanded use of felony probation and the growth of halfway houses and pre-release centers. Prisoners also benefitted from furloughs (weekend or holiday passes to their families), work release, educational release, and counseling and treatment in the community.

Reintegration pushed community-based, non-secure alternatives and treatment programs. Advocates argued that this approach was appropriate for the majority of convicted felons. Prisons ought to be reserved for the hardcore, dangerous few from whom society truly needed to be protected. Prison had its place, but it was not a very good place, and most criminals did not need to go there. If the ones who did go there needed programs, these should be provided in the community to the maximum extent possible.

## Warehousing

For a few years, especially after the decline of rehabilitation, reintegration was a dominant correctional model. The number of people coming under correctional supervision was increasing, but most of the increase was in probation. The national incarceration rate (the number in prison per 100,000 population) had peaked at 139 in 1939, gone down sharply during the war, and did not reach the pre-war peak again until 1981. What should have been a noticeable increase in prisoners in the 1970s was being temporarily diverted through reintegration.

In the early 1980s, the penal mentality took a hard right turn. The **War on Crime**, declared by President Lyndon Johnson in 1965 as part of his Great Society social program, was refocused to become a **war on criminals**. This meant punishments would be made severe and imprisonment would be preferred over other options, like probation. The politics of punishment flowered under Republican President Ronald Reagan, who held office from 1981 to 1989. His administration popularized the "get tough on crime" mentality that spread to state and local governments. New laws required mandatory prison sentences, abolished or restricted parole, and lengthened prison terms. Most significant, in its effect on prison populations over the next decade, was a new war--the **War on Drugs**.

Although illegal drug use had escalated in the 1960s and 1970s, comparatively few people went to prison for drugs; fewer than 10 percent of the prison population was made up of drug criminals in the early 1980s. Under Reagan, federal and state policies changed dramatically. Strict enforcement of drug laws swept huge numbers of men and women into the criminal justice system. The drug of emphasis, from about 1985 on, was crack cocaine. It was viewed as the most evil drug, for its addictive effect and for its relationship with inner-city gangs, turf wars, drive-by shootings, and other violence.

In the 15 years between 1980 and 1995, the prison population more than tripled. Half of the increase was drug criminals. From the 1970s to the 1990s, the percentage of violent criminals in prison decreased sharply, from 60 percent to 40 percent, while drug criminals flooded state and especially federal prisons. By 1999, toward the end of the second decade of the War on Drugs, more people were in prison for drug crimes--320,000--than had been in prison, *period*, 20 years earlier.

What was the purpose of prison in this policy? The most common term was **warehousing**. To warehouse is to place, deposit, or store in a controlled environment for a period of time, and then to remove. To prisoners this meant that their removal from society was solely for public safety. Nothing beneficial to them was expected to result. The Federal Bureau of Prisons's term for this view was the **balanced model**. The BOP's position was that prison serves multiple objectives, including retribution, deterrence, incapacitation, and rehabilitation.

Under the balanced model, rehabilitation was the least important objective, both because rehabilitation programs had been deemphasized and because sheer numbers overwhelmed programs that remained. The other purposes reflected society's interests and were compatible with the **icebox model** which rationalizes warehousing. This model views prison as a large icebox in which "bad eggs" are stored (preferably for as long as possible) before being taken out for another look.

Such was the role of the American prison at the beginning of the twenty-first century. The prison population had increased every year since 1972 and, at the end of 2001, stood at 1,330,000. Politicians argued about the escalating costs of imprisonment, and the long-term social consequences of warehousing America's social misfits, most of them young, poor, black and Hispanic men. As the new century began, prison officials and policy makers were once again asking, "What are prisons for?"

## Specialized Correctional Institutions

In the 1800s, the "corrections system" was the local jail holding pre-trial and short-term prisoners and the state penitentiary--a maximum security fortress. Here and there, the progressive states added specialized new institutions, founded on the argument that certain criminals deserved differential treatment.

Juvenile **houses of refuge** for boys and girls opened in larger cities in the 1820s. These combination schools/ shelters/workshops confined young criminals, runaways, orphans, abandoned children, and "wayward" children. State-operated **training schools**, also known as industrial schools or reformatories (not to be confused with the reformatory for adults), were separate prisons for juveniles. Massachusetts opened the first training school for boys in 1847 and the first for girls in 1856.

Women also began to get separate, if not always better, treatment about this time. The **Indiana Reformatory Institute** for Women opened in 1873 before the first separate reformatory for men. Others followed in Massachusetts, New York, and elsewhere in the early twentieth century, culminating in the Federal Industrial Institution for Women at Alderson, West Virginia, which opened on November 14, 1928. These female prisons were generally smaller, less security conscious (no walls), and provided dormitory or cottage housing.

Reformatories for young men came into common usage in the late 1800s. While reformatories confined prisoners in cells and employed strict discipline, their inmates got the benefits of schooling, vocational training, religious instruction, physical conditioning, recreation, and inmate clubs. With the indeterminate sentence and parole, they also got out of prison faster than penitentiary prisoners.

As the American prison population increased steadily in the early years of the twentieth century, the diversity of prisons within a state depended on two key circumstances--the number of prisoners in custody, and prison officials' and politicians' views on the need for specialized treatment.

After World War II, when rehabilitation programs became widely available, several states built separate prisons to provide treatment for certain types of criminals--the mentally ill, drug addicts, and sex criminals, for instance. The federal prison system and several states built prison hospitals for old or sick inmates. Reception centers were needed to classify new prisoners. States also began to build more medium- and minimum-security prisons-- smaller in size and capacity, fences replacing walls, fewer security and more rehabilitation staff, with dormitories and rooms replacing cellblocks. The prisoner population gradually shifted from almost entirely maximum security to predominantly medium and minimum security.

Other small, separate prisons flourished during the reintegration era of the 1970s--work release centers, halfway houses, pre-release centers, and so on. These were usually located in urban areas to house men or women nearing the end of their sentences (or after release), and were classified as **open institutions**, meaning they had no armed guards, no fences. A convict living there only had to walk away to escape.

These small reintegration facilities should not be confused with the variety of **camps**--road camps, forestry camps, and "pea" farms--that were found in many states, particularly in the South and West. The role of these camps varied. Some held trusties in low security and were called "honor camps." Others were like tiny maximum-security prisons in a forest or on a farm.

While some states had large penitentiaries, small specialized prisons, and, possibly camps as well, other states did not. Those with small prison populations, such as Montana, New Hampshire, and North Dakota, had only one small prison that held all convicted felons. Georgia and South Carolina relied heavily on a decentralized network of county prisons. Several Southern states operated plantation prisons. Louisiana and Mississippi operated penal systems centered on one huge prison farm in each state, Angola in Louisiana and Parchman in Mississippi, with smaller satellite farms. Each state system developed its own personality over time.

## State Corrections Departments

Prisons originally were independent institutions, each with its own warden or superintendent appointed by the governor, its own agenda, and its own management style. They were acknowledged to be political institutions. Officials were hired and fired as political administrations changed, and no civil service existed to protect the jobs of prison employees. Everything depended on political affiliation and personal relationships.

After World War II, as the number of specialized prisons grew and probation and parole became more established, centralized corrections bureaucracies emerged as the dominant penal authorities in the states. The new bureaucracy was most often called the state **department of corrections**. Departments could be unified to include adult and juvenile prisons, probation, and parole, though not all did. Probation often remained under the control of county judges. In some states, training schools and juvenile probation were put in a different agency or left with the welfare department. Other states grouped juvenile and adult corrections with mental hospitals and social-service institutions--such as schools for the blind and deaf and homes for orphans, the mentally retarded, and pregnant girls--in departments of charities and institutions.

Even following the unified department model, no two state systems are the same. Most corrections departments have authority over all aspects of juvenile and adult corrections, but some split these functions. Local jails, probation, and juvenile justice complicate the picture. American corrections today is 51 distinct systems, one for each state and one federal, not a unified national system.

## The Corrections System Today

From its elementary origins two hundred years ago, the modern prison has grown into the centerpiece of today's correctional system, an enterprise that provides diverse forms of social control never imagined by Enlightenment reformers. Three of every 100 Americans, juveniles and adults, are under correctional supervision--in jail, prison, or in the community--at any given time. To provide the supervision and the necessary administrative, treatment, and related functions, a vast network of correctional organizations has evolved. Estimates have put the economic cost of today's correctional bureaucracy--public and private--at upwards of $60 *billion* a year, a huge expense that continues to grow as this network, already the largest of any on earth, continues to expand year by year. Many people, scholars and prison officials alike, question the role this system of formal social control has come to play in modern American society. But, given the social and political conditions of today, it is difficult to imagine that it will shrink significantly in size anytime soon.

## SELF TEST

## Multiple Choice

1. In the model of the industrial prison of a century ago, the greatest emphasis was placed on:
   a. inmate education
   b. psychological counseling
   c. hard labor
   d. spiritual development
   e. physical conditioning

2. Four of the following features were associated with the Big House; which one was NOT?
   a. high stone walls
   b. industrial shops
   c. concrete and steel construction
   d. guard towers
   e. low security dormitory housing

3. The combined effect of the Hawes-Cooper and Ashurst-Sumners Acts was to:
   a. establish parole in America
   b. prohibit capital punishment except for murder
   c. create the reformatory
   d. end the shipment of prison-made goods
   e. encourage higher education of prisoners

4. The federal prison official closely associated with the medical model in federal corrections was _____.
   a. George Beto
   b. Marcus Welby
   c. James Bennett
   d. Clinton Duffy
   e. Lewis Lawes

5. Four of the following were cited in McGee's study of causes of the 1950s prison riots; which one was NOT?
   a. idleness
   b. media agitators
   c. lack of programs
   d. overcrowding
   e. political neglect

6. In the medical model, the first step was called _____, when the prisoner's needs were assessed.
   a. restriction
   b. classification
   c. pacification
   d. importation
   e. confrontation

7. When rehabilitation fell out of favor in the 1970s, the era that followed it was known as:
   a. reintegration
   b. reparation
   c. regulation
   d. resistance
   e. religion

8. In the War on Crime, the big boost in prison population in the 1980s and early 1990s came from the:
   a. Attack on Terrorism
   b. Campaign against Sexual Assault
   c. Crusade against Pornography
   d. Rally against Satanism
   e. War on Drugs

9. Since the end of World War II, state prisons are most likely to be collectively grouped in a bureaucracy known as the _____.
   a. prison bureau
   b. justice agency
   c. corrections department
   d. welfare department
   e. human rights division

10. At one time, prisons sold most convict-made goods on the open market, and the prison used the money in its own operation; the term for this model was the:
    a. employer model
    b. franchise sales
    c. convict lease
    d. public account
    e. public works

**True or False**

_____ 11. Robert Martinson and Norval Morris both argued that rehabilitation would work if prisons spent a lot more money on programs.

_____ 12. Convict leasing flourished in the South after the Civil War.

_____ 13. The most intense period of rioting in American prisons came immediately after the Civil War and forced all prisons to turn to maximum security housing and physical punishments.

_____ 14. The federal anti-convict labor laws of the 1930s banned the sale of any prison-raised agricultural products, which wiped out prison farms.

_____ 15. Most prison factories that geared up for war production during World War II kept right on producing military goods for several years after the war ended in 1945.

_____ 16. The houses of refuge that appeared in large cities in the 1800s were primarily intended for women who were victims of domestic violence.

_____ 17. Most of the prison riots of the 1950s were nothing more than botched mass escape attempts.

_____ 18. Labor unions were generally in favor of convict labor, calling prisoners "our brothers in toil" and urging fair wages for convict laborers.

_____ 19. The American prison population began climbing in the 1970s and continued to climb through the end of the century.

_____ 20. Prison camps were generally small and both a specific type of inmate population and a specific work purpose, such as farming or forestry.

**Fill In the Blanks**

21. The historical event that most closely associated with federal laws banning the interstate shipment of prison-made goods was _____.

22. Many of the problems of American prisons since the end of World War II are related to the lack of _____ in prison after the end of the industrial prison.

23. _____, the federal prison director of the 1930s, warned that riots were likely if inmate idleness was allowed to persist.

24. Related to warehousing, the _____ model suggests that prisons exist to hold convicts in cold storage.

25. The previous name of the American Correctional Association was the American _____ Association.

26. The failure of rehabilitation is measured by what is called the _____ rate.

27. The Indiana Reformatory Institute and the Alderson prison were early examples of prisons for _____.

28. The change goal that preceded rehabilitation in American correctional philosophy was _____.

29. The federal prison system replaced the medical model with the _____ model.

30. A prison classified as a(n) _____ institution has no armed guards or perimeter security.

**Discussion**

31. What were the advantages of the industrial prison?

32. If the industrial prison was such a good idea, what reasons did the opponents of prison labor give for abolishing its practice of hard labor?

33. What were the arguments behind the creation of specialized correctional institutions to complement the penitentiaries?

34. In terms of the perceived purpose of imprisonment, what ideologies dominated American corrections from World War II through the end of the twentieth century?

35. In the era of the industrial prison, what different systems of prison labor were used to work convicts and financially benefit from their work?

36. Explain the theory of the medical model in corrections.

37. American prisons of the 1950s were marked by a period of widespread rioting; what were these riots all about?

38. What good reasons can you give for combining all of a state's correctional institutions into a state department of corrections?

39. Thought question: If you had been a convict in 1910, how would your life have been different from that of a convict of today? Which period do you think you would have preferred?

CHAPTER FOUR

# Ideologies and Sentencing

For the convicted criminal--felon or misdemeanant--sentencing is a critical event. It means the difference between freedom and confinement. It controls the future, often for many years to come. In a few cases, it means life or death. But for many of us, including the political officials who make and enforce the laws as well as the ordinary citizens to whom the laws are applied, sentencing is a murky area, based more on ideology or personal feelings than any objective knowledge of cause and effect. After reading this chapter, you should be familiar with:

      1. Principal objectives of punishment.
      2. Sentencing models important in contemporary criminal justice.
      3. Common sentencing options, from probation to imprisonment to death.
      4. The sentencing decision.
      5. Sentencing issues and reforms.
      6. Impact of sentencing on corrections.

## Key Terms

| | |
|---|---|
| punishment | mitigating circumstances |
| retribution | proportionality |
| retaliation | gatekeeper function |
| *lex talionis* | trial judge |
| utilitarianism | probation officer |
| deterrence | pre-sentence investigation report (PSI) |
| incapacitation | prosecutor |
| reformation | bureaucratic model |
| rehabilitation | judicial imperialism |
| ideology | appellate courts |
| conservative ideology | governor |
| liberal ideology | parole board |
| radical ideology | pardon board |
| model | good time |
| non-system | earn time |
| rehabilitation model | gain time |
| reintegration model | indeterminate sentencing |
| crime control model | determinate sentencing |
| due process model | sentencing discretion |
| justice model | disparity |
| just deserts model | discrimination |
| neoclassical model | mandatory minimum sentences |
| selective incapacitation | presumptive sentencing |
| logical consequences | habitual offender enhancement |
| restorative justice | three strikes and you're out |
| balanced and restorative justice (BARJ) model | supervised release |
| victims' rights movement | truth in sentencing |
| model muddle | courtroom work group |
| plea bargaining | sentencing guidelines |
| capital crime | Model Penal Code |
| *Furman v. Georgia* | sentencing institutes |
| *Gregg v. Georgia* | sentencing councils |
| bifurcated trial | natural life sentences |
| aggravating circumstances | |

## The Objectives of Sentencing

What are we trying to accomplish through apprehending criminals and convicting them in court? The most common answer in American society today would probably be **punishment**, which has to do with the imposition of a penalty of some kind as a result of a rule or law violation. Punishment derives from the Latin *poena*, translated as penalty or pain.

Our notions of punishment as what is due the criminal derive from historical practice. The pre-Christian historical societies provided economic sanctions, slavery, banishment, corporal punishment, and death as sentences for guilty criminals. Early Christian societies continued the same punishments in their fight against sin. All these outcomes certainly qualify as punishment, and most of them were physically painful as well.

Legal scholars agree that punishment in ancient societies was based primarily on **retribution**, or **retaliation**, for the harm done by the crime. The concept of retribution is equivalence, returning to the victim what is due. Punishment under *lex talionis*, the law of retaliation, was *limited* punishment. It was intended to replace the use of the blood feud and vendetta that had marked early family and tribal relations. Instead of vengeance or revenge, which were personal and unbalanced and often led to extended conflict, as one party sought to gain the upper hand on another, retribution sought to bring about an impartial, equitable resolution of conflict. The punishment, whether economic or physical, settled the score.

Retributive justice prevailed into the 1700s, when the ideas of the Enlightenment gave rise to **utilitarianism**, "the greatest good for the greatest number." Popularized in the writings of such scholars as Cesare Beccaria and Jeremy Bentham, utilitarianism emphasized the effects of punishment on the larger society. Three modern objectives of punishment grew out of utilitarian thought--deterrence, incapacitation, and reformation (later rehabilitation).

**Deterrence**, which in Beccaria's argument was to be achieved through the certainty of imprisonment, was the discouraging effect that punishment has on those who may contemplate committing a crime. We avoid the conduct, or the criminal avoids its repetition, because we know the consequences. We are restrained by our fear of punishment.

**Incapacitation** is the protective effect of punishment on society. A criminal who in the early days was banished or who is imprisoned today cannot harm society. Society is safer because criminals have been removed.

**Reformation**, in the twentieth century **rehabilitation**, posits that punishment reduces or eliminates future criminal behavior through individual change during confinement (reformation), or through programs designed to motivate law-abiding behavior (rehabilitation).

But which purpose is more important, in comparison to the others? This becomes a matter of ideology. An **ideology** is a body of belief and doctrine that guides how an individual or a larger group sees the world. In America today, three contrasting ideologies are often compared to describe different philosophies of punishment. The **conservative ideology** is said to be "tough on crime." Conservatives want more severe criminal penalties and greater use of imprisonment. Think bigger, tougher prisons. The **liberal ideology** views most criminals as disadvantaged members of society. Liberals want more resources put into rehabilitation and crime prevention. Think nicer, more helpful prisons. The **radical ideology** takes an economic or class view of crime; the legal system is designed for social control. Radicals concentrate on attacking the ills of society--racism, poverty, materialism, and the overreach of the criminal law--and would significantly decrease (or abolish) the use of imprisonment. Think very tiny prisons filled with corrupt corporate executives and politicians and a few murderers and sex criminals.

## Sentencing Models

If an ideology is a way of thinking, then a **model** takes these beliefs or assumptions and turns them into a design for action. A model is a representation of a system based on what one believes and knows--it is a framework for putting ideas to work.

As criminal justice, described by the President's Crime Commission in 1967 as a **non-system**, has grown more systematic over the years, models have become more important in conceptualizing how the system ought to work. The **rehabilitation model** was very important to prisons from the early 1950s through the 1970s. It emphasized institutional programs to correct the problems and disadvantages criminals needed to overcome if they were to live crime-free lives.

The **reintegration model** was particularly influential in the 1970s. Its emphasis on real-world programs, as opposed to rehabilitation programs offered within prison walls, and its preference for probation and other community-based forms of supervision were instrumental for several years in expanding non-custodial alternatives and holding down prison populations.

Herbert Packer discussed criminal justice in 1960s America as incorporating two contrasting models--crime control and due process. The **crime control model**, which in this era focused more on efficient law enforcement and case processing leading to criminal conviction, emphasized the system's part in maintaining social order. Later, enlargement of the prison system would be argued as a necessity in housing those criminals who became persistent threats to the social order. Packer contrasted crime control with the **due process model**, which emphasized the rights of criminal defendants in the legal system. Due process was very important at this time, as the U.S. Supreme Court under Chief Justice Earl Warren made many landmark decisions extending Constitutional protection to state court defendants.

Tension between the crime-control and due-process models is important. As Frank Schmalleger has suggested, American criminal justice is *crime control through due process*, incorporating individual protection within crime control. But the emphasis on one or the other, particularly the critical role of the courts as intervening authorities, can change significantly over time.

In the 1970s, construction of an ideological framework for a new sentencing model (or the renovation of an old model) began. David Fogel's **justice model** argued against rehabilitation and in favor of a rationalist, retributive approach that relied on a carefully constructed scale of crimes and punishments. Fogel's sanctions were on the lenient side. He believed, as Beccaria did 200 years ago and most criminologists do today, that certainty of punishment is more important than severity. This idea of imprisonment as primarily retributive punishment was taken a step further by Andrew von Hirsch and other advocates of the **just deserts model**, which supported more consistently applied punishments and great use of imprisonment.

One aspect of American crime, high levels of illegal drug use, was a concern of the **neoclassical model** popularized in the 1980s. Drawing on Beccaria and Bentham and other members of the Classical School of Criminology of late eighteenth and early nineteenth centuries, neoclassicists asserted the value of deterrence. What was needed, especially with drug criminals, was more extensive use of imprisonment. "Prison, not probation," was the neoclassic battle cry. The "War on Drugs," begun in Reagan's first term and perpetuated by succeeding presidents, became the prime force driving America's imprisonment rate upward.

Habitual criminals would soon have their own model--**selective incapacitation**. Deriving from the research of Peter Greenwood and others, this model focused on high-risk or high-rate criminals. It sought to identify criminals fully committed to a criminal lifestyle. If our capacity to confine is limited, selective incapacitation argued, we do society the most good by imposing long prison terms on the criminals who commit the most crimes. Selective incapacitation inspired "three strikes" laws in many states over the next decade or so, resulting in the long-term incarceration of many habitual offenders.

Juvenile criminals were not immune from model changes. The **logical consequences** model was developed to tighten controls over juveniles who did not respond favorably to supervision. It emphasized discipline, accountability, and certainty of action. "If you do this, this will happen." Restating deterrence in a form applicable to juveniles, logical consequences sought to bring adult-like management to young criminals. Its result was to put more juveniles behind bars and increase supervision over those who remained in the community.

At the end of the twentieth century, a new justice model appeared on the scene. Called **restorative justice**, or the **balanced and restorative justice (BARJ) model**, its vision of justice was healing rather than punishment, a triangle of "three Cs"--community, crime victims, and criminals. The community needed to be more "interested" and involved. Crime victims, whose exclusion from the system had been at the heart of the politically aggressive **victims' rights movement** of the eighties and nineties, should be better informed and allowed more participation. The goal of restorative justice is to achieve a restoration to all parties, to repair the damage done.

Models are important to justice in America, but they have to be seen in the context of a very disorganized and multilayered criminal justice system. In a system made up of federal, state, and local government agencies, each supplemented by many private organizations and individuals, many divergent models may be pursued at the same time, some of them often at odds or directly contradictory to one another. Harry Allen and Clifford Simonsen have referred to this **model muddle** as a defining characteristic of corrections in America. Corrections is often not going in any one direction, but in several different directions at once, depending on where you happen to look. In this landscape, politics is more important than rationality.

## Sentencing Options: Non-Custodial

Most criminals will never go to prison. Their crimes are not serious enough. Of the more than 10,000,000 persons arrested each year in the United States, about 500,000 end up in prison. Five percent go to prison, 95 percent go elsewhere (or nowhere, as half of all arrests are disposed of without a conviction).

Criminals can be divided into three offense types--traffic, misdemeanor, and felony. Traffic violators are most likely to get a fine. If an additional punishment is tacked on, it is likely to be community service or a suspended jail sentence.

Misdemeanor offenses call for a penalty of up to a year in jail and a fine prescribed for each offense. Misdemeanors include thefts, assaults, vandalism, possession of marijuana, disturbing the peace, and so forth. Convicted misdemeanants, like traffic violators, often get fines and suspended sentences. Repeaters are likely to get short jail terms. Community service, court costs, restitution, and probation supervision are also misdemeanor punishment options.

Special counseling ("treatment") programs have been developed for certain types of traffic and misdemeanor criminals in recent years. Involvement in domestic violence in many locales may result in referral to counseling. Traffic violators may be sent to driver improvement training. Persons involved in assaults and "road rage" incidents may be assigned to anger management classes. And huge numbers of persons convicted of alcohol and drug crimes are sentenced to substance abuse counseling.

Felons are the third type of criminals. In recent years about a third of convicted felons have been sentenced directly to probation. These are predominantly first-time felons convicted of property and lesser drug crimes, though a few violent criminals, mostly those convicted of assault and battery, may also get probation. About 20 to 25 percent of felony offenders get a combination sentence--jail time followed by probation. These people are often held in jail pre-trial until their case comes to court. They plead guilty, with credit for time served, and get released from jail directly to probation.

## Sentencing Options: Imprisonment

What Harry Allen and Clifford Simonsen have called the correctional filter takes most lesser criminals (and a good number of greater criminals against whom evidence is lacking) out of the system and returns them to the community from whence they came. But for someone arrested for a felony in which the evidence is strong, the odds of imprisonment increase. If the charge sticks at the felony level, the defendant (particularly one who has a prior criminal history) has an even chance of going to prison.

A felony is generally defined as a crime for which the penalty is a year or more in a state or federal prison. Felony sentences over the past decade have averaged about five to six years. Violent criminals get longer terms, while property, drug, and public-order criminals get shorter terms. According to state court records for 1998, 928,000 adults were convicted of felonies. The great majority--94 percent--pleaded guilty, often as a result of **plea bargaining** (reaching a deal about the length of the sentence, the specific charge, or the number of charges). The other six percent were convicted at trial.

Convicted felons drew three dispositions:
1. Probation--32 percent.
2. Local jail term (often time served, with probation to follow)--24 percent.
3. State prison term--44 percent.

By categories, state court felons were convicted of:
1. Drug crimes--34 percent.
2. Property crimes--31 percent.
3. Violent crimes--18 percent.

4. Public order crimes--18 percent.

The likelihood of imprisonment varied considerably by crime of conviction:
1. Murder--94 percent.
2. Robbery--76 percent.
3. Rape--70 percent.
4. Burglary--54 percent.
5. Drug trafficking--45 percent.
6. Auto theft--43 percent.
7. Drug possession--36 percent.
8. Fraud--35 percent.

Federal courts sentenced 50,000 felons in 1998, the majority for drug trafficking (38 percent) or fraud (17 percent). Four out of five federal felons got prison time. Their average sentence was just over five years.

About two-thirds of felons entering state prisons each year are serving new sentences. The other third are parole or probation violators who have had their conditional status revoked and now have to serve their "old" prison sentence, or the rest of it.

## Sentencing Options: Death

Death was once commonly applied to a wide variety of criminals. Under English common law, almost every felony eventually became a **capital crime**. In all Western societies through the eighteenth century, death sentences were frequently imposed and executions common public events. No more. In August 2002, the United Nations and the Death Penalty Information Center identified 111 countries as abolitionist in law or practice--76 for all crimes, 15 for all but military crimes or crimes against the state, and 20 de facto (the penalty is on the books but never used). About 84 countries are retentionist, still imposing death sentences, some sporadically, some frequently. Only a handful of countries--China, the Congo, Iran, Iraq, Saudi Arabia, and the United States --routinely carry out more than 20 to 30 executions a year.

Most Americans--from 60 to 70 percent--according to the most recent polls, support the death penalty. In the 1960s, public support was much lower. The number of executions in America had declined steadily from the 1930s on, slowing to a trickle by the 1960s, and more Americans were opposed to the death penalty in 1966 than in favor of it. The U.S. Supreme Court, in *Furman v. Georgia* (1972), ruled that the death penalty as it was then being applied violated the Eighth Amendment's prohibition against "cruel and unusual punishment."

Opponents of capital punishment thought the death penalty had been abolished. But public concern over high levels of violent crime promoted a resurgence of political enthusiasm for capital punishment, and four years later, in *Gregg v. Georgia* (1976), the Supreme Court approved reinstatement of the death penalty, provided a structured process was followed. Today, 38 states, the federal government, and the military follow the steps approved by the Court almost 30 years ago. They include:
1. A narrow definition of the crime of first-degree or capital murder, usually defining specific circumstances such as a felony murder (like a robbery), a multiple homicide, or the killing of a police officer.
2. A two-part trial, called a **bifurcated trial**, with a guilt phase followed by a separate penalty phase.
3. Presentation of **aggravating circumstances** and **mitigating circumstances** in the penalty phase. Aggravating circumstances, such as torture, prior criminality, victim impact, or future dangerousness, make the crime worse. Mitigating circumstances, such as the criminal's youth, family history, or mental disability, show that he may not deserve the death penalty.
4. Automatic appeal to the state supreme court, which reviews the trial record for errors and to insure **proportionality**, the concept that a similar crime elsewhere in the state might also have resulted in a death sentence.

Local prosecutors, who exercise the **gatekeeper function** in filing capital charges and seeking death sentences in court, seek the death penalty in less than 10 percent of all homicides. Death sentences averaged about 300 per year in the 1990s. For any single homicide during this time, the national odds of getting a death sentence ranged year to year from about one in 50 to one in 80. The odds on eventually being executed, after receiving a death sentence, are no more than one in three or four, though this varies greatly from state to state.

Support for the death penalty has dropped again recently as publicity about the extent of innocent men and women on death row has undercut public and political confidence in the legal process. The numbers of both death sentences and executions have fallen. Two U.S. Supreme Court decisions, *Atkins v. Virginia* (2002), prohibiting the execution of the mentally retarded, and *Ring v. Arizona* (2002), requiring juries--rather than the judge-- to impose a death sentence, have each removed defendants from death row. The biggest hit to America's death row population was in January 2003, when Illinois governor George Ryan, citing a "terribly broken" legal system, commuted the death sentences of all 167 inmates on Illinois's death row. The Court has allowed the practice of executing juveniles as young as 16 (at the time of the crime) to stand, although only seven states, all in the South, have actually done so in the past two decades.

As the death row population declined to about 3,500 in 2003, some have asked yet again if the death penalty is finally on the way out. The answer is not anytime soon. It remains popular nationally and hugely popular in the South, where about two-thirds of death row inmates are found and where about 90 percent of executions occur. The death penalty is more about symbolism and politics than it is crime control, but it is one part of American culture that many citizens continue to hold dear to their heart.

## The Sentencing Decision

When the criminal has been convicted, who decides the sentence? Most people would probably respond, "the judge," because the robed figure on the podium is the one who imposes it. That used to be true, but today's judges face more constraints in imposing sentences.

Under English common law and European civil law, the **trial judge** was the sentencing authority. Judges enjoyed wide discretion in deciding sentences, which for felonies could range from outright discharge to death. The sentence was quickly carried out, and few cases were appealed or subject to the intervention of the king.

In the twentieth century model of the American felony court, the judge ordered a **probation officer** to complete a **pre-sentence investigation report (PSI)**, like a background investigation into the crime and the defendant, providing information to the judge and recommending a sentence.

This option is still available today, but most convictions--90 to 95 percent or more in virtually all courts--are obtained through plea bargaining. The plea bargaining model transfers sentencing power from the judge to the **prosecutor**. The prosecutor negotiates an appropriate sentence for the defendant, who pleads guilty. The judge can ratify or reject this bargain, but the sentence is really the prosecutor's call. This compromise or **bureaucratic model**--involving prosecutor, defendant, defense counsel, and judge in a collaborative effort to impose punishment while avoiding costly and time-consuming trials--is a much more accurate representation of how sentencing works today. So while district attorneys, victims' advocates, and legislators (who actually make the laws others execute) protest **judicial imperialism** and leniency in sentencing, prosecutors have much more control over outcomes than judges do.

In about half the states, state **appellate courts** can review the sentence imposed by the trial court. They have the power to shorten the sentence if they believe an unduly severe sentence has been imposed. The **governor** and two authorities that are part of the state's correctional system, the **parole board** and the **pardon board**, also influence sentencing. The parole board has limited authority to allow the conditional release of the criminal from prison before his sentence is up. The pardon board can recommend to the governor a pardon to set aside a conviction or a commutation to shorten the sentence of someone in prison.

Finally, the prison itself affects sentence length through its use of **good time**, time deducted from a prisoner's sentence for good behavior. This practice, which started as a way of reinforcing positive behavior at Auburn prison in 1817, was universal in American prisons throughout the twentieth century. State prisoners could often shorten their sentences by a third or half. Good time today is often called **earn time** or **gain time** when it is tied to specific achievement on the prisoner's part, such as participation in vocational training or education programs, rather than merely avoiding disciplinary misconduct.

To say that the judge decides the sentence ignores the significant impact of numerous other less-visible participants. The judge is really just a stage actor in a much larger production, though he is likely to be blamed when anything goes wrong with the outcome of a sentence.

## Sentencing Issues and Reforms

Early penitentiaries used **determinate sentencing**. If you got two years for theft, you served every day of the two years. The advent of good time (adopted not to help inmates but to maintain order) changed this calculation, making it possible for well-behaved prisoners to get out early. The rise of the reformatory in the late 1800s was also important. It used parole to expand early release of reformed (later rehabilitated) men and women back into society.

As Michael Tonry has pointed out, determinate sentencing evolved into a model of **indeterminate sentencing** that prevailed in state and federal courts from the 1930s into the 1970s. This model allowed for two forms of criminal sentencing. In some states, such as California, a defendant would be sentenced to an open-ended term, such as one to 15 years for auto theft. In others, such as Louisiana, the judge would select a specific term, say five years, from a much longer range provided in the statute. But in both states, the criminal would be parole eligible and would earn good time, so he would usually stay for no more than one-third to one-half the maximum possible length of the sentence imposed.

The indeterminate sentence allowed for individualization of both the original sentence and time actually spent in custody. The key to its use was **sentencing discretion**, which was allowed under the traditions of both English common law and European civil law. The critics of contemporary sentencing argued that discretion had become **disparity**, in which widely divergent penalties were applied to criminals convicted of similar crimes. Sometimes disparity resulted from **discrimination**, based on race or other variables, but often it could not really be explained. It seemed a part of the sentencing culture that developed over time in a locale and was then applied by judges who differed sharply in particular cases. Some judges were tough on crime, or certain crimes, such as drug offenses, while others were lenient. And it was all perfectly legal, so long as the sentence fell within the range provided by law, which was often very broad.

The way to attack disparity was to limit discretion, mostly judicial discretion but also discretion in the hands of other officials. The most direct way to reduce discretion in sentencing and correctional practice was to change the laws under which discretion was exercised, and this is what state legislatures and the federal Congress did during the 1980s and 1990s. The objective was to return to the old determinate sentence of the 1800s.

One of the ways to make punishment more certain was to abolish the probation option for several types of crimes --gun crimes, selling drugs, or sex crimes, for instance. Conviction required mandatory prison terms, or what were more often called **mandatory minimum sentences**. On the other end of the spectrum--discharge from prison--the federal government and about 15 states abolished discretionary release from prison on parole. This change could not be retroactive to prisoners held under prior sentences, but it could be made effective as of a certain date: from that date on, no convicted felons would be eligible for parole. Many other states also cut back on parole by eliminating eligibility for specific types of offenders--murderers, sex criminals, or repeat offenders, for instance--or by increasing the portion of the sentence that had to be served before the eligibility date was reached (such as from one-third to one-half the sentence).

California and other states moved in this direction by adopted **presumptive sentencing**, which establishes a base line sentence but allows a judge to give a greater or lesser sentence within a specified range based on specified aggravating or mitigating circumstances. In 1993, Washington passed the first new **habitual offender enhancement** provision, commonly known as **three strikes and you're out**, which provided an automatic life term for the third serious felony conviction. It attempted to apply selective incapacitation as a practice. Drawing on the baseball analogy--and going far beyond the old habitual offender statutes already in use--three strikes laws targeted repeat felons for long, mandatory prison terms. California's law, enacted in 1994, gave a mandatory sentence of 25 years to life to any violent felon convicted of two prior felonies of any type, violent or not, and doubled the sentence for the second felony conviction. It is the most inclusive in the country and has had great impact on that state's prison population.

Violent criminals were targeted as well by reduced good-time provisions. In new sentencing provisions that took effect in 1987, Congress mandated that all federal criminals had to serve 85 percent of their prison terms. Parole was abolished and, after good-time release, **supervised release** was added as a replacement. Twenty-eight states and the District of Columbia, enticed by federal funding of jail and prison construction, adopted the 85-percent standard for violent criminals by the end of the 1990s.

The term commonly used for reducing good time is "truth in sentencing," the implication being that sentencing was previously a lie, that people were fooled into thinking that criminals were going away for a much longer time. Perhaps they were. But members of the **courtroom work group**--prosecutors, defense attorneys, and judges--knew how good time and parole worked, and they agreed on sentences accordingly.

Another significant method of reducing discretion was the use of **sentencing guidelines** (or sentencing grids). The two most influential models, developed by Minnesota in 1980 and the U.S. Sentencing Commission in 1987, set up a table arranging crimes from most serious to least serious on one side; across the top is a scale that considers the criminal's prior offense history. Where the two lines of crime and criminal history cross, a penalty is designated, usually a narrow range from within which the judge must choose. Sentencing thus becomes mathematical rather than a matter of discretion.

Before the movement to take away judicial discretion began, numerous other reforms had been offered to eliminate disparity by making the decision-making process more systematic or standardized. The **Model Penal Code** proposed by the American Law Institute in 1962 put forth a uniform set of criminal laws and penalties for the states to consider. Suggesting that imprisonment should be used as a last resort, it did not get a lot of attention in the post-1970 crime control era. Sentencing institutes and sentencing councils for judges were also proposed as ways to reduce disparity. New judges, who in America usually come to office without prior training, were supposed to be sent off to **sentencing institutes** to learn how to sentence properly; this training was intended to at least expose these officials to the principles of proportionality and fairness. **Sentencing councils** were groups of judges who would review cases coming up for sentencing and share their views, resulting in sentences that reflect group discretion. Councils have been used in an advisory capacity but are no longer highly thought of today. Indeed, discretion in any form remains a bad word in the politics of sentencing today, except for the relatively hidden and totally unaccountable discretion of prosecutors.

## The Impact of Sentencing on Corrections

The corrections system has been profoundly affected by sentencing changes of the past 30 years. Nationwide we have far more people behind bars and under supervision in the community than we have ever had before. This condition is the result of several related changes in sentencing practices:

1. More convicted felons going directly to prison.
2. Sharp increases in the imprisonment of drug criminals after 1980.
3. Longer prison terms, particularly for violent criminals, habitual criminals, and drug traffickers.
4. Criminals serving more of their terms, as parole and good time were cut back.
5. More formal control of misdemeanants and felons under community supervision, imposing more conditions on them, and locking them up more often if they fail to comply.

One notable example of the overall trend toward greater punitiveness is the growth of **natural life sentences** in state and federal prisons--a punishment rarely used anywhere else in the world. Before the 1970s, there was no such thing as a true life sentence in American prisons. By 2001, according to the *Corrections Yearbook*, about 117,000 inmates, nine percent of the total prison population, were serving life sentences. Of these, 31,000 (or 26 percent) were natural lifers. Georgia had almost 6,000, Pennsylvania and Louisiana 3,600 each. The Louisiana State Penitentiary at Angola has become a lifers prison; 85 percent of its inmates come there to serve terms that will last until they die in prison. No other prison in the world can make such a claim.

What is next for criminal sentencing? Many practitioners and corrections scholars would like to see a model of criminal sentencing that uses shorter sentences and more community-based alternatives. These goals may be unreachable in the short term. To whatever degree sentencing disparity has been reduced over the past three decades, the result has been the destruction of individualized sentencing. In the course of eliminating "leniency" by imposing sentences that are equally severe, we have driven our jail and prison populations to all-time highs. Many citizens and most politicians evidently want this trend to continue, even if the reasons for the policies are irrational or erroneous.

## SELF TEST

### Multiple Choice

1. Punishing one offender as an example to discourage other offenders is called:
   - a. rationality
   - b. transference
   - c. monasticism
   - d. genetics
   - e. deterrence

2. Which one of the following best states the purpose of indeterminate sentencing?
   - a. To keep the prison population as small as possible
   - b. To move all offenders through the system as quickly as possible
   - c. To frighten young people into avoiding lives of crime
   - d. To provide early release for rehabilitated inmates
   - e. To separate the mentally ill from the general prison population

3. A sentence that requires the offender to serve a prison term, such as for committing a crime of violence using a firearm, is called a(n):
   - a. preemptive sentence
   - b. concurrent sentence
   - c. exclusive sentence
   - d. reductive sentence
   - e. mandatory sentence

4. The purpose best served by the three strikes and you're out laws is:
   - a. reintegrative
   - b. restorative
   - c. incapacitative
   - d. eclectic
   - e. diminutive

5. If you were protesting sentencing disparity, you would most likely be making which one of the following statements?
   - a. Criminals are not given enough help to change their behavior
   - b. Penalties for the same offense vary too much from one offender to another
   - c. Judges ought to have more discretion rather than less in imposing penalties
   - d. Victims have too much influence over sentencing
   - e. It is hard to tell whether a specific sentence has much effect on the offender

6. Who usually prepares the presentence investigation report?
   - a. the judge's law clerk
   - b. the deputy court clerk
   - c. a police detective
   - d. the probation officer
   - e. an assistant district attorney

7. A recent restatement of retributive justice--viewing prison time as pain to be meted out--is known as:
   - a. just deserts
   - b. due process
   - c. lock psychosis
   - d. habeas corpus
   - e. corporal time

8. In the penalty phase of a capital trial, the defense attorney normally presents _____ circumstances to show why the defendant does not deserve death.
   - a. inflammatory
   - b. commendatory
   - c. mitigating
   - d. associative
   - e. pacifying

9. Recent sentencing trends include four of the following; which one does NOT fit?
   - a. More convicted felons going directly to prison
   - b. Prisoners serving more of their terms before release
   - c. Longer prison terms for habitual offenders
   - d. Declining use of life sentences
   - e. Increased imprisonment of drug criminals

10. In the BARJ model, the key word seems to be _____.
   a. alternative
   b. judgment
   c. agreement
   d. bureaucratic
   e. restorative

## True or False

_____ 11. The shift to determinate sentencing is intended to give judges more discretion in tailoring sentences to fit offenders.

_____ 12. The conservative ideology is generally associated with policies resulting in higher rates of imprisonment.

_____ 13. The idea of equivalence is most closely associated with the incapacitation theory in corrections.

_____ 14. Most of the world's nations today do not regularly employ the death penalty to punish criminals.

_____ 15. Indeterminate sentencing gave correctional authorities a lot of power to determine how long the offender actually remained in custody.

_____ 16. In general, the prosecutor is more important in determining criminal sentences than the judge is.

_____ 17. Sentencing today emphasizes rehabilitation to a greater extent than it ever has previously.

_____ 18. Truth-in-sentencing laws generally require offenders to serve a greater portion of their sentence in prison before release.

_____ 19. Today everyone convicted of a felony crime has to go to prison.

_____ 20. In *Furman v. Georgia* (1972), the Supreme Court struck down all death penalty statutes then in existence in the United States.

## Fill In the Blanks

21. If it worked perfectly well, the _____ approach should reduce prison population by identifying and confining the high-rate offenders who commit the majority of serious crimes.

22. The juvenile version of deterrence was known by the term _____.

23. The 1970s model that tried to take (or keep) criminals out of prison and deal with their problems using community resources was known as the _____ model.

24. When parole is done away with, the principal remaining way for a convict to get early release is _____.

25. The general argument against discretion in sentencing suggests that allowing too much discretion results in _____.

26. If a state legislator was making a speech about "imperialism" in sentencing, he would probably be criticizing the power of _____.

27. A table with a list of crimes on one side and a scale of prior criminal convictions across the top would be an example of sentencing _____.

28. Discretionary release is most often associated with the action of _____ boards.

29. The great majority of _____ offenders would expect to get a fine and probation or a suspended sentence.

30. In regard to the death penalty, the gatekeeper function is said to be performed by the _____.

## Discussion

31. What does sentencing disparity mean, and how can we get rid of it?

32. Why is the perception that judges have almost total control over sentencing not accurate?

33. Explain the rationale of the shift from indeterminate to determinate sentencing.

34. If you were a judge looking over a presentence investigation report on an offender you knew nothing about, what information in the report would you find most important?

35. What important standards were established by the Supreme Court decision of *Gregg v. Georgia* (1976)?

36. Explain how the different ideologies--conservative, liberal, and radical--view the use of imprisonment.

37. Define a model for individual sentencing if rehabilitation were the prime objective of criminal sentencing,

CHAPTER FIVE

# Jails

Most Americans have never been inside a prison, but practically everyone would know where to find the nearest jail.  Jails in America are typically locally operated by county or city governments.  They are defined by extremes--from tiny to huge; from primitive to ultra-modern; from one or two cells to multi-story high rises; from isolated rural settings to downtown complexes; from no services at all to services equal to the best provided in state prisons.  As the entry point into corrections, jails hold an eclectic mix of adults (and a few juveniles) at all stages of the criminal justice process. Federal jail inspector Joseph Fishman in 1923 called the jail "a melting pot" for the worst elements in the criminal world; it remains much the same, only much larger, today.  After reading this chapter, you should be familiar with:

    1. The jail's place in corrections.
    2. The jail's historical role.
    3. The American jail system today.
    4. The legal status of jail inmates.
    5. A profile of jail inmates.
    6. Jail design and architecture.
    7. Jail problems.
    8. Contrasts between urban and rural jails.
    9. Proposals to improve the jail.

## Key Terms

detention
gaol
jail
keeper
fee system
gaol fever
dumping ground
rabble
Walnut Street Jail
Wickersham Commission
county sheriffs
lockups
state-operated jails
detention centers
holdback inmates
detainer
bus terminal
trusty
detoxification centers
John Howard Society
linear/intermittent surveillance design
bullpen
drunk tank
first-generation jail

podular/remote surveillance design
pods
second-generation jail
podular/direct supervision design
third-generation jail
new-generation jail
custodial convenience
enforced idleness
overcrowding
staffing
per diem
Special Operations Response Team (SORT)
accreditation
American Jail Association
supervised pretrial release
Pretrial Services Resource Center
price-tag justice
special courts
drug courts
weekenders
community service
pretrial alternatives
community correctional center

## The Jail in History

The jail is the oldest correctional facility, though some would argue vehemently against the idea that the jail has ever had much of a correctional purpose.  The jail's historical role was to hold prisoners awaiting trial or punishment.  Today we call this role **detention**, the part of corrections that takes place before conviction and the imposition of sentence.  The English institution that provided this function was called a **gaol**. The American pronunciation is the same but the spelling is **jail**.

The Assize of Clarendon of 1166 required all sheriffs in English counties to construct jails to hold prisoners awaiting trial. The jail was nominally under the control of the sheriff, who was the king's chief administrative officer at the county level. Sheriffs contracted the jail out to a **keeper** who was directly responsible for custody of inmates. Although the keeper was paid no salary, the contract was considered desirable in that it provided the keeper an income from fees charged inmates and the contract itself could be sold for an exorbitant price.

The **fee system** endured for several hundred years. It put the responsibility for financing the jail not on the government--local or national--but on the inmates, or their families, friends, or charitable sponsors. Urban jails, then as now, were often overcrowded. Today we have tuberculosis, hepatitis, and HIV; early English jails had **gaol fever** (typhus), pneumonia, smallpox, starvation and a host of other ailments related to malnourishment, no medical care, and infectious diseases that spread rapidly in close quarters. Women inmates and children, who were mixed in population, were subject to sexual exploitation by keepers and other inmates.

Linda Zupan called the medieval English jail a **dumping ground** for social outcasts, misfits, and those for whom no care options existed at the time, such as the insane and the diseased, particularly lepers. In *The Jail* (1985), John Irwin argues that the jail's role in controlling **rabble**, society's underclass, has always dominated its role in holding real criminals. In English jails, the majority of those confined were vagrants, debtors, the poor and unemployed, runaways, and the mentally ill; criminals awaiting trial or sentence were in the minority.

The English sheriff and jail reformer John Howard sought major jail reforms in the 1770s and 1780s:
  1. Segregation of prisoners by age, sex, and severity of crime.
  2. Cells for prisoners to reduce moral and physical contamination.
  3. Salaried staff to prevent extortion by keepers.
  4. Appointment of chaplains and medical officers to promote the spiritual and physical well-being of prisoners.
  5. Prohibitions against the sale of liquor to prisoners.
  6. Provision of adequate clothing and food to prisoners to ensure their continued good health.
Howard's reforms, while popularly received, were put into practice long after his death--from gaol fever--in 1790.

Colonial American jails were based on the English model. They were under the control of county sheriffs, they charged prisoners fees for necessities and luxuries, and they were found as stone or wooden structures located downtown in the county seats. The most influential colonial jail, Philadelphia's **Walnut Street Jail**, considered the birthplace of the penitentiary regimen, was closed in 1835 and eventually completely demolished.

While the American penitentiary developed as a state institution in the 1800s, the jail remained a local institution --primitive, understaffed, and poorly funded. Its only correctional motivation was avoidance: no one would want to come back. But surprisingly (and sadly) enough, many of its customers were regulars--the habitual drunks, riffraff, and petty troublemakers who lived on the fringes of modern urban society, John Irwin's rabble.

In most parts of the country, the jail was still a single local institution, under the direction of the sheriff, serving the dual purposes of custodial confinement and misdemeanant punishment. An advisory report submitted to the National Commission on Law Observance and Enforcement (better known as the **Wickersham Commission**) in 1931 called local jails "dirty, unhealthy, unsanitary--and ill-fitted to produce either a stabilizing or beneficial effect on inmates." Half a century later not much had changed, except that overcrowding was worse in the larger jails: Attorney and author Ronald Goldfarb subtitled his classic 1976 book on jails "The Ultimate Ghetto." This was the condition of the American jail in the early 1970s, when it held about 100,000 inmates. As the "War on Crime" got underway, these numbers would soar, to over 600,000 by 2001, aggravating jail problems that were centuries old.

## The American Jail System Today

The structure of the jail system in America is not much different from what it was a hundred years ago (or from its origins in England a thousand years ago). The jail is a unit of local government. Most jails are operated by **county sheriffs**; indeed, although the sheriff may perform diverse law enforcement, civil, and court-related functions, more sheriffs' employees work in jails than in any other function.

A jail was defined by the "National Jail Census, 1970" as "any facility operated by a unit of local government for the detention or correction of adults suspected or convicted of a crime and which has the authority to detain longer than 48 hours." This definition is still used today, except that it makes reference to detention after the first court appearance and increases the holding period from 48 hours to 72 hours.

Two types of facilities are excluded from this definition. **Lockups** are short-term facilities typically operated by local police under municipal authority. A lockup is most commonly a cell or group of cells in the back of a police station. An arrested person might be held there for a few hours or overnight pending questioning, release, or transfer to the county jail. Also excluded are **state-operated jails**. Six states--Alaska, Connecticut, Delaware, Hawaii, Rhode Island, and Vermont--operate combined jail/prison systems (Alaska also has 15 locally operated jails) in which local, pre-trial inmates are housed in state-run facilities.

The Justice Department's detailed jail census counted 3,365 jails in 45 states (including Alaska) in 1999. They held 605,943 inmates, or an average of 180 inmates each, which on the surface appears to be a cozy, manageable number. An estimated 11 million persons were admitted to jail in 1999. By 2002, the jail inmate count was up to 665,475, an increase of 10 percent in three years.

Most jails hold far fewer than 180 inmates; 63 percent in the 1999 survey had a capacity of under 100 inmates. The 2,100 jails in this category held only 71,000 inmates, or about 34 each. These were the jails that had the most empty beds, averaging about 71 to 85 percent of capacity. The 300 largest jails in America, on the other hand, housed 48 percent of the total inmate population, almost 300,000 inmates, under the most congested conditions. They were at 97 percent of capacity overall. The 50 largest jail systems, all of them in urban counties or cities, housed nearly a third of all jail inmates--209,847 as of June 30, 2002.

## Jail Inmates: Legal Status

Most arrested adults will be booked into jails--most of them locally operated but a few state or federal--as their entry point into the legal system. Juveniles are generally housed in separate **detention centers** or detention homes or halls, but some facing adult trials or living in rural areas where juvenile facilities are not available will be confined in adult jails.

The 1999 jail census identifies these functions by type of inmate:
1. To receive individuals pending arraignment and hold them awaiting trial, conviction, or sentencing.
2. To readmit probation, parole, and bail-bond violators and absconders.
3. To temporarily detain juveniles pending transfer to juvenile authorities.
4. To hold mentally ill persons pending their movement to appropriate health facilities.
5. To hold individuals for the military, for protective custody, for contempt, and for the courts as witnesses.
6. To release convicted inmates to the community upon completion of sentence.
7. To transfer inmates to Federal, State, or other authorities.
8. To house inmates for Federal, State, or other authorities because of crowding of their facilities.
9. To relinquish custody of temporary detainees to juvenile and medical authorities.
10. To operate community-based programs with day reporting, home detention, electronic monitoring, or other types of supervision.
11. To hold inmates sentenced to short terms (generally under one year).

At mid-year 2002, about 60 percent of jail inmates were held in pre-trial detention. They were supposed to be detained and not punished, but it is not easy to tell the difference in many jails where they are mixed with other inmates serving sentences. Except for the ranks of what Harry Allen and Clifford Simonsen call **holdback inmates**--those felons serving state time--the sentenced inmates are misdemeanants, which means large numbers of people convicted of DWI, theft, assault, and minor drug crimes. Jails also hold large numbers of probation and parole violators under **detainer**, meaning that they cannot be released until a revocation hearing is held. In the miscellaneous category, you might find a few material witnesses, a few people in contempt of court, and, more recently a growing number of people behind on their child support payments--so-called "deadbeat dads." Finally, jails hold inmates awaiting transfer to other state prisons or to federal facilities, including alien deportation centers and military jails. Little wonder that the jail has been called the **bus terminal** to the rest of the corrections system. It is here that people make connections to wherever they are going.

An average jail stay in recent years is reportedly about 20 days but, like the average number of inmates per jail, this is a deceptive figure. Ninety percent or more of jail inmates turn over rapidly. They are in and out within

41

a few hours. The other ten percent stay longer. They are accused felons unable to make bail, misdemeanants serving short sentences, felons serving longer sentences in those states (such as Louisiana and Kentucky) where state prisoners have been housed in local jails, and probation and parole violators awaiting revocation hearings. So jails do have a semi-permanent population, some of whom will be assigned **trusty** status to do the cooking, cleaning, and maintenance work. Trusties (not "trustees," who oversee financial or legal affairs) often live in better housing and are given more privileges; at one time they ran many jails.

## Jail Inmates: A Profile

Many minor offenders never go any farther than their one local jail, though they may go in and out of it many times during their lifetimes. In their "dumping ground" function, jails until recently held a diverse group of drunks, the mentally ill, vagrants and derelicts (before they became "homeless people"), juvenile runaways, and anyone else the police wanted to detain until they could decide what to do with them.

Although **detoxification centers** have had significant impact in removing habitual drunks and some offenders high on drugs from the drunk tank to the treatment ward, substance abuse remains the most common immediate problem of jail inmates. Local jurisdictions have cracked down on DWI offenders in recent years, and urban jails are now full of men and women arrested on drug charges--not drug dealing, necessarily, just simple possession of various illegal drugs.

Mental illness is also prevalent among jail inmates, especially among the homeless people finding their way back into jail as police crack down on disorderly conduct in public places--trying to drive transients off the streets. If a drunk, or an addict, or a homeless person commits a crime and is arrested, he still goes to jail; if he cannot make bail, he stays.

If you went through the jails and eliminated the offenders without serious, documented problems with alcohol and drugs and without a history of mental health issues, you would not have many people left in most jails. Jails deal with many troubled people, as you see in jail death statistics--suicide trailing only natural causes as the leading cause of inmate deaths, and AIDS deaths occurring at a rate several times higher than in the free world.

Jail inmates remain predominantly male--88.4 percent versus 11.6 percent female--although the number of female inmates has increased more rapidly than that of men over the past 20 years (since the War on Drugs began). At midyear 2002, nearly six in ten local jail inmates were racial or ethnic minorities. Whites made up 43.8 percent of the jail population; blacks 39.8 percent; Hispanics 14.7%; and other races (Asians, American Indians, Alaska Natives, Native Hawaiians, and other Pacific Islanders) 1.6%.

The jail's inmate population continues to evolve. Drug crimes have brought more women to jail. AIDS, tuberculosis, and hepatitis, all of which are strongly associated with drug usage and unhealthy lifestyles, have brought a lot more sick inmates into jails, and have escalated the costs of jail medical care. Jails are still cheaper to operate than prisons, because of lower guard-to-inmate ratios and the lack of rehabilitation and support services, but the cost differential is narrowing. Reform groups, such as the **John Howard Society** (or Association), named after the English sheriff, advocate a much broader role for the jail in dealing with criminal behavior. Jails touch far more lives than prisons do but often have few resources to address their inmates' problems.

## Jail Design and Architecture

Jails come in all types and designs, influenced most by age and intended capacity. The old county jails featured what is now called the **linear/intermittent surveillance design**--multi-person cells arranged in long tiers like prison cellblocks. Guards walked up and down the corridors outside the cells observing inmates through the bars. These jails featured such cells as the **bullpen**, which might hold from half a dozen to twenty or more inmates in a single cell; the **drunk tank**, a foul, smelly cell where drunks were kept until they sobered up; a padded cell for mental cases; and separate cells or tiers for juveniles and women. These **first-generation jails** practiced little classification of inmates; a middle-aged businessman arrested for traffic violations might be thrown into a bullpen with murderers and rapists who had been in jail for years.

In the 1960s, the **podular/remote surveillance design** was developed. Cells were arranged in sections commonly called **pods** (from podular), sharing a common floor space used for eating and other group activities; inmates spent most of their time in this common area, not locked in their individual (usually two-man or larger) small cells. These **second-generation jails** were designed to provide indirect surveillance of inmates by jailers who watched from glassed-in control booths. One jailer would typically be watching a pod that contained 20 or 50 or 100 inmates. Jailers were only in direct contact with inmates when they went into the pod.

In the mid-1970s, three model federal jails, called Metropolitan Correctional Centers, applied the **podular/direct supervision design** in which the correctional officer is placed inside each housing unit or pod with no bars or glass separating him from the inmates. Many of the newer, larger urban jails now apply the principles of direct supervision. They are called **third-generation** (or **new-generation**) jails. They look very different from the old jails laid out in cellblocks. In the third-generation design, the jailers are locked inside the pods with the inmates. The jailer mans a console or a desk where he can observe and talk to inmates directly at all times. This approach increases security and also promotes interaction between jail guards and inmates. The podular cell design is now being supplemented by direct-supervision dormitories in many county jails, providing a less costly medium-custody alternative to cell housing for ordinary inmates.

## Jail Problems

The problems of the jail are diverse and enduring. When we look at why it has been so difficult to improve the jail, three aspects of the jail's operation stand out:

    1. The jail is predominantly a local institution, meaning it often lacks the political and economic resources to better itself.

    2. The jail's clientele--characterized as rabble, drunks, nuts, dopeheads, and losers--do not rate very far up the scale of social concern.

    3. The short-term duration of the jail experience, in contrast to longer-term imprisonment, diverts attention away from jail conditions; the perspective is that even if jails are awful, most people will not be in them very long anyway.

In the past, poor physical facilities often went hand in hand with poor staffing. Most jails were operated by county sheriffs or municipal police departments that considered the jail a nuisance function. Most jails were small, averaging fewer than 25 inmates with only one jailer on duty at any given time. The jailer was a police officer or deputy sheriff who was also the booking officer, dispatcher, and records clerk. Jail staff were often the newest officers in training or older men not fit for road duty. In many jurisdictions even this minimal level of staffing was not a certainty. Jails were left unattended or in the care of trusties--inmates with the keys to the cells of other inmates.

Hans Mattick, in his influential research of the 1960s and 1970s, referred to jail administration in this era as guided by the principle of **custodial convenience**, defined as "everyone who can, takes the easy way out and makes only the minimal effort." Jailers concentrated on preventing escapes and left inmates to work out their own internal order, not unlike conditions in English jails several hundred years earlier.

Without treatment or work, the jail environment was one of **enforced idleness**, meaning that inmates were kept in cells with no activities or programs. They could talk, smoke, play cards and dominoes, read, eat, and sleep; if you spent a day in jail or 180 days in jail, the routine was the same (and still is in many jails). As Harry Allen and Clifford Simonsen wrote recently, "A lot of 'doing time' is dead time."

Poor staffing, inadequate physical facilities, and the absence of programs were tolerable so long as jails were small and legally invisible. But when jail populations began to increase in the 1970s and jail overcrowding became a continuing problem, especially in urban jails, inmates began to file and win lawsuits in the federal courts. They attacked jail conditions as violating the "cruel and unusual punishment" provision of the Eighth Amendment. They also sued for damages under the civil rights provisions of Section 1983, Title 42, U.S. Code.

Overcrowding became a major problem for the largest jails by the early 1980s. In Ken Kerle and Dick Ford's influential 1982 report, *The State of Our Nation's Jails*, jail administrators listed their top five problems--personnel, modernization, overcrowding, recreation, and funding. Among the jails under state or federal court order to improve jail conditions at the time, the top five reasons were crowded conditions, recreation, structure (modernization), medical, and visitation.

Jail officials today continue to identify overcrowding and staffing as their two major problems. Even if they are no longer under court order, many large jails are always at or over capacity, which affects inmate medical care, food services, physical conditions, security, classification and segregation, and mental health services. Inmates in urban jails live together in jammed-together idleness, their existence defined by the culture of overcrowding.

Staffing remains a critical concern. Most people who work in American jails are deputies employed by local sheriffs. Most of them have no particular qualifications or interests in corrections. Most jail employees are guards whose job is to maintain security. Jails have few professional staff to provide programs for inmates. Many improvements have been made in the quality of jail staff, particularly in regard to training, but many jails remain both understaffed and badly staffed by employees who, like inmates, would rather be some place else.

Sheriffs are commonly paid a **per diem** rate by county government (a descendant of the old fee system) for housing local prisoners. This rate is typically pitifully small; sheriffs use their own revenues, often supplemented by payments from state and federal authorities for housing their prisoners, to maintain decent living conditions.

## Big Jails

The five largest jail systems in America--Los Angeles, New York, Cook County (Chicago), Maricopa County (Phoenix), and Philadelphia--held over 60,000 inmates at midyear 2002, about 10 percent of the nation's total jail population. These five cities each have more people in jail (7,000+) than 18 states have in their prison systems. With the turnover rate for individual jails averaging 1,000 to 1,500 percent or even more annually, these jails regularly process from 100,000 to 300,000 inmates each year--the population equivalent of a large city flowing in and out of their doors.

The largest of these, Los Angeles County, has maintained an average daily inmate count of more than 19,000 for the past three years, has faced major internal problems. To deal with gang conflicts brought in from the streets, it started "Operation Jail Safe" to isolate and pacify gang members who were often involved in violent incidents within the jail. Faced with increasing numbers of inmates testing positive for tuberculosis, Los Angeles County began taking chest x-rays of inmates placed in population. Los Angeles County had so many inmates with TB, HIV, hepatitis, and drug addiction (often leading to multi-drug resistant TB, or MDRTB), that it resorted to the more expensive but also more thorough and more quickly available x-ray testing.

The jail also attracted attention late in 2001 by allowing an outside group to distribute condoms to about 300 gay inmates in the Central Jail. The sheriff's official policy was that the department was not condoning sex in jail (which is a felony under California law), but that high rates of HIV, syphilis, and other sexually transmitted diseases warranted the condom distribution program as a public health measure. Only four other large jails were known to have policies providing condoms to inmates.

New York City's jail complex, Rikers Island, held about 14,600 inmates in the year 2000. This jail complex, which is often called "the world's largest penal colony" because its ten jails make up a complex filling a small island less than one mile square. Journalist Jennifer Gonnerman called the jail a "city-run superghetto kept out of the public eye." She found that about 30 percent of prisoners had been homeless within three months before they were locked up. Twenty-five percent received some mental health services. Twenty percent of the women and seven percent of the men were HIV-positive. And 90 percent were high school dropouts. Three-quarters of the inmates were pre-trial detainees held because they could not make bail; they spent a year or two in jail waiting to plead guilty.

The Cook County Jail in Chicago has a troubled past marked by gang violence and overcrowding, and a troubled present that looks much the same. More than 11,000 inmates were held in the downtown jail in 2002, making it the largest single correctional facility in the United States. Larger jail maintain a version of a SWAT team to deal with cell extractions, hostage situations, disturbances, and shakedowns. Cook County's **Special Operations Response Team (SORT)** was accused of raiding a maximum-security cellblock for the sole purpose of beating and terrorizing gang members, then filing false reports to cover it up, according to *Chicago Tribune* reports. After an almost four-year internal investigation, 14 deputies were charged with wrongdoing in the incident. In the meantime, overcrowding has worsened, and investigators were looking into a later incident in which several deputies were injured and inmates claimed to have been beaten.

Maricopa County is more famous for its sheriff than its jail. The sheriff is Joe Arpaio, an ex-DEA agent who is called "America's Toughest Sheriff," a nickname given him by the media (or possibly by himself) for hardcore anti-crime and anti-criminal practices. He is famous for his get tough policies: housing 1,200 inmates in a tent city; chain gangs for men, women, and juveniles; only two meals a day, and these very cheap and plain; banning smoking, coffee, movies, porn magazines, and unrestricted television in jail housing units. The sheriff runs a fabulous public relations campaign about himself and his conservative philosophy, but his jail continues to have many of the same problems other large jails have, including frequent lawsuits.

At one time the Philadelphia Jail was reputed to be one of the worst in America, a jail run by inmate gangs who routinely beat and raped new inmates thrown into the jail's tanks. Poor conditions in the jail persisted for many years, eventually resulting in a federal judge imposing a court order on the jail system. Jail population, once capped by the courts at 3,750, had risen to 7,695 by March 2003, partly as a result of new jail construction. Jail critics were concerned that old problems would begin to emerge again once federal court supervision was ended.

## Small Jails

At the opposite end of the scale from these huge complexes are the smaller jails that proliferate at the city and county level. As the big jails' problems originate in high volume and overcrowding, the small jails' problems lie in meager resources and limited services.

The Kotzebue Regional Jail Facility in Kotzebue, Alaska, is an example of a modern small jail. Opened in 1995, the jail's capacity is 12 inmates in one pod and two individual cells. The one or two correctional officers on duty double as police and emergency dispatchers. Busy times often see well over 100 bookings per month, and jail population has gone over 30 at peak times.

Small jails in Kentucky have been experiencing another problem common in local jails--inmate suicides. Jails still have a suicide rate estimated at nine to ten times higher than the free world rate, though this has declined sharply in some jails with better screening and prevention procedures in recent years. The inmates in Kentucky apparently did not get the word, as 17 of them killed themselves in a recent 30-month period.

Lawsuits are common in jail death and injury cases. When fire swept through the Mitchell County Jail in North Carolina on September 5, 2002, eight inmates were killed, seven of them trapped in a second-floor holding cell. The county agreed to pay two million dollars to families of the victims, and lawsuits were pending against the state, whose inspectors failed to detect safety violations in the jail.

## Improving the Jail

Steve Ingley, the executive director of the American Jail Association, has said: "Jails have been required to do a lot more, with a whole lot less. They have a huge responsibility, without the resources. If we're going to continue on this path of putting away people, we're going to have to deal with this." How *do* you deal with this, particularly the fundamental problem of economics that has hampered local jails for a thousand years? Joel Thompson and Larry Mays, in *American Jails* (1991), provide a list of eight recommendations to improve the jail:

1. States should provide aid to local governments for jail construction and renovation.
2. States should develop mandatory jail standards.
3. Inspection and enforcement provision should be developed to compel compliance with standards.
4. States should support cooperative agreements to build regional jails.
5. Local governments should educate citizens about jail functions and conditions.
6. Local officials should develop long-term financial plans for the jail.
7. Jails should be required to have written policies and procedures.
8. Communities should explore alternatives to incarceration.

Mandatory jail standards accompanied by inspection provisions apply in about 35 states today. The major indicator of high standards in jail operations today is the achievement of **accreditation** through the American Correctional Association. This process, which involves self-study according to national correctional standards and auditing by outside experts, is rigorous enough that few jails make the effort. By mid-2003, fewer than 100 (about three percent) of the more than 3,300 local jails were ACA-accredited. The other professional organization important to jails is the **American Jail Association (AJA)**, formed in 1981and dedicated to improving the conditions and systems under which such persons are detained, advancing professionalism and standards, and providing leadership.

Many of these jail professionals have advocated the establishment of larger regional jails to serve multi-county areas. When sheriffs and political officials make such proposals or want to make other improvements to staffing or inmate services, they find that these changes are a hard sell--especially if they cost money in the form of higher taxes or revenue bonds. Most people accept the role of the jail as is. Even in well-off communities, jail are often given the most meager local resources to work with, which obliges them to look to higher levels of government for supplemental funds.

## Alternatives to Jail

As overcrowding and other problems persist in local jails, authorities explore alternatives that would reduce jail populations. **Supervised pretrial release**, or release on recognizance (ROR), has been used in many jurisdictions to release without bail low-income, non-violent lesser defendants who demonstrate strong community ties. The **Pretrial Services Resource Center** in Washington, D.C., is a clearinghouse that sends consultants to work with local jails and courts in establishing guidelines to accomplish two objectives--diverting pre-trial offenders from the jail into treatment and supervision options, and making sure offenders show up for disposition or trial as scheduled.

But turning people loose without bond runs head-on into the traditional and politically-entrenched practices associated with **price-tag justice** in America. We tend to think that offenders with money or property should get out of jail on bail. Poor people, even those who are stable local residents not likely to flee, should stay in. The image of the jail was, and is, that of the appropriate social institution for controlling poor people in the cities.

**Special courts** have been created in many localities to deal with certain types of offenders through diversion and treatment programs. The most prolific growth over the past decade has been in **drug courts**, which try to connect offenders with treatment and social services as an option to conviction and jail or prison time, but other special courts deal with domestic violence, mental health, juvenile, and traffic cases.

For people sentenced to jail time, jails have explored such alternatives as intermittent sentences, in which offenders called **"weekenders"** spend weekends in jail and weekdays at home working, and performing **community service**, which obliges offenders to put in hours on charitable or public service projects. **Pretrial alternatives** and expanded sentencing options administered by a full-service community correctional center would provide increments of increased control over offenders, who could replace idle time with time spent more productively in the community.

## The Jail of the Future

What will the jail of the future look like? Current trends suggest that it will be a larger, more diverse institution than the jail of a few years ago. In rural areas, it will be a regional jail shared by several counties. Many jails will offer a greater range of treatment programs and non-custodial alternatives. The jail might actually become the hub for many forms of correctional intervention at the local level, eventually evolving into the **community correctional center** scholars and jail professionals have imagined for years. Some people would be locked up, pretrial and serving sentences, but far more people would be on pretrial release and work release, coming in to take part in diversion and treatment programs, performing community service, providing restitution to victims, and leading useful lives under supervision in the community.

The two underlying difficulties in imagining this expanded role for the jail are, first, its local nature, and second, money. It is often difficult (or impossible) to get local authorities to work toward this model, especially when multiple jurisdictions are involved. County government officials in America are not famous for working together toward a common goal. Money is always a problem: who is going to pay for the facilities and staff needed to provide this higher level of services? Even with a vision of where they want to go, jail officials see a road cluttered with obstacles.

**SELF TEST**

**Multiple Choice**

1. If you were in a cell with three other inmates in a long row of fifteen cells fronting onto a corridor, which type of facility would you be in?
   - a. a halfway house
   - b. a first-generation jail
   - c. a second-generation jail
   - d. a third-generation jail
   - e. a generation-X jail

2. Most jails are operated by which authorities?
   - a. county sheriffs
   - b. municipal police departments
   - c. state corrections departments
   - d. the Federal Bureau of Prisons
   - e. private contractors

3. This English practice put the cost of jail operation on the offenders housed in it:
   - a. the day fine
   - b. transportation
   - c. discounting
   - d. the fee system
   - e. the bounty

4. What was the basic purpose of the early jail?
   - a. rehabilitation
   - b. reformation
   - c. deterrence
   - d. diversion
   - e. detention

5. The most pervasive problem resulting in state and federal court supervision of local jails has been:
   - a. overcrowding
   - b. lack of recreation
   - c. brutality by guards
   - d. lack of screening for HIV
   - e. limitations on visiting

6. Most jail inmates are in which legal category?
   - a. probationers and parolees under detainer
   - b. sentenced to state custody
   - c. pretrial
   - d. sentenced to federal custody
   - e. convicted and awaiting sentencing

7. The greatest number of American jails have a rated capacity of how many inmates?
   - a. over 1,000
   - b. 501-1,000
   - c. 251-500
   - d. 100-250
   - e. 1-100

8. A living unit of a new jail is most often called a:
   - a. pod
   - b. hub
   - c. clink
   - d. cage
   - e. wheel

9. In his use of the term "rabble," John Irwin was suggesting that most jail inmates are:
   - a. mean and rebellious
   - b. infected with diseases
   - c. poor and unimportant
   - d. not going to stay in jail very long
   - e. known to have long criminal histories

10. The John Howard Society would best be described as an organization that promotes:
   - a. more rights for victims of crimes
   - b. a return to the fee system
   - c. free dope for jail inmates
   - d. jail reform
   - e. abolition of the federal prison system

## True or False

_____ 11. John Howard became famous as the inventor of the fee system, which raised money to finance better jails.

_____ 12. Jails generally have a better physical environment and better services for inmates than prisons do.

_____ 13. A second-generation jail would practice indirect monitoring of inmates, typically with a guard in a glassed-in control booth.

_____ 14. The fifty largest jail systems in the United States hold almost a third of all jail inmates.

_____ 15. In the city jails of the modern era, the "tank" was considered the nicest cell, where trusty inmates were put to reward good behavior.

_____ 16. Most of the new jails feature inmate living quarters that keep individual offenders in extended solitary confinement, much like the early Pennsylvania penitentiary.

_____ 17. Although the number of female inmates is rising, males continue to make up almost 90 percent of the jail inmate population.

_____ 18. Jails have more people locked up at any one time than do prisons.

_____ 19. In most states, the state corrections department is taking over jail operations to improve the quality of services provided inmates.

_____ 20. Research suggests that the use of detoxification centers has virtually eliminated people with alcohol problems from local jail populations.

## Fill In the Blanks

21. English sheriff John Howard's own death was "jail-related;" he died as a result of _____.

22. One option often used for misdemeanor offenders in lieu of a jail term and sometimes a fine is an assignment to some type of public works project. This is called _____.

23. The largest single correctional facility in the United States today would be found in the city of _____.

24. The employees patrolling the pods of most American jails today wear the uniforms of what governmental agency? _____

25. In its expanded role of the future, the jail would become known as the _____.

26. If you had to pinpoint the one most significant personal problem of jail inmates, you would point to _____.

27. The other major problem of jail inmates, most noticeable in larger urban jails, is that large numbers of inmates have _____ concerns.

28. If holdback inmates were not in jail, they would be in _____.

29. The jail version of SWAT in the Cook County Jail is known as _____.

30. One common way of reducing the jail population is by providing _____ as an option to money bail for those indigent inmates who have strong community ties and are not considered dangerous.

## Discussion

31. What problems are traditionally associated with jail operations?

32. Describe the operation of a "typical" American jail today.

33. How have jail designs changed in recent decades? What is the dominant thinking in jail design at present?

34. How is the jail population different from the prison population?

35. What are the worst problems of large urban jails?

36. What alternatives are commonly used to reduce jail populations?

37. As someone who has just been arrested and booked into a county jail, you are put into a pod with about two dozen other inmates. What are their backgrounds like?

38. Imagine that you were a progressive sheriff who really wanted to do something to help jail inmates with their problems. What circumstances do you see that would limit your ability to do so?

# CHAPTER SIX

# State and Federal Prisons

Adults convicted of felony crimes may be imprisoned in one of the approximately 1,800 state, federal, local, or private prisons in America. Of the more than 1,300,000 felons in prison in 2003, the great majority were held in state prisons in various levels of security, from open to supermax. After reading this chapter, you should be familiar with:

1. The reasons for the growth of state prison systems in recent years.
2. The differing security levels in state and federal prisons.
3. Variations in the institutional makeup of state systems.
4. Close-ups of several state prison systems.
5. The history of federal prisons.
6. The different types of federal prisons.
7. Recent changes in the federal prison system.
8. The role of local and private prison systems.

## Key Terms

prisons
Gaol at Wymondham
Walnut Street Jail
Jeremy Bentham
panopticon
Pennsylvania model
Auburn model
industrial prison
agricultural prison
work camps
prisonization
maximum security prisons
close/high security prisons
medium security prisons
minimum security prisons
open security facilities
multilevel prisons
supermax
special housing unit (SHU)
San Quentin
Huntsville
*Ruiz v. Estelle*
Angola
Three Prisons Act
U.S. penitentiary
Fort Leavenworth
McNeil Island
Atlanta
Alderson
Federal Bureau of Prisons
Justice Department
Sanford Bates
BOP
Lewisburg

Alcatraz
country club prisons
James V. Bennett
Federal Prison Industries, Inc.
UNICOR
Norman Carlson
master plan
unit management
mandatory literacy
gender-neutral employment
balanced model
medical model
family culture
legal standards
Butner
Oakdale
Mariel Boatlift
minimum security
low security
medium security
high security
administrative security
Administrative Maximum
community corrections offices
U.S. Sentencing Commission
Sentencing Reform Act
supervised release
cream of criminals
white-collar criminals
political criminals
Club Fed
Cook County Department of Corrections
New York City Department of Corrections
Philadelphia Prison System

## The Growth of State Prison Systems

**Prisons** confine felons serving sentences of longer than a year. They are primarily operated by state governments, although the Federal Bureau of Prisons confines federal offenders, three large cities operate their own prisons, county jails in several states now house felony prisoners, and private prisons hold contracts to house state and federal prisoners. Virtually all prisons are at or above 100 percent capacity.

The state prison systems of today were founded on the model of the nineteenth century penitentiary, which embodied the legal reforms of the eighteenth century Age of Enlightenment. The first penitentiaries were developed in England and America in the late 1700s. Sir Thomas Beever opened the **Gaol at Wymondham**, in Norfolk, England, in 1785, incorporating principles of isolation, work, and penitence to change the nature of confinement. The Philadelphia Society for Alleviating the Miseries of Public Prisons, led by Dr. Benjamin Rush and other civic reformers, incorporated Beever's ideas into the design of the **Walnut Street Jail**, the first so-called penitentiary in America, which opened in Philadelphia in 1790.

**Jeremy Bentham**, the Utilitarian philosopher, proposed his model **panopticon**, a huge prison with a glass top for improved lighting and better supervision of inmates. But what developed in practice was the **Pennsylvania model** or separate system, and then the **Auburn model** penitentiary, which became the American prototype because of its cheapness and economic productivity. The Northern and Midwestern states perfected the Auburn model of the **industrial prison** that lasted into the Great Depression of the 1930s. The Southern states of the post-Civil War era developed the contrasting model of the **agricultural prison**, the giant prison farm applying the plantation mentality to managing prison labor. States in the South and West also developed prison **work camps**, in which inmates worked on public roads, cleared forests, and completed other public works projects.

People borrowed ideas and then built institutions to try to apply the new ideas. The people who built the next generation of institutions tried to improve upon the existing institutions of their time. Thus what we have, in the prison system of today, is an ongoing social experiment in which men and women of "good intentions" use confinement of criminals as a principal means of controlling crime.

## State Prisons Systems Today

The heart of the state correctional system and generally its most costly component is its adult prisons. Most states started their prison systems with one institution, a penitentiary based on the Auburn model, and then expanded the system by building additional prisons as the population increased and the need for special purpose facilities (such as those for women, younger offenders, or drug addicts) was accepted.

Early penitentiaries practiced maximum security; indeed, the enduring image of a "prison" is derived from the architecture of these institutions--high walls, guard towers, cellblocks stacked in tiers, massive concrete and steel construction. It is these prisons--the oldest, largest, and most secure--that define imprisonment in America. It is these prisons to which Donald Clemmer applied the term **prisonization**, meaning the inmate's adaptation to the culture of the penitentiary. The more profoundly artificial and different the prison is from the outside society, the more the prison inmate is set apart from the values of conventional society.

Today prisons are graded according to security levels:
1. **Maximum security prisons**. These are often the older, larger, walled penitentiaries with the most rigorous security procedures and the lowest ratio of inmates to guards. They hold about 12 percent of state inmates, almost entirely in one- or two-man cells.
2. **Close/high security prisons**. In some states, these are considered a kind of maximum security, though the security measures are less restrictive and the ratio of inmates to guards may be higher. About 16 percent of state inmates are held in this classification.
3. **Medium security prisons**. These are usually the smaller, newer prisons, with double fences instead of walls and dormitory or pod housing rather than cells. The inmate-to-guard ratio may be twice that of the maximum security prison. About 35 percent of state inmates are held in this classification, which is now the usual starting place for new inmates who are not perceived as dangerous or escape risks.
4. **Minimum security prisons**. These newer, smaller prisons have minimal perimeter security and fewer internal controls. The inmate-to-guard ratio is even higher, and inmates may live in rooms or dorms with more privacy and more amenities. About 31 percent of state prison inmates are held in minimum security. They have usually worked their way down from higher classifications; many are "short-termers" approaching release.
5. **Open security facilities**. Not usually called prisons at all, these are non-secure facilities such as work release centers, pre-release centers, halfway houses, and other types of community-based facilities. They have no armed guards and no fences; to escape all you have to do is walk away and not come back. When they catch

up with you later, you will be put in maximum security as an escape risk. About five percent of state inmates are in open classification.

Many state prisons are called **multilevel prisons** because they provide two or more of these levels of security within the same institution. Inmates can change from one grade to another without having to transfer to another prison. The general trend today is toward expanding the lower security grades, especially medium security.

In the decade of the 1990s, the term "supermax" entered the prison management vocabulary. **Supermax** refers to the highest level of security that can be applied to a prison housing unit. Inmates are kept in single-person cells, generally locked down twenty-four/seven. It is an earned status, based mostly on what the inmate does *after* he gets to prison, rather than what he has done before. Most supermax inmates do not have work assignments, nor do they have access to ordinary prison recreation, inmate organizations, or programming. Visiting is restricted. Privileges are minimal. Contact with other people, including staff, is very limited. The inmate is isolated in his cell as much as possible, with brief outdoor exercise periods in a small, individual exercise yard. Supermax refers as much to a type of inmate (who is perceived as a threat requiring control measures beyond maximum security) as it does to a particular prison architectural or management style. Less than two percent of the American prison population is confined in supermax housing.

Many prisons have a **special housing unit (SHU)** with security conditions similar to supermax, but housing disciplinary offenders for shorter periods rather than long-term security and control problems. Special housing would once have been called "the hole," where inmates were subject to physical punishments, restricted diets, and sensory deprivation.

Most of the new prisons built in the twentieth century have incorporated lower levels of security--medium security, minimum security, and open. The new prisons tend to be smaller than the old penitentiaries, and because they are of more recent construction they are much more modern in their design and amenities. Fences have replaced walls, and the ratio of guards to inmates is lower. Most corrections officials agree that only about 15 to 25 percent of prisoners require maximum security; the rest do fine in lower security institutions.

State prison systems range in size from North Dakota, which has just over 1,000 people in prison, to the huge systems of California and Texas, each with more than 150,000 in prison. Rates of imprisonment vary greatly as well. They are highest in the South and lowest in the North. A vast gulf separates Maine and Minnesota, with imprisonment rates of 137 and 139 per 100,000, from Louisiana and Mississippi (and until last year Texas), with rates over 700 per 100,000. For the 50 states, the average was about 425 per 100,000 on June 30, 2001.

## North Dakota

North Dakota has the nation's smallest prison system--three prisons housing 1,168 inmates as of June 30, 2002. As recently as 1981, the system was small indeed, 280 inmates, which would hardly register as a blip on the prison radar screen today.

Although North Dakota's imprisonment rate (167 per 100,000 in 2002) is well below the national average and its prison population tiny in comparison to other states, the rapid growth of felons sentenced to imprisonment has been an important political issue over the past decade. The 2001 state legislature established an interim committee to study future prison needs. The average daily inmate population had nearly doubled in the previous eight years, from 567 in 1993 to 1,095 as of June 2001. The committee was to examine several key issues:
    1. Relieving prison overcrowding, which required state prisoners to be housed in rehab centers, local jails, and a private prison in Minnesota.
    2. Rescinding mandatory sentences for drug crimes and other offenses. The average sentence for drug offenders had risen from 40 months in 1993 to 60 months in 2000.
    3. Providing more substance abuse treatment for prisoners. About two-thirds of North Dakota's inmates were alcohol or drug dependent, and few were able to get into treatment.
    4. Building a separate prison for women. The number of women inmates had increased from 20 in 1990 to about 100 a decade later, presenting housing problems at the two men's prisons where they shared space. Legislators are concerned that continued population increases and additional housing costs will cut into treatment funds and make it difficult to maintain the state's traditionally low--about 20 percent--recidivism rate.

## California

On the opposite end of the scale from North Dakota are the nation's two largest state prison systems, California and Texas. In 2001, California held 160,315 state prisoners and Texas 158,131; Florida and New York were way back with 73,000 and 67,000 prisoners in custody.

The history of the California prison system dates to the early 1850s, when inmates confined on the prison ship *Wapan* built the prison which came to be known as **San Quentin**. It housed both male and female inmates until 1933, when the women's prison at Tehachapi was built. Despite periodic schemes to shut it down, San Quentin--"the prison that would not die"--held nearly 6,000 inmates in 2003. Folsom State Prison, California's second oldest prison (dating from 1880), held 3,600.

In the federal system and many international prison systems, the prevailing theory for a long time favored smaller prisons, following the reasoning that mass institutions made management more difficult and individualized treatment nearly impossible. Six hundred was often used as a maximum desirable prison population.

When you look at California's prisons today, you see just the opposite. California prisons are small towns behind walls and fences. In 2003, California's correctional system consisted of 33 state prisons, 28 camps, 16 community correctional facilities, and five prisoner/mother facilities. They held in total 160,000 inmates, the 33 prisons holding 148,000 of these--averaging about 4,500 inmates per prison. Most prisons are multilevel institutions, many of them broken up into entirely separate facilities practicing unit management. The two largest California prisons in 2003 were the Correctional Training Facility at Soledad and Avenal State Prison. Divided into South, Central, and North Facilities, Soledad held 7,000 men. Avenal held just over 7,000.

California prisons use five classification levels:
     I. Open dormitories without a secure perimeter.
     II. Open dormitories with secure perimeter fences and armed perimeter security.
     III. Individual cells, fenced perimeters, and armed perimeter security.
     IV. Cells, fenced or walled perimeters, electronic security, armed officers inside and out.
     SHU. Security Housing Unit, the most secure area within a Level IV prison.
The system also uses designations for special populations. *RC* is for men and women undergoing classification in reception centers. *Camps* designates the minimum security inmates assigned to the system's forestry and firefighting centers; 20 such centers housing 2,200 male and female inmates operate out of the Sierra Conservation Center in Jamestown. *Condemned* is for the 560 male inmates on death row at San Quentin and the 14 female inmates on death row at Chowchilla.

From post-World War II through the 1970s, California was recognized as one of the most progressive state prison systems. It offered probably the widest variety of vocational and educational programming of any state prison system. These features are still around today, but the system is better known as for its great success in locking people up than for its treatment effectiveness.

In 1981, California had 29,000 men and women in prison. Twenty years later the system was five times larger. California built 21 new prisons and added housing units to existing facilities. Prison costs increased to the point that California was spending more on prisons than on its famous system of higher education. The state has recently changed its approach in dealing with drug criminals to use more non-secure treatment alternatives, but its prison population continued to grow in 2001 before leveling off in 2002. A growing percentage of inmates have very long terms (under "three strikes" laws) that will keep them behind bars until they are elderly or dead. The California prison system's reputation for progressiveness has been another casualty of the War on Crime.

## Texas

The Texas prison system long consisted of a central prison and a network of prison farms scattered around it. The central unit in **Huntsville** was established in 1849; the farms were spread around Houston and Huntsville up to a hundred miles or more away from "The Walls."

When George Beto became director of the Texas Department of Corrections in 1962, it was still a loose confederation of maximum security prison farms. When he left ten years later, Beto had transferred power from the wardens to the central office of the TDC, creating what John DiIulio has called the control model in Texas prisons. This model emphasized farm work and strict discipline within a centralized bureaucratic environment.

Like many Southern prison systems with a higher ratio of inmates to guards, Texas had relied on inmate trusties-- called building tenders or BTs--to maintain internal order. Unlike the other states, when federal courts began to abolish the practice of convicts controlling other convicts, Texas fought to keep its old-fashioned system intact. It lost. In *Ruiz v. Estelle* (1980), federal Judge William Wayne Justice dismantled the building tender system and ordered other major changes, including reducing overcrowding and staff brutality and improving inmate classification and legal access.

The removal of the BTs, the induction of huge numbers of inexperienced security officers, and the abrupt collapse of the control model caused tough times in Texas prisons in the mid-1980s. Violence increased dramatically, and Texas prisons lost the sense of purpose forged under Beto's leadership. Prison populations soared. Texas went from third place, with 13,000 inmates in 1967 (well behind California and New York and just slightly ahead of Ohio) to first place, with 30,700 inmates, by 1980. By the early 1990s, its prisons were well over capacity and another 30,000 inmates were being stored in county jails. The legislature got voter approval to sell bonds financing new prisons--47 units holding 100,000 inmates.

By early 2003, the system was nearing capacity again, with 158,000 inmates in prison, 10,000 of these in private prisons. TDCJ officials were projecting the need for another 14,000 prison beds by 2008. Crime had dropped steadily for a decade, but prisons were still growing, and legislators were debating their options–more prisons, increased use of parole, privatization, more money spent on rehabilitation, or housing state inmates in the cheaper county· While the legislature debates its options, the incoming tide of inmates rises higher. Texas will soon be passing California again.

## Louisiana

Louisiana has earned its title as "The Inmate State" over the past decade. With a population of 4.2 million, Louisiana held more than 50,000 people in jail and prison in 2001. Canada, with 30 million people, confined 36,000 prisoners. Japan, with a population of 125 million, locked up 67,000. Over the 30-year period from 1971 to 2001, Louisiana's prison population increased from about 3,500 to 36,000, a 1,000 percent increase that marked the most dramatic growth of any state prison system in the country. Its prison incarceration rate, about 800 per 100,000, and jail incarceration rate, about 400 per 100,000, are each the highest in the country. At any given time, one of every 80 people in Louisiana is behind bars, the highest rate of confinement in the world today.

In prison circles, Louisiana is best known for its state penitentiary at **Angola**, one of the largest and most enduring prison farms in America. Originally one of a cluster of private plantations along the Mississippi River northwest of Baton Rouge, Angola was used to house convicts under the private lease that prevailed in Louisiana after the Civil War. Angola was the sole destination of Louisiana's convicted felons--men and women, boys and girls--into the 1950s.

Several features of convict leasing carried over to state operation of Angola--cheapness, hard labor, isolation, brutality, segregation, no rehabilitation, and the profit motive--making the prison a tough place to do time (or to stay alive) for much of the twentieth century. Federal court intervention in 1975 caused the state to build a new system of medium-security institutions in rural parishes across the state. When it ran out of money to build new prisons, Louisiana began storing its surplus prisoners in parish jails. They are serving state time but in the custody of parish sheriffs, who are compensated by the state--at a current rate of $23 per day--for keeping them. It is much cheaper for the state to pay sheriffs to keep state inmates in jail than for the state to care for them in a state prison.

In the new system, Angola is no longer the main prison. Its role is now that of the long-termers' prison, confining 3,400 natural lifers and other inmates serving long sentences. Angola, as the national model of the lifers' prison now emerging in America, has the oldest inmate population of any major prison in the country. They expect to live out their lives and die on "The Farm;" many of them will be buried in the prison cemetery.

54

## Minnesota

If Louisiana's prison system has the reputation of being a bloated system full of lifers and drug and property criminals, Minnesota's prisons have the opposite reputation--a small, rational system focused on locking up the most dangerous criminals. On June 30, 2002, Minnesota, with a population of 4.5 million, held just under 7,000 people in prison; its rate of 139 per 100,000 was the second lowest in the country behind Maine.

As a percentage of its state budget, Minnesota's prison system is the cheapest in the country. It relies heavily on probation to keep the numbers behind bars down, and it uses prison space to hold violent criminals. Its prison terms, following the sentencing guidelines adopted in 1980, have been among the longest in the country for this reason. Since 1987, sex offenders have comprised the largest category of the inmate population, making up 19 percent of the population on January 1, 2001.

The mission statement of the Minnesota Department of Corrections is one simple statement: "It is our mission to develop and provide effective correctional practices that contribute to a safer Minnesota." The eight adult prisons are divided into a six-level custody classification system; some prisons have multiple custody levels.

Minnesota's politicians and corrections officials take pride in having avoided the most extreme approaches of the "get-tough-on-crime" agenda of the past two decades--truth-in sentencing and three strikes and you're out provisions, for instance. But recently they have noticed that Minnesota is not completely immune from the punitive ethos. Its prisons are full, double bunking of single-person cells is underway in some prisons, and officials are discussing the need to build two new prisons by 2010.

Most of this increase is attributed to drug offenders. In 1990, 219 offenders were in Minnesota prisons for drug crimes (seven percent of the total prison population); by 2001, this number had increased to 1,066 (17 percent). The state is exploring ways to deliver more effective treatment to both sex and drug offenders in community-based settings and in prison to reduce recidivism. It already proclaims a very low prison recidivism rate of about 20 percent, comparable to North Dakota.

## The Birth of the Federal Prison System

At one time there were few federal crimes and the few criminals serving federal time were housed in state and local institutions. After the Civil War, the numbers of both offenses and offenders began to climb. Congress passed the **Three Prisons Act** in 1891. The first **U.S. penitentiary** was the old military prison at **Fort Leavenworth**, Kansas, which began to house federal prisoners in 1895. **McNeil Island**, Washington, an older prison already in use, was designated a U.S. penitentiary in 1907. The third penitentiary, **Atlanta**, was the first newly-constructed federal prison. It opened in 1902. In the 1920s, Congress authorized a reformatory for young men at Chillicothe, Ohio, which opened in 1928, and the first federal prison for women at **Alderson**, West Virginia, which opened the same year.

Mabel Walker Willebrandt, an assistant attorney general in the Justice Department, had laid the groundwork for establishing a unified federal prison system in the 1920s. The **Federal Bureau of Prisons** was created by an act of Congress signed into law by President Herbert Hoover on May 14, 1930. It was established as an office within the federal **Justice Department**, where it remains today. **Sanford Bates** was appointed the first director of the new Bureau of Prisons, which quickly became known in corrections as the **BOP**. Bates consolidated control over the separate institutions in the new system and centralized policy-making authority.

At the end of 1930, the new system was made up of 14 institutions with just over 13,000 inmates. Bates oversaw the rapid expansion of the system over the next decade. The U.S. Penitentiary at **Lewisburg**, Pennsylvania, considered the most advanced institution of its kind in America, opened in 1933. The federal prison medical center at Springfield, Missouri, opened the next year. Federal prison camps to provide minimum security housing and work assignments in forestry and road building began to open.

In 1934, the most famous of the federal prisons, **Alcatraz**, was opened, ironically against the wishes of the BOP central office, who considered the prison more trouble than it was worth. The old military prison on Alcatraz Island in San Francisco Bay was converted to confine civilian prisoners. Alcatraz is often identified as the first "supermax" prison (a title that more appropriately belongs to the United State Penitentiary at Marion, Illinois, that opened in 1963), though its reputation for both the meanness of its clientele and the impossibility of escape was always exaggerated. Bureau management were pleased to shut it down in 1963.

## Developing A Model System

Throughout its history, the Bureau of Prisons has often been admired as a model system. Federal prisons have been called **country club prisons**; the assumption was that they got a "better class of prisoner" and then threw money at the prisons to make them nice places to do time. John DiIulio and others have disagreed. "Management is the key," they have argued--stable, visionary, professional leaders who were able to minimize political intervention in prison affairs.

Since it was created in 1930, the Bureau of Prisons has had only seven directors:
Sanford Bates, 1930-1937
James V. Bennett, 1937-1964
Myrl Alexander, 1964-1970
Norman Carlson, 1970-1987
J. Michael Quinlan, 1987-1993
Kathleen Hawk Sawyer, 1993-2003
Harley Lappin, 2003 to present

**James V. Bennett** completed the original construction of the bureau in his long tenure, which was marked by three important features:
1. **Federal Prison Industries, Inc.** Originally authorized by Congress in 1934, the BOP's industrial component has been a mainstay of the system since. Known since 1978 by the trade name **UNICOR**, this enterprise produces goods used by the military and the federal bureaucracy; since these goods are not sold directly to the public, they do not run afoul of the federal prison labor laws that so devastated state prisons in the 1930s. About 18 percent of federal inmates work in UNICOR jobs.
2. The federal inmate classification system. Bennett guided the development of a prisoner classification system intended to rationalize inmate management and promote individualized treatment.
3. The medical model. Although it would later be officially abandoned as a policy, it did result in the expansion of educational, vocational, and treatment programs open to inmates.

The long tenure of **Norman Carlson** as director is noted for modernizing the management practices of the BOP. Under Carlson the BOP was restructured into five (later six) regions and adopted a **master plan**--a set of principles establishing the direction in which it wished to be moving:
1. **Unit management**. This approach broke larger prisons down into smaller, autonomous units (based on housing units) in which security, treatment, and other staff were expected to work closely together.
2. **Mandatory literacy**. Increasing to high school equivalency by 1991, this program requires inmates to participate in literacy training to get better work assignments within the federal prison system.
3. **Gender-neutral employment**. Men and women are hired for all staff positions in every institution solely on their perceived ability to do the job.
4. The **balanced model**. After 1975, the bureau turned away from the **medical model** and adopted this composite model combining rehabilitation, deterrence, retribution, and incapacitation.
5. The "**family culture**." Through seminars, agency meetings, expanded training, reassignments, and moves, the bureau sought to promote a close-knit relationship among its staff and their families.
6. **Legal standards**. Anticipating the prisoners' rights movement, the bureau provided higher standards of care and custody before being ordered to do so by the courts.

One of the new prisons that opened under Carlson was the Federal Correctional Institution (FCI) at **Butner**, North Carolina, which opened in 1976. Butner was designed to apply the post-rehabilitation prison management ideas of criminologist Norval Morris. It offered a more open environment and voluntary treatment programs.

J. Michael Quinlan, the attorney and warden who succeeded Carlson as director in 1987, was welcomed to office by the two most destructive prison riots in federal history. Cuban inmates awaiting deportation at **Oakdale**, Louisiana, and serving time at USP Atlanta rioted because they wanted to stay in federal prisons rather than being sent back to Cuba. Many of the rioting inmates had come to the U.S. in the **Mariel Boatlift** of 1980. Some of these Cuban prisoners, stuck in immigration limbo, have never been released from custody.

Quinlan and his successor, Kathleen Hawk Sawyer, continued the rapid expansion of the federal prison system. When Sawyer retired in 2003, the system had grown to more than 100 institutions housing 140,000 inmates. In addition, another 15,000 prisoners were held in privately managed prisons, and another 11,000 were held in local jails or in open facilities in the community. The BOP under current director Harley Lappin is the biggest prison system in America, and it is continuing to grow steadily while state systems are stabilizing in size or experiencing marginal growth. The BOP had more staff in 2003, 34,000, than it had inmates 20 years earlier.

## Security Levels in Federal Prisons

Since 1979 the Bureau of Prisons has used a five-level security classification system for inmates. The BOP's classification philosophy is to place inmates in the least restrictive security level in the institution closest to home. From lowest to highest, with inmate-to-staff ratios decreasing steadily up the line (officially from 10:1 in minimum security camps to 2:1 in the high security penitentiaries), the levels in 2003 were:
    1. **Minimum security**. These federal prison camps (FPCs), usually located adjacent to other federal prisons or military bases, held 19.6 percent of inmates.
    2. **Low security**. Called federal correctional institutions (FCIs), these prisons, featuring double fences and dormitory housing, held 38.8 percent of federal prisoners..
    3. **Medium security**. These FCIs, with stronger perimeters, cell housing, and greater internal controls, held 24.6 percent of prisoners.
    4. **High security**. These U.S. penitentiaries (USPs), which look very much like everyone else's penitentiaries, held 10.8 percent of inmates.
    5. **Administrative security**. This category, including special-purpose inmates, such as illegal aliens awaiting deportation and medical cases, held 6.2 percent of inmates. Among these were 500 federal prisoners-- the highest security threats in the federal system--held in the **Administrative Maximum** unit at the U.S. Penitentiary in Florence, Colorado.

Federal offenders not in prison are managed through 28 **community corrections offices (CCOs)** spread across the country. Each CCO has a community corrections manager, whose job it is to deal with contract agencies such as local jails, halfway houses, prerelease centers, and other organizations--both public and private--that provide services to federal offenders outside of prison.

The sentencing guidelines adopted by the **U.S. Sentencing Commission** in 1985 have limited the use of probation for federal offenders and increased the length of sentences applied to many offenders, particularly those convicted of crimes of violence and drug offenses, by narrowing the sentencing discretion of federal judges. The **Sentencing Reform Act** (1984) dramatically changed good-time provisions; federal inmates now serve 85 percent of their actual sentence, getting no more than 15 percent sentence reduction for good behavior. The same law abolished parole. Most federal judges now impose a new condition called **supervised release** on offenders after their discharge from secure custody. Supervised release, as an add-on period of supervision performed by federal probation officers, is practically identical in its effects to parole; it just happens to be imposed by the court instead of by a discretionary parole board.

## What's Different About Federal Prisons

As John DiIulio found in his research, federal prisoners are collectively hardly the "**cream of criminals**," though they are on the whole much less likely than state prisoners to be confined for crimes of violence. The percentage of drug criminals in federal prisons peaked at 61 percent in the mid-1990s and declined to about 55 percent by 2002. The next two leading criminal categories are illegal possession or use of weapons or explosives and arson, and immigration law violators, each making up more than 10 percent of the total population.

A small number of federal prisoners, well under 10 percent, could be defined as **white-collar criminals** or **political criminals.** The four-term governor of Louisiana, Edwin Edwards, 75, serving 10 years for racketeering, conspiracy, and other crimes related to casino gambling, is one of them. In a 2003 interview at the Federal Medical Center at Ft. Worth, Texas, Edwards pointed out that his institution is not "**Club Fed**," and he was not on vacation. His home is a medium security prison. After 16 years in the governor's mansion, Edwards's work assignment is as a prison janitor, and his wife has filed for divorce with his consent.

The makeup of the federal prison population has changed significantly over the past 20 years. Three of every ten federal inmates are foreigners, most from Mexico, Columbia, Cuba, the Dominican Republic, and other Central and South America countries, but really from around the world. The "war on drugs" has brought into the federal system a large number of drug users and street-level drug dealers who would once have gone to state prisons. They bring with them their medical problems and gang affiliations.

Federal prisons manage their inmate populations by better classification, not by having more correctional officers. The national average of prison inmates to correctional officers in 2001 was 5.4:1; in the federal system, the ratio was 9.7:1. Salaries of federal correctional officers were above the national average but far below what some state systems, particularly in the Northeast and West, pay their COs. The money not put into CO salaries leaves more for other professional staff. In the year 2000, the national average cost of imprisonment per inmate per day was $61.04; the federal cost was $59.02, about two dollars a day less. The BOP did spend slightly above the national average on both food and medical care, two aspects of prison life that matter greatly to inmates.

Several other features favor federal prisons--newer prisons, better physical plants, UNICOR, and a greater variety of activities and rehabilitation programs. But federal prisons remain well above 100% capacity at present, and new prisons are being built as fast as Congress appropriates the funds. The BOP is still looked to as a leader in the corrections field, but today it is driven by the same punitive mood that affects state corrections systems. Good management can only do so much to counterbalance hard sentencing. The Bureau of Prisons expects to be in an expansion mode for at least the next decade.

## Local and Private Prisons

Not all felons sentenced for state crimes end up in state prisons. In another of those historical anomalies, three large cities operate their own prison systems housing a portion of the felons their courts sentence to prison time. They supplement rather than replace state prisons. These are:
> the **Cook County Department of Corrections**.
> the **New York City Department of Corrections**.
> the **Philadelphia Prison System**.

These cities operate prison systems larger than the systems of many states. They have jail systems for pre-trial and misdemeanor inmates, but some of their convicted felons stay in local prisons rather than entering state custody.

It has also become much more common, over the past decade, for felons to serve state time in local jails, both in-state and out. This practice is due primarily to overcrowding of state prisons and to the economic incentive for local sheriffs to house the overflow of state prisoners in their county jails. In 2001, local jails held almost 48,000 state prisoners. The practice is especially common in the South. Louisiana has been housing state prisoners in parish jails since the 1970s, resulting in a prison system that by 2003 housed almost as many felons (16,000) in local jails as it did in state prisons (20,000).

Privately-operated jails and prisons have also flourished recently. In 1983, no prisoners were held in secure institutions operated by private companies. Twenty years later, the approximately 160 private prisons and jails held about 140,000 inmates.

## Alternatives to Prison Building

As we face a continuing influx of new prisoners, amounting to a minimum increase of 15,000 to 20,000 new state and federal prison beds annually, we have to ask about the wisdom of pursuing the bricks-and-mortar solution in corrections. Prisons are very expensive to construct. The more secure they are, the more expensive they are to build and to operate after opening. Furthermore, prison beds, once made available, are very difficult to empty. We continue opening new prisons, but we rarely shut down old ones--until they fall down from old age. The more we pursue building new prisons as the appropriate way to punish convicted felons, the more we commit to a future mind-set that encourages high rates of incarceration instead of alternative community-based programs or other crime prevention alternatives. If we have the prison beds available, we are highly likely to fill up the empty spaces first before we consider other options.

# SELF TEST

## Multiple Choice

1. Agricultural prisons were found predominantly in:
   - a. the South
   - b. the Far West
   - c. New England
   - d. the North
   - e. the Midwest

2. In which security classification are the greatest number of state prisoners held?
   - a. open
   - b. minimum
   - c. medium
   - d. close/high
   - e. maximum

3. The minimum security prison provides a model for those inmates who are:
   - a. near the ends of their sentences
   - b. mentally ill
   - c. too violent for general population
   - d. first-time offenders
   - e. serving life sentences

4. The first federal penitentiary was located at:
   - a. Lewisburg, Pennsylvania
   - b. El Reno, Oklahoma
   - c. Fort Leavenworth, Kansas
   - d. Marion, Illinois
   - e. Springfield, Missouri

5. Which model was officially deemphasized by the Bureau of Prisons after 1975?
   - a. brutality
   - b. work
   - c. medical
   - d. agricultural
   - e. confinement

6. For which category of offenses are the most prisoners confined in federal prisons today?
   - a. robbery
   - b. white-collar
   - c. interstate theft
   - d. homicide
   - e. drugs

7. The largest category of criminals in Minnesota's prison system are _____.
   - a. sex offenders
   - b. juvenile offenders
   - c. illegal aliens
   - d. white-collar criminals
   - e. domestic violence offenders

8. In which federal department is the Bureau of Prisons located?
   - a. State
   - b. Interior
   - c. Treasury
   - d. Justice
   - e. Homeland Security

9. Which state has the highest rate of imprisonment (prisoners per 100,000 population)?
   - a. Ohio
   - b. Louisiana
   - c. North Carolina
   - d. New York
   - e. California

10. If you wanted to visit the smallest prison system in America (a system you could easily tour in one day), you would go to which state?
   - a. Idaho
   - b. North Dakota
   - c. West Virginia
   - d. Utah
   - e. Nebraska

59

## True or False

_____ 11. The federal prison system was established before any state prison systems were in existence.

_____ 12. The federal system has announced plans to do away with its high security penitentiaries as being unnecessary to maintaining adequate control over prisoners.

_____ 13. The federal prison system has so few women inmates that it does not have a separate prison for women.

_____ 14. The unit management system used in federal prisons means that the prison is broken up into smaller, semi-autonomous operating units featuring a team management approach.

_____ 15. A federal prison camp is a minimum-security institution.

_____ 16. Most convicted felons serving prison terms are in the custody of the states.

_____ 17. The trend today is toward substantially increasing the percentage of inmates confined in maximum security.

_____ 18. The Auburn penitentiary is considered the model of the modern American maximum security prison.

_____ 19. A gang leader suspected of ordering hits on rival gang leaders in prison would be a prime candidate for supermax housing.

_____ 20. The original San Quentin prison in California was built by gold miners to house claim jumpers during the California gold rush days.

## Fill In the Blanks

21. The two states with the largest numbers of prison inmates are California and _____.

22. The old penitentiaries built in the 1800s were intended to house inmates under _____ security conditions.

23. The institution called the first penitentiary in the United States was located in the city of _____.

24. The prison system that coined the term "balanced model" to describe itself was the _____ system.

25. If you picked up an item that had been manufactured in a federal prison, it should be marked with the corporate symbol _____.

26. Of minimum, low, medium, and high security classifications in the BOP, the smallest number of inmates are in _____ security.

27. The longest serving director of the BOP (and the person most responsible for the adoption of the medical model) was _____.

28. The largest number of foreign citizens in federal prisons come from the country of _____.

29. Alcatraz and Leavenworth were alike in their origins as _____ prisons before they became part of the federal prison system.

30. The federal prison in Louisiana that was seized and burned in a 1987 riot by Cuban prisoners was _____.

## Discussion

31. How are federal prison inmates different from state prison inmates?

32. Why was the Federal Bureau of Prisons created?

33. What is the importance of Federal Prison Industries, Inc.?

34. Briefly outline the different security levels used in the federal prison system.

35. Explain the purposes associated with each of the major levels of security you would find in a typical state prison system.

36. How did the model of the American penitentiary develop?

37. If you were asked to sum up the most distinctive feature of each of the five state prison systems discussed in this chapter--North Dakota, California, Texas, Louisiana, and Minnesota--what would you say?

38. A state legislator says, "We ought to make all prisons maximum security again."  What criticisms can you direct at his proposal?

# CHAPTER SEVEN

# Management and Custody

As a formal, complex organization, the prison presents unique management concerns, particularly in its efforts to balance the competing interests of custody and treatment. Although custody is the most important function of a prison or jail, and more people work in security than in all other functions combined, administrative and treatment functions are also ongoing and require the services of significant numbers of staff. After reading this chapter, you should be familiar with:

1. The prison warden's role today.
2. The evolution of management styles to the present.
3. The importance of custody (and the lesser role of treatment) in the correctional setting.
4. The influence of the prison environment on management and custody.
5. The important themes of correctional management.
6. The methods of secure custody in prison.
7. The problems of managing custody and treatment in prison.
8. Support staff common in the American prison.

## Key Terms

warden
secure custody
perimeter security
Elayn Hunt Correctional Center
C.M. Lensing
Warden Norton
unit management
empowerment
Management by Walking Around (MBWA)
scientific management
human relations
Theory X
Theory Y
autocratic style
Elam Lynds
Thomas Mott Osborne
bureaucratic style
Joseph Ragen
internal environment
external environment
George J. Beto
James V. Bennett
Ross Maggio
treatment
"nothing works"
initial classification
institutional needs
political hack
the count
sally port
contraband
frisk search

strip search
body cavity search
shakedown
razor wire
electrified fences
lockdown
snitches
trusties
inmate guards
the yard
towers and walls
gates
escorts
Corrections Emergency Response Team
 (CERT)
assaults
escapes
walkaways
total institutions
infantilization
overcrowding
prison gangs
unit team management
correctional officers
the Captain
blue flu
turnover rate
custody oriented
prison chaplain
ombudsman
counselor
case manager

## The Prison Warden Today

The head of an American prison is typically called a **warden**, a title derived from an English term for a keeper of animals. In this view, the warden is essentially a gatekeeper. In any secure prison, the warden's chief objective is to maintain **secure custody** of prisoners, but secure custody involves much more than **perimeter security**, or merely keeping inmates confined within the walls and preventing escape. The contemporary warden's role has become one of balancing competing interests--the inmates, the staff, political officials, and the public--while maintaining physical and internal security, administering the prison, and providing positive programs to change behavior.

**Elayn Hunt Correctional Center** is located in St. Gabriel, Louisiana, 15 miles south of Baton Rouge along the River Road. Hunt is a men's prison which opened in 1979. Its warden is **C.M. Lensing**, Jr., a native of north Louisiana who has worked in corrections since completing a graduate degree in criminal justice at Northeast Louisiana University in 1975. Lensing was appointed warden at Hunt in 1989.

When he speaks to students about contemporary prison management, Warden Lensing often begins by asking if they know **Warden Norton** from *The Shawshank Redemption*. Most do. Norton was warden of Shawshank, the fictional state prison in Maine (though based on the old, now-demolished Thomaston Penitentiary) where Andy Dufresne spent the 19 years from 1947 until 1966. That style of warden no longer exists, Warden Lensing points out.

Warden Lensing defines the contemporary warden's role as consisting of two parts: the traditional warden's role and the CEO role. The traditional warden's role--focused on institutional security--is now divided among several assistant wardens who oversee the prison's different operating units. Hunt has practiced **unit management** (or unit team management) since 1994. This approach decentralizes management authority by housing units, breaking down the centralized control into smaller operating units. The goal is to get custodial, rehabilitation, and support staff working more closely together with the inmates they supervise.

Warden Lensing's remarks about his CEO role often draw surprised looks from students. He points out that the budget of his prison in 2002 was over $40 million, over 80 percent spent on staff. The institution has 800 staff members, 582 of them correctional officers working in security. In the last few years, the percentage of women correctional officers at Hunt has increased from 18 percent to over 40 percent. Warden Lensing indicates that he spends far more time with staff matters than with inmates--and that his staff cause him far more problems than the inmates do. Staff turnover, sometimes at the rate of 40 percent annually, is his worst problem.

When students ask Warden Lensing about his management philosophy, he responds by listing several key elements: empowerment, safety, professionalism, secure resources, and unit management. **Empowerment--** "giving people control over their own work and lives"--is the foundation, applying to inmates as well as staff.

Warden Lensing practices his version of **MBWA, Management by Walking Around**, which takes him out of his office to visit each of the compounds that make up his prison. He meets regularly with what he calls his "management team," the deputy wardens who act as division heads and the assistant wardens who run the housing units, but he makes it a point to get out and see people in the units most days that he is in his office.

He tells students that the focus on rehabilitation and the individual criminal offender has turned around 180 degrees in the time he was worked in corrections. Victims have come to the forefront in criminal justice. Where attention was once focused on rehabilitation and recidivism, it is now directed more toward public safety and reducing victimization. The programs may still be the same in many instances, but the focus is less upon their effects on the individual criminal and more upon their outcomes once the criminal is back in society.

## Prison Management Then and Now

Correctional administrators draw from a wide range of sources as they manage their employees and perform their correctional functions. When management first began to develop as a science a century ago, one of the first major schools of thought was in fact called **scientific management**. In Frederick Taylor's *The Principles of Scientific Management* (1911), the ideal manager was a skillful manipulator of basically uncooperative, deficient human beings. People needed to be constantly supervised, corrected, and time-managed.

The scientific management model, which still has influence in factory and assembly-line settings, was supplanted by the **human relations** movement of the 1930s. Human relations viewed human beings not as obstacles to be overcome but as social beings who wanted to work and produce. The human relations movement focused on the informal organization, on human relationships and morale as determinants of productivity.

Douglas McGregor's *The Human Side of Enterprise* (1960) proposed two contrasting theories of human behavior, Theory X and Theory Y. **Theory X** assumed that the average person disliked work, had to be coerced and threatened to produce, and avoids responsibility. **Theory Y**, in contrast, assumed that people are motivated to work, will accept and seek responsibility, and will freely adopt organizational goals.

Prison managers refer to the **autocratic style** of earlier prison wardens, who were Theory X managers in the extreme. The dictionary definition of *autocrat* is "an absolute ruler." The warden of the 1800s and early 1900s had absolute authority, if he chose to use it. His only allegiance was to the governor who appointed him and the state legislators who approved his budget.

The prototype of the autocratic warden was undoubtedly Captain **Elam Lynds**, the warden of both Auburn and Sing Sing prisons in New York in the 1820s. His system of strict control emphasized three principles: "industry, obedience, and silence." He said the secret of prison discipline was to maintain uninterrupted silence and uninterrupted labor; he viewed the use of physical punishment as essential to instilling fear in convicts.

Many other early wardens would have agreed with Lynds about the need for absolute authority in running a prison. Even such a progressive reformer as Zebulon Brockway, the founder of the reformatory, believed in extreme discipline and regimentation as the basis of reform. On the other hand, **Thomas Mott Osborne**, who became warden of Sing Sing in 1914, was a prison reformer before he became warden. Warden Osborne liberalized prison rules, allowed inmate self-government, and established a token economy. The convicts apparently loved his Theory Y approach, but conservative political officials did not. He was indicted for neglect of duty and resigned his office in 1916.

Management historians say that the autocratic management style of early penitentiaries began to yield to the **bureaucratic style** of today after World War II, when centralized state corrections bureaucracies were established and other changes outside of prisons took away the independent authority wardens had previously enjoyed. In *Stateville: The Penitentiary in Mass Society*, James Jacobs chronicles 50 years in the life of Stateville Penitentiary, Illinois's largest maximum security prison. He focuses on the management style of one of the last autocratic wardens, **Joseph Ragen**, known as "Mr. Prison" in Illinois, and its long-term effect on the prison.

Robert Freeman has discussed the correctional manager as operating within both internal and external environments. The **internal environment** consists of three primary influences--the inmate social culture, the prison's physical environment, and the prison staff culture. The contrasting **external environment** is made up of outside forces that interact with the internal environment--the department of corrections, the media, state officials, the civil service department, the courts, victim and prisoner advocacy groups, families of prisoners, and representatives of special needs inmates and rehabilitative programs.

When a group of state and federal prison wardens met a few years ago to define the warden's role, they listed twelve major duty areas, headed by managing human resources and managing the external environment. The earlier autocratic wardens maintained their positions by maximizing their control over the internal environment and minimizing external influences. By the 1960s and 1970s, it was clear that the prison was no longer an insular institution. External influences became more dominant, and prison management became less of a one-man show and more of a team effort.

Prison wardens today are usually products of the system, college-educated professionals who have moved around from one institution to another and have no particular ties to any institution. A 2002 American Correctional Association profile of over 2,000 wardens and superintendents in state prison systems showed that the numbers of women wardens are increasing steadily, to about 25 percent in the most recent survey. Almost 20 percent of the wardens surveyed were black, and another 10 percent were Hispanic or other ethnic minorities. And about one in four wardens were cross-gender managers, most commonly, women managing men's prisons.

Although today's wardens are rarely well-known public figures, some do emerge to speak out on correctional policies and issues. **George J. Beto**, the director of the Texas Department of Corrections, was one such figure. Beto developed the control model of corrections, emphasizing work, discipline, and education in a rigorously controlled prison setting. **James V. Bennett**, who headed the Federal Bureau of Prisons from the 1930s through the early 1960s, is another such figure. Bennett, who advocated individualized treatment of inmates, built the federal prison system into an influential organizational model. In Louisiana, **Ross Maggio** was called "Boss Ross" for his authoritative public style as warden of the Louisiana State Penitentiary at Angola. Maggio used the power of a federal court order to clean up Angola after a period of internal violence and disorder in the 1970s. He built a professional management team and minimized political intervention in prison affairs.

## Treatment versus Custody

We often use "treatment" and "rehabilitation" as synonymous terms. In the narrow definition, **treatment** would be the services--such as counseling, casework, and therapy--offered by the professional staff to change the behavior of prison inmates. Treatment is one part of rehabilitation, along with academic education, vocational training, recreation, religion, outside visitors, and inmate self-help activities. In its broadest definition, treatment can be anything positive that happens to an inmate in prison, even if neither the institution nor the inmate knows what it is or how important it is at the time. There has been a kind of skepticism about the effectiveness of treatment in the correctional setting for more than two decades. "What works?" Robert Martinson asked in reporting his research findings in 1974. "**Nothing works**," he replied, or at least, "Nothing works consistently enough to apply it across the board with any reasonable expectation of success."

We say that institutions then gave up on treatment, but in fact treatment had always been incidental to secure custody in prison. Treatment got what was left after custody, administration, and work programs took their share of the budget. This typically amounted to no more than five percent to ten percent of the institution's budget, which is hardly a firm commitment to change. Wardens get fired when prisoners riot or escape; no prison warden has ever been fired for failing to rehabilitate inmates. After two centuries of locking up felons to serve prison terms, we still do not know whether prison wardens *can* rehabilitate inmates.

## Classification and Assignment in State Prisons

In the complex, multi-level state prison system of today, incoming inmates usually go to a specific facility for classification upon entry into the system. These facilities are called by various names--reception centers, diagnostic centers, reception and evaluation centers, or classification centers. Inmates are tested, interviewed, and monitored; their criminal history files are reviewed and prison records brought up to date. The **initial classification** is geared toward determining the level of security the inmate should be placed in. Is he an escape risk? A protection case? Is he dangerous to himself, to other inmates, or to staff? Does he have enemies?

Classification was originated as a tool to match the institution's programs to the needs of the prisoner, but it became over time more a device of security--to match the inmate to the **institutional needs** of the prison. It determines what prison the inmate will be sent to, what security level he will be housed in, what his work assignment will be, and what programs he will be allowed to take part in.

## Custody As a Way of Life

The person in charge of custody has long been the key figure in day-to-day prison operations. In some states, the deputy warden for custody was the mainstay of institutional continuity. Especially in the South, wardens were considered **political hacks**, meaning that they were political appointees who got their jobs without any particular skills or interests, or without any expectation that they would actually *perform* as wardens. They were paid to be figureheads. The security warden ran the prison. Wardens came and went; security was forever.

The custodial staff, then as now, relied on a variety of devices and techniques to maintain secure control of inmates. Among these measures are:
1. The **count**. The most important task of the custodial staff, most authorities acknowledge, is counting inmates to determine their whereabouts. The frequency of counting varies with the prison and the custody level.
2. The **sally port**. Basically a double gate, a sally port is used to control vehicle and pedestrian traffic into a prison. Only one gate can be open at a time; in theory prison security is always maintained.
3. Prison rules. Usually provided the newly arrived inmate in a handbook during classification or orientation, the rules define categories of offenses, disciplinary actions, and grievance procedures.
4. Control of **contraband**. Contraband is anything not authorized by prison rules, including items that are allowed but of which the prisoner has too many. Most contraband comes into prison through guards. Common contraband items smuggled in would include drugs, alcohol, pornography, weapons, and money.
5. Searches. The **frisk search** is most common. It is a pat down search of the inmate's outer clothing. The **strip search** requires the inmate to remove his clothing so that both his body and the clothing can be

inspected more closely. Inmates suspected of hiding contraband in their rectum--a practice called "keestering," may be subjected to a **body cavity search** by medical personnel or more recently by scanning machines.

6. Tool and key control. To prevent inmates from gaining access to items that could be used as weapons or as tools of escape.

7. Shakedowns. A **shakedown** is a search of an area, such as a cell or tier of cells, a dormitory, a work place, or a communal area such as the library, the dining hall, or the chapel. Prisons have shakedown crews of guards whose job it is to carry out thorough searches.

8. Walls and fences. Old prisons have walls, new prisons have fences, usually double fences topped with **razor wire**. Guards armed with rifles man towers that surveil stretches of wall or fence. Several states, led by California, are using **electrified fences**, which can be as lethal as a rifle shot. This is called perimeter security, to distinguish it from internal security within the walls.

9. Lockdowns. A **lockdown** means that one or more inmates, from a cellblock to a dormitory to an entire prison, are confined to their living quarters for a period of time. This is done after an incident of violence or when trouble is anticipated. Extended lockdown is used to hold the most troublesome inmates in long-term isolation.

Not on this list but of even greater importance to the old-style security warden were **snitches** and **trusties**. Snitches cultivated by guards were said to be the key to knowing what was going on in the old penitentiary. Trusty work assignments were given to favored inmates. In most prison systems at one time, these inmates were given direct control of other inmates, including making assignments, charging fellow prisoners fees for services and special favors, and, most commonly in the South, acting as **inmate guards** armed with guns.

In a contemporary prison, the security staff will be divided among shifts (usually three or four) and several types of job assignments:

1. Inmate living quarters, a critical assignment given experienced officers who get along well with inmates because it involves the most direct contact.

2. Work sites, another assignment involving lots of direct contact with inmates.

3. The **yard**, important as the site of the most open social interaction among inmates.

4. **Towers and walls**, often viewed as a monotonous, undesirable assignment for new officers or officers who do not get along well with other officers or inmates; sometimes a disciplinary assignment.

5. **Gates**, which control movement within the facility.

6. Visiting, important as an entry point for contraband.

7. Dining hall, another important group congregation area.

8. Hospital, treatment units, and recreation areas, all controlled access areas.

9. **Escorts** and transports, which move inmates around or take them outside the prison for legal or medical visits.

10. Training and administration, often assignments for officers believed to have management potential.

11. Roving security patrols and **Corrections Emergency Response Teams** (CERT teams, or SORT teams, like SWAT teams outside) that deal with uncooperative inmates, hostage incidents, riots, and other crises.

To the custodial staff, the two most serious events in prison are **assaults** and **escapes**. According to *The 2001 Corrections Yearbook*, about 50,000 assaults of inmates and staff (two-thirds inmates, one-third staff) were officially reported in American prisons in 2000. About 19 percent required medical attention (at least an examination). In the same year, 55 inmates but no prison staff were killed in assaults by inmates. The murder rate within prison, incidentally, was about 4.5 per 100,000 in 2000, compared to the national homicide rate of 5.6 per 100,000. Prisoners are generally much safer from serious injury or death from assaults in prison than they were on the street.

Over 7,000 prison escapes were reported in 2000, but 90 percent of these were from open, nonsecure facilities, primarily involving work release, prerelease, and furlough inmates. These are often called **walkaways** rather than true escapes. About 65 to 70 percent of walkaways and escapees are recaptured quickly, picking up new criminal charges upon recapture.

## The Social System and Custodial Models

Prisons, especially maximum security penitentiaries, are **total institutions**. They take away individual responsibility and autonomy and attempt to make the inmate completely submissive to prison authority and totally dependent on prison routine. Prisoners are as dependent as newborn babies. Babies grow and mature, but prisoners will still be treated like babies--like very bad babies--years later. This **infantilization** of inmates is a serious limitation of the custodial approach in corrections.

The social system of the prison has been significantly affected in recent years by two circumstances. First, prisons in most states are at or over capacity. **Overcrowding** aggravates the natural conflicts that would occur in prison, it escalates tensions and the potential for violence, it gives prison officials fewer choices about how to place individual inmates (especially the ones who cause trouble), and it makes the task of keeping the prison safe and secure more difficult. Second, the rise of **prison gangs** has divided the social system into competing factions and further heightened the violence potential. Prison gangs are predominantly a problem in the Southwest, where Hispanics are found in prison in greater numbers. Most prison violence occurs for personal reasons that have nothing to do with gang affiliation, but those states that have serious gang problems recognize that inter-gang and intra-gang conflicts make the problem of prison violence worse.

In American prisons, the reliance on the paramilitary model of custody has led to two enduring principles of prison operation:
     1. Custody rules. All facets of prison life, including treatment, are subordinate to the custody function.
     2. Custodial staff only do custody. They guard; they don't help, advise, counsel, treat, or express any interest in the inmate as a human being. To them he is an alien with a number, and all that matters is the count.

Contemporary prisons have explored different approaches to getting the custodial staff and the program staff to work more effectively together. The approach pioneered in the federal prison system and now used in many state systems is called **unit team management**. This decentralized approach breaks the prison up into quasi-autonomous parts, usually based around residential quarters. The idea is to break down barriers between specialists and get staff to take a broader role with inmates. Some correctional officers like this concept; many want no part of it. Custody and treatment remain more often adversaries than allies.

## Correctional Officers

The people who work in security run the prison. Generally speaking, the higher the security level of the prison, the lower the ratio of inmates to **correctional officers**. State averages of inmates to COs range from about 3.5 to 1 up to 8 to 1, with a national average of 5.4 to 1 in 2000. Because security is an around-the-clock operation, the number of officers is always divided among shifts. The basic mathematical calculation is that each security post requires from five to five-and-a-half people to man it continuously year round, because of sick days, holidays, training, and other assignments. So if a big prison has a thousand security officers, about 160 to 200 would be scheduled to work at any given time.

In the old days, the head of security was often called **"the Captain."** The captain ran the prison day to day. He interacted with inmates, made assignments, disciplined and punished, and saw to it that the work got done. Prisons were typically located in rural areas. The guards were often farmers working in the prison to make ends meet. The convicts were most likely to be street criminals from the big city. These cultural differences were often heightened by differences of race and ethnicity as well.

The correctional officer of today is different from the guard of a hundred years ago. Correctional officers are men and women, white, black, and Hispanic. In 2001, 23 percent of correctional officers were women, 21 percent were black, and six percent Hispanic. These numbers are increasing steadily; of the new correctional officers hired in 2000, 35 percent were female and 39 percent minorities. Two states, Mississippi and Arkansas, already have more women than men correctional officers, and several other Southern states are moving in this direction. Men's prison are increasingly staffed and managed by women. What would Elam Lynds think?

More than 250,000 correctional officers worked in state and federal prisons in 2001. Their average starting salary was just under $24,000 a year; New Jersey's starting salary of $36,850, the highest in the country, was more than twice that of Louisiana, the lowest, at $15,324. Correctional officers in several states are unionized but not allowed to strike. Prison employee groups have used sick-outs or attacks of **"blue flu"** to support their demands for recognition or improved working conditions.

Forty-eight of the 50 states have some requirement for preservice training for new correctional officers (the state average is 262 hours, more than six weeks), 47 have a probationary employment period averaging about ten months, and requirements for inservice training have increased steadily also, averaging almost 40 hours per year. Despite efforts to professionalize the correctional officer's role, the **turnover rate** for COs remains high, about

16 percent in 2000, after averaging between 12 and 16 percent for the decade of the 1990s. Advancement opportunities in corrections, with the comparatively high turnover rate and the continuing expansion of the system to deal with overcrowding problems, has made corrections an attractive career field for the time being.

Are today's correctional officers, with all their training, higher salaries, and professionalism, really different from the prison guards of earlier times? The prison guard of the past was **custody oriented** and worked in a maximum security environment. In the lower security prison of today, the security staff, male and female, may play more of a "human relations" role requiring them to be more empathetic with inmates, more interested in their problems, more involved in rehabilitation programs, and more suited to serving as role models. Interaction with inmates and management of inmates are more important than authority and coercive power; lower security prisons strive for "normalcy." Prison guards saw prisoners as objects; correctional officers are supposed to see them as people. Most prison staff working in security today prefer to be known as correctional officers. "Don't call me guard," they say. But which are they? Is a CO just a more politically correct term for a guard, or is there a genuine role difference?

## Prison: Basic Services

Prisons of all security levels, even maximum security in which custody is most emphasized, provide inmates with many services and activities beyond simply being locked up. When people object to the provision of these services--"convict coddling"--correctional managers have four ready responses:
  1. Convicts are not on the street any longer. When they give up their freedom, the state assumes the responsibility for their welfare and safety.
  2. Prisons are obligated to maintain constitutional living conditions. To do otherwise would invite costly lawsuits and court intervention.
  3. In the old days, when prisons did not provide services and activities, inmates spent all their free time trying to exploit each other and escape. Positive activities make the institution easier to manage.
  4. The special programs may actually make inmates better human beings. Isn't it worth spending a little more if criminality is reduced as a result?

The prison provides three basic services--medical, religious, and education and training--and a wide variety of staff is needed to deliver them. The custodial staff still dominate in numbers and in their influence on inmates (the influence of COs in the housing units and on work sites is particularly important), but many inmates have been helped and redirected by a prison teacher, a counselor, a psychologist, a vocational instructor, or a chaplain.

Religion is an important prison activity. Some inmates fake it, to get to go to church and hang out with their buddies. Others, who never took the time to seek out religion when they were running the streets, find that prison religious programs change the whole direction of their lives. Many prisons have thriving religious communities, from Black Muslims to Eastern religions to every variety of Protestantism, Catholicism, and Judaism. The **prison chaplain** has been a staple of the institution since the days of the Walnut Street Jail, when ministers were part of the effort to induce penitence. Some prison chaplains are dedicated, highly regarded men and women who have a special calling to work with prisoners; others are viewed as uninspired hacks who are little more than snitches for security.

The chaplain is one of many specialized careers required by prisons that people on the street rarely consider. Among the other non-security staff positions necessary to the daily operation of the prison are these:
  Facility manager. The person responsible for maintaining the prison's buildings and grounds. The director of the physical plant.
  Food service manager. The person responsible for procuring food supplies and supervising the kitchen and dining facilities. Meal preparation is very important to inmates, right at the top of their daily concerns.
  Health system administrator. The manager of the institution's health care and medical programs. Usually he or she is an administrator, not a physician.
  Industrial specialist. The person who supervises the inmates working in a prison industry. Generally this is someone who has special training or work experience in the specific work supervised.
  Medical officer. A doctor licensed to practice medicine in the state, either a general practitioner or a specialist.
  **Ombudsman.** A person who receives and investigates inmate (and sometimes staff) complaints. Only a few states have this position; others have a grievance officer or investigator who looks into complaints.
  Recreation specialist. A specialist in physical or other forms of recreational activities. Because most

prisoners are young men, recreational programs are very important in prison.

Teachers and vocational educators. A person certified in education or a specialized vocational training skill. Prisons need teachers with certifications from lower elementary through high school. Most large prisons have several vocational training classes open to inmates.

The delivery of treatment services in the more narrow sense may involve the participation of several kinds of professionals from the behavioral sciences:

Psychologists, who do testing and measurement of inmates, construct personality profiles, and provide counseling.

Psychiatrists, who are few in number and not highly regarded in prisons. They do more diagnosis than treatment in most prisons.

Sociologists, who do more research and monitor the effectiveness of treatment programs, rather than treating offenders directly.

Social workers, often called caseworkers, whose tasks include assessing needs, assigning and conducting programs, and evaluating progress.

**Counselors**, a job title for a person who may apply one of a number of treatment modalities--such as reality therapy, transactional analysis, behavior modification, and guided group interaction--but is more likely to take a generic counseling approach as opposed to a rigorously therapeutic treatment regimen.

**Case managers** or classification officers, usually assigned by housing units. Their job is to look after the inmates' overall welfare, paying particular attention to any personal matters that affect life in custody.

### Is Prison Treatment Possible?

The greatest debate among treatment professionals over the past two decades or more is whether treatment, in the broadest sense, is either possible or desirable within the prison setting. The institutional model keeps large numbers of inmates locked up in secure institutions; treatment programs are built into the custodial routine. Many behavioral scientists would much prefer to see a reemphasis on the reintegration model, which sends offenders out into the community for treatment programs.

Treatment within prison is more likely to appear incidental to custody; treatment in the community is more likely to feel like the real thing. If the intent is to keep prisoners isolated and focused on the prison experience, we should continue as is; if we want them to look beyond the boundaries of the prison, we should explore every possibility of contact with the outside world. Treatment within prison can probably be improved, but it will always be under the domination of custody. Treatment in the community is much closer to how we want the offender to live for the rest of his life.

## SELF TEST

### Multiple Choice

1. A decentralized, housing-unit based style of management often used to break down traditional barriers between custody and treatment in prison is called _____ management.
   a. functional
   b. unit team
   c. priority
   d. experiential
   e. ensemble

2. In a typical prison, how much of the operating budget would be devoted to treatment programs?
   a. less than 10 percent
   b. about 20 percent
   c. about 30 to 35 percent
   d. exactly 40 percent
   e. more than 50 percent

3. Which one of the following services to prison inmates is probably most recent in origin?
   a. psychological counseling
   b. medical care
   c. academic education
   d. vocational education
   e. religious services

4. The institutional model of programming is often said to be in conflict with the _____ model.
   a. deterrence
   b. logical consequences
   c. control
   d. reintegration
   e. revisionist

5. Which one of these prison officials would have been most closely associated with penitence in the Walnut Street Jail?
   a. the social worker
   b. the teacher
   c. the doctor
   d. the ombudsman
   e. the chaplain

6. Most prison wardens today would identify the principal objective in operating their prison as:
   a. rehabilitation
   b. secure custody
   c. deterrence
   d. retribution
   e. humanitarianism

7. Which of the following types of personal searches would be considered most invasive or intensive?
   a. frisk
   b. metal detector
   c. strip
   d. pat down
   e. body cavity

8. The national turnover rate among correctional officers has averaged closest to _____ percent in recent years.
   a. 2
   b. 6
   c. 14
   d. 25
   e. 38

9. The principal purpose associated with use of the sally port is to:
   a. maintain a secure perimeter at all times
   b. separate mentally ill offenders from the general population
   c. train new guards
   d. isolate gang members
   e. search large areas, such as dormitories or cellblocks

10. Wardens generally identify _____ as their most important concern.
    a. state politics
    b. the courts
    c. human resources
    d. the media
    e. victims' advocacy groups

**True or False**

_____ 11. Custody and treatment both thrive in a bureaucratic system.

_____ 12. Classification of new inmates is used far more for the benefit of treatment than it is for custody.

_____ 13. Prison administrators have generally been very open and accessible individuals who have not minded representing their institutions in the public eye.

_____ 14. Chaplains were banned from early penitentiaries because they were said to bring too much hope to prisoners.

_____ 15. Correctional officers are generally not allowed by law the right to strike as part of any labor union job action.

_____ 16. Until after World War II, the prison guard was usually an uneducated minority male from a poor urban neighborhood.

_____ 17. Most of the old wardens tried to eliminate snitches from the inmate population, believing they were destructive to the inmate social system.

_____ 18. About one in four correctional officers today is female, and the numbers continue to increase.

_____ 19. Several state prison systems employ a staff member called an ombudsman to receive and investigate inmate complaints.

_____ 20. Most prisons assign their best correctional officers to tower or wall duty, viewing this as the most skilled duty position.

## Fill In the Blanks

21. The originator of the control model in Texas prisons, _____ became a well-known public figure as the director of the Texas corrections department.

22. Diagnostic and reception centers are generally designed to process _____ inmates.

23. Wardens describe two recent developments that have made custody's job of managing the inmate social system more difficult; these problems are _____ and _____.

24. The most important task for which the custody staff is responsible is _____.

25. The management style of the early prison warden was said to be _____, meaning that he had absolute authority over inmates and staff.

26. Correctional officers are always looking for _____, meaning anything that inmates are not allowed to have in their possession.

27. If a disturbance broke out in a prison dormitory, the first response force that would be called to the scene would likely be the institution's _____ team.

28. _____ was an early twentieth century prison warden who practiced democratic values and humane prison rules to a degree unusual for his time.

29. One practice of many prison wardens today is known by the term _____; it suggests that wardens must get out of their offices and into the housing and operating units of their institutions to see what is going on.

30. Of maximum, medium, minimum, and open security prisons, the greatest number of escapes occur from _____ security.

## Discussion

31. Why is custody so much more important than treatment?

32. What are the basic traditional services the prison provides its inmates?

33. Make a convincing argument for unit team management in prison.

34. Why was (and is today) the position of the deputy warden for custody so powerful?

35. What are the main custodial devices and techniques used to maintain security in a maximum custody prison?

36. What evidence can you cite of the prevalence of the "paramilitary model" in prison operations?

37. How is the makeup of the correctional officer work force different from a century ago?

38. Guards or correctional officers--which is the correct term?

## CHAPTER EIGHT

# Corrections Policies and Issues

The most consequential issue in American corrections since the early 1980s has been the extent of use of incarceration itself as a crime control measure. Is America better off in 2003 with more than 2,000,000 behind jail and prison bars than it was in 1980 when that number was about 400,000? We will come back to this issue in the international context in Chapter 16 at the end of the text. In this chapter, we will look briefly at several other issues that have dominated policy debates regarding institutional corrections in the past decade:

     1. Professionalization and the accreditation movement in corrections.
     2. Prison health care.
     3. Responding to population increases.
     4. Privatization.
     5. Race and imprisonment.

## Key Terms

professionalization
accreditation
American Correctional Association
Professional Development Department
certification
Best in the Business
Commission on Accreditation
  in Corrections (CAC)
HIV
AIDS
tuberculosis
multidrug-resistant tuberculosis (MDR-TB)
hepatitis B virus (HBV)
hepatitis C virus (HCV)
*Estelle v. Gamble*
adequate medical care
principle of equivalence
principle of less eligibility
deliberate indifference
penal harm
bricks-and-mortar solution
front-end solution
double-bunking
back-end solution
alternative storage
parallel universe

double standard
punishment for profit
correctional/industrial complex
corporate demon
contract
private for-profit
private nonprofit
charitable organizations
contractors
employer model
convict leasing
slaves of the state
low-security custodial facilities
surveillance technologies
electronic monitoring
Corrections Corporation of America (CCA)
Wackenhut Corrections Corporation (WCC)
quick fix
underclass
focal concerns theory
beyond rehabilitation
social dynamite
superpredator
thug life
self-fulfilling prophecy
cycle of doom

## Professionalization and Accreditation

Professionalization and accreditation have become important terms in correctional administration in the past two decades. **Professionalization** has to do with gaining professional status for persons working in corrections, while **accreditation** seeks comparable status for their employing organizations.

Erika Fairchild has identified six key indicators of professionalism--merit hiring, training, advanced technology, incorruptibility, equal treatment of citizens, and close adherence to the law. To her list we might add other criteria, such as pre-service education, ethical standards, public service orientation, and the public's view of the occupation's practitioners. Where does corrections stand on the professional scale? Close to a million people work in the corrections field, full- or part-time; would most meet professional standards?

Most institutional jobs in corrections are filled through merit hiring--but with workers who have a high school diploma or GED, and no other pre-service preparation. The main motivation for many people working in corrections is "to get a job" or the benefits that go with civil service employment. Most people express no particular calling for the field. Training is basic. In the year 2000 at least 46 of the 50 states required an average of six-and-a-half weeks (262 hours) of recruit training, ten months of probationary status, and a week (38 hours) of annual in-service training for new correctional officers in operational positions. Probation and parole staff training requirements varied more widely from state to state in 2000, but 46 of the 50 states required an average of about four weeks (170 hours) of pre-service training and a week (37 hours) of annual in-service training. Advanced technology has become more important, as managers search for ways to improve monitoring and security and hold down personnel costs, sometimes to the point that equipment receives more emphasis than staff, or technology is emphasized while human deficiencies are ignored.

Other indicators having to do with ethics, law, orientation, and treatment of citizens are more difficult to evaluate in their correctional context. One need not search very hard to find examples of corruption, discrimination, and illegal conduct in corrections. Indeed, the front page of the leading corrections web site, *corrections.com*, lists links to recent news articles about misconduct by corrections staff, operational and administrative, some of it resulting in litigation. But people whose corrections careers have spanned the last 30 to 40 years would generally agree that both the ethical standards of corrections staff and the legal framework within which they operate are much stronger today than they were a generation ago.

The leading advocate of corrections professionalism today is the **American Correctional Association**, which originated in the National Congress on Penitentiary and Reformatory Discipline meeting in Cincinnati in 1870. The ACA's **Professional Development Department** takes its direction from Article 7 of the 1870 Declaration of Principles: "Special training, as well as high qualities of head and heart, is required to make a good prison or reformatory officer. Then only will the administration of public punishment become scientific, uniform and successful, when it is raised to the dignity of a profession, and men are specially trained for it, as they are for other pursuits." Since 1999, this department has provided a professional certification program leading to four different levels of **certification**--as a corrections executive, manager, supervisor, or correctional officer. Certification is viewed as a way of teaching a standardized body of professional knowledge to individuals who enter corrections work at different levels with very divergent backgrounds.

The ACA also promotes professionalism through seminars conducted at its conferences twice each year. It publishes the monthly journal *Corrections Today*. One of the regular features of the magazine is a **"Best in the Business"** section that highlights the accomplishments of corrections workers at all levels. The ACA also publishes the bi-monthly refereed journal, *Corrections Compendium*, presenting scholarly research articles.

The other major advance in corrections promoted by the American Correctional Association over the past 25 years is known as accreditation. The **Commission on Accreditation in Corrections (CAC)** developed the national standards to be used in granting organizations accredited status before accreditation officially began in 1978. The ACA cites several benefits to accreditation, including improved management, reduced legal liability, enhanced public credibility, an improved working environment, and the establishment of criteria that can be used in comparing organizations nationwide. Accreditation follows a prescribed sequence of steps–assessment, application, self-evaluation, and official audit. Accredited status is granted for three years, to be followed by reaccreditation, going through the audit again, for an additional three years.

Accreditation started slowly but really accelerated by the 1990s. Today the ACA publishes standards manuals for 21 different types of correctional functions. By 2003, the ACA indicated that more than a third of all state prisons but less than five percent of local jails were accredited. Critics point out that accreditation in and of itself is no guarantee of organizational performance. In corrections, it is not hard to find accredited institutions where systematic mistreatment of prisoners has occurred. Critics also point out that standards may be set too low in many instances (the "lowest common denominator" concept), and that no real enforcement mechanism exists, except for the denial of reaccreditation, which is virtually unheard of.

Accreditation's adherents, including upper echelon officials of the ACA, take a contrary view, pointing out that corrections is obviously much better off because of accreditation than it would have been without it. They also cite the importance of professional national standards available to practitioners, something that is particularly important in the decentralized American corrections system. In this view, accreditation is one of the important forces driving correctional organizations forward.

## Correctional Health Care

One of the persistent problems of prison health care is that the prison draws its population from the least healthy part of the general population--the urban poor, often referred to today as the underclass. As James Marquart and his colleagues noted, "Research shows marked variations in health status and access to health care by socioeconomic status. The poor exist in 'triple jeopardy,' for they are typically uninsured, generally live in medically underserved areas, have difficulty obtaining needed health care services, and continue to have higher mortality rates than higher income persons."

The concentration of large numbers of unhealthy, poor minorities in prison provides a foundation of concern. The federal report "Medical Problems of Inmates, 1997" indicated that nearly a third (31 percent) of state inmates and a quarter (23.4 percent) of federal inmates reported having a physical impairment or mental condition. Most of the impaired inmates said that they suffered from multiple impairments or that they were limited in the kind or amount of work they could do.

The National Commission on Correctional Health Care, a nonprofit group that works for improved health care in prisons, issued a report on serious, contagious diseases among inmates in the mid-1990s:
> 1. An estimated 34,800 to 46,000 inmates (about 2.0 to 2.5 percent of the jail and prison population at the time) were infected with **HIV**, with an estimated 9,000 with full-blown **AIDS**.
> 2. An estimated 98,500 to 145,500 HIV-positive inmates were *released* from prisons and jails back into society during this time.
> 3. As much as one-fifth of the inmate population of two million could be infected with hepatitis C.
> 4. There were an estimated 1,400 active cases of **tuberculosis** in jails and prisons in 1997, and as many as 12,000 inmates carrying the disease were released that same year.

Even people who could not care less about what happens to prisoners ought to be concerned about the flow of sick inmates back into society. Jonathan Shuter, former medical director at Rikers Island in New York City, has pointed out that prisoners are not a separate population. "Inmates cycle in and out of these places. They're not staying there." Shuter saw a dramatic increase in tuberculosis and HIV cases at Rikers Island. Nationwide, women in custody are much more likely to be HIV-positive than men (3.6 percent to 2.2 percent, according to the Bureau of Justice Statistics in 2000), and New York has by far the highest rate of HIV-positive inmates in the country (8.5 percent). One-fourth of the women admitted to Rikers Island when Shuter was there had the virus, half of them unaware that they were infected.

Although in decline behind bars since 1995, HIV and AIDS remain at least four times as prevalent in prison as in the general population. Drug users who inject drugs are often infected with multiple diseases, blood-borne, such as hepatitis and HIV, and air-borne, such as TB. Inmates who are in and out of custody often stop taking their drugs after release, so their symptoms may be alleviated but they are not completely cured. This is particularly important for inmates with tuberculosis, who may develop what is called **multidrug-resistant tuberculosis (MDR-TB)**, which has been on the upswing in poor parts of several large American cities-- Washington, D.C., New York City, Los Angeles--with large concentrations of intravenous drug users.

With HIV in decline at present and TB concentrated in urban areas, the greatest health care threat behind bars has become hepatitis, the term for several viral infections affecting the liver. At one time the focus in prisons was on the **hepatitis B virus (HBV)**, which is spread by sexual contact and blood. It has a long incubation period and can cause serious long-term liver damage. But in the past decade, attention has shifted to the apparently much more widespread **hepatitis C virus (HCV)**, a blood-borne virus spread by intravenous drug use or blood transfusions before improved screening began about 1990.

Less than two percent of the free world population in the United States is HCV-infected. Among the prison population, the infection rate is estimated at 18 percent, 10 times higher, because of the concentration of intravenous drug users in prison. Often lying dormant for decades, Hepatitis C causes liver disease in 20 percent of its victims, and eventually kills five percent of those infected. Hepatitis C requires lengthy treatment--at least one full year--with expensive medication, costing $10,000 to $25,000 annually per patient, with uncertain success rates. Many prisoners expect to die without ever getting this treatment.

What is the prison's obligation in providing health care to inmates? The standards of today are very different from those of yesterday. Jails and prisons of the past enjoyed poor reputations as health care providers. If you

74

had asked a convict of a generation or two ago, "What happens to you when you get sick in prison," the answer would be, "You die." Prison medical services were minimal, and jail services were sub-minimal.

This image began to change in the 1960s and 1970s. Litigation attacking poor conditions in confinement often put medical care near the top of the list, usually just below overcrowding and poor security. One of the early landmark prisoners' rights cases, *Estelle v. Gamble* (1976), established a standard that remains in effect today: prisoners are entitled to **adequate medical care**. What does "adequate" mean? It does not mean the best, or excellent, or superior, or even good. It means suitable for people in their circumstances with two circumstances being particularly important: They are poor and they are locked up. So what prisoners get is a minimalist standard of medical care--public health for the poor as modified to fit prison.

Michael S. Vaughn and Leo Carroll have contrasted two opposing arguments in regard to prison health care. One side, occupied by health care professionals, prisoner advocates, some correctional administrators, and sick prisoners, argues the **principle of equivalence**: with respect to medical care no distinction should be made between inmates and citizens of the free world. The contrasting view, more popular with the public and political officials who pass laws and make policies, is the **principle of less eligibility**: prison conditions must always be "a step below the minimum standard of living of people working or on welfare" in the free world; to make prisons less attractive, prisoners must be treated worse than the lowest law-abiding citizens outside.

The courts, as part of the political system shaping the application of punishment, recognize that prisoners are entitled to some level of medical care, while the public outside is entitled to a higher standard. Prisoners are entitled to less, and when mistakes happen, it is more difficult for them (or their survivors) to collect damages for bad medical care. *Estelle v. Gamble* established the standard of **deliberate indifference** in federal courts dealing with prison medical malpractice litigation, a much higher standard--amounting to gross negligence or recklessness--than the standard of negligence that would apply in free world medical malpractice claims.

The **penal harm** advocates of today argue that deficient medical care, including suffering and death, is a deserved corollary of penal confinement. They argue that prison life should be made harder, or tougher. They would reduce medical services to a bare minimum. In dealing with the medical problems of older inmates, for instance, their policy would be to confine them securely, ignore their complaints, and let nature take its course. Many people in politics and society share this view.

Prison medical care, focused on a population that is both older and more prone to serious illness than earlier populations, is an expensive proposition. Most states estimate that about 10 to 15 percent of their prison budget goes for medical care. Jails used to spend much less, but in recent years urban jails have had to deal with more sick, debilitated drug users, homeless people, and mentally ill; jails have had to lay out large sums to upgrade their medical and mental health services. Corrections officials, recognizing that health care behind bars is in crisis, want to provide more and better services, but when they need more money they have to turn to political officials who are prioritizing budget cuts in tough economic times. Sick prisoners are low on the priority list.

**Responding to Population Increases**

Prisons cost money in two ways--capital outlays for construction, and annual operating costs, which are primarily (75 to 90 percent) personnel costs. Average construction costs for new prisons vary from $10,000 per bed to over $100,000 per bed, depending on the security level of the institution, prevailing construction wages, and other costs. Thus a new 1,000 bed prison might cost anywhere from $10 million to $100 million, depending on where it was located and who it was designed to hold.

Average operating costs also vary widely depending on salaries, the distribution of inmates in various custody levels (maximum or supermax costing two or three times as much as minimum), and the provision of medical care and rehabilitation programs. Alabama's average cost of $25.19 per inmate day in 2001 was the cheapest in the country; Alaska's daily cost of $111.89 was the most expensive. The national average per inmate day in 2001 was $61.04, or $22,279 to keep one inmate in prison for a year. The federal prison system was slightly cheaper, averaging $59.02 per day or $21,542 annually.

Although corrections officials have looked for ways to hold down prison costs--both construction and operation-- corrections has taken an increasingly large slice of the state budget pie year by year over the past two decades or more. Any prison remains an expensive cathedral to public safety, and state policy has consistently been not to build new prisons (the **bricks-and-mortar solution**) in anticipation of growth; instead they wait until existing prisons are full, and then build new facilities to relieve overcrowding.

To avoid new prison construction, states have traditionally been presented with three principal options--front-end solutions, double-bunking, and back-end solutions. The **front-end solutions** emphasize probation and community-based alternatives to imprisonment. **Double-bunking** has to do increasing efficiency by putting more people into existing space. The **back-end solutions** allow the early release of inmates when prisons get badly overcrowded.

By the 1990s, as warehousing had settled in as the dominant purpose of imprisonment, prisons developed a fourth option--**alternative storage**. Included in this option are private prisons (in-state and out-of-state), prisons in other states, and jails (usually in-state but sometimes in other states also). The theory here is that the prisoner is a commodity to be stored. When limits are reached and breached within your own system, you turn to other secure facilities as a temporary measure, waiting for the population to go down or new institutions to open.

At the end of 2002, 73,500 state prisoners, about 5.8 percent of the total state prison population, were held in private facilities. A much smaller number of state prisoners, estimated at about 5,000, were held in the prisons of another state, the majority of them in Virginia.

The other alternative storage facility, beyond the private prison and the prison in another state, is the local jail. By the end of 2001, over five percent of all state prisoners, 67,760 inmates, were housed in jails, either temporarily or permanently through contractual arrangements with local sheriffs. Six states--Alabama, Kentucky, Louisiana, New Jersey, Tennessee, and Virginia--each held more than 3,000 state prisoners in local jails.

Beginning in the 1970s, when its state prison at Angola was placed under federal court order to improve conditions and reduce overcrowding, Louisiana started storing its excess inmate population in parish jails. Initially considered a temporary move, it became permanent after 1990, when the state stopped building new prisons. The per diem rate paid sheriffs for housing state prisoners in parish jails was raised several times, eventually to $22.39, and the sheriffs found that with their lower operating costs they could make a tidy profit from housing state inmates, while the department of corrections found it could house inmates at least one-third cheaper in local jails than in state institutions.

What started as a stopgap measure became a **parallel universe**. The result of carrying out this policy over the long term was apparent in the numbers of 2003. Of the 36,000 convicted felons in Louisiana, 17,000 were held in state prisons, 3,000 were held in two private prisons, and 16,000 were held in local jails. Louisiana is the only state to hold less than half of its state prisoners in state-operated institutions. Its focus on reducing costs has taken it further along the alternative storage path than any other state.

How is this alternate universe plan working? Jails--even the bigger, modern jails of today--are still not prisons, and most cannot provide the level of services, security, or supervision that prisons can. The Louisiana Department of Corrections acknowledges that a **double standard** of care exists for prisoners housed in parish jails versus those in state prisons.

From the point of view of inmates serving state time in the parish jails, local time is dead time. Most inmates spend practically all their time sitting in dorms or cellblocks doing nothing. Security is more lax, so the jails have greater problems with escapes, assaults, and minor misconduct than the prisons do. They also have much greater problems with contraband; some jails are notorious within the prison system for allowing inmates access to marijuana, other illegal drugs, and alcohol--while they are locked up serving felony sentences.

The alternate universe plan has now been in effect for such a long time it would be difficult to dismantle it. It has changed the landscape of jailing in Louisiana, particularly in rural parishes, where the sheriff's jail warehouses have become a major industry. The sheriff's department has grown from a small public safety organization to a commercial enterprise--in several rural parishes the largest employer in the local economy.

But the boom times may be ending. State officials are attempting, through legal and policy changes, to rein in the prisoner population--to eventually have inflow match outflow to reach a level of stasis. Sheriffs built new jails anticipating an uninterrupted supply of state prisoners. For the first time, the state has more local jail beds than it has state inmates to fill them. Quite apart from whatever sheriffs are not doing for prisoners, their financial precariousness, built on human trafficking, threatens them with ruin in the years ahead. They are put in the position of pressuring the legislature to send *more* people to prison, to fill their jails up again. Or, failing there, their marketing people can get on the phone--to Idaho, South Dakota, wherever prison are full--and rent their empty beds to prisons in other states, which is exactly what many of them are trying to do at this moment. Warehousing prisoners is more and more an interstate commerce.

## Privatization

In 1980, no secure, privately operated jails or prisons existed in America. By 2001 about 150--100 prisons and 50 jails--were open for business, holding about 120,000 prisoners, or six percent of the jail and prison population. What is responsible for this sudden development?

In the early 1980s, the entrepreneurs who founded Corrections Corporation of America, the first private prison company, argued that they could operate prisons in several ways better--cheaper, faster, more efficiently--than public authorities. Advocates of privatization attacked corrections as an inefficient public bureaucracy, arguing that they could save the public 10 to 20 percent in the operating costs of jails and prisons.

Critics of privatization, including political officials, corrections officials, and social scientists, objected to transferring secure custody of prisoners--for a long time a public responsibility--to private corporations motivated by economic concerns--cost and profit. They most often attacked the ideology of **punishment for profit** and cited the danger of a **correctional/industrial complex**--a network of private corporations, politicians, and corrections officials--that would promote public policies to continue the growth of the corrections industry.

Critics sometimes conjure up images of a **corporate demon**, scheming in the boardroom to keep the public afraid of crime, to keep politicians passing new laws getting tougher on criminals, to keep widening the net of offenders brought under formal control, and to keep locking up more offenders in secure facilities. Robert Lilly and Mathieu DeFlem, in their article "Profit and Penality: An Analysis of the Corrections-Commercial Complex," warn of the monetary colonization of criminal justice. Profit supersedes human values, and economic interests drive justice decisions.

Joseph Hallinan, author of *Going Up the River: Travels in a Prison Nation* (2003), describes the close relationship between private prison owners and state and local politicians. Private corporations make big contributions to influential politicians, who then approve the contract necessary for private prison operations. Public policy--expensive public policy--emerges from this symbiotic relationship.

The proponents of privatization strongly resist efforts to portray them as the dark side of the force. They point out that it is government and not private entrepreneurs who establish corrections priorities, and government controls private corrections with a detailed **contract**; fail to live up to the contract, and you get fired or sued or both. They also argue that privatization of jails and prisons is a worthwhile experiment; why should anyone be afraid of a little competition?

Before this movement to privatization of secure custody, private involvement in corrections had taken three traditional forms:
      1. **Private for-profit.** A few halfway houses and many drug and alcohol treatment facilities are operated for the profit of their owners. Many individual service providers--such as therapists and counselors--simply contract or bill for their services, often at an hourly rate.
      2. **Private nonprofit.** This is a corporation organized to perform a specific function, such as operating a work release facility for inmates completing state prison sentences. The corporation is managed by a board of directors that gets no income from their civic work.
      3. **Charitable organizations.** Often a branch of a larger national organization, such as the Salvation Army or Boys Town, this organization usually has a broader funding base and operates a network of related programs.

Many other individuals and organizations are corrections **contractors**. They contract with jails or prisons to provide services the institutions either cannot or do not want to provide--medical care, psychiatric treatment, specific types of counseling, education and vocational training, and food service.

77

The traditional role of the private sector in corrections was not a happy story. Early English sheriffs and their wardens were essentially profiteers who operated their jails to make money from the fees charged inmates. Entrepreneurs transported indentured servants from English jails to hard labor in the American colonies. Private businesses once operated factories within prison walls and contracted for prison labor. This is a practice similar to the so-called **employer model** of today, in which businesses move production centers to prisons and hire prisoners to work in them. **Convict leasing**, primarily in the South, rented out convicts to private lessees, who in effect owned the convicts lock, stock, and barrel. Convict leases--in which mostly black inmate populations labored as "slaves of the state" (from *Ruffin v. Commonwealth*, an 1871 Virginia case) at agricultural labor, railroad building, levee building, cutting trees, building roads, indeed any form of labor they were directed to by the private businessmen who owned them--lasted into the early years of the twentieth century. Local jail inmates labored on private property at the direction of their sheriffs until very recently. The exploitation of prison labor for the profit of prison officials, politicians, and sharp businessmen is a principal reason for the poor image of privatization in corrections today.

Although the greatest controversy in private corrections recently has been in regard to the operation of high-security jails and prisons, privatization has had more impact on other applications. Harry Allen and Clifford Simonsen suggest that private organizations are most involved in treatment programs, **low-security custodial facilities** and non-secure residential settings, and **surveillance technologies** for offenders not incarcerated. Private sector treatment programs, often directed at chronic substance abusers, can be either residential or non-residential. Low-security and open facilities are the greatest part of the institutional business of private corrections. Private contractors have also moved quickly into the application of surveillance and control technologies. Private drug-testing labs support many community-based corrections programs. A number of electronics firms offer **electronic monitoring** devices--everything from bracelets to home video monitors with breath-testing capabilities--to suit many levels of supervision.

**Corrections Corporation of America (CCA)**, formed in 1983, remains the largest private prison operator in America. With a capacity of 62,000 inmates in its 60 American jails and prisons in 2001, CCA houses just over half of all adult prisoners in private secure institutions. Its nearest competitor, **Wackenhut Corrections Corporation (WCC)**, while concentrating more on the overseas market, maintains a 21 percent share of the American market with 26,000 beds. Together CCA and Wackenhut control 75 percent of the private prison beds in America.

Thirty-one states had at least one privately operated jail or prison by 1998, led by Texas with 43 and California with 24. By the end of 2002, several states in the South and West, led by New Mexico (43 percent), Wyoming (30.3 percent), Alaska (30.9 percent), Montana (29.3 percent), and Oklahoma (27.7 percent), held more than a quarter of their prison population in private facilities.

What was behind this rapid growth? Many of the state and local governments that turned to private companies were in a position comparable to a heroin addict suffering withdrawal pains--they were looking for a **quick fix**. In the case of prisoners, the attraction of the private companies was based on their ability to bring new prisons on line quickly without investment of public funds in capital outlay. For about 15 years, then, private jails and prisons were one of the stopgap measures used to lessen some of the financial burdens of pursuing the brick and mortar solution to criminal sentencing--the massive expansion of the jail and prison system.

As James Austin and Garry Coventry pointed out in their 2001 monograph, *Emerging Issues on Privatized Prisons*, the longer private prisons operate, the more they look like public prisons. In their early years, private prisons effected most of their savings in salaries and benefits, where 75 to 90 percent (or more) of a prison's budget typically goes. They paid lower salaries in general and provided fewer fringe benefits. But over time, the once new staff have acquired seniority and more benefits comparable to those paid in public institutions. Private prisons have also had their share of management and security problems, including several well-publicized incidents involving escapes and violence, showing that they are as equally capable of mismanaging prisons as the public sector.

Political officials, except at the federal level, seem more skeptical of the sales pitches of private corrections corporations. The numbers of inmates in custody are growing very slowly or declining in most states; the sense of crisis in needing new beds has passed in most places. The major private corporations, CCA and Wackenhut, are looking to expand their overseas operations, though it remains to be seen if American prisons, like American cigarettes, are easily exportable. Some private corporations are trying to expand their involvement in the new forms of intermediate sanctions and community-based programs that are developing today. They believe that the peak of private involvement in operating secure prisons has already passed.

## Race and Imprisonment

If you visit virtually any prison in America, you will be struck almost immediately by the overrepresentation of racial and ethnic minorities in the population. Black inmates alone made up 45 percent of incarcerated felons at year end 2002, compared to 34 percent white, 18 percent Hispanic, and three percent all others. Why do race and ethnicity play such a big part in imprisonment?

Two recent Bureau of Justice Statistics reports describe prisoners and trends in imprisonment in detail. "Prisoners in 2002" provides the following figures for rates of imprisonment by race and gender. These numbers represent the number of sentenced prisoners per 100,000 in the American population in each category.

|          | Male  | Female |
|----------|-------|--------|
| White    | 450   | 35     |
| Black    | 3,437 | 191    |
| Hispanic | 1,176 | 80     |

These figures indicate that in comparison to white males, the imprisonment rate for Hispanics is about two-and-a-half times higher, while the rate of black imprisonment is eight times higher. For females, the comparable rates are two-and-a-half and five-and-a-half times greater. Black males are 100 times more likely to be incarcerated than white females.

The second report, "Prevalence of Imprisonment in the U.S. Population, 1974-2001," estimates that about one in 17 white males, one in six Hispanic males, and one in three black males (32.2 percent) will do prison time during their lifetime, if current incarceration rates remain unchanged. This is *imprisonment* in a state or federal prison, mind you, not just a felony conviction that might carry only a short jail term or probation. If we add this group to the total, then the majority of black males born in 2001 will be convicted of a felony at some time in their lives. The comparable figure for white males would be about 10 percent.

Most research into disparity in imprisonment, such as Scott Christianson's *With Liberty for Some: 500 Years of Imprisonment in America*, has emphasized the historical linkage between the lower class and imprisonment. From colonial times through the 1960s, indentured servants, slaves and free people of color, immigrants, ex-slaves and their descendants, and the urban poor who make up the bulk of the present day **underclass** have dominated jail and prison populations. Crime and imprisonment have been a part of the normal life of the urban poor since the founding of the republic.

The gap between white and minority imprisonment rates, already wide in the 1970s, began to accelerate, particularly for Hispanics, who began immigrating to this country from Mexico and other Latin American countries in great numbers from the 1960s on. In the early 1970s, the overall percentage of men who had done prison time was 2.3 percent--1.4 for whites, 8.7 for blacks, and 2.3 for Hispanics. By 2001, the white percentage had almost doubled (to 2.6 percent), the black percentage had likewise almost doubled (to 16.6), but the Hispanic percentage had more than tripled (to 7.7 percent).

What is responsible for the persistence of this wide gap between white and minority imprisonment rates? Some would argue it proves the continuing importance of racism in the criminal justice system, while others suggest the influence of economic class and other factors, including social disadvantages and high crime rates among the poor, the persistence of a significant subculture of poverty in the United States, and, particularly in regard to drug crimes, the politics of selectivity in bringing offenders into the system.

Steven Spitzer in 1975 used the term **social dynamite** to describe those members of the deviant population in society who are viewed as particularly threatening and dangerous; people so labeled tend to be more youthful, alienated, and politically volatile. Regarded as more in need of formal social control, they are more likely than less volatile offenders to be formally processed through the criminal justice system.

Darrell Steffensmeier and his colleagues over the past several years have researched the **focal concerns theory** of judicial decision making in Pennsylvania courts. This theory emphasizes three "focal concerns" in sentencing: the offender's blameworthiness, protection of the community, and practical considerations, such as cost and family effects. Judges tended to see the criminal records of young black males being more serious and more indicative of future criminal behavior; they also saw young black males as lacking the social bonds that would reduce the likelihood of future criminality.

Coming from more dysfunctional social environment, with fewer resources to fall back on, and perceived as being culturally less inclined to change, black and Hispanic criminals are less likely to be dealt with leniently by the justice system--to get non-incarcerative sentences and shorter terms behind bars. Researchers who have looked at the processing of youthful offenders through the juvenile courts have stressed the importance of the concept of **beyond rehabilitation**, meaning that a juvenile is much more likely to be punished severely or transferred to the adult court for processing if he or she is perceived to no longer be amenable to rehabilitation. The court looks at specific circumstances--family involvement, performance in school, gang ties, extracurricular interests, and "attitude"--in deciding whether to keep working with the juvenile or give up and deal with him as an underage but almost certain future adult criminal.

Judicial decision making is based on both reality and image. In the 1990s, the image of the **superpredator**, the violent, inner-city, teenager and young adult, often a gang member heavily involved in drug dealing, and almost always black or Hispanic, proliferated in music and film, was culturally popularized in the term **thug life**. Although there were not many of them and they were concentrated in the poorest parts of a few large cities, the superpredators' image--and their popularity with American youth in general--was enough to scare hell out of the political system.

Some researchers emphasize the selectivity of crime control policies. From the 1980s through about the mid-1990s, the War on Drugs brought far more minorities than whites into prison for drug crimes; since then, violent crimes, particularly homicide, robbery, and assault, have continued to bring much greater numbers of blacks and Hispanics than whites into prison. Two-thirds of all arrests for homicide and felony assault, and three-quarters of all arrests for robbery, are of black and Hispanic offenders. These crimes, except for armed robbery, typically involve victims of the same racial or ethnic group as the offenders.

For many felons leaving prison, even those with a mind set to follow the law and stay out of trouble, the barriers to entering mainstream society are formidable. They make it difficult for ex-cons to get a good job, to get the assistance they need to get out of poverty, to maintain stable family lives as spouses and parents, and to live productive lives in their communities. A generation ago, the term **self-fulfilling prophecy** was often used to mean a consequence that came about because it was expected or predicted. An example would be black children not doing well in school because they were said to be not as smart or not trying as hard as white children, which was used to explain why many minority-dominated schools were deficient, and also to justify avoiding serious efforts to make them better. Today, with criminals, the concept is more like a **cycle of doom**, in which young black males (and to a lesser extent, young Hispanic males) are foretold to live unproductive lives of crime and poverty on the fringes of society. At current rates of imprisonment, more than half of all the black boy babies born in America this year will grow up to be convicted felons.

# SELF TEST

## Multiple Choice

1. In the alternate storage universe, Louisiana has become famous for storing large numbers of its inmates in:
   a. other states
   b. local jails
   c. other countries
   d. private prisons
   e. federal prisons

2. The most widespread and potentially most costly disease among prison inmates today is:
   a. hepatitis C
   b. diabetes
   c. tuberculosis
   d. Alzheimer's
   e. influenza

3. The leading professional journal for corrections practitioners is:
   a. *Behind Bars*
   b. *Crime and Punishment*
   c. *Justice Journal*
   d. *Corrections Today*
   e. *Pros and Cons*

4. The process through which correctional organizations are recognized for compliance with national standards is known as:
   - a. monitoring
   - b. dispersion
   - c. judication
   - d. accreditation
   - e. circumscription

5. Private agencies such as the Salvation Army and Boys and Girls Town that operate facilities to assist criminal offenders are called _____ organizations.
   - a. self-serving
   - b. exploitative
   - c. charitable
   - d. discretionary
   - e. subversive

6. The motivation of private prison corporations is often summarized as punishment for _____.
   - a. pain
   - b. profit
   - c. fun
   - d. the elite
   - e. rehabilitation

7. The response to prison population increase that emphasizes putting more people into existing prison space (even in overcrowding results) is known as:
   - a. custodial zoning
   - b. sensory deprivation
   - c. double-bunking
   - d. back-end solution
   - e. gerrymandering

8. Blood-borne diseases such as hepatitis and HIV are most likely found in prisoners who are:
   - a. vampires
   - b. mentally ill
   - c. drug users
   - d. elderly
   - e. middle class

9. The landmark case of *Estelle v. Gamble* (1976) required prisons to provide _____ medical care to inmates.
   - a. kind and loving
   - b. superior
   - c. subhuman
   - d. income-adjusted
   - e. adequate

10. In 2001, the national average cost to keep an inmate in prison for a year was closest to:
   - a. $6,400
   - b. $14,800
   - c. $37,900
   - d. $10,500
   - e. $22,300

**True or False**

_____ 11. A higher percentage of jails than prisons are accredited by the ACA.

_____ 12. The prevalence of HIV/AIDS continues to rise in prisons, increasing to epidemic proportions.

_____ 13. Penal harm advocates believe that no real effort should be made to improve prison services to a level comparable to the free world.

_____ 14. As a percentage of the state budget, states are spending much less on corrections today than they were 25 years ago.

_____ 15. Most states have no training requirements for new corrections officers.

_____ 16. The corporate demon concept is mostly directed at corruption among state prison wardens.

_____ 17. The federal prison system spends more per inmate than any state prison system.

_____ 18. State prisoners assigned to local jails would expect a better living environment and better services than they would be provided in prison.

_____ 19. Private prison corporations have been careful to avoid any appearance of political impropriety by avoiding all except necessary contact with the political officials who approve their contracts.

_____ 20. At current imprisonment rates, black males are about 10 times more likely to be imprisoned in comparison to white females.

## Fill In the Blanks

21. _____ is to the individual corrections worker what accreditation is to the corrections agency.

22. The oldest and largest private prison corporation is _____.

23. According to the principle of _____, prisoners must be treated worse than the lowest level of society outside prison.

24. The term commonly applied to the poor urban minorities from which the bulk of the prison population is drawn is _____.

25. At present rates of imprisonment, the estimate is that one in _____ black males born today will do prison time.

26. In the juvenile court, the phrase _____ is important in identifying someone deserving adult punishment as a highly probable future criminal.

27. In the South, the practice that allowed private contractors to exploit prison labor was known as _____.

28. The most difficult to treat form of tuberculosis is known as _____-TB.

29. If you are a strong advocate of expanding probation supervision instead of adding new prison beds, you would be said to favor _____ solutions.

30. The legal status of convicts during the era when they were expected to perform involuntary hard labor in prison is summed up in the phrase _____.

## Discussion

31. Why do you think many citizens (and some prisoners) might believe that private prisons are inherently superior to public prisons?

32. Explain the application of the concept of the self-fulfilling prophecy as it applies to young black males and imprisonment today.

33. Why are prisoners sicker than ordinary citizens?

34. If you were a prison warden, would you seek accreditation for your institution? Explain your decision.

35. As an outsider looking in, what do you see in corrections workers that supports or hinders the notion of professional status?

36. Your state's prison population has been static but is starting to go up again. Briefly, what are your options? Which do you recommend for the short-term future?

37. If you were a judge routinely sentencing criminals to probation, jail, and prison, what factors would you look at in making decisions? Do you think the factors that would lead to imprisonment would tend to be concentrated in certain population groups, or would they be evenly distributed among all defendants?

CHAPTER NINE

# Male and Female Prisoners

This chapter is about people behind bars--the more than 2,000,000 men and women in America's prisons and jails. What are they like? What kinds of paths did they follow to get locked up? What are their problems? What do they have in common? And how do they differ from the rest of us? After reading this chapter, you should be familiar with:
1. The background of men in prison.
2. The profile of a typical state prisoner.
3. The background of women in prison.
4. The profile of a typical female prisoner.
5. How state and federal prisoners differ, and how jail and prison inmates differ.

## Key Terms

chronic offender
first offender
functionally illiterate
substance abuse history
regular drug user
broken family
cycle of violence
root cause of crime
sociopath
anti-social personality disorder
caste system
Jean Harris

preferential treatment
chivalry
hidden crime
prostitution
Elizabeth Gurney Fry
Alderson
Mary Belle Harris
liberation theory
equal opportunity imprisonment
parenting
rabble
criminalization of the mentally ill
transinstitutionalization

## Men in Prison: Criminal Histories

Prisons hold two-thirds of America's prisoners, jails the remaining third. If we look closely at the more than one-and-a-third million people in state and federal prisons as of 2003, what commonalities do we see? The great majority of people in prison are male repeat offenders. Most have been in criminal trouble before, many of them consistently since early adolescence. Research by Marvin Wolfgang and others has supported the **chronic offender** concept. Following birth cohorts, people born in a locale in a given year, Wolfgang found that a relatively small number of persons in society, perhaps five or six percent, was responsible for the majority of all arrests and an even greater majority of violent crime arrests.

About one in three boys and one in seven girls will be arrested at least once as juveniles (under age 18) according to current estimates, which on the flip side means that most juveniles (even many caught in an act of wrongdoing) will never be formally taken into custody. Juveniles arrested three or more times are at high risk to continue to be arrested as adults. The great majority of adult criminals have not only committed felonies but also been arrested at least once by age 21. After age 25, arrest rates fall off sharply, even for people previously arrested.

Among state prisoners in 1997, 23 percent were in prison as first offenders, 32 percent had one or two prior felony sentences, and 42 percent had three or more prior felonies. The number in prison as first offenders (we should remember that **first offender** means first time caught and processed as a felon, not first time actually committing a crime or being arrested; "first felony convictee" is probably a more accurate term) had increased from 19 percent in 1991, most likely as a result of reduced sentencing discretion in the courts. But essentially about three in four people in state prisons in the 1990s had prior felony convictions involving either probation or imprisonment.

Imprisonment is a status directly related to criminal violence and prior conviction record. The "Survey of State Prison Inmates, 1991," indicated that 94 percent of inmates had been convicted of a violent crime or had a previous sentence to probation or incarceration; this would mean that only six percent of the prison population was made up of non-violent first offenders in for drug, property, or public order crimes. Of the six percent who were non-violent neophytes, the majority (61 percent) were in prison for drug trafficking or possession, while 12 percent were imprisoned for burglary.

The crimes for which people have been imprisoned have shifted over the years. In the 1970s, when incarceration rates were much lower and prison systems much smaller, persons convicted of crimes against persons made up about 60 percent of the state prison population, property criminals 30 percent, and drug and public-order criminals together the remaining 10 percent. These numbers underwent a remarkable change during the 1980s after the War on Drugs was declared. By the mid-1990s, the number of persons imprisoned for violent crimes had declined to about 40 percent, property and drug offenders were about 25 percent each, and public-order criminals (including such crimes as weapons and explosives violations, DWI, escape, commercialized vice and morals offenses, and other regulatory crimes) made up the remaining 10 percent. After the mid-1990s, the number of drug criminals began to decline and the number of violent criminals went up again.

By 2001, this was the breakdown of sentenced inmates in state prison systems by category and offense:

| | |
|---|---|
| Total | 1,208,700 |
| Violent offenses | 596,100 (49.3%) |
|     Murder | 159,200 |
|     Manslaughter | 16,900 |
|     Rape | 30,900 |
|     Other sexual assault | 87,600 |
|     Robbery | 155,300 |
|     Assault | 118,800 |
|     Other violent | 27,400 |
| Property offenses | 233,000 (19.3%) |
|     Burglary | 104,700 |
|     Larceny | 45,500 |
|     Motor vehicle theft | 18,000 |
|     Fraud | 33,700 |
|     Other property | 31,100 |
| Drug offenses | 246,100 (20.4%) |
| Public-order offenses | 129,900 (10.7%) |
| Other/unspecified | 3,600 ( 0.3%) |

The single largest group of convicted felons, greater in number than either murders or robbers, is drug traffickers. About two-thirds of the 246,100 drug felons (or more than 160,000) were convicted of various crimes related to drug distribution, and in over 70 percent of these cases the drug was either crack or powder cocaine. In many state prison systems today, even as the War on Drugs supposedly wanes, the number one category of new admissions remains people convicted of distributing cocaine.

The sentences that imprisoned offenders are serving have grown longer over the past two decades. The court-set sentence length has declined slightly, but as truth-in-sentencing policies, tougher parole standards, and the abolition of parole have kicked in among the states and at the federal level, the length of time served before release has increased sharply--by about 10 percentage points or six months overall for all offenses. An average term today is about three years. Release statistics are based on inmates *released*, not the figures for inmates remaining in prison. The ones still in prison have done more time and served a greater portion of their sentences than the ones getting out; the new ones coming in now will serve terms perhaps twice as long (in real time) on average as the ones who came in back in the 1970s.

## Men in Prison: Personal Demographics

A 1997 comprehensive profile of state prisoners reported these statistics on race and age:

| Race | | Age Group | |
|---|---|---|---|
| White | 33.3% | Under 25 | 19.8% |
| Black | 46.5% | 25-34 | 38.1% |
| Hispanic | 17.0% | 35-44 | 29.4% |
| Other | 3.2% | 45+ | 12.7% |

Federal prisoner statistics show more Hispanics and others in population (and fewer blacks and whites), and federal prisoners are a few years older. If the median age of state prisoners now is about 33, the median age of federal prisoners is about 37. In the 1970s, whites outnumbered blacks in the prison population, but continuing high rates of violent crime (murder, assault, and robbery) among blacks and the anti-drug focus on crack cocaine have driven the numbers of blacks in prison much higher since then. As the numbers of Hispanics living in the United States have shot up since the 1960s, the numbers of Hispanics in prison have increased at a rate even higher than that of blacks.

Although in absolute numbers the number of women in prison has increased sharply--from fewer than 10,000 in the early 1970s to nearly 100,000 30 years later--the fact is that state and federal prisoners remain overwhelming male. Males made up 93.7 percent of state prisoners in 1997 (down from 94.5 percent in 1991) and 92.8 percent of federal prisoners in 1997 (up from 92.2 percent in 1991). Fewer than seven of every 100 prison inmates are women. Between 1995 and 2002, the total number of male prisoners grew 27 percent, the number of female prisoners by 42 percent. Women remain much less likely to be arrested for the violent crimes that are growing in statistical prevalence among prison inmates.

Prisoners are much more likely than the general population to be unmarried and undereducated. Only one in six state prison inmates and three in ten federal prison inmates are married. Most state prison inmates have never been married. In 1997, 68 percent of black inmates, 54 percent of Hispanic inmates, and 43 percent of white inmates had never been married.

The 1997 education breakdown by categories was as follows:

| Education | |
| --- | --- |
| Less than high school | 39.7% |
| GED | 28.5% |
| High school graduate | 20.5% |
| More than high school | 11.3% |

Almost 70 percent of state prisoners did not graduate from high school, compared with about 18 percent of adults not in prison. Prisons are full of high school dropouts who begin prison life functioning at elementary school literacy levels. These inmates are said to be **functionally illiterate**.

Along with their educational deficits, prisoners have long been notoriously underemployed. In 1997, 55 percent were working full-time, 12 percent part-time, and 33 percent were unemployed before imprisonment. At a time when national unemployment rates have been in the five to six percent range, prisoners were about six to eight times more likely to be unemployed or working only occasionally, often at transient labor jobs.

Lack of work translates into low income. In surveys conducted in 1986 and 1991, only 11 percent (1986) and 15 percent (1991) of prisoners were earning $25,000 or more annually before they came to prison. Twenty-seven percent (1986) and 22 percent (1991) were earning less than $3,000 a year before they came to prison. Well over half in both surveys had annual incomes of less than $10,000, below even what a college student living on loans and a part-time job can live on. If a prisoner's lawful income is this low, it is easy to see that crime, especially selling drugs, becomes a covert "hustle" to pick up the money needed to meet basic necessities of life.

**Men in Prison: Life Histories**

Thus far we have established that most prisoners are young to middle-aged men, predominantly lower-class minorities, with lengthy criminal histories and poor education and employment records. What other disadvantages might they have? The most significant burden many prisoners carry around is a history of substance abuse; the extent to which alcohol and illegal drugs influence their lives is perhaps the main feature setting prisoners apart from mainstream society.

Although most drug criminals are in prison for crimes related to powder or crack cocaine, their **substance abuse histories** and those of other inmates not in prison for drug crimes are diverse. They start earlier in life, drink alcohol to excess and use drugs more often, and experiment with a greater range of hard drugs than non-prisoners, right up to the time of their arrest. For many prisoners, time spent in jail is the first time they have been sober in years.

About half of all prison inmates claim to have been under the influence at the time of the crime leading to their arrest. Surveys from 1986 and 1991 showed these results:

|  | Percent of inmates | |
|---|---|---|
| Under the influence of: | 1991 | 1986 |
| Alcohol only | 18 | 18 |
| Drugs only | 17 | 17 |
| Both alcohol and drugs | 14 | 18 |
| Total | 49 | 54 |

In a 1997 survey, alcohol was the single most influential drug by itself (36.5 percent), followed in descending order by marijuana (14.8 percent), the "other drugs" category (8.4 percent), crack cocaine (8.3 percent), powder cocaine (7.4 percent), and heroin (5.5 percent). The inmates who were drinking immediately before their crimes, which has consistently been about a third of all prisoners, had consumed on average about three six-packs of beer or two quarts of wine, drinking for a median time of about six hours, before going out to commit their crimes.

About 80 percent of inmates reported using illegal drugs at least once in their lives, and 60 percent or more identify themselves as **regular drug users** at some point in their lives. These figures do not include alcohol. Prisoners take drug abuse much farther than people in society. About one in four prisoners has used heroin or other opium derivatives, and about one in four has used a needle to inject drugs, most often heroin, cocaine, or crank. This explains most of the hepatitis and HIV among prison inmates.

The composite effect of drugs and alcohol on imprisonment is profound:

Inmates under the influence of drugs or alcohol at the time of the imprisonment crime--50 percent.

Inmates in prison for drug and alcohol crimes--22 percent.

Inmates committing their crime to get money for drugs--17 percent.

These categories overlap, obviously, but even so it is apparent that if substance abuse could be prevented or treated more effectively, the numbers of people in prison would be reduced substantially.

Prisoners drink and use drugs. Where do these habits begin? Most prisoners are products of the **broken family** that is associated with a range of social ills--poverty, substance abuse, physical abuse, and criminality. The 1997 inmate survey reported that inmates were almost as likely to be raised by a mother only (38.5 percent) as by two parents living together (43.7 percent), and the two-parent figure is inflated, including parents who were not married to each other, step-mothers or step-fathers, and live-ins who acted as surrogates. Perhaps three out of four prisoners did not grow up living in a stable household with their two natural, married parents.

Family fragmentation is most noticeable among black inmates. The decline of marriage in the black community over the past forty years has resulted in two generations of black children growing up in single-parent households. By 2000, far more black inmates were products of single-mother households rather than two-parent households.

About one in three state prisoners in 1997 grew up in a household where a parent abused alcohol or drugs or both (according to the prisoners' own definition of "abuse"). Physical and sexual abuse and domestic violence are prevalent in inmate families. In research involving men and women inmates in a large urban jail in the early 1990s, two-thirds of the men and almost half the women reported serious domestic violence in their childhoods: "Both violence and non-violence tend to be continuous. If you had a violent family life as a child, you are very likely (in the range of 90 percent) to have a violent adult family life as well. If you had a non-violent family life as a child, your adult family life is likely to be non-violent also, unless you happen to hook up with a spouse (more likely a male than a female) who proceeds to give your life a violent turn."

In her research into the connection between childhood abuse and adult criminality, Cathy Spatz Widom used the phrase **cycle of violence** to suggest that a childhood history of physical abuse predisposes the survivor to violence in later years. She found that documented abuse or neglect as a child increased the likelihood of arrest as a juvenile by 53 percent, as an adult by 38 percent, and for a violent crime by 38 percent.

Patrick Fagin of the Heritage Foundation has explored the social influences on crime and violence in his writings for more than a decade. Whereas others tend to focus on race or socioeconomic variables in explaining crime, Fagin sticks to a family structure explanation. He identifies seven family conditions leading to crime:

1. Fatherless families.
2. The absence of a mother's love.

3. Parental fighting and domestic violence.
4. The lack of parental supervision and discipline.
5. Rejection of the child.
6. Parental abuse or neglect.
7. Criminal parents.

These family conditions lead to higher rates of juvenile delinquency and in time adult criminality, which when concentrated in a specific geographical locale, such as a minority lower-class urban ghetto, can destroy the sense of community necessary to sustain the neighborhood. Although we may use poverty or race as the markers, the real **root cause of crime** in these areas, as Fagin sees it, is broken families.

We are very aware today that crime runs in families. Four in ten prisoners have immediate family members who have served prison time, which is one of the more striking features of their background. Among young black inmates, given the increased likelihood of imprisonment among blacks, the chance of another family member having been in prison is almost even.

To further complicate their social disabilities and personal limitations, many prisoners have personality or attitude problems that make it difficult for them to get along with people. They used to be called **sociopaths**; today the more common term is **anti-social personality disorder**, meaning that they exhibit such characteristics as impulsiveness, poor self-control, lack of remorse for wrongdoing, lack of empathy with others, manipulativeness, irresponsibility, superficial charm, exaggerated sense of self-worth, and disregard of the consequences of their behavior--one important consequence being repeated imprisonment.

Prisoners are predominately poor minorities--the underclass--with limited prospects. When they are not in prison they are likely to be found living in the densest, poorest urban neighborhoods where crime and substance abuse flourish. They live there because that is where their families and friends live. If America had a **caste system**, prisoners would be on the bottom level, even without the one final impediment to moving upward toward mainstream society--a felony record. When you look at where prisoners came from, and what they have to return to when they get out, it should be no surprise that half of them end up back in prison within five years, either on new convictions or as parole violators. For these men, prison is a normal life experience.

## Women in Prison: Personal Features

**Jean Harris** came to prison with a not so typical prisoner background in some respects--a middle-aged white schoolteacher with a drug problem, arrested only once in her life, but that arrest for murdering her lover in an argument. Harris wrote about her sisters in New York's Bedford Hills Prison, in *Stranger in Two Worlds (1986)*: "The chasm between me and the other women was wide and deep when I came to Bedford. In some ways I have bridged the gap. In many others I have not and never could. I am almost 40 years older than the other women here, and I am considered `rich' because I am white, and because I have been widely publicized as `social.'"

The characteristics of women in state and federal prisons in 1998 were reported as follows:

|  | State Prisons | Federal Prisons |
| --- | --- | --- |
| Number of prisoners | 75,200 | 9,200 |
| | | |
| Race/Ethnicity | | |
| White | 33% | 29% |
| Black | 48% | 35% |
| Hispanic | 15% | 32% |
| Other | 4% | 4% |
| | | |
| Age | | |
| 24 or younger | 12% | 9% |
| 25-34 | 43% | 35% |
| 35-44 | 34% | 32% |
| 45-54 | 9% | 18% |
| 55 or older | 2% | 6% |
| Median age | 33 | 36 |

| Marital status | | |
|---|---|---|
| Married | 17% | 29% |
| Widowed | 6% | 6% |
| Separated | 10% | 21% |
| Divorced | 20% | 10% |
| Never married | 47% | 34% |
| | | |
| Education | | |
| 8th grade or less | 7% | 8% |
| Some high school | 37% | 19% |
| HS graduate/GED | 39% | 44% |
| Some college or more | 17% | 29% |

Seventy-five percent of women's felony convictions in state court in 1996 were for property crimes (mostly fraud and larceny) and drug crimes. Of women passed along to imprisonment in state prisons in 1998, the leading category of offenses was drug crimes (34 percent), followed by violent crimes (28 percent), property crimes (27 percent), and public-order crimes (11 percent). So while half of all men are in prison for crimes of violence, over 70 percent of women are in prison for non-violent crimes, and generally with a less prominent criminal history than men sentenced to imprisonment.

Although news accounts often give the impression that women of today are more violent, the number of women convicted of homicide and robbery has fallen off steadily in recent years. The most common violent crime for which women are arrested is the misdemeanor simple assault, typically against an acquaintance, friend, or family member. Women are much less likely to commit or be charged with predatory violent crimes against strangers. The female murder rate in 1998 (1.3 per 100,000) was less than half what it had been in 1976 (3.1 per 100,000). The male murder rate was 11 per 100,000, about nine times the female rate.

Researchers into women's criminality have found two distinctive features marking the lives of women prisoners-- abuse and drugs. Joycelyn Pollock has reported research consistently showing that a substantial percentage of incarcerated women have been abused, both sexually and physically, as children. A study conducted by the Oregon Department of Corrections (1993) found that 45 percent of its female inmates reported physical abuse, 66 percent reported sexual abuse, and 37 percent reported abuse before 18. Similar research in Oklahoma found that about two-thirds of women inmates reported being abused at some point in their lifetimes. The Oklahoma study was notable in showing the continuity of abuse: women who were physically or sexually abused as children were likely to be abused as adults as well.

The use of drugs and alcohol is higher among victims of abuse, which relates to significant drug abuse histories among women prisoners. Women evidently are more likely than men to abuse drugs, while men are more likely to abuse alcohol. In a recent report, 60 percent of female prisoners said they used drugs in the month before the offense, 50 percent were daily users, 40 percent were under the influence at the time of the offense, and nearly one in three committed an offense to get money for drugs.

Women prisoners are sicker than men, at least partly because of intravenous drug use. Women prisoners are much more likely to be HIV positive and to be infected with Hepatitis B and C than men are. At year end 2000, 3.6 percent of all female inmates were HIV positive, compared to 2.2 percent of males. Hispanic female inmates reported the highest HIV infection rate of any group in prison.

The personal histories of women prisoners, in comparison to men, seem even more filled with sadness and misfortune. The 1993 Oregon study of its female prisoners gave this summary: "This survey presents a picture of women inmates characterized by low achievement, early delinquency, and high experience of abuse. The women have generally low education levels, worked at unskilled jobs as teenagers, and a high percentage used alcohol and drugs as teenagers." Barbara Owen, who wrote *In the Mix: Struggle and Survival in a Women's Prison*, based on her work in a California prison, offered this observation: "The offense profile also suggests that women tend to commit survival crimes to earn money, feed a drug-dependent life, and escape brutalizing physical conditions and relationships."

# Women in Prison: Theories of Crime and Punishment

In the history of the penitentiary, which is to say the modern history of punishment, why have so few women been imprisoned? Many scholars of the criminology of women believe that women once received **preferential treatment**--translated as leniency--within the legal system. There were several reasons cited for this favorable treatment, including the non-violent nature of women's crimes (except for murder, which when committed by females usually involved family members or loved ones as victims), the lack of serious prior criminal histories among most women offenders, and the condition of motherhood, still prevalent today (about 80 percent of women in jail and prison are mothers, the great majority of these with minor children still living with them). Judges were said to take a paternalistic view of women offenders, dealing with them like fathers deal with bad children.

Otto Pollak suggested in *The Criminality of Women* (1950) that the legal system practiced **chivalry**, meaning that the male-dominated system treated women protectively. Pollak also suggested that much of women's criminality was **hidden crime** in that it involved victims who were family members or friends of the offender. They would presumably be less likely to call the crimes to the attention of the system (or demand punishment) because of their relationship with the criminal.

The early biophysical criminologist Cesare Lombroso said the only crime to which women were well suited was **prostitution**, not only because it was so prevalent at the time but also because it was passive and required little skill. The early women's prisons, which were only separate wings of larger men's prisons, were full of women who were whores, thieves, and consorts of criminal men. Many correctional reformers of the 1800s, such as the English Quaker **Elizabeth Gurney Fry**, advocated dealing with these women in special facilities, run for and in some cases by women (though usually under the direction of men).

The first all-female prison was the Indiana Reformatory Institute, which opened in 1873 and applied Zebulon Brockway's reform methods. The first federal prison for women, at **Alderson**, West Virginia, opened in 1927. The woman sometimes identified as the first female warden (though other women held other titles as heads of other early women's prisons), **Mary Belle Harris**, was its head. These and other prisons set the tone of women's corrections--the idea that women prisoners were immoral beings, unduly influenced by men, who needed to be reformed but did not present much of a physical threat to safety and security.

Prostitution remains an important criminal offense today, though generally not a felony for which the offender is put in prison. But many practitioners of prostitution get in trouble for other crimes--for crimes of violence related to their work, for drug-related offenses, and for other crimes related to their hustling lifestyles.

The differential treatment of women did not always mean better treatment, particularly once a woman actually ended up in prison. Women's prisons were smaller, less restrictive, and less secure, but they were also typically more demeaning to women offenders and less inclined to offer support services and rehabilitation programs.

**Liberation theory**, which is based on analysis of the changing roles of women in society as exemplified in the impact of the women's liberation movement, suggests that women are not as likely to be given preferential treatment or differential treatment today. They are more likely to be viewed as the criminal equals of men, in a system where women are moving more into important decision-making roles as well. Laws that treat all offenders equally, particularly drug laws, have greatly reduced the likelihood that women, even the mothers of small children, will get favorable treatment by the system.

Despite these professions of **equal opportunity imprisonment**, the truth is that the prevalence of women in the prison population would not have increased significantly over the past three decades were it not for the War on Drugs. At the end of 2002, when 97,500 women were in state and federal prisons, the two leading crimes among women inmates were drug trafficking and drug possession, accounting for one-third of the women in state prisons and two-thirds of the women in federal prisons.

Imprisonment for drugs has particularly affected the numbers of minority women in prison. Recent Bureau of Justice Statistics estimates suggest that about 11 of 1,000 women will go to prison in their lifetime. This likelihood varies by race--five out of 1,000 white women, 15 out of 1,000 Hispanic women, and 36 out of 1,000 black women. What is most interesting here is that the projected imprisonment rate of white males, 44 per 1,000, is not that much higher overall than that of black females. At current imprisonment rates and life expectancies, black females have almost the same lifetime prospect of imprisonment as white males.

As the number of women in prison has increased so rapidly in such a short time, the number of women's prisons has also increased quickly. California alone has gone from one women's prison holding a thousand inmates in the early 1970s to five prisons holding more than 10,000 in 2002. The two largest women's prisons in America, Valley State Prison and the Central California Women's Facility, both located outside Chowchilla, hold more than 7,000 inmates; these two prisons could have housed every female felon imprisoned in America 30 years ago.

The five states with the highest incarceration rates for women in 1998 were:

|  | Inmates per 100,000 Women Residents |
| --- | --- |
| Oklahoma | 122 |
| Texas | 102 |
| Louisiana | 94 |
| Mississippi | 77 |
| California | 67 |

The 1980s was the biggest single decade in the history of building prisons for women; 34 new prisons for women were built in this decade. Many of the new prisons are designed with more maximum security features to house a deeper-end, more long-term and hard-core population. Women's prisons are said to be "nicer" than men's prisons, but women in prison are still routinely described as harder to manage and more difficult to deal with day-to-day than men in prison. Correctional officials do not mean that the women are more violent or escape prone, but they say women complain too much, get involved in too many petty disputes, and do not adapt as well to prison routines.

Knowing that about eighty percent of women in prison are mothers, it is no surprise that women prisoners report that separation from their children and family outside ranks as the greatest pain of imprisonment. Visiting is often limited or restricted, with little opportunity for prisoners to meet privately with their children, their mothers, and their sisters.

Jean Harris resolved, shortly after she entered Bedford Hills, not to let the prison--either the administration or the inmates--beat her down. She began working in the prison's Children's Center, where visiting took place. When she was asked to teach a **parenting** class, she did not know what the term meant: "I had never heard the word--parenting--before I went to prison." Observing prison mothers with their children was an eye-opening experience, she found. "It was the lack of gentleness toward their children that struck me first, even though they were loving mothers. They had been smacked when they did something wrong and now they were doing the smacking." Gentleness became the core of her parental instruction.

## State versus Federal, Prisons versus Jails

America has three types of secure custody institutions for adult criminals--state prisons, federal prisons, and local jails. If you were an inmate in a state prison, you would most likely be confined in a medium custody institution with other criminals who are about equally likely to be locked up for a violent or non-violent crime. More of the violent criminals serving long-term sentences, or those criminals who have been involved in violent incidents or serious disciplinary infractions since coming to prison, will be passed up the chain to the maximum security or close/high security institutions.

The federal prison system is now larger than any single state system and has a lot more prisons to move inmates around in if it wishes to do so. The two most distinctive features of federal criminals are, first, most are drug criminals, and, second, many are citizens of other nations. In 2001, about 55 percent of federal prisoners were convicted of drug crimes. Immigration offenses (10.5 percent) and weapons crimes, such as possession of a firearm by a convicted felon (8.8 percent), were the second and third most common offenses, followed by robbery (7.2 percent) in fourth place.

Almost a third of the federal prison population is made up of foreign nationals, mostly from Mexico and other Latin American countries. If you plan to either work in or become an inmate in the federal prison system, you should definitely learn to speak Spanish before you get to prison. Federal prisoners are also in general a few years older than state prisoners, more likely to be married, and substantially better educated. These variables, while not necessarily making them "nicer" inmates, do make them in general easier to manage.

Jails are another matter. The most correct way to think of the jail population is to think of two different groups, a short-term population, the ones who will be here today, and a long-term population, the ones who will still be here in 90 days. The short-termers include those who are released on bail or other options soon after arrest, and the members of the urban underclass--the urban poor, adolescents and young adults, homeless street people, prostitutes, alcohol and drug abusers, and the mentally ill--who make up John Irwin's rabble. They may not stay in jail very long on any particular charge, but when you examine their life history, some have spent more time behind bars than most felony offenders. These habitual misdemeanor offenders are often assigned to trusty positions in the jail doing the cooking, the laundry, the cleaning, and maintaining the sheriff's vehicle fleet.

The long-term inmates in the jail population are of several types--misdemeanants, probation and parole violators, felony arrestees whose crime and prior record make them good prison candidates, and, most commonly in the South, felony state prisoners serving their terms in local jails. The jail itself does not divide its inmates into short- and long-term according to how long they are expected to remain behind bars. If it is a larger jail, it may place offenders in housing units--either cellblocks or pods--by level of dangerousness; in a smaller jail, everyone may be mixed together.

Primarily because of the number of misdemeanants in jail, the demographics of jail inmates differ slightly from those of prison inmates. The percentage of women in the jail population is higher--11.6 percent, compared to 6.7 percent in prison. The numbers of whites (43.8 percent) have climbed again recently so that they are now more numerous than blacks (39.8 percent) or Hispanics (14.7 percent).

The jail is closer to the street than the prison is; it gets a lot of inmates who are still high on drugs or alcohol when they come in. It also gets more inmates who are mentally ill, some of them dangerously so. About one in six jail inmates held in jail at any given time is estimated to have a serious mental illness--more than 1,000,000 persons a year. Jails now hold more people receiving psychiatric treatment than public psychiatric hospitals do. More than 30 years ago, Dr. Marc Abramson, a California psychiatrist, originated the term **criminalization of the mentally ill** to describe what he saw as people who had been held in state hospitals were turned loose and entrusted to the care of community mental health clinics. Many of these former mental patients ended up homeless, psychotic, arrested, and in jail. Today we often call this process **transinstitutionalization**, referring to the transfer of mental patients from hospitals to jails. In 1999, about nine percent of jail inmates were taking some type of psychotropic medication, a number similar to those receiving some kind of mental health therapy or counseling.

Although jail suicide rates have fallen by more than fifty percent in the past 20 years, jails still have more suicides each year than prisons do. About 35 percent of inmate deaths in jail in 1999 (324 of 919 total) were by suicide (the rate was 54 per 100,000 inmates), compared to 11 percent of prison deaths (26 per 100,000 inmates). Jail inmates are also sicker than prison inmates, coming off the streets with diseases such as hepatitis, tuberculosis, and HIV that require immediate treatment. Much of this is related to the high incidence of substance abusers in the jail population. When sheriffs say they are treating more mentally ill people than community mental health clinics are, they can also say they are treating far more substance abusers than all community facilities combined.

In comparison to prisons, the greater diversity (and more rapid turnover) of the inmate population is one of the jail's two most striking features. The other is the almost complete absence of anything purposeful to do. "Jail time is dead time," observers have said for a century, and the statement remains just as true in jails today.

# SELF TEST

## Multiple Choice

1. When judges are described as having paternalistic attitudes toward women offenders, it means the judges treat the women like:
   a. sex objects
   b. children
   c. mad dogs
   d. illegal aliens
   e. the mentally ill

2. About what percentage of women in prison are mothers?
   a. 11-12 percent
   b. 20-22 percent
   c. 35-38 percent
   d. 53-55 percent
   e. 75-80 percent

3. The most prevalent "traditional" female crime of the 1800s was probably:
   a. burglary
   b. prostitution
   c. infanticide
   d. arson
   e. robbery

4. Barbara Owen has said that women's crimes, fed by drugs, poverty, abuse, and poor relationships with men, are best characterized as:
   a. survival crimes
   b. crimes of pleasure
   c. political crimes
   d. hate crimes
   e. identity crimes

5. In a 1997 survey, male prisoners reported that _____ was the drug that had most influenced their behavior before incarceration.
   a. heroin
   b. alcohol
   c. methamphetamine
   d. cocaine
   e. LSD

6. Prisoners were once called sociopaths; the more common term today is:
   a. bipolar
   b. psychotic
   c. anti-social personalities
   d. schizophrenic
   e. obsessive/compulsive

7. About what percentage of prison inmates today are black and Hispanic?
   a. 17 percent
   b. 30 percent
   c. 46 percent
   d. 65 percent
   e. 84 percent

8. The greatest number of men are in prison today for:
   a. murder
   b. drug crimes
   c. assault
   d. robbery
   e. burglary

9. As Patrick Fagin sees it, the "root cause" of crime is:
   a. political corruption
   b. poor schools
   c. deteriorating cities
   d. racial discrimination
   e. broken families

10. The most accurate definition of first offender as it is used describing someone in prison is:
    a. under age 21
    b. first time arrested
    c. first time prosecuted
    d. first felony conviction
    e. first violent crime committed

**True or False**

_____ 11. Women offenders agree that separation from their male partners is the worst part of doing prison time.

_____ 12. Research in Oregon and Oklahoma prisons has established that the majority of female inmates were victims of either sexual abuse or physical abuse (or both) before incarceration.

_____ 13. There are more women in prison for prostitution than for any other single crime.

_____ 14. About half of male prison inmates today are confined for crimes against persons.

_____ 15. According to the idea of chivalry or preferential treatment, men got more lenient punishments than women because judges tended to view women as being the cause of men's criminal behavior.

_____ 16. Prisoners on the whole are slightly better educated than the general population outside prison.

_____ 17. Jails have much higher suicide rates than prisons do.

_____ 18. Most authorities do not believe any definite connection exists between family violence in childhood and family violence in adulthood.

_____ 19. Most inmates agree that alcohol and drug abuse became problems for them only *after* their first prison term.

_____ 20. Inmates would agree that jails provide more work, programs, and other purposeful activities than do prisons.

## Fill In the Blanks

21. Most of the increase in the number of women in prison over the past 20 years is due to the increased incarceration of _____ offenders.

22. Women make up about _____ percent of the total prison population.

23. Many prisoners lacking basic reading and writing skills are said to be _____.

24. After drug offenses, the second greatest number of male inmates are in prison for the crime of _____.

25. Otto Pollak is often cited for his suggestion that women's criminality was _____ crime because women were more likely to victimize family members and friends.

26. Some researchers believe the social movement known as women's _____ has had significant impact on women's criminality, whereas others argue it has missed women criminals almost entirely.

27. Serving her prison term for murder, Jean Harris found meaning in teaching _____ classes to inmates.

28. Discharging inmates from mental hospitals only to put them in jail is known by the term _____.

29. Elizabeth Gurney Fry and Mary Belle Harris are historically associated with prisons for _____.

30. Cathy Spatz Widom's term for the perpetuation of childhood physical abuse into adult criminal violence was the _____.

## Discussion

31. Are men and women different as criminal threats in society?

32. How is the background of women in prison today different from the background of men in prison?

33. "Prisoners have the same chance in life as everyone else," the politician says. Agree or disagree.

34. Federal prisoners are quite different from state prisoners; what are the key differences?

35. If you are attacking the behaviors that eventually lead to imprisonment, what would be your first priority? Why?

36. Prisoners often report that jail life is much more "annoying" than prison life. Why would they use this word in contrasting the two environments?

## CHAPTER TEN

# Prison Life

This chapter considers life behind bars as it is lived by men and women serving terms in prison. Each year 600,000 or more men and women enter prison as newly-convicted felons or parole violators. Everyone who enters prison experiences prisonization, in Donald Clemmer's term, but the experience differs depending on individual circumstances--what the inmate brings to prison, and what he or she finds there. After reading this chapter, you should be familiar with:
1. The evolution of prison life.
2. Sociological views of prison life.
3. Prison life today.
4. The life of women in prison.
5. Prison violence.
6. Sex in prison.
7. Prison gangs.
8. Death in prison.
9. Perspectives on prison life.

## Key Terms

rehabilitation
recreation
self-improvement
prisonization
convict code
convict
free world
inmate
prison argot
bug
fish
screw
shiv
universal factors of imprisonment
clique
institutionalized
the yard
corruption of authority
deprivation
pains of imprisonment
cigarettes
rat
center man
gorilla
merchant
wolf
punk
fag
ball buster
real man
tough
hipster
total institution
disculturation
institutionalization
importation

administrative segregation
disciplinary detention
protective custody
mental health housing
affectional starvation
dyad
prison family
kinship
femme
stud broad
kite
the life
the cool
the square
the mix
vengeful equity
goon squad
SORT
prison riot
mass rebellion
Attica riot
Santa Fe riot
monosexual
asexual
co-correctional prison
gang rape
galboy
jailhouse turnout
Prison Rape Elimination Act of 2003
furlough
conjugal visiting
prison gang
security threat group (STG)
Mexican Mafia
Nuestra Familia
Texas Syndicate

| state-raised youth | Mexikanemi |
| square john | Aryan Brotherhood |
| jailing | Black Guerilla Family |
| doing time | Bloods |
| gleaning | Crips |
| governmental perspective | bus therapy |
| general population | prison hospice |
| special management | |

## The Evolution of Prison Life

Public views of prison life tend to extremes. On the one hand, you have the old Big House prison of *The Shawshank Redemption*, replete with violence, homosexual rape, guard brutality, and corruption; on the other, the "country club prison," a sort of prison resort where convicts golf and play tennis, enjoy conjugal visits, and idle away their time at public expense. Which perspective is more real today? The Big House view of prison life on which *Shawshank* is based is surely more realistic, particularly for its time, the 1940s to the 1960s, than the country club view ever has been. Prisons have always come much closer to the sense of dread and terror implicit in the Big House than to the notion of comfort and relaxation associated with the country club prison. But in fact most prisoners today live in an environment not much like either of these views.

For the convicted felon, prison life has changed as the nature of the institution itself has changed--from the pre-penitentiary jail, to the penitentiary, to the Big House, to the correctional institution, to the contemporary prison warehouse. In the late 1700s, life in confinement was life in jail waiting for trial, sentencing, or punishment. The themes of life in this institution, the predecessor to the penitentiary, were degradation and idleness. Even for temporary housing of the rabble of society, jails were beneath the standards of civilized men and women.

The penitentiary of the early to late 1800s was intended to be an improvement over the worst features of the jail. For most inmates, penitentiary life was safer and more healthy. The physical punishments and solitary confinement could be brutal, but not many people went there, and if you could deal with the isolation, silence, and monotony you would not do a lot of time.

As the reformative ideals of the penitentiary yielded to the more practical objectives of economic productivity and efficient management, the Big House model emerged by the early 1900s. This prison was a bureaucratic, high-walled, maximum security factory in which most prisoners worked long hours six days a week. But the demise of the industrial prison in the 1930s created the quandary dramatized by the prison riots of the early 1950s: If work was no longer the main focus of imprisonment, what other activities could replace it? Over the next two decades three types of activities developed as answers to this question:

    1. **Rehabilitation.** Prisons began to offer a much broader range of programs--vocational training, educational, religious, and treatment-oriented--open to far more inmates than previously.

    2. **Recreation.** Sports, movies, arts and crafts, and free time activities proliferated.

    3. **Self-improvement.** Inmates were allowed more time and resources to read and study on their own and to form clubs and other organizations devoted to particular interests--twelve-step, literary and political discussion, civic, dramatic and performing arts, social, and religious.

This period is often called the rehabilitation era, when the prison was transformed into the correctional institution. Prisoners were no longer so isolated from the free world. Society took a greater interest in prisons, and activists found it easier to visit men and women in prison. The civil rights movement, which broke down the barriers separating the races in society, reached into prisons as well. And prisoners, who had previously enjoyed few legal rights, began to get greater access to the courts. Judges intervened in prison operations to deal with bad living conditions and abuses of power by prison officials.

These important changes--social, racial, and legal--undermined the remnants of the old social order of the maximum security prison. Prisons went through periods of internal turmoil in the 1960s and 1970s--violence, litigation, and agitation aggravated by overcrowding of the old prisons--before the prison warehouse began to emerge from the fog, creating a contemporary form of prison life in a structured, moderate environment the founders of the penitentiary would not recognize.

## Sociological Views of Prison Life

In his classic text, *The Prison Community* (1940), Donald Clemmer wrote about the maximum security prison as a social organization. His premise was that prison is a microcosm of society--a particularized setting in which inmates create a social system based on life outside of prison but within the limitations imposed by the prison environment. Prisoners underwent **prisonization**, which he defined as "the taking on in greater or less degree of the folkways, mores, customs, and general culture of the penitentiary."

The conduct of prisoners in the penitentiary was measured against the **convict code**: "The fundamental principle of the code may be stated thus: Inmates are to refrain from helping prison or government officials in matters of discipline, and should never give them information of any kind, and especially the kind which may work harm to a fellow prisoner. Supplementary to this, and following from it, is the value of loyalty among prisoners in their dealing with each other."

The rules of the code could be expressed like commandments: "Do your own time." "Don't be a rat." "Be a man." "Don't interfere." "Don't talk to the guards." Men who followed the code often called themselves **convicts**; those who did not, or who obviously identified with the values of the **free world**, were called **inmates**. Calling a convict an inmate was a fistfighting insult.

Clemmer compiled a dictionary of common words of the **prison argot**--the language of imprisonment, shared by prisoners and staff, including these common examples:

> **Bug**: an insane person.
> **Fish**: one newly arrived in prison.
> **Screw**: a guard.
> **Shiv**: a knife, usually hand-fashioned and contraband.

Clemmer pointed out that every inmate was subject to the **universal factors of imprisonment**--acceptance of an inferior role, the facts concerning the prison's organization, new habits of daily life, the local language, the idea that the environment should minister to his needs, the desire for a good job to make it easier for him to "do his time and get out."

Prison society was often viewed as being shaped like a pyramid, or more correctly a diamond. At the top were the professional criminals, assisted by their lieutenants in the second level. The bulk of ordinary cons made up the bulge around the middle. Squares, rats, and bugs made up the lower level. At the very bottom were the child molesters ("baby rapers"), who as the lowest of the low often got paid back in kind in prison for what they had done outside.

Some prisoners, particularly those focused on reentering the free world, kept to themselves and did not associate much with other prisoners. Others, including those who had lost touch with the outside world, were associated with influential prison **cliques**, or social groups, that controlled gambling, contraband, and the sexual exploitation of younger inmates. In time many inmates became **institutionalized**; they were so acclimated to prison routine, so comfortable in prison, that it had become their normal life. Freedom was too scary to think about; when they were discharged, they did not stay out of the concrete womb for long.

In the penitentiary as Clemmer was observing it, a long-term process was at work. Big House prisoners still worked hard, typically long hours six days a week, and they lived (and often worked as well) under strict racial segregation; but they were beginning to have more free time, and they were allowed to spend this time with other inmates--in multi-man cells, in recreation, and particularly in the center of prison social life, on **the yard**, the open space in the middle of the quadrangle of prison buildings.

Inmates not only had more freedom of association, but they had also been absorbed into the prison work force. Trusty inmates assumed full-time responsibilities as part of the prison administration, and, more important, they took direct control of other inmates. They made work and housing assignments, maintained records, dispensed medicine, food, and property, and provided special favors, with or without the supervision of prison staff. In the South, gun-toting convict guards worked other inmates in the fields. Trusties took orders from staff, and they also took orders--and bribes--from other inmate leaders whose authority was independent of the prison administration.

96

In *The Society of Captives* (1958), Gresham Sykes wrote about the evolution of the prison social system from absolute to shared authority. He refers to the accommodation of custodians and prisoners within prison walls as **corruption of authority** --"the imperfect enforcement of the organization's regulations and orders with the tacit acceptance of the officials"--and he sees it not as an evil but as a necessity to the prison of this era:

The struggle between prison guards and inmates, Sykes argued, is in part due to the practice of **deprivation** in prison operations. Deprivation means "the removal or withholding of something," usually something that the person would otherwise be entitled to. The **pains of imprisonment** result from several important deprivations:
1. Liberty, or freedom of movement.
2. Goods and services, particularly their material possessions from the free world.
3. Heterosexual relationships.
4. Autonomy, the freedom to make choices.
5. Security, or the safety of his person and property.
In the absence of money (still contraband in many prisons today), an alternate economy developed. The principal medium of exchange was **cigarettes**.

Like Clemmer, Sykes was interested in prison language, or argot, pointing out that it provided "a map of the inmate social system." Criminal argot, he argued, was not about secrecy (because the guards understood it as well as the inmates did) or symbolic membership in the underworld; it was a way to structure the prison experience. Sykes reported several argot terms that are still often used in discussing prison life by both prisoners and outsiders:
**Rat** or squealer: one who betrays the inmates to the guards, because it benefits him or because he identifies with the guards.
**Center man**: an inmate who shares the viewpoint of the guards.
**Gorilla**: an inmate who takes what he wants by force or intimidation.
**Merchant** or peddlar: an inmate who sells material goods to other inmates.
**Wolf**: a masculine, aggressive homosexual.
**Punk**: an inmate who may not appear feminine but who becomes a passive homosexual in prison.
**Fag**: a feminine homosexual who engages in homosexuality because he likes it. ("Punks are made, but fags are born.")
**Ball buster**: a rebellious inmate who challenges the authority of the guards unnecessarily.
**Real man**: the standard of the code, the convict who endures imprisonment with dignity.
**Tough**: a touchy, unstable inmate who "won't take anything" from other inmates.
**Hipster**: an inmate who talks toughness or leadership but is hollow at the core.

Sykes discusses the interaction of inmates and guards within the unstable prison social system, and the corruption of authority that occurs over time, "finally reaching a point where the inmates have established their own unofficial version of control. The custodians, in effect, have withdrawn to the walls to concentrate on their most obvious task, the prevention of escapes." Prison riots took place when this balance was disturbed and officials attempted to regain the authority they had ceded to the prisoners.

In his book *Asylums: Essays on the Social Situation of Mental Patients and Other Inmates* (1962), sociologist Erving Goffman defined a **total institution** as a "place of residence and work where a large number of like-situated individuals, cut off from the wider society for an appreciable period of time, together lead an enclosed, formally administered round of life." If the inmate stays too long within this system, Goffman suggested **disculturation** occurs. By this he means that he inmate undergoes an "untraining" that makes him temporarily (or permanently) incapable of managing certain features of daily life on the outside, if and when he gets back to it. The more common term for this experience is **institutionalization**.

The concept of a monolithic prison social system, developed within the isolated prison in response to the deprivations of prison life and training new "fish" in its values, was challenged by the research of John Irwin. In *The Felon* (1970), Irwin suggested an **importation** model, in which convict norms, status, and roles are brought into the prison from the outside world. The premise would be that most convicts are already criminal, sharing "age-old criminal norms and values," long before they get to prison. Irwin offered eight criminal identities defining world views *before* people get to prison--the thief, the hustler, the dope fiend, the head, the disorganized criminal, the **state-raised youth**, the lower-class man, and the **square john**.

Irwin saw the prison social system as a mix of all these identities, a mix further complicated by the prisoner's mode of adaptation to prison life. He identified three principal modes:

      1. **Jailing**: cutting yourself off from the outside world and attempting to construct a life within prison.

      2. **Doing time**: making no effort to change your life patterns, but trying to live comfortably in prison while maintaining outside contacts.

      3. **Gleaning**: looking outside the prison and trying to improve yourself using the resources the prison has to offer.

The prison Irwin observed was a prison in transition, the Big House being transformed by modern ideas on rehabilitation, classification, and management into something that was less than the sum of its parts--a greater institution broken down into its components without the dominant ethos that had once marked its life. The old, maximum security penitentiary had been supplanted by its successor, the modern "correctional institution," which would in turn be replaced by the contemporary prison warehouse.

## Prison Life Today

Changes over the past 25 years have limited the most destructive features of prison life, particularly as they affected the physical safety of inmates. While both inmates and staff agree there is such a thing as an inmate social system or subculture, particularly in the older, maximum security prisons that are least susceptible to unit management, they recognize that it is not as strong as it once was. Prisoners today are far from isolated, unless they choose to be. Through the entertainment and news media, and through liberal visitation policies, they are more in contact with the outside world. Levels of staffing are much higher in most state systems than they were in the Big House days, and inmate trusties no longer have direct control over other inmates. Court intervention has resulted in improvement of prison living conditions.

In determining the nature of life in the contemporary prison, some researchers, most notably John J. DiIulio, Jr., are more likely to study prison administrators than relations among inmates. DiIulio's 1987 book, *Governing Prisons: A Comparative Study of Correctional Management*, sets out what he calls a **governmental perspective** on prisons. In this perspective, he argues, "... the key actors in any prison setting are the prison administrators, from the director to the warden to the most junior correctional officer in the cellblock. They are the government of the prison, and it is assumed that the quality of prison life will depend mainly, if not solely, on what they do or fail to do. It is the government of keepers, not the society of captives, that is of primary importance."

A safe, orderly, well-run prison is one with a good administration that has the resources to carry out its mission; an unsafe, disorderly, chaotic prison is one with a poor administration lacking such resources (or mismanaging the resources if it has them). In the latter institution, power passes into the hands of the inmates, and living and working in prison become high-risk endeavors once again.

What is prison life like for most inmates in American prisons today? Over 1,000 new prisons have opened in the past 30 years, most of them medium to low security and open facilities. The result is that 75 percent of inmates today live not in the old fortress prisons ("Gothic monoliths," as Harry Allen and Clifford Simonsen describe them) but in fenced, less secure prisons, where they are housed in dorms and rooms, not cells. Many prisons today are multi-level, meaning they hold inmates in two or more different security levels. California's prisons, which are by far the largest in the world, averaging 4,000 to 5,000 beds each, are built on this model. One warden is in charge overall, but the prison applies unit management to each of several smaller housing units. The several thousand inmates are never all in one place at one time.

This is the breakdown of prisons by type, by capacity, and by average population in 2001:

| Type | Number | Capacity | Average Population |
|---|---|---|---|
| Open/Community | 194 | 46,128 | 238 |
| Minimum | 325 | 141,771 | 436 |
| Medium | 327 | 275,417 | 842 |
| High/Close | 92 | 76,234 | 829 |
| Maximum | 95 | 120,357 | 1,267 |
| Multi-level | 302 | 270,006 | 894 |

The maximum category includes most of the old Big House prisons still in use, including such famous names as Auburn, Sing Sing, San Quentin, Trenton, and Leavenworth. About 50 of these old penitentiaries dating back to the 1800s remain open today. The new prisons are typically one- or two-story dormitories in which 50 to 100 inmates live in bunk beds, rooms, or cubicles with a common dining area and recreation area built into each dorm. They resemble low-rise versions of college dormitories built during the same period. They have the normal amenities, including electricity, running water, central heating, and cable TV.

Life in the new prisons is pretty much lived in the congregate; one of the rights you give up as an inmate--perhaps the one right those of us who are not imprisoned would miss the most if we were locked up--is the right to privacy. It is difficult to impossible in most prisons ever to be completely alone, to get away from everyone else-- to have your own space. A general rule of supervision in a medium or maximum security prison is that each prisoner is to be either in his cell or in the line of sight supervision of a staff member at all times. While this works well for security (if it is actually practiced), it does not do much for one's sense of privacy.

Regardless of security level, prisons run on routine. If an inmate is not working, he is likely to be in one of three other places--at home, which is his bed, room, or cell; in the housing unit common area, which might include a dayroom, recreation area, hobby shop, or TV room; or on the yard, an outdoor area where inmates gather to talk and sometimes play sports.

The prison day is highly structured: three meals (two hot, one cold); work in the morning and afternoon (about two-thirds of prisoners have some kind of work assignment, with food services, dorm orderlies, grounds keeping, the laundry, the warehouse, and maintenance the most common); half a day of class or training if you are in school; visitation in an assigned block of time usually once a week; club meetings, church, sports, TV, hobby crafts, and free time evenings and weekends; all of this taking place within the same circle of people grouped together by the institution's choice.

Prisons today are very big on rules. New inmates are given a rule book during classification. Inmates who break the rules are subject to disciplinary write-ups--"getting a ticket." Inmates average about 1.5 to 2.0 disciplinary tickets a year. Inmates who are written up will face a disciplinary hearing before one officer or a board of up to three members, depending on the seriousness of the offense and the institutional practice. Inmates face minor punishments, from loss of privileges or visitation to extra duty, or major punishments, such as loss of good time, lockdown, or reassignment from one housing unit to another or to another prison.

Most inmates prefer to be in population, or **general population**, a status that is least restricted and that allows the most freedom of movement. Most large prisons have **special management** housing units. The American Correctional Association uses these terms to define four types of housing:

  1. **Administrative segregation**: an inmate removed from general population as a threat to security or to the safety of other inmates and staff. This is a long-term status but it is not a punishment for a disciplinary violation.
  2. **Disciplinary detention** (or disciplinary segregation): an inmate removed from general population for committing serious violations of institutional rules.
  3. **Protective custody**: an inmate removed from general population who requests or requires separation from other inmates for his own safety.
  4. **Mental health housing**: an inmate removed from general population because of serious mental disorders that make it impossible for him to mix with other inmates in open housing.

## The Life of Women in Prison

Is the prison experience for women different than it is for men? Until recently there were few women in prison, and they did not draw a lot of research interest. David Ward and Gene Kassebaum's *Women's Prison: Sex and Social Structure* (1965) compared the social roles of women in prison with those of men in prison. Instead of a cohesive subculture, the women's prison was divided into small, intimate family groups centering on homosexual relationships. Ward and Kassebaum suggested that women prisoners suffered from "**affectional starvation.**" Their emotional and sexual needs for men led to the creation of a prison culture of **dyads** (or two-person relationships) based on male and female roles.

Rose Giallombardo's *Society of Women: A Study of a Women's Prison* (1966), argues against the deprivation or pains of imprisonment thesis and for the Irwin and Cressey's importation thesis, suggesting that the social order of the women's prison is based on identities brought in from the outside world. Much of *Society of Women* is concerned with the explication of the **prison family** or **kinship** networks. These are groups, small or large, similar to families in the free world, but based on females playing all the parts--husbands and wives, sisters and brothers, grandmothers and grandfathers, aunts and uncles, and so on.

Giallombardo looks at social roles and sex roles in detail. She describes such roles as the "snitcher," the "square," the "jive bitch," the "rap buddy," and the "homey." She defines several sex roles in what she calls the "homosexual cluster," particularly the roles of **femme** and **stud broad**, who are the female and male roles in an ongoing homosexual relationship. Giallombardo collected prison **kites**, or letters between inmates, many of which were love letters. She also included a glossary of prison terms in use by Alderson inmates at the time. Many of these terms are the same as terms from the argot of men's prisons, focusing on sex, drugs, the legal system, and criminal careers.

In *Making It in Prison: The Square, the Cool, and the Life* (1972), Esther Heffernan found, as had previous studies, that the substitute family (in other settings also known as the play family or make-believe family) was a critical element to the social order of the women's prison. She defined three basic orientations to prison life:

   1. **The Life**: the habitual deviant criminal, often with a background in prostitution and drug abuse, who settles comfortably into the internal life of the prison.
   2. **The Cool**: the professional criminal who tries to control the prison environment while maintaining contacts with the outside world.
   3. **The Square**: the non-criminal tied to conventional norms and values.

In the 1960s, when the early sociological studies of women's prisons were completed, fewer than 10,000 women were in prison in America. By 2002, the number of women in prison had increased to more than 97,000. The two largest women's prisons in America (perhaps the two largest in the world) are California's Valley State Prison for Women (3,500 inmates) and the Central California Women's Facility (3,100 inmates). These two new prisons--"sister institutions" each located on one square mile of land outside Chowchilla, California-- alone would have held every female state and federal prisoner in the country as recently as 1973, when 6,004 women were in prison at the end of the year.

We have looked earlier in this text at reasons for the rapid increase in the numbers of women in prisons, emphasizing changes in sentencing, legal decision-making, and the War on Drugs. But how has prison life changed for women as the system has been flooded with new inmates? Several scholars, most notably Barbara Bloom, Meda Chesney-Lind, and Joycelyn Pollock, have written extensively about policies and practices in imprisoning women over the past two decades.

The best recent book to focus on the "new" culture of the big women's prison is Barbara Owen's *"In the Mix": Struggle and Survival in a Women's Prison* (1998), which is based on three years of observation, interviews, and research in the Central California Women's Facility. What did Owen see in CCWF? She saw mostly women from the economic and social margins of American society, women whose lives were shaped by the overlapping dimensions of drug use, crime, and, often, violence. For these women, crime is a survival skill, and they see the prison they were sent to as a tough, impersonal place.

The women in CCWF believe that their prison is less violent than a men's prison, with less allegiance to a convict culture. Race and security classification are not considered barriers to inmate interaction, and the inmates described fairly cooperative relationships with prison staff, about two-thirds of whom were men. Owen uses the phrase **the mix** to mean behavior that causes trouble and conflict with staff and other inmates. The mix is centered on the prison yard, where inmates hang out; to avoid the mix, inmates stay to themselves, in their own housing or even better in their own rooms.

Women often indicate they have a harder time "doing time" than men do. They miss their children and their families, they resent their subservient status in prison, and they do not find prison treatment programs or medical care to be useful. They do adapt to imprisonment, but they think of the prison experience as being harder on them than it is on men. This is particularly true as prison systems today adopt the policy that Meda Chesney-Lind calls **vengeful equity**-- treating women offenders as though they were men, particularly when the outcome is punitive (as in imprisonment), in the name of equal justice.

## Prison Violence

Although violence is less common today than a generation ago, it remains a part of the prison experience. Scholars who study prison violence have divided it into five types:

1. Self-violence, in the form of suicidal gestures and attempts.

2. Staff-to-inmate violence, which was once the norm for running a tightly disciplined prison. Most prisons had their guard **goon squads** to administer physical punishment to inmates until recently (in some prisons, perhaps yesterday). Today the preferred term is **SORT**, for Special Operations Response Team, used most often to subdue uncooperative inmates without inflicting extraneous damage.

3. Inmate-to-inmate violence, in the form of assaults and homicides.

4. Inmate-to-staff violence, in the same form.

5. Collective violence against authority, in the form of disturbances and riots.

Physical violence is more of a threat than a daily occurrence in most prisons today, and when it occurs it is at a much lower level than in the past. The prison homicide rate in the year 2000 was 4.49 per 100,000, compared to the national homicide rate of 5.6 per 100,000; prisoners were less likely to be murdered in prison than on the street. *The Corrections Yearbook 2001* reported about 50,000 assaults in state and federal prisons in the year 2000. About a third were against staff, the other two-thirds against inmates. Most of these were simple assaults --basically fights not involving weapons. About 4,200 assaults (split 45 percent against staff, 55 percent against inmates), or less than five percent of the total reported, were referred for prosecution as criminal offenses. The rate of serious assaults is prison is estimated to be the same or lower than the rate outside prison.

What are the causes of violence in prison? Many people assume that prisons are tinderboxes in which psychotic inmates fueled by racial, ethnic, gang, political, and various other animosities attack people as targets of symbolic hatred. First, few prisons are tinderboxes, and second, most violence is personal and has nothing to do with larger issues. Inmates fight with other inmates they don't like for personal reasons--conflict has nothing to do with politics, culture, or race, and in most states very little to do with gangs. The nature of prison life surely aggravates violence. In the free world, we do have some choice of our associates, and if certain people annoy us, we try to avoid them. Prisoners often have no such freedom of choice.

Individual acts of violence against staff or other inmates are one concern; prison disturbances and riots against the authority of the institution are another. Prison historians often cite a rebellion in the underground Simsbury, Connecticut, prison in 1791 as the first prison riot in America. Many prison disturbances from the early 1800s through World War II were not so much political demonstrations as they were escape attempts, some of them leading to successful mass escapes.

The prison riots of the early 1950s were a different matter. These actions were about calling attention to prisoners' complaints. They followed a pattern: inmates seizing a building, taking available guards hostage, presenting a list of demands, publicizing their complaints about the prison as much as possible, then capitulating when their demands were met or when the use of overwhelming force appeared imminent. Some political officials had proposed a **mass rebellion** theory as the cause of these riots, but the American Prison Association commission that reviewed them rejected this idea and identified other causes– inadequate financial support and official and public indifference, excessive size and overcrowding of institutions, substandard personnel, enforced idleness, unwise sentencing and parole practices, lack of professional leadership and professional programs, and political domination of management.

Strikes, disturbances, and riots that focused on media attention and political demands recurred in another cycle at the end of the 1960s, leading up to the most famous and most deadly prison riot in American history, the **Attica riot** of September 9-13, 1971. After three days of negotiations, an assault force of state police and guards was sent in to recapture the prison. They killed 39 people (10 hostages and 29 inmates); three other inmates and one guard were killed by prisoners during the riot. Attica became known as the classic example of how not to handle a prison riot, especially in the general rampage of shooting that brought it to an end.

If Attica was the political riot, then the riot at the New Mexico State Penitentiary in February 1980 was the "apolitical prisoner" riot, or some said the "prison code" riot. In the **Santa Fe riot**, prisoners took over the control center and held hostages, some of whom were tortured and brutalized. But the rioters vented their greatest rage upon other inmates, particularly snitches and weaker inmates in protective custody. Thirty-three men were mutilated and murdered, and hundred of others were raped, beaten, tortured, or terrorized in what remains the most savage prison riot in American history.

## Sex in Prison

There is no sex in prison. Or that's what the rules say. "Unofficial" prison sex is generally divided into three types--self-sex, or masturbation; heterosexual sex, involving male and female inmates or staff; and homosexual sex, involving either male or female inmates or staff.

Of the three types, masturbation is by far the most common and widespread, with more than 90 percent of men and women inmates admitting in surveys that they practice it in prison. Masturbation is a disciplinary writeup. The inmate is reminded that prison life is not only monosexual, but it is also **asexual**--without sex.

Sex between prison staff and inmates is illegal in about 46 states today, although it is acknowledged to be a common problem. In the old days it was typically male guards taking advantage of female inmates; today, as more women go to work in men's prisons, sex between male prisoners and female staff is a more frequent occurrence. It is a serious disciplinary violation and a crime, and it also creates compromised relationships between those maintaining security and those affected by it.

Heterosexual sex can also take place between male and female inmates, if they happen to be among the few American prisoners held in so-called **co-correctional prisons** that allow regular interaction between inmates of opposite genders. Fewer than 100 such prisons operate in the United States; they are small, special purpose facilities that combine males and females in the same population for treatment, pre-release, work release, education, or some other specific function. These institutions do not condone sex between inmates, any more than same sex prisons allow sex between inmates.

When most people think of prison sex, they think of homosexual sex, usually between men and commonly violent and coerced. To outsiders, the typical prison sexual encounter is the **gang rape** in which sexual predators beat a younger inmate into submission and force him into anal sex. How prevalent is this scenario in real prison life today? Stop Prison Rape, Inc., the most important national activist group interested in this issue, gives what it calls a "conservative" estimate of 300,000 males sexually assaulted behind bars annually.

Most prison officials are in total disbelief at this estimated number of sexual assaults. Recent research by Cindy Struckman-Johnson and David Struckman-Johnson surveyed inmates and staff in seven state prisons. Seven percent of the inmates had been victimized in circumstances that would meet the legal definition of rape--forced sex and penetration. The great majority of these were one-to-one encounters, not group attacks. Another 14 percent had experienced some other type of pressured or forced sex.

Several other findings from this research were notable. In about 20 percent of the incidents, the sexual aggressor was a male or female staff member. In six of the seven prisons, the staff estimates of inmates coerced into sex were much lower than the inmate estimates. Several factors were identified by the inmates as creating a climate in which sexual coercion was more likely--large prison population, a high percentage of inmates incarcerated for a crime against persons, barracks housing, racial conflict (involving black aggressors and white victims), and lax security (including a "permissive" environment in which staff allowed sexual exploitation to occur).

Louisiana prison journalist Wilbert Rideau wrote about sex in Southern prisons of a generation or more ago. In these understaffed (or trusty staffed) institutions, sexual exploitation was taken for granted. The guards allowed older inmates to turn young inmates into **galboys** to maintain order within the prison. Sexual favors were also used as currency to settle debts and earn cash for the cons who pimped out their "kids." Rideau interviewed inmates who were comfortably settled into prison homosexuality. Some had been homosexual before imprisonment, while others--**jailhouse turnouts**--adopted homosexuality as a way of dealing with the oppressive climate of fear within the prison. He described prison rape was an act of "violence, politics, and an acting out of power roles," an act of conquest and demasculation, stripping the male-victim of his status as "man." The aggressor reinforced his sense of manhood and personal worth by dominating the weaker inmate, and the prison of that time either could not or would not do anything about it.

Congress recently passed the **Prison Rape Elimination Act of 2003** providing for gathering national statistics about the problem and developing guidelines for states about how to address prisoner rape. Some authorities have advocated greater reliance on such methods of approved sexual contact as **furloughs** and **conjugal visiting**. Furloughs for home visits are used extensively by prisons in many foreign countries, but they have been out of fashion in the United States since the 1980s. Conjugal visiting, sometimes called family visiting to indicate that it is about more than just sex in a trailer, is allowed in only six states--California, Connecticut, Mississippi, New Mexico, New York, and Washington--and then only to married inmates with good disciplinary records in certain levels of custody. A very small percentage of inmates qualify for and make use of conjugal visits.

For practically all prisoners, including those in the conjugal visiting states, prison remains the asexual place it has been since the creation of the penitentiary. This is obviously not to say that sex does not go on, only that it is repressed and covert rather than openly acknowledged. Most prisoners today, and most prison officials, believe that most prison sex is consensual rather than coerced, even if most participants would not call themselves homosexual outside of prison.

## Prison Gangs

Once prisoners were allowed to congregate together in housing units and on the yard in their idle time, men and women began to form primary groups, variously known as cliques, tips, or in women's prisons families. In their most extreme form in the contemporary prison, they are called **prison gangs**, or in the argot of prison officials, **security threat groups (STGs)**. A gang would be a street term for a group of people who hang out together, commit crimes together, socialize together, and consider a particular geographical area their home turf. The STG designation is reserved for a group of inmates who belong to a tightly knit organization that attempts to manipulate the internal life of the prison to the benefit of the organization's members.

The dominant prison gangs in America are Hispanic. They include:
    1. The **Mexican Mafia** (La Eme). Said to be California's first prison gang, it formed in the 1950s among Chicano teenagers in the custody of the California Youth Authority, later expanding to Folsom and San Quentin.
    2. The **Nuestra Familia**. Founded in the 1960s in Soledad prison, its members were Hispanic inmates from Northern California who organized to protect themselves from the Los Angeles-based Mexican Mafia.
    3. The **Texas Syndicate**. Appearing at Folsom and San Quentin in the 1970s, its membership consisted of Texas Mexican Americans who hung together to reduce harassment by the California-based gangs.
    4. The **Mexikanemi** (or Texas Mexican Mafia). Organized in the early 1980s, this is the largest gang in the Texas prison system.

In opposition to these and other Hispanic gangs of the Southwest were several other gangs with ethnic origins. These include:
    1. The **Aryan Brotherhood** (or AB). The leading white supremacist prison gang, organized in San Quentin in the 1960s to oppose the growing dominance of Hispanic and black gangs. It is the most widespread white gang in American prisons today, with branches in several states and the federal system.
    2. The **Black Guerilla Family**. Revolutionary inmate George Jackson is credited with uniting several black groups into this California supergang of the late 1960s. Politically charged and belligerent, it was the prison contemporary of the Black Panthers on the street. It later disintegrated.
    3. The **Bloods** and **Crips**. Offshoots of the Los Angeles street gangs, these groups formed in California prisons in the 1980s and were exported to other states as their members were imprisoned there.

Illinois is reported to have the most gang-dominated prison system in America today; more than half of its inmates, concentrated in high security prisons, are reportedly gang members, mostly with ties to black Chicago-based street gangs. By January 1, 2001, 37 states and the federal prison system reported monitoring and managing prison gangs (as security threat groups) within their prison systems. About 5.1 percent of inmates were identified as having had some type of gang affiliation (through self-admission, criminal history, or tattoos), while about 1.7 percent were classed as prison gang members.

Several popular gang-management strategies have emerged in recent years--segregation, isolation of gang leaders in supermax housing, **bus therapy** (transferring inmates to other prisons), jacketing gang members' files, and compiling gang databases. Although prison officials have been successful in reducing the numbers of assaults and homicides attributed to gangs in recent years, it is not reasonable to expect that they can wholly eradicate gangs from their prisons. The permanent street gang, with lifetime membership, has become a part of the criminal culture of many American cities. When its members are concentrated in the volatile environment of a high security prison, it seems logical to expect that the intense, "blood-in, blood-out" philosophy of the ethnic prison gang would develop. The prison management strategy becomes one of containment, not eradication.

## Death in Prison

Death in prison is increasingly death from old age or death from the diseases of substance abuse. *The 2001 Corrections Yearbook* reports this distribution of inmate deaths in the year 2000:

| Type | Total | Average/State |
|------|------:|------:|
| Natural Causes | 2,509 | 48 |
| Suicide | 201 | 4 |
| AIDS | 195 | 4 |
| Unknown/Other | 118 | 2 |
| Execution | 85 | 2 |
| Homicide | 55 | 1 |
| Accidental | 39 | 1 |
| Escape | 1 | 0 |
| Total Deaths | 3,203 | 62 |

The steady increase in the number of natural causes deaths in prison over the past decade is attributed to two main causes: The general aging of the inmate population and the increasing use of long sentences, including natural life sentences, since the early 1980s. There really are lots of old men and women in prison, and more of them are dying in prison because they are not eligible for release. Deaths from heart disease, cancer, stroke, and other ailments associated with aging have increased accordingly. AIDS deaths in prison have dropped sharply since the mid-1990s peak of over 1,000 per year, while deaths from hepatitis have increased steadily and now are more numerous than those from AIDS.

Three American prisons have established **prison hospices** licensed by the American Hospital Association. One such program, begun at Louisiana's Angola prison in 1998, provides end-of-life care for up to six inmates at a time. The hospice volunteers are a group of about 15 to 20 inmates, mostly lifers who know that they will one day be likely candidates for hospice care themselves. The prison nurse who oversees the hospice says most hospice patients die from cancer or complications related to hepatitis C. In a prison where more inmates die than get paroled each year, hospice provides more attention than dying inmates could expect in the past.

The suicide rate in prisons nationwide has averaged about 14 to 16 deaths per 100,000 for the past decade. The overall suicide rate for men in the United States in 1999 was 19.7 per 100,000, so in general, men in prison have *lower* suicide rates than men in the free world--whether because they are tougher, happier, more closely watched, lethal weapon-deprived, or getting better mental health care we cannot say.

## Perspectives on Prison Life

In trying to understand prison life today, and how it has changed over time, we can look to various sources from inside prison walls and from outside. Many books, written at different times and reflecting varying viewpoints on imprisonment, can illuminate the darkness of our ignorance as we seek to learn more about prison life. But a word of caution: each work, especially if it speaks about prison from inside the walls, has to be put in its time and place. No work speaks for all prisoners in all prisons, particularly not in the highly differentiated prison system of today. Watch a prison movie from the Big House era, and then relate it to what you see when you visit a medium security state or federal prison today. The environments are radically different.

The recent text that provides the best general guide to contemporary prison life is *Behind Bars: Surviving Prison*, by Jeffrey Ian Ross and Stephen C. Richards. Both are PhD criminologists; Ross worked in prison for four years, Richards served 11 years in prison and on parole as a convicted drug dealer. Ross and Richards write, in their introduction, "Prison bears little resemblance to what you've seen in movies or read about in books." Their point is well-made: public perceptions of prison life are shaped by the most popular accounts, which are often the most extreme and sensationalized. The most violent, sociopathic inmate who tells the most depraved stories of his prison experiences in maximum security and supermax may get all the attention, because his stories are the most *interesting*--murders, rapes, escapes, riots, brutality. The prison film that tells the biggest lies and most distorts the truth, particularly if it shows a convict who triumphs over an unjust legal system and lives happily ever after, is the one that gets all the attention and wins the awards. The ordinary prisoner in the predominant low- to medium-security prison of today leads a much less interesting life. The account of his days looks like the diary of a house cat: "ate, slept, peed, and looked out the window." Who would buy his story? So outsiders, seeing the movies and reading the popular books, tend to think that all prisoners live the lives of the two extremes--either the very worst or the very best--when in fact the lives of most prisoners in confinement are characterized by humdrum monotony, boredom, and dead time strung out for years on end.

# SELF TEST

## Multiple Choice

1. The most famous of the political prison riots took place at this prison in New York in 1971:
   a. Sing Sing
   b. Alhambra
   c. Albany
   d. Auburn
   e. Attica

2. The first of the major Hispanic gangs to develop in California prisons was the:
   a. Braceros
   b. Mexican Mafia
   c. Vaqueros del Norte
   d. Latin Kings
   e. Hermanos Pistoleros

3. Four of the following would fit the old inmate code; which one would NOT?
   a. "Do your own time."
   b. "Be friendly to the guards."
   c. "Be a man."
   d. "Don't be a rat."
   e. "Don't exploit other inmates."

4. Gresham Sykes suggested that prison riots and disturbances occur because control of the prison passes from the administration to the inmates; he called this concept:
   a. corruption of authority
   b. latent omnipotence
   c. executive concession
   d. imminent absolutism
   e. dynamics of compromise

5. In prison slang, the inmate who practiced the principles of the inmate code would be known by this term:
   a. merchant
   b. hipster
   c. real man
   d. gorilla
   e. wolf

6. The scholar who defined the three main modes of adaption to prison life as jailing, doing time, and gleaning was:
   a. John Irwin
   b. Gresham Sykes
   c. Harry Allen
   d. Donald Clemmer
   e. Stephen Richards

7. Four of the following are standard words of prison vocabulary; which one is NOT?
   a. quark
   b. screw
   c. fish
   d. bug
   e. shiv

8. In Barbara Owen's research, the social environment in which trouble started was known as the:
   a. posse
   b. mix
   c. jam
   d. games
   e. train

9. John DiIulio's premise takes what is called a _____ perspective on prison life, arguing that correctional managers, not inmates, determine the quality of prison life.
   a. faith-based
   b. nonintervention
   c. imperative
   d. governmental
   e. pacification

10. Erving Goffman described the prison and the asylum as examples of what he called the _____, where individuals are isolated under strict, formal controls.
    a. country club
    b. deviant colony
    c. total institution
    b. secular monastery
    e. protective island

**True or False**

_____ 11. Most of the studies of women's prisons have found that women tend to associate with other women in what are called prison families.

_____ 12. Statistics on assault and homicide suggest that inmates are safer in prison than they would be on the street.

_____ 13. Almost all states allow some inmates, usually trusties, to participate in heterosexual sexual activities through a formal conjugal visiting program.

_____ 14. Although AIDS deaths in prison are declining, deaths resulting from hepatitis are increasing.

_____ 15. Donald Clemmer used prisonization to refer primarily to coercive acts by prison guards intended to break the spirit of prison inmates and force them to adjust to prison routine.

_____ 16. Sexual relations between prison staff and inmates are generally against the rules but not a violation of the law.

_____ 17. The Aryan Brotherhood is one of the most important prison self-help groups that tries to help inmates prepare for life after prison.

_____ 18. The commission that investigated the prison riots of the early 1950s placed the blame on Communist agitators who had infiltrated the prison population.

_____ 19. An inmate who is said to be institutionalized is more at home in prison than in the outside society.

_____ 20. The practice of "bus therapy" would be used primarily to relocate a troublesome inmate from one prison to another; it is really for security rather than therapeutic.

**Fill In the Blanks**

21. Meda Chesney-Lind's term for the concept that female prisons are being modeled directly on male prisons is _____.

22. The term applied to the young convict who has spent most of his life in foster care, group homes, and juvenile institutions before coming to prison is _____.

23. Congress recently passed the Prison _____ Elimination Act to deal with this troublesome aspect of prison life.

24. The _____ prison riot is considered an example of the old code; in this riot, prisoners tortured and killed other prisoners who were snitches or were being held in protective custody.

25. Reformers suggest that two practices, conjugal visiting within prisons and _____ to go home to visit families, would help reduce the incidence of prison homosexuality.

26. The idea that there is a vocabulary of words and slang terms common to prisons and prisoners has given rise to the compilation of what is called a prison _____.

27. The term _____ suggests that the inmate subculture derives from the inmates' efforts to replace those aspects of outside life denied them by the prison.

28. The administration's general term for prison gangs today is _____.

29. In the contemporary prison it might be called a SORT-team and be used to subdue an unruly inmate; in the old prison it was a group of guards called a _____ and used to apply physical punishment.

30. In both men's and women's prisons, the general term for an inmate who identifies with the values of the free world would be _____.

## Discussion

31. How has the prison subculture changed since Donald Clemmer first described it in the 1940s?

32. How does the popular view of sex in prison contrast with reality?

33. If you were an inmate, what would be the advantages of being in a co-correctional facility?

34. Even if both men and women have been involved in criminal activities before they come to prison, how would you expect the experience of imprisonment to be different for women than it is for men?

35. One of your friends argues that prisons today have become "country clubs." How do you respond?

36. What were the important pains of imprisonment identified by Gresham Sykes?

37. What are the different types of special management housing that would be used in a contemporary prison?

38. Thought question: So, if you were an inmate just deposited into a contemporary prison, how would you spend your time?

# CHAPTER ELEVEN

# Special Needs Prisoners

This chapter concentrates on special needs prisoners who have disabilities or limitations that present special problems in confinement; it also considers the prison system's response to these needs. The special needs prisoners to be discussed include:

1. Juvenile prisoners.
2. Mentally ill prisoners.
3. Substance abusing prisoners.
4. Mentally retarded or developmentally challenged prisoners.
5. HIV/AIDS prisoners.
6. Sex criminals.
7. Protective custody prisoners.
8. Older prisoners.

## Key Terms

chancery court
*parens patriae*
ward
juvenile delinquency
superpredator
juvenile gangs
differential association
juvenile
dangerous classes
delinquent juvenile
status offenders
incorrigible juveniles
PINS
neglected
dependent
juvenile court
intake
petition
adjudication
disposition
rehabilitation
*Kent v. United States*
*In re Gault*
due process
Juvenile Justice and Delinquency
  Prevention Act
decarceration
deinstitutionalization
decriminalization
Jerome Miller
custody philosophy
diversion
net-widening
probation
staff-secure facilities
group homes
treatment centers
experiential programs
shelters

boot camp
aftercare
zero-tolerance policies
asylum
insanity
M'Naghten rule
right from wrong
insanity defense
not guilty by reason of insanity (NGRI)
temporary insanity
incompetent to stand trial
guilty but mentally ill (GBMI)
mental illness
Community Mental Health Act
deinstitutionalized
transinstitutionalization
treatment units
psychotropic medication
therapeutic community
triple whammy
Alcoholics Anonymous
Narcotics Anonymous
Center on Addiction and Substance Abuse
separate unit
addiction groups
relapse prevention
mentally retarded
borderline mentally retarded
developmentally challenged
Americans with Disabilities Act (ADA)
*Atkins v. Virgina*
AIDS
HIV
HIV-positive
environment of risk
sex criminal
sex offense
crime against nature
sex offender

locked facilities
detention center
house of refuge
training school
the least restrictive alternative
hidden system
jail and lockup removal
sight and sound separation
waiver
beyond rehabilitation
cottage style
dormitory style
treatment modalities

child abuser
child molester
sexually violent persons (SVP)
stage concept
castration
Depo-Provera
protective custody (PC)
protection cases
commitment lag
baby-boom generation
geriatric inmates
geriatric prison
one-size-fits-all

## Juvenile Criminals

The origins of American juvenile law can be traced to English common law, which in general viewed anyone age 14 or older as an adult subject to punishment in the criminal court. Children under seven could not be held criminally responsible. With seven- to fourteen-year-olds, the issue was whether they understood right from wrong; if they understood their act was wrong, they were punished as adults.

As the common law developed, a special civil court called the **chancery court** was created. One of its functions was to provide for the welfare of minor children, such as those left orphaned or abandoned. The doctrine of *parens patriae*, meaning "the state as parent," gave the king, as the father of the country, authority to manage the affairs of dependent children through the courts. The child was called a **ward** of the state. Thus the concept of state intervention in the lives of children was established long ago, though it was not until the 1800s that modern behavioral scientists defined the concept of **juvenile delinquency**. The modern juvenile court represents a merger of the old authority of the chancery court and more contemporary ideas about causes of behavior.

Today we take the existence of the juvenile court for granted. If you are a juvenile--meaning under the age of adult criminal responsibility, which in the majority of states is 18--you will be dealt with by a separate system that processes only juveniles, under special rules and procedures. The only exceptions would be those persons legally juveniles who are transferred to the adult courts for prosecution, usually either as habitual offenders or as defendants charged with the most serious violent crimes.

Each year about one-third of arrests for the FBI's Index crimes and one-sixth of arrests for the Index violent crimes were of persons under 18. The arrest rate, which is the likelihood that a person of a certain age will be taken into custody, is highest for persons in the 15 to 18 age group and declines substantially over the next few years into the mid-twenties, where it declines even further. Present estimates are that about one in six boys and one in twelve girls will be referred to juvenile court before their eighteenth birthday.

The perception that today's youth are meaner than those of even a few years ago has led to calls to "get tougher" on juvenile criminals. In the 1990s, our political vocabulary expanded to include the term **superpredator**, referring to a violent, inner-city minority youth who is also a gang member, to define our fear of juvenile criminality. As **juvenile gangs** have become more involved in drug trafficking, particularly crack cocaine, their neighborhood turf battles, centered around schools, have become more deadly.

The greater accessibility of firearms to juveniles and the enhanced cultural support for the use of deadly force to resolve disputes make life in the poorest parts of many large cities much like living in a war zone. Edwin Sutherland's influential 1930s social learning theory of criminality, **differential association**, suggested that juveniles learn criminality from their peers and reject the more conventional values of middle-class society.

The juvenile court stepped into the lives of the young urban poor at the very beginning of the twentieth century. **"Juvenile"** comes from the Latin *juvenis*, meaning young, and it applies to children under the age of adult majority. The role of the state, through the juvenile court, was to provide protection or salvation, which developed over time into the contemporary idea of rehabilitation. We think of the juvenile court as handling criminals, but in fact a sizable number of juvenile court cases deal with juveniles not charged with crimes. The historical evidence suggests that the juvenile court was really intended to deal more with petty criminals and non-criminals, especially the children of the **dangerous classes**--poor immigrants and minorities, who were flooding American cities by the end of the 1800s.

The juvenile court would in time divide its clientele into three main types of cases:
      1. A **delinquent juvenile** is a minor who has committed a crime for which an adult could be arrested.
      2. A **status offender** has engaged in acts that are specifically wrong for underage youth but not against the law for adults--running away, curfew violations, truancy and school misconduct, disobeying or threatening parents, sexual promiscuity, and underage drinking. Often referred to in the statutes as **incorrigible juveniles**, status offenders are identified as **PINS**, Persons In Need of Supervision, or CHINS or CINS, Children In Need of Supervision, or MINS, Minors In Need of Supervision.
      3. A category of "deprived, neglected, or dependent children," according to the Uniform Juvenile Court Act. These juveniles' problems lie with their parents' failure to provide for them. They may be termed either **neglected**, meaning their parents are at fault for not taking proper care of them, or **dependent**, meaning that the parents, through no fault of their own (such as sickness or mental illness or extreme poverty) have failed to provide a proper home environment. Children in either category can end up wards of the state, under *parens patriae*.

The original **juvenile court** was deliberately different from the adult criminal court of the time. The first American juvenile court began operating in Chicago (Cook County), Illinois, in 1899. Its principal features were:
      1. Traditional courtrooms were not used; all that was actually required were a table and chairs where the judge, the child and his or her parents, and probation officers could sit together and discuss the case.
      2. Children could be brought before the court on the basis of complaints of citizens, parents, police, school officials, or others.
      3. The children's hearings were not public and their records were kept confidential because children coming before the court were not considered criminal.
      4. Proof of the child's criminality was not required for the child to be found in need of the court's services.
      5. The court had great discretion in determining what kind of services the child required and had wide latitude in determining a disposition.
      6. Lawyers were not required because the hearings were not adversarial.
      7. The standards and procedures long in use in adult courts were missing in the juvenile courts; the standard of proof beyond a reasonable doubt was not required, and hearsay was permitted.

The juvenile court system today continues to use different terminology and operates (at least in theory) under a premise different from the adult criminal court. Juveniles brought into the system are screened through a process called **intake**. The majority of all juveniles taken into police custody are released or handled through other informal alternatives at this point; the more serious or chronic offenders will have a petition filed. The **petition** is the legal document that specifies the basis for juvenile court action. The juvenile who goes to court is entitled to two hearings, though they are often collapsed into one. The first is called **adjudication**, which proves guilt, like an adult trial; the second is **disposition**, which determines the proper sentencing alternative.

Although the juvenile justice system was founded on the hope of **rehabilitation**, over time it became the most neglected part of the criminal justice system. It was the worst-funded and least-supported. The legal process in the juvenile court was highly informal, lacking any relation to due process. Criminals and non-criminals were dealt with as if they had similar problems and needs and were equally deserving of confinement. This mix gave rise to the frequent observation that what were intended to be reform schools became **crime schools** which made their young residents much worse.

In the 1960s and 1970s the courts, the federal government, and many state governments began to address the problems a half-century of neglect had created in the juvenile courts. The first two in a series of important United States Supreme Court decisions, *Kent v. United States*(1966) and *In re Gault*(1967), addressed the legal rights of juveniles. *Kent* was an important background case that it reviewed the history of second-rate juvenile court operations. The *Gault* case was much more important, applying adult standards of due process to what had previously been an informal legal environment. With *Gault*, juveniles got the right to counsel, to notice of charges, to an adversarial proceeding, and to the privilege against self-incrimination that had been lacking previously. Other cases over the next decade further clarified the juvenile's rights to **due process** in court.

In 1974, Congress passed the **Juvenile Justice and Delinquency Prevention Act**. This important piece of legislation had great impact on the states, requiring several important changes of direction in juvenile justice if the states wished to continue receiving federal crime control money:

1. Non-criminal status offenders, and other non-criminals, were not supposed to be mixed with criminal delinquents in secure custodial settings.

2. Juveniles were not supposed to be mixed with adult offenders in jails and prisons.

3. A policy of **decarceration**, often called **deinstitutionalization** in its application to non-criminal juveniles, which involved reducing the number of young people held in secure custody, resulted in larger numbers of young people being dealt with through community-based alternatives rather than in secure settings.

4. **Decriminalization** of deviant behavior resulted in the removal of non-criminals from the juvenile court and particularly from secure institutions such as detention homes and training schools.

Jerome Miller of Massachusetts went ever further, closing his state's juvenile training schools in the early 1970s. His policy was to try to work with almost all delinquents, including violent offenders, in community-based programs. Miller rejected the **custody philosophy**, suggesting that for rehabilitation secure custody did far more harm than good. Other jurisdictions pushed diversion programs designed to take lesser offenders and non-criminals out of the process early on. Seeking to avoid the effects of labeling, **diversion** allows the offender to avoid a conviction by participating in a program providing treatment, community service, or some other alternative disposition. Diversion programs are sometimes accused of **net-widening**, that is, pulling minor offenders into supervision within the system, but these options remain popular with local juvenile justice officials.

About 2.3 million persons under age 18 were arrested in 2001--about 17 percent of all arrests and 15 percent of all violent crime arrests. Juvenile arrests for violent crime dropped sharply after 1994, resulting in a juvenile violent crime Index rate in 2001 that was the lowest since 1983. About 70 percent of arrested juveniles were sent on to juvenile court. The remainder were dealt with through dismissal of charges, diversion, or referral to adult court. Juvenile courts processed about two million petitions--about 1.7 million delinquency cases based on arrests, the other 300,000 involving either status offenders or dependent and neglected children. About one in every four juveniles arrested is eventually formally adjudicated delinquent. The four common dispositional alternatives used in these cases were **probation** (62 percent), out-of-home placement (24 percent), other disposition (10 percent), and release without sanction (4 percent).

If placement is made to what are called **staff-secure facilities**, meaning non-secure or no locked doors or gates to keep juveniles in custody, four basic options are available:

1. **Group homes**. Mostly privately operated, by non-profit, for profit, or religious organizations; often used for status offenders.

2. **Treatment centers**. Many also privately operated, but some public; the focus is on juveniles with substance abuse and mental health problems.

3. **Experiential programs**. Also often privately operated; includes wilderness programs, such as Outward Bound and Vision Quest, and other programs that remove juveniles from their home environment for enriching experiences.

4. **Shelters**. Both private and public, housing short-term populations of neglected and abused children, runaways, and other juveniles, predominately non-criminals.

Two main types of publicly-operated **locked facilities** house about two-thirds of all juveniles in placement:

1. The **detention center**. This facility, sometimes called by such names as the detention home or juvenile hall, is the jail for juveniles. It is typically a smaller, locally operated facility housing juveniles pre-court and those awaiting transfer to other facilities. It is the descendant of the **house of refuge**, historically used to house poor children in the cities.

2. The **training school**. This facility, sometimes called the industrial school, reform school, or training institute, is the juvenile prison. It developed as a state-operated alternative to the penitentiary for younger criminals in the latter part of the 1800s.

The guiding principle of juvenile placement is supposed to be **the least restrictive alternative**, which deemphasizes secure custody. The farther along the scale of placement alternatives you go, from private to public, from staff-secure to locked, the more the population resembles the population of the adult prisons in a given state. This means minority males who are repeat offenders; they are younger versions of the adult prison population. Status offenders, females, whites, middle-class juveniles, and those from two-parent families are more likely to be held in the private and staff secure facilities that Clemens Bartollas and Stuart Miller have referred to as the **hidden system**, an option for the more amenable-to-treatment middle-class juveniles.

111

We should keep in mind that at any given time fewer than 10 percent of juveniles under correctional supervision are in secure custody, compared to about 30 percent of adults under correctional supervision. With its guiding principles of leniency, community-based alternatives, and second chances (principles bruised but still in place as the crime war abates), the juvenile justice system uses secure custody much more narrowly.

Detention centers hold juveniles between arrest and disposition or placement. Most of them are small, holding fewer than 50 boys and girls (in separate housing), though some large city centers may hold 100 to 200 or more in a single facility. The juvenile courts tend to move more rapidly than the adult courts, so the average length of stay in custody is short. An average stay is about two weeks; 86 percent of juvenile in detention stay less than 60 days.

In 1997, an estimated 9,100 youths under age 18 were held not in detention centers but in adult jails. This practice, common at one time, was strongly discouraged by a provision of the Juvenile Justice and Delinquency Prevention Act of 1974 requiring **jail and lockup removal**. Short-term exceptions were allowed if the jail met **sight and sound separation** requirements--basically housing any juveniles in a separate unit where they had no contact with adults. Many of these juveniles were in the process of being passed along to the criminal court for prosecution as an adult. This action, called **waiver**, transfer, or certification, is generally based on a combination of two circumstances, age and serious criminality, such as a fourteen-year-old who commits a rape and murder, or a sixteen-year-old who is an habitual burglar.

Fewer than one percent of juveniles processed to court after arrest have been waived into the adult courts; in 1990 the total was 8,300, in 1999 7,500. They are not necessarily the most violent but rather those whom court officials believe to be **beyond rehabilitation**, meaning that they have been through the system several times and show little sign of changing. Youths convicted as adults go into the adult prison system, not to juvenile training schools. About 7,000 juveniles fit into this category in 1996. The typical offender in this category is a 17-year-old minority male convicted of robbery, aggravated assault, or drug trafficking.

Most youths kept in locked facilities as delinquents go to state training schools. Training schools, described as mini-prisons with schools, average about 100 to 200 residents each, though several of the older institutions are larger and many special-purpose facilities are smaller. Two models prevailed in the past, the **cottage style** with several small residences grouped around a hub of administrative buildings, and a **dormitory style** similar to a military barracks. Juveniles were rarely housed in cells, though this has changed in the new training schools built in the past two decades. The result is that the newer institutions often look more like real prisons.

The routine of training school life is similar to imprisonment. Incoming juveniles are classified and assigned to a housing unit. They go to school in levels--pre-literacy, literacy, pre-GED, and GED or the preferred high school diploma. Most training schools have an abundance of recreational programs--the less they have of other activities, the more they rely on sports to keep their residents busy. Others follow a variety of **treatment modalities**, from one or two sessions of group therapy a week to daily substance abuse counseling to highly structured behavior modification programs. Boys and girls do not stay as long in training schools--the average was about six months in 1997--so days have to be full to get everything in. **Boot camp** programs, which proliferated at the end of the 20th century, are particularly regimented; they cram a lot of discipline, physical fitness, and behavior therapy into a 90- to 180-day program. Most juveniles are serving indeterminate sentences; they are released early, to **aftercare**, the juvenile version of parole.

Many juvenile facilities today have adopted **zero-tolerance policies** on the use of violence by residents and staff. The objective is to create an environment to enhance rehabilitation--education, vocational training, counseling, and treatment. But most juveniles in locked facilities are a stubborn bunch to rehabilitate. Few are first offenders; most have been through the courts and other non-custodial placements several times. They have done poorly in school; many have dropped out or been expelled for disruptive behavior. Their families are disorganized or non-functional. They have no job or social skills. Many of them have personal and family histories marked by violence and physical and sexual abuse, aggravated by their own abuse of drugs and alcohol.

The premise of juvenile justice is that no child should be consigned to a wasted life before he reaches adulthood; the people who work in this system continue to advocate the goal of rehabilitation. Some political officials have proposed abolishing the juvenile court and simply treating all juveniles as adults, including punishing them with adult sentences. That was what we used to do, before the 1800s, and it failed to deter or prevent the emergence of juvenile delinquency as the growth of the city defined a new social order.

The impression is that today's juvenile courts have turned more punitive than previously, though it is a selective punitiveness directed at the more hardcore juvenile criminal--the urban minority youth with the long criminal record and the absence of family or other resources to intervene on his behalf. While small numbers of juveniles are waived to adult courts for trial, most continue to be handled by a juvenile justice system committed to helping and promoting change.

## Mentally Ill Prisoners

The mentally ill or mentally disturbed have been placed in social institutions since the 1500s, when the **asylum** first appeared in Europe. But mentally ill criminals were punished right along with ordinary criminals, until the development of the concept of insanity. **Insanity** is a legal term for a mental condition. The most influential definition of insanity was the **M'Naghten rule**, established in 1844 after delusional Englishman Daniel M'naghten tried to assassinate Prime Minister Robert Peel, killing Peel's male secretary by mistake. The jury found M'Naghten not guilty by reason of insanity, and the appellate judges agreed that M'Naghten could not be held criminally accountable because he did not know right from wrong. He was insane.

Today the states use several different specific definitions of insanity, but all of them center around the person's ability to know **right from wrong** and behave accordingly. The **insanity defense** is used infrequently, generally in only a fraction of one percent of criminal cases, most commonly in crimes of violence led by assault and murder. To have much of a chance of getting a **not guilty by reason of insanity (NGRI)** verdict, the defendant must typically have a fairly well-documented history of mental disorders. The defendant enters a plea of NGRI and then must prove that he did not know right from wrong at the time of the crime. Extreme anger or **temporary insanity** does not work here, though this defense was allowed in a few jurisdictions until recently. The court will almost always hear testimony from mental health expert witness, such as psychologists and psychiatrists--who often offer completely opposing opinions, testifying for the prosecution and the defense, as to the defendant's mental state at the time of the crime. Some defendants do not deny they were sane when they did the crime but argue that they have subsequently gone insane--they are **incompetent to stand trial,** typically because they do not understand the proceedings against them and cannot aid their lawyer in the defense. The trial must be delayed until the defendant regains competency.

A person who is found NGRI at trial is not convicted of a crime; he or she has no criminal record. Such a person is rarely discharged and sent home; he is much more likely to end up in secure confinement within a state or private mental hospital. His discharge from custody becomes a medical decision, subject to the court's approval.

In March 1981, John Earl Hinckley attempted to assassinate President Ronald Reagan, seriously wounding Reagan and three other men in the attack. After Hinckley was found not guilty by reason of insanity at his trial in 1982, the federal courts and several states abolished the insanity defense and created the optional verdict of **guilty but mentally ill (GBMI)**. Offenders get an ordinary sentence but serve it in a prison treatment unit--if space is available--or a regular prison if it is not. They are prisoners first, patients second, and they are not legally insane. They are serving finite sentences (except for the lifers) and will eventually be returned to society in whatever mental state they are in at the time of discharge.

Correctional and mental health authorities estimate that about 15 percent (one in six) prison inmates is mentally ill; the percentage among jail inmates, who are closer to the street, is estimated to be even higher. Recent estimates suggest that prisons hold about three times as many mentally ill persons as do civil mental hospitals, and that the prevalence of severe and chronic forms of **mental illness** (defined as serious impairments in everyday functioning) is from two to four times higher among prisoners than among the free world population, depending on which state (geographically, not of mind) you happen to be in.

The number of mentally ill prisoners has increased dramatically over the past 30 years, as public mental hospitals were downsized after the adoption of the **Community Mental Health Act** of the 1970s. Only the non-functioning and dangerous (to themselves and others) inmates were to remain hospitalized. The others were to be **deinstitutionalized**--returned to the community and treated through clinics on an out-patient basis. Many thousands of mentally dysfunctional former patients have undergone **transinstitutionalization**--leaving the asylum for the jail and prison.

Human Rights Watch has written that doing time in prison is particularly difficult for prisoners with mental illnesses that impair their thinking, emotional responses, and ability to cope. They have unique needs for special programs, facilities, and extensive and varied health services. Compared to other prisoners, moreover, prisoners with mental illness also are more likely to be exploited and victimized by other inmates.

Most states have established special **treatment units** for the more troublesome mentally ill in their prisons; the larger states have entire separate prisons for this purpose. Three basic treatment options apply:
1. Twenty-four-hour care: 1.6 percent of inmates were housed in special units for the most seriously mentally ill, where they were continuously monitored and provided intensive treatment.
2. Therapy/counseling: 12.8 percent of inmates participate in some type of regular therapy or counseling sessions, most often group counseling. Some of these participants may be attending for reasons other than mental illness, such as substance abuse or sex offender treatment.
3. **Psychotropic medication**: 9.7 percent of inmates were taking one or more mood-altering drugs-- antidepressants, stimulants, sedatives, tranquilizers, or other anti-psychotic drugs--to alter their mental state.

Some prisons use the **therapeutic community** model to house and treat the mentally ill, particularly those suffering from the **triple whammy** of serious mental illness, substance abuse, and criminal behavior. The therapeutic community views the prisoners, under staff supervision, as being the primary therapists for one another. In an institutional treatment unit or in a community-based setting, therapeutic communities have been successful in providing intensive treatment to alcoholics and drug addicts where less drastic approaches have failed.

## Substance Abusing Prisoners

The most pervasive aspect of the pre-imprisonment lives of both men and women prisoners is the influence of substance abuse. If you took a group of 100 prisoners and asked them, "How many of your lives have been significantly affected by your use of alcohol or drugs," about 80 would raise their hands. If you took this group of 80 and asked them this followup question, "How many of you would cite alcohol or drugs as being directly involved in the crime that brought you to prison," about 40 to 45 would raise their hands. Alcohol tends to be more important for men, while drugs are more of a problem for women, but for the majority of prisoners, substance abuse is closely linked to criminal behavior.

Despite the prevalence of substance abuse among the prisoner population, most institutions do very little to educate prisoners about substance abuse or to help prevent the use of drugs and alcohol in the future, other than allowing inmates to participate voluntarily in self-help groups such as **Alcoholics Anonymous** or **Narcotics Anonymous**. Although prison officials recognize that most inmates have problems with alcohol or drugs, people are no longer high in prison and prisons are for punishment, not treatment-- prisoners first, patients second. The institution's human and fiscal resources are directed toward secure custody rather than future behavior. The prison is far more interested in what you do *in* prison than what you might do later *out* of prison.

The long-term prospect on dealing more actively with substance abusers in custody as special needs inmates is not encouraging. The **Center on Addiction and Substance Abuse (CASA)** has estimated that about 70 to 85 percent of inmates need some level of substance abuse treatment. But in 1996, only 13 percent of state inmates were undergoing any such treatment. Only 10 percent of federal prisoners and 8 percent of jail inmates were in treatment. The number of prisoners in treatment declined in the 1990s, partly for philosophical reasons but partly for economic reasons as well: money was shifted from treatment to security as the prison population increased steadily during this period.

By the early years of the twenty-first century, there were signs that drug treatment was being emphasized once again, especially through the growth of drug courts at the local level. But most of the treatment emphasis was focused *outside* of prison, on persons not in custody, rather than inside. Participation in prison drug treatment programs at the beginning of 2001 was broken down as follows:
1. **Separate unit**: about 48,000 inmates lived in a prison housing unit with other prisoners getting stepped-up treatment.
2. **Addiction groups**: about 54,000 inmates took part in regular therapy as a member of a group being treated for drug addiction.
3. Counseling only: about 41,000 received individual or group counseling only.

CASA called the absence of drug treatment for the prison population a missed opportunity: "Preventing drug and alcohol abuse and providing effective treatment for drug- and alcohol-abusing inmates hold the promise of significant savings to taxpayers and reductions in crime. CASA estimates that it would cost approximately $6,500 per year, in addition to the usual incarceration costs, to provide an inmate with a year of residential treatment in prison and ancillary services, such as vocational and educational training, psychological counseling, and aftercare case management." Most states have no such program for action, though several have moved to more focused treatment, especially what is called **relapse prevention** to inmates immediately before discharge.

## Mentally Retarded Prisoners

Recent estimates suggest that about four to ten percent of a state's prison population is mentally retarded, which is considerably higher than the one to two percent of the population outside prison. The definition of **mentally retarded** is an IQ of below 70; an IQ in the range of 70 to 85 is said to be **borderline mentally retarded**. The problem with placements in these categories is that test scores may vary by several points from one time to another, and on different scales--verbal versus cognitive--within the same test, so it is hard to make precise judgments based on test scores.

Many experts say you have to look at the person in the social context. Joan Petersilia suggests that mentally retarded persons have a childlike quality of thinking, coupled with slowness in learning new material. Mentally retarded persons have little long-term perspective and little ability to think in a causal way to understand the consequences of their actions. They are not insane. Though some of them may also be mentally ill, they do know right from wrong. They are often referred to as **developmentally challenged**, meaning that they function at a lower mental age, often a pre-adolescent age. They are usually followers, easily manipulated, and often used by others with more intelligence and/or experience.

In the landmark case of *Ruiz v. Estelle* (1976), officials estimated that about 10 to 15 percent of the Texas prison population was retarded. These inmates were observed to be more abnormally prone to prison injuries and more likely to be found guilty of disciplinary infractions. Other research in different systems has found that mentally retarded prisoners suffer from other adjustment problems:
1. More frequent physical abuse and victimization.
2. Economic exploitation and theft of property.
3. Greater involvement in fights, as a response to victimization.
4. Adjustment problems often result in lockdown, higher security classification, and, for victims, protective custody.
5. Lack of participation in and completion of programs.
6. Lower rate of selection for parole and early release options.

The **Americans with Disabilities Act (ADA)**, passed in 1990, prohibits discrimination based on disability, including the intellectual disability implicit in mental retardation. States have been sued on behalf of mentally retarded inmates. Prisons have been required by the courts (or have voluntarily changed their policies) to screen inmates and make certain that prison programs are open to eligible inmates with disabilities.

In *Atkins v. Virginia* (2002), the United States Supreme Court ruled that severely mentally retarded murderers cannot be executed. This judgment would involve an estimated 150 to 200 of the 3,500 defendants on death row.

## HIV/AIDS Prisoners

The first reports of **AIDS**--Acquired Immune Deficiency Syndrome--in American prisons were among drug injecting inmates in New York and New Jersey in 1981 and 1982. By the end of the 1980s, as medical knowledge of **HIV**, the human immunovirus resulting in AIDS, increased, the vast increase in the numbers of intravenous drug users coming into prison made AIDS not just the "gay disease" but also the "prisoners' disease." The number of **HIV-positive** prisoners and the number of prison deaths from AIDS increased steadily until 1995, when about 25,000 known HIV-positive inmates were held in custody (2.3 percent of state and federal prisoners), and over 1,000 state prisoners died of AIDS. By the year 2000, the number of HIV-inmates was holding steady at just over 25,000 (the percentage decreasing to 2.0), while the number of deaths had declined sharply to 174.

HIV infection rates in prison remain about four to six times higher than HIV infection in society. New York has the greatest number--about 6,000--of HIV-positive inmates and also the largest percentage of its prison population--8.5 percent--infected. AIDS is more of a problem where large numbers of poor drug users are in custody; rates are also higher for women (3.6 percent) than men (2.2 percent), and among minorities than whites.

In 48 of the 50 states and the federal system, HIV inmates are generally distributed throughout all prisons in the system. Two states, Alabama and Mississippi, segregate HIV-positive inmates in special housing units comparable to protective custody. Medical privacy laws prohibit authorities from identifying HIV inmates to other inmates and staff. Indeed, the majority of the states do not know who is HIV-positive among their inmates because they do not test them to find out. Twenty states test everyone entering their system, and 11 more test designated "high-risk" groups. The states with the largest HIV populations do not employ mandatory testing.

The result is that as a prison inmate you do not know who among your fellow or sister inmates is HIV-positive unless they tell you directly or unless you are so informed by a third party. If you live or work in prison, you know that somewhere between one and five percent of the inmates around you are HIV-positive, but you don't know for sure who they are. What flows from this is an **environment of risk**. If inmates choose to inject drugs or have sex with other inmates, these at-risk behaviors, besides resulting in the possibility of disciplinary action, can also result in HIV infection. The risk is always there.

AIDS presents two particular problems in prison management. Some prisoners take out their hostilities on possibly or openly HIV-positive inmates who happen to be around them in population. Some are homophobic, or AIDS-phobic; others simply do not want to have contact with "sick" prisoners, even if the inmates still appear healthy enough on the surface.

In addition to the problems relating to the interaction of HIV-positive inmates with other inmates and staff, prisons also have to worry about the special needs of inmates with AIDS. About one in four HIV inmates has confirmed AIDS. The medical care and medication needs of the estimated 6,500 prison inmates with AIDS set them apart from other inmates. Medications alone used in some AIDS regimens may cost $10,000 to $20,000 per year, without factoring in other costs of medical care and security.

## Sex Criminals

Fewer than ten percent of American prison inmates are imprisoned for crimes involving sex acts--about 2.5 percent for forcible rape, 6.0 percent for other sexual assaults, and a lesser number for other non-violent sex crimes. All of these can be labeled as **sex criminals**, though under the laws of most states certain types of sex criminals are singled out for particular attention.

Broadly defined, a **sex offense** can be any criminal act of a sexual nature. On one end of the scale is the violent offense of forcible rape; on the other end are such minor crimes as window peeping, indecent exposure, and prostitution. In between are lesser sexual assaults, child molestation, incest, and offenses in the **crimes against nature** category rarely prosecuted today--sodomy, buggery, and bestiality.

A **sex offender** is by definition anyone convicted of a sex offense. Offenders who sexually victimize children have been targeted for close scrutiny recently. The general trend over the past generation of two has been to deal more severely with **child abusers**, who physically abuse children; incidents that had previously been viewed as private family matters or punished minimally in court are now viewed very differently. **Child molesters** have fared even worse under the law of late. Even though the reported short-term (three-year) rate of new convictions for offenders convicted of sex crimes other than forcible rape is the lowest of any category of offenders, public support for the imprisonment, identification, regulation, and treatment of sex offenders victimizing children is very strong--and likely to remain so.

In the decade after Megan Kanka was murdered by a paroled sex offender in New Jersey, all states adopted some form of "Megan's Law" requiring sex-offender registration; almost all have a community notification requirement as well. A number of states have passed laws giving prisons the authority to keep dangerous sex offenders locked up even after their prison term expires, in effect holding them in extended quarantine as if they were mentally ill.

These **sexually violent persons (SVP)** laws tend to focus upon criminals who have served prison terms after victimizing multiple victims--adults or children. At the end of their prison term, those criminals deemed at high risk to reoffend, through a formal review process, are civilly committed to a state-run treatment program--in a locked facility--until the treatment staff recommend their release. The committing judge, as in mental health commitments, has the final release authority.

All current SVP programs use the **stage concept** of treatment. The Kansas Sexual Predator Treatment Program uses five stages or levels--entry phase; the core phase teaching critical concepts that allow residents to identify their thought and behavior patterns before, during, and after their crimes; the advanced phase, teaching the resident to apply in his daily life the concepts learned in the core phase; the honor phase, in which the resident works on a relapse prevention plan; and the awaiting transition phase, in which the residents undergo transition to a structured environment, such as a halfway house.

States have also intensified research into in-prison and out-of-prison treatment programs for sex offenders trying to find more effective control models. Most follow traditional therapy models, using a progression through levels over time. A few courts have allowed offenders to volunteer for **castration**, which involves surgical removal of the testicles. A handful of states require--and several others allow--chemical castration through the use of the drug **Depo-Provera,** a birth-control hormone that kills or sharply reduces a male offender's sex drive.

## Protective Custody Prisoners

**Protective custody (PC)** is both a status and a housing, a label and a place. To a prisoner, PC means that he has been identified as a likely victim and cannot remain in general population; he will thus be removed from population and placed in a housing unit--a dormitory or cellblock--populated by other inmates like himself.

Who are the people most likely to end up in PC? Convict journalists Ron Wikberg and Wilbert Rideau said PC units house "what most prisoners perceive and refer to as snitches, queers, punks, rats, faggots, and gal-boys." But this perception of PC inmates as either sexual deviants or violators of the convict code was affected by other growing concerns, Wikberg and Rideau observed, including "overcrowding, violence developing from debts, drugs, a growing number of sex offenders, prison informants, a more youthful and violent offender coming into the prison system, and the growth of gangs."

The steady increase in the number of inmates placed in protective custody during the 1970s and 1980s can be attributed to one basic rationale: PC was safer than general population. Inmates who had been victimized, sexually or physically, or who lived in fear of victimization, or whom prison authorities identified as likely victims, requested PC (or were assigned directly with no choice) to avoid the violence and exploitation expected to result if they remained in population. PC was sanctuary, and many inmates sought it.

By the 1990s, the prison's management of PC inmates had undergone important changes. Classification was used more effectively to separate **protection cases** as they entered the system. The American Correctional Association has established the following model policy on protective custody: "It is the policy of the Department of Corrections to provide specialized housing for inmates who require protection from other inmates in order to ensure their personal safety when no other reasonable alternative is available. This is typically done by affording them protective custody status in the facility's administrative segregation unit."

While ACA guidelines stress that PC is not a punitive measure, prisoners know that life in PC is not a piece of cake. Although ACA policies specify that protective custody conditions--including visitation, correspondence, food service, recreation, and programs--should approximate those provided to the general population, it is often impossible to maintain comparability in a small locked unit. Journalists Wikberg and Rideau pointed out: "The conditions of life within the PC units make up the largest consistent complaint expressed by those assigned to it. Because of the more restricted and isolated environment, prisoners with PC at the Louisiana State Penitentiary have little or no social activities, organized sports or recreation, and they are prohibited from any academic or vocational training despite a great number of them being relegated to protection status for many years."

How many inmates are in protective custody today? Most prison authorities say far fewer than in the old days, though the numbers are hard to pin down. *The 2001 Corrections Yearbook* estimates that only about 1.2 percent of inmates in the states responding to their survey were held in PC. But about three times that number were held in ad seg; many of these were on their way to PC and would be sent along when space was available.

PC is not always a safe haven. Inmates in PC sometimes abuse or exploit others in their units. And there is the problem of leaving PC to reenter general population. Inmates assume that something is wrong with another inmate who has been in PC, and they often want to find out what it is. The stigma stays with you after you leave the unit.

## Older Prisoners

When we think of the crime problem in America, we think of young men. Crime remains a young man's game, for the most part. Arrest rates for both violent and property crimes peak out in the late teen years and decline sharply after the early twenties. Punishment rates, or more specifically imprisonment rates, lag behind arrest rates, primarily because we are more lenient on younger offenders, often giving them one or sometimes several chances to stop committing crimes (the official term is desistance) before we resort to imprisonment. Harry Allen and Clifford Simonsen have called this phenomenon the **commitment lag**--the gap of several years before active young criminals pick up their first prison term.

In the 1970s, the average age of state prisoners was reported as 26 or 27. It has increased steadily since then, reaching 34.7 by 2001. This is an average increase of seven to eight years, within a relatively short period of time. Researchers have cited four major reasons for the aging of America's prison population:
   1. The aging of the general population from which prisoners come. The **baby-boom generation** (referring to children born from 1946 through 1960), which is widely cited for its impact on crime rates in the 1960s and imprisonment rates in the 1970s, is now middle-aged.
   2. The accumulation of men and women who have aged in prison while serving exceptionally long sentences.
   3. The focus on career criminals with previous incarceration histories through the application of "three strikes and you're out" laws and other statutes aimed at repeat offenders.
   4. As the legal system concentrates on homicide, drug distribution, and sex offenses, more middle-aged and elderly criminals are entering prison as first-time felons but with sentences long enough to keep them in prison until they are dead or nearly so.

The prison population is aging, and the number of inmates over age 55 has grown dramatically, increasing tenfold from 1979 to 2001. In most states, it is the fastest growing segment of the inmate population. The *Corrections Yearbook 2001* indicates that by 2001 7.9 percent of the prison population was age 50 or older. In five states and the federal system, the percentage is already above 10 percent.

Cost is a major concern associated with aging populations. Various studies indicate that elderly inmates cost two to three times as much to house as younger inmates, primarily because of more costly medical care and medication. A California study found that the cost of younger inmates was about $21,000 annually, while it was $60,000 for inmates over the age of 60. The primary reason for the high cost of older inmates is medical care. Those over age 65 are likely to spend twice as much time in medical facilities and have three times the health care costs of younger inmates.

At least 16 states have designated a "special needs" facility for infirm or disabled **geriatric inmates**. Louisiana's **geriatric prison**, Forcht-Wade, opened in 1998 as a branch of a larger prison in north Louisiana. It operates as a nursing home for the elderly and disabled, holding about 400 minimum custody inmates who require extra care in reduced custody status.

As more prisons move into the nursing home business, coping with older inmates will be a huge problem for cash-strapped state governments in the years ahead. Ronald Aday wrote in *Aging Prisoners* (2003), "In addition to health care issues, work assignments, [Medicare] co-payments, nutritional requirements, concerns for victimization, end of life issues, and appropriate staffing are concerns that will have to be addressed. The task is a daunting one."

## A Word on Special Needs Prisoners

The management of special needs prisoners in population creates complications both for them and for prison managers. Many special needs prisoners cannot hold their own with other inmates in the repressive, closed-in environment of prisons; they are more likely to be victimized and exploited, to "cause trouble" that is often not of their own making. The **one-size-fits-all** approach to imprisonment--downplaying individuality and emphasizing uniformity--that prevails today fails to take into account the differences among prisoners with special needs; many of these inmates do their time without ever having their special problems addressed in meaningful treatment programs that would help them avoid future criminal behavior after they get out of prison.

We should also consider that special needs are not distributed one per inmate. A juvenile criminal may also be both mentally retarded and mentally ill; a sex criminal may be isolated as a protection case not because he is a pervert but because he is HIV positive. In the prison environment, these special needs--making their bearers targets for victimization--can be even more defining than they are on the street.

# SELF TEST

## Multiple Choice

1. If your mother was a crack-head prostitute who ran the street and left you, at ten years old, alone in your apartment for days at a time, you might be brought into juvenile court as a:
    a. delinquent
    b. neglected child
    c. incorrigible juvenile
    d. status offender
    e. emancipated child

2. The Latin phrase meaning "the state as parent," used as the basis of the authority of the juvenile court, is:
    a. *vox populi*
    b. *sub judice*
    c. *parens patriae*
    d. *non compos mentis*
    e. *particeps criminis*

3. Four of the following are juvenile status offenses; which one is NOT?
    a. running away
    b. curfew violation
    c. possession of a concealed weapon
    d. truancy
    e. ungovernability

4. A policy of decarceration, if followed seriously over a period of years, would result in the population of juveniles in confinement:
    a. going down
    b. remaining stable
    c. being made up more of habitual offenders
    d. containing more violent and property offenders but fewer drug offenders
    e. increasing rapidly

5. What institution is described as a long-time dumping ground for the mentally disordered?
    a. the hospice
    b. the prison hospital
    c. the asylum
    d. the jail
    e. the community mental health clinic

6. Yesterday's ambulatory, non-criminal mental patient is today's:
    a. hopeless lunatic
    b. political official
    c. homeless person
    d. drug addict
    e. cult member

7. The greatest number of sex offenders in treatment programs are:
    a. young men
    b. mentally retarded
    c. homosexual women
    d. people who have sexually abused animals
    e. juveniles confined in training schools

8. The new insanity verdict of the 1980s, which several states used to replace the "not guilty by reason of insanity" verdict, was:
    a. "diminished capacity"
    b. "totally deranged"
    c. "crazy but culpable"
    d. "exceptional personality"
    e. "guilty but mentally ill"

9. The rate of HIV infection in prison, in comparison to the outside world, is most related to:
   a. needle sharing
   b. prostitution
   c. child abuse
   d. homosexuality
   e. poor nutrition

10. If you were discussing "transinstitutionalization," you would be suggesting that the mentally impaired had been removed from mental hospitals and put into:
   a. private homes
   b. work camps
   c. suspended animation
   d. shock therapy
   e. jails and prisons

## True or False

_____ 11. One of the principles of the common law was that persons under 18 could not be punished in the criminal court for violating the law.

_____ 12. The law provides that any juvenile who commits a felony can be locked up in an adult jail and mixed with adult offenders.

_____ 13. In the juvenile court, a "juvenile delinquent" is any child whose behavior fails to conform to the expectations of the police or other social institutions.

_____ 14. The basic purpose of the Community Mental Health Act was to remove more homeless people from the street by confining them in jails for treatment.

_____ 15. Most inmates who come to prison HIV positive are male homosexuals.

_____ 16. The number of elderly inmates in prison, as a percentage of the total population, is in decline as prisons try to make room for younger, more violent offenders.

_____ 17. A person with an IQ of 69 or below is generally acknowledged to be retarded.

_____ 18. Female inmates are much less likely to be HIV positive than male inmates are.

_____ 19. The case of *Ruiz v. Estelle*, which dealt with the issue of medical care provided to Texas prison inmates, found that less than one percent of these inmates were mentally retarded.

_____ 20. Diversion is a legal maneuver used to sentence a juvenile to secure custody without going to court first.

## Fill In the Blanks

21. The English common law court that was given jurisdiction over "unattached" children was the _____.

22. The shelter for juveniles found in American cities in the 1800s was the _____.

23. The 1974 federal legislation said to have changed the direction of the juvenile justice system was the _____ Act.

24. A defendant found not guilty by reason of insanity would ordinarily be found in a(n) _____ within a few weeks after the trial.

25. About 16 states have designated a facility known as a(n) _____ prison for incapacitated older inmates..

26. The purpose, at least in theory, of the modern juvenile court is said to be _____.

27. The M'Naghten rule is most related to those criminal defendants who are _____.

28. The drug Depo-Provera would be used in treating _____ offenders.

29. Offenders suffering from the triple whammy are marked by criminal behavior, mental illness, and _____.

30. The sex offenders targeted by recent civil commitment statutes that subject them to involuntary "treatment" at the end of their criminal sentences are commonly designated as _____.

**Discussion**

31. Briefly explain the origin and meaning of the concept of *parens patriae*.

32. How are juvenile training schools different from adult prisons?

33. Explain what happened to cause more mentally ill persons to wind up in correctional facilities.

34. What problems is the developmentally challenged offender likely to experience in prison?

35. What are the different types of sex offenders you would find in greatest numbers in prison treatment programs?

36. What problems do HIV positive inmates present in prison?

37. Why has the number of older prisoners increased so dramatically in recent years?

38. As an inmate who has just been moved into protective custody housing, how is your life going to be different from inmates in general population?

39. What impact do special needs offenders have on the operation of the prison?

# CHAPTER TWELVE

# Prisoners' Rights

The convicted felon in confinement exists in a legal world much different from that of free people outside prison. Prisoners give up many rights upon conviction, and the rights they retain are constrained by the nature of confinement. The loss of citizenship rights also applies to felons who do not go to prison, and to ex-offenders after their release from prison. After reading this chapter, you should be familiar with:

1. The historical legal status of the convicted felon.
2. Recent developments in prison litigation.
3. Leading cases in prisoners' rights--access to courts, discipline, medical care, and personal rights.
4. Effects of litigation on jail and prison administration.
5. Alternatives to litigation.
6. Post-release consequences of a criminal conviction.
7. Civil rights commonly denied felons.
8. Registration and civil commitment of ex-offenders.
9. Methods of erasing criminal records and restoring offenders' rights.

## Key Terms

civil death
outlaw
non-person
*Ruffin v. Commonwealth*
penal servitude
slave of the state
hands-off doctrine
appeals
torts
criminal charges
writ of mandamus
administrative appeals
*habeas corpus* petitions
civil rights lawsuits
Eighth Amendment
cruel and unusual punishments
Bill of Rights
incorporation
Fourteenth Amendment
due process
equal protection
Warren Court
due process revolution
class-action lawsuits
totality of conditions
*Holt v. Sarver*
Section 1983 lawsuit
under color of state law
court order
injunction
court master
monitor
contempt power
activist
consent decree
access to courts
jailhouse lawyer

*Cooper v. Pate*
Religious Freedom Restoration Act of 1993
legitimate penological interests
gender equity
differential treatment
disparate treatment
parity of treatment
parity model
vengeful equity
equal treatment
special needs
grievance procedures
ombudsman
exclusionary rule
*Morrissey v. Brewer*
frivolous lawsuits
Anti-Terrorism and Effective Death Penalty Act
  (AEDPA)
Prison Litigation Reform Act (PLRA)
rights era
deference era
*Bell v. Wolfish*
judicial deference
*Gregg v. Georgia*
*Rhodes v. Chapman*
*Turner v. Safley*
*Wilson v. Seiter*
*Lewis v. Casey*
reasonable relationship
recreational litigation
ex-offender
ex-con
collateral consequences
invisible punishments
civil disabilities
annulment
registration of criminals

law library
*Wolff v. McDonnell*
liberty interest
DB Court
*Estelle v. Gamble*
deliberate indifference
right to refuse treatment
informed consent
medicate to execute
personal rights
First Amendment
Black Muslim

yellow card
Megan's Law
community notification laws
national sex offender database
civil commitment
sexually violent predator (SVP)
*Kansas v. Hendricks*
medicalization of deviance
executive clemency
pardon
expungement
erasure of record

## The Convicted Felon in History

For hundreds of years under common law, a felon had no commonly accepted legal status. The concept of **civil death** meant that the felon lost his legal standing as a citizen; he no longer had the civil rights of other persons. He became an **outlaw** or what would later be termed a **non-person** in the eyes of the law and society.

This legal status, or lack of legal status, continued into the days of the penitentiary. A well-known 1871 Virginia appellate court decision, ***Ruffin v. Commonwealth***, declared that the convicted felon had forfeited his rights-- "for the time being the slave of the State." In describing the condition of **penal servitude** and defining the prisoner as the **slave of the state**, this case seems authoritative in restating the "convict-as-social-outcast" principle that had endured for centuries.

Not everyone agrees with this historical view. Donald Wallace, for one, has found several cases in the 1800s and early 1900s in which courts took the position that felons had some legal standing. If you accept Wallace's view, which runs contrary to much of the general commentary on the prisoner's legal status during this era, the convicted felon, if not exactly a dead man, was surely on a legal frontier--a remote place where the rules that applied to everyone else did not generally apply to him.

In practice convicts were lost in the penitentiary's dark womb. If anything happened to them, if they fell sick and died from neglect, if they were harmed by another inmate, or if they were killed by a guard, no explanation was necessary. The state was not liable for any misadventure that befell a felon in prison, nor was it required to meet standards of decent care. Bad management or deliberate abuse of prisoners had no legal consequences.

By the 1940s and 1950s, the widespread legal philosophy was that the courts left prison operations alone. Court officials acknowledged that they lacked the expertise to tell prison officials how to run their institutions. This concept, called the **hands-off doctrine**, allowed prison wardens to run their institutions with legal impunity. Prison officials were not accountable in either state or federal courts for their actions or for conditions within their institutions. Not until the 1960s, when social and legal changes shook up the existing order of American society, would the hands-off doctrine be abandoned and prisoners begin to find courts more concerned about their rights as citizens in confinement.

## Legal Actions Open to Prisoners

Christopher Smith has provided an overview of legal actions that prisoners may file in state and federal courts:
   1. **Appeals**. Anyone convicted at trial (a small percentage of all convictions, in comparison to guilty pleas in which appeals are less readily available) has the right to appeal the conviction into higher state and federal courts. The great majority of appeals result in decisions against the convicted criminal.
   2. **Torts**. Based on negligence or intentional actions, a tort suit is simply a lawsuit for damages filed in the state or federal court that would have jurisdiction over the place of confinement.
   3. **Criminal charges**. Inmates or prison staff who commit crimes against prisoners could have criminal charges filed against them, if the prisoner can convince a local district attorney or U.S. district attorney with jurisdiction over the prison to accept charges.
   4. **Writ of mandamus**. Mandamus is a another old common law legal action. A person asks a court to order a public official to perform his or her lawful duty.

123

5. **Administrative appeals**. Applying mostly to internal actions within the prison such as disciplinary hearings, classification, and transfers, these appeals would be carried forth into a court when they could not be resolved within the internal workings of the prison or corrections bureaucracy.

6. Other legal actions. This category would include a broad range of other civil and administrative actions that a prisoner might be involved in because of events *outside* of prison, including such legal matters as divorce, child custody, real estate transactions, Social Security, and veterans benefits.

State and local prisoners, who make up over 90 percent of all prisoners in custody, have two common means available to litigate their confinement in the federal courts--*habeas corpus* **petitions** and **civil rights lawsuits**. *Habeas corpus*--Latin for "you have the body"--is an old English legal remedy. As it was used in English and American courts for a long time, it allowed a court to review the legality of a prisoner's confinement. After the appeal was over, prisoners could file *habeas corpus* petitions in a state court or a federal court asking the judge to review constitutional issues related to the legal process and conduct of the trial. A state prisoner who files a *habeas corpus* petition is likely to be asking the federal courts to review his conviction; but he could be asking for a review of the conditions under which he is serving his prison term.

Over the past 40 years, the more common form of litigation attacking prison conditions or treatment has arisen in the federal courts under the Federal Civil Rights Act (Section 1983 of Title 42 of the U.S. Code). Prisoners found this law comparatively simple to use, and it covered a multitude of prison conditions and procedures. They also tended to favor the federal courts, whose judges were not part of the state political system that the prisoners blamed for their legal problems.

## The Eighth Amendment: Cruel and Unusual Punishment

The **Eighth Amendment** to the Bill of Rights of the U.S. Constitution contains these provisions: "Excessive bail shall not be required, nor excessive fines imposed, nor cruel and unusual punishments imposed." For almost two centuries, the "**cruel and unusual punishments**" clause had no application to prisoners. The **Bill of Rights**, adopted to limit the power of the federal government and its officials, had no application to state prisoners--only federal prisoners--as originally applied. In including it in the Bill of Rights, the draftsmen of the American Constitution were more concerned with torture--common practice at the time--and other physically excessive means of punishment.

In this era the death penalty was an accepted punishment. When the Court was asked to rule on New York's new electric chair in *In re Kemmler* (1890), it held the Eighth Amendment inapplicable to the states and added the following comment: "Punishments are cruel when they involve torture or a lingering death; but the punishment of death is not cruel within the meaning of that word as used in the Constitution. It implies there something inhuman and barbarous, something more than the mere extinguishment of life."

In the 1960s, the Supreme Court, through the more frequent application of a legal doctrine known as **incorporation**, began to apply the provisions of the Bill of Rights to the states, including local jurisdictions within the states. The mechanism for incorporation was the **Fourteenth Amendment** to the Constitution, adopted in 1868 after the Civil War. Section One provides in part: "No State shall make or enforce any law which shall abridge the privileges or immunities of citizens of the United States; nor shall any State deprive any person of life, liberty, or property, without due process of law; nor deny to any person within its jurisdiction the equal protection of the law."

The **due process** and **equal protection** provisions of the Fourteenth Amendment made citizens subject to state laws--such as criminal defendants and convicted criminals--also subject to federal constitutional standards. The Bill of Rights applied as much to state cases as it did to federal cases. In landmark cases such as *Mapp v. Ohio* (1961), *Gideon v. Wainwright* (1963), *Miranda v. Arizona* (1966), *In re Gault* (1967), *Brady v. Maryland* (1968), and dozens of other cases in this decade and the early part of the next, the Court moved to set consistent national standards where only widely varying state standards had existed previously.

Most of the early decisions dealt with criminal suspects pre-trial and at trial, not in confinement after conviction. But as the **Warren Court** undertook what is called the **due process revolution** at the national level, federal district judges began to accept lawsuits filed by state prisoners alleging unconstitutional prison conditions in state prisons and local jails. The most influential of these cases were **class-action lawsuits** filed by a small group of inmates but on behalf of a larger group--such as all inmates in a treatment unit, or all inmates in a jail or prison, or all inmates in all the jails of a particular county or the prisons of a particular state.

During the 1970s, virtually every state prison system and most urban jails would be sued in inmate lawsuits arguing that confinement in these institutions constituted cruel and unusual punishment under Eighth Amendment standards. The South was hardest hit. In state after state across the South, federal district judges heard Eighth Amendment and Fourteenth Amendment suits charging that prisons were overcrowded, dilapidated, violent, and failing to provide needed care, particularly in regard to medical care and mental health services.

The suits often became **totality of conditions** actions in which several different lawsuits with different complaints would be rolled into one mega-case examining the whole prison or in several states the entire prison system. Then the federal judge would issue a court order for prison reform in the name of the lead case. In Arkansas it was *Holt v. Sarver* (1970); in Alabama it was *Newman v. Alabama* (1972); in Mississippi it was *Gates v. Collier* (1972); in Louisiana it was *Williams v. McKeithen* (1975); in Texas it was *Ruiz v. Estelle* (1980).

*Holt v. Sarver* was the first state-level totality of conditions Eighth Amendment case. The federal court found in *Holt* that the Arkansas prison system was in violation of the cruel and unusual punishments clause in several key aspects:
1. The prison was largely run by inmate trusty guards who breeded hatred and mistrust.
2. The open barracks within the prison invited widespread physical and sexual assaults.
3. The isolation cells were overcrowded, filthy, and unsanitary.
4. There was a total absence of any program of rehabilitation and training.
Similar conditions were found in other Southern prisons and in many jails around the country in this era, typically leading to federal court orders to eliminate those conditions found to be violative of basic constitutional requirements.

## Section 1983: Civil Rights Litigation

Although the Eighth Amendment and Fourteenth Amendment litigation had the more profound impact in accomplishing broad institutional reform during the 1970s and 1980s, the most common form of prisoners' rights litigation during this era, and continuing today, is through what is commonly called a **Section 1983 lawsuit**. Title 42 of the U.S. Code, Section 1983, provides: "Every person who, under color of any statute, ordinance, regulation, custom or usage, of any State or Territory, subjects of causes to be subjected, any citizen of the United States of other person within the jurisdiction thereof to the deprivation of any rights, privileges or immunities security by the Constitution and laws, shall be liable to the party injured in an action at law, suit at equity, or other proper proceeding for redress."

This statute was enacted in 1871 but only began to be applied to local or state criminal justice officials in 1961. Section 1983 actions proliferated by the early 1970s. From about 200 filings in 1966, the number jumped up to 5,000 in 1972, and the numbers increased steadily for the next 25 years, roughly paralleling the increase in state prisoner population, to more than 40,000 in 1996. The premise of these actions is that a state or local government official acting **under color of state law** has deprived a prisoner of a constitutional right. The two most common circumstances cited in these lawsuits are physical security--when a prisoner is attacked by other prisoners or by corrections officers--and medical treatment.

Hanson and Daly, in their review of the approximately 25,000 Section 1983 lawsuits filed in 1992, found that about 94 percent were dismissed by the court. About six percent of the total filings, or 1,500 cases, survived the initial review. Four percent were dismissed with the prisoner's agreement, sometimes because of a settlement. Of the two percent went to trial, prisoners won fewer than half. So out of 25,000 lawsuits filed, prisoners won outright less than one percent, and settled to their advantage another small percentage, the victories totaling fewer than 1,000 out of 25,000 filed. Most prisoners got nothing for their lawsuits, except the satisfaction of taking up court time and messing with prison officials.

## Federal Court Intervention

By the 1970s, hands off had been transformed into a very definite hands on. Hundreds of jails and prisons ended up operating under a federal court supervision. This ordinarily involved the imposition of a **court order** giving the court controlling authority over some aspect of the institution's operations and requiring that certain steps be taken to eliminate unconstitutional conditions. Sometimes the court granted an **injunction**, a legal order to stop an action or practice that was ruled improper. If the intervention was broad-based and would go on for an extended period, the court would appoint an official usually termed a **court master** or **monitor** to oversee the institution's response to the order. The master, someone outside the system but experienced in corrections, did the leg work for the judge.

The court's authority ultimately resided in its **contempt power**, its ability to impose a jail term or a monetary fine upon officials who violated its order. Because the orders came from a federal district court, where some judges might be considered too "liberal" or **activist**, meaning that they were siding with the prisoners against the administration, it was common for prison officials to appeal unfavorable rulings to the federal appeals courts and eventually to the U.S. Supreme Court. These legal battles were often protracted struggles that went on for decades. The goal of the court order was to achieve a formal agreement, called a **consent degree**, in which both sides agreed (through their attorneys) on the actions to be taken to resolve the litigation. When the court determined that the institution had met the requirements of the court, as written down in the consent decree, the court order was terminated. The institution could operate on its own again, without federal court supervision.

## Prisoners' Rights: Access to Courts

In the "good old days" of the penitentiary, prison officials had complete control over the prisoner's contact with the outside world. If the warden did not want a letter or legal document complaining of prison conditions to get out, he simply destroyed it and locked the prisoner in "the hole" for daring to criticize the prison. All of the prisoner's other rights thus depend on this first right of **access to courts**--to bring a complaint to the attention of authorities who will require prison officials to follow the law. In *Ex parte Hull* (1941), the Supreme Court struck down a Michigan prison regulation that gave prison officials the right to review all prisoner legal filings *before* they were sent to court--and destroy any found objectionable. The Court ruled that a prisoner's right to petition a federal court for a writ of *habeas corpus* could not be abridged or impaired.

Prisoners would argue later that the right of access was meaningless if they did not have legal assistance and access to legal resources in preparing writs and briefs and submitting materials to the courts. The Supreme Court, in *Johnson v. Avery* (1969), was asked to consider the case of a Tennessee prison inmate who was transferred for acting as a **jailhouse lawyer**, assisting other inmates with legal matters. Since prisoners were not entitled to professional attorneys, the district court ruled, "for all practical purposes, if such prisoners cannot have the assistance of a `jail-house lawyer,' their possibly valid constitutional claims will never be heard in any court." The Supreme Court ruled that the state could not enforce a regulation barring inmates from furnishing assistance to other prisoners.

A few years later, the issue of research materials was addressed in the North Carolina case of *Bounds v. Smith* (1977), often called the **law library** case because it required prison authorities to assist inmates in the preparation and filing of meaningful legal papers by providing prisoners with adequate law libraries or adequate legal assistance from persons trained in the law. A later ruling in this same case, *Smith v. Bounds* (1987), defined an "adequate" prison library as consisting of inmates trained as paralegals, photocopying materials without charge, and access to the library for all inmates.

The requirement of access to legal materials by all inmates has often been a problem for prisoners held in special housing units, such as segregation or mental health. It has also been an issue for inmates whose first language is not English. In a later case reviewing the intervention of an Arizona district court into these issues--*Lewis v. Casey* (1996)--the conservative Supreme Court of the 1990s overturned the detailed requirements the lower court had established for prison library operations to serve specific targeted populations. It said that without a showing that these inmates were actually being harmed by inadequate legal resources, the court should defer to the judgment of prison authorities.

## Prisoners' Rights: Discipline and Due Process

As prison officials once had complete control over prisoners' contacts with the courts, so they once had complete authority in internal disciplinary and punishment matters. The key Supreme Court case to address procedures in imposing punishments for violating prison rules was *Wolff v. McDonnell* (1974), which replaced informal, spontaneous punishments with more structured proceedings. It was only six years before *Wolff*, in *Jackson v. Bishop* (1968), that the U.S. Eighth Circuit Court of Appeals had finally struck down corporal punishment of prisoners in Arkansas, a common practice in numerous other states into at least the 1950s.

In *Wolff v. McDonnell*, Nebraska prison inmates sued over the informality of prison misconduct proceedings that could result in the loss of good-time credits. The Supreme Court ruled that prisoners were protected by the Fourteenth Amendment's due process clause; the Court provided that the prison must extend basic elements of due process to prisoners in disciplinary proceedings (specifically if they involve a possible **liberty interest**, such as loss of good time or punitive segregation). The required safeguards include advance written notice of the charges; a written statement by the factfinders as to the evidence relied on and reasons for the disciplinary action; opportunity for the inmate to call witnesses and present documentary evidence in his or her defense; counsel substitute (either a fellow inmate or staff member) to assist the inmate with the hearing; and an impartial prison disciplinary board.

*Wolff* had great impact on prison and jail operations. The increased formality of disciplinary proceedings works to reduce arbitrariness and personal abuses--and likely reduces as well the number of such violations that might be written up and forwarded to the disciplinary board. The DB Court--for disciplinary board--meeting on a regular schedule, has become a standard part of the internal disciplinary system of all secure custodial and community residential facilities since *Wolff*.

## Prisoners' Rights: Medical Care

Access to medical care and the quality of care provided are important issues to prisoners, who suffer from a broad range of health problems related primarily to poverty and substance abuse. Although prison health care before the reform era was inconsistent and often "shockingly substandard," according to law professor Sheldon Krantz, not until the Texas case of *Estelle v. Gamble* (1976) did the Supreme Court address medical care by itself as an Eighth Amendment issue. The court reviewed the history of Gamble's medical treatment and determined that his case did not rise to the level of **deliberate indifference** to the serious medical needs of inmates--"the unnecessary and wanton infliction of pain." Gamble lost, but the Court established the deliberate indifference rule that became the foundation of later Section 1983 litigation of all types, not just medical care. Deliberate indifference, which is comparable to gross negligence or recklessness, focuses on the motives or thoughts of prison officials responsible for the injury, which in medical cases results from the bad care provided.

*Estelle v. Gamble* is said to have established a general right to "adequate" medical care in prisons, meaning that the medical needs of prisoners cannot be completely ignored or botched. Prisoners do have a right to treatment, even if it is not constitutionally protected at the same level as the right of private citizens. But what of the opposite right, the **right to refuse treatment**? Treatment of prisoners against their will often ventures into the subject area of mental incompetence. If a patient--free or in prison--is mentally competent, he or she has the right to refuse treatment. This is a right to privacy decision called the **informed consent** doctrine. People have the right to decide what will and will not be done to their bodies. That includes the right to decide whether to take medication or permit surgery.

This issue has come up again recently in connection with inmates on death row. The 1986 decision in *Ford v. Wainwright* had ruled that to be executed inmates must be mentally competent--at least to understand their crime and the punishment. Can inmates be medicated against their will to remain functional enough to be processed along toward their execution date? Does the state have the authority to **medicate to execute**? Some states do not allow this, but this far no Supreme Court ruling prohibits the practice.

## Prisoners' Rights: Personal Rights

The **personal rights** of prisoners are commonly placed under the **First Amendment** of the Bill of Rights, which reads: "Congress shall make no law respecting an establishment of religion, or prohibiting the free exercise thereof; or abridging the freedom of speech, or of the press; or the right of the people peaceably to assemble, and to petition the Government for redress of grievances."

Religion is very important to many prisoners, the center of their prison life. Some of the most important early prisoners' rights cases in the 1960s dealt with the right of inmates to practice an established religion, in these cases the **Black Muslim** faith in Illinois and California prisons. One of the leading cases--the first Section 1983 case decided in a prisoner's favor--was *Cooper v. Pate* (1964), a lawsuit filed by Thomas X. Cooper, a former Catholic turned Black Muslim in Illinois's Stateville Prison. While the prisons saw the Muslims as an adversarial political group, the courts ruled that prisoners had to be allowed to practice their faith and not be punished for doing so.

The free exercise of religion is an important issue in American society. Congress passed a new law, the **Religious Freedom Restoration Act of 1993**, which was intended to force the government to provide compelling justifications for insisting that any law or policy was more important than people's religious practices. Although this law was declared unconstitutional by the Supreme Court in 1997 on the basis that Congress lacked the authority to enact such legislation, several states have adopted or considered the adoption of similar laws since.

Contact with the outside world is also important to prisoners. The courts have generally ruled that prisons can limit (or forbid) prisoners' direct contact with outside media, such as TV reporters or journalists. What general rights do prisoners have to communicate with or visit with other persons, including family and friends? Prisoners who want to maintain family and friendship ties face severe limits on the frequency, duration, and type of contact allowed in visiting. Many prisons (and even more jails) still enforce rules on non-contact visits, and in many institutions the display of any kind of personal affection is a write-up. Visitation is regarded as privilege rather than a right. Sexual contact is absolutely forbidden, except in the six states that allow conjugal visits for at least a portion of the inmate population, usually trusties or medium security inmates who are married and have good conduct records.

Applying the **legitimate penological interests** rule first formulated in *Turner v. Safley* (1987), prison authorities regulate correspondence and publications received by inmates. Mail can be opened and inspected for contraband but is generally not censored. Publications must be on an approved list (or not be on the disapproved list, such as porn magazines). Books and periodicals must be sent directly from the publisher or a bookstore, and not from a private person. Publications detrimental to the security, good order, or discipline of the institution--such as those relating to weapons, escape, physical violence, or pornography--are prohibited.

## Prisoners' Rights: Women in Prison

Women prisoners and their advocates have often made two general claims about the management of women in prison: Women generally have fewer programs and treatment options open to them than men do, and the programs and options that do exist are not gender-specific; they are designed for men rather than for women. The basic argument is that the focus of prison management is so much on men that women are incidental, not deserving of equal attention. This deals with the concept of **gender equity**.

Several courts have found **differential treatment** of male and female prisoners in the recent past. The landmark case here is *Glover v. Johnson* (1979 and 1987). In this Michigan case, a U.S. district court found that female inmates were offered educational and vocational programs which were markedly poorer than those offered to male prisoners. The court applied the equal protection clause of the Fourteenth Amendment to say that male and female inmates must be provided comparable conditions of confinement and access to rehabilitative programs. If **disparate treatment** had marked the imprisonment of women to this time, **parity of treatment** became the subsequent goal.

Many of the scholars who write about the imprisonment of women are not certain that the **parity model** is a good idea in practice. The parity model that evolved from 1970s litigation treated women prisoners *as if they were men* (to use Barbara Bloom and Meda Chesney-Lind's emphasis), applying a male standard to women at sentencing and in prison. From differential treatment, which often disadvantages women prisoners through neglect, the prison system has moved to **vengeful equity**, in which women are treated exactly as men are--with regard to chain gangs, medical care, and family visitation, for example.

The argument about policy goals in managing the imprisonment of women today is often said to come down to a contrast between the **equal treatment** model and the **special needs** model: "... equality is defined as rights equal to those of males, and differential needs are defined as needs different from those of males." A few cases have supported the special needs model, particularly with regard to medical care and visitation with their children, but in general the equity model is more prevalent. The huge increase in the numbers of women in jail and prison over the past 30 years--from about 15,000 to approaching 200,000--has also provided an impetus to treat female prisoners as a clientele more deserving of equitable attention.

## Prisoners' Rights: The Effect on Jail and Prison Administration

Before the due process revolution, incarceration was a closed, internal world. Court intervention has changed this world in several important ways, as James Jacobs wrote in 1980:
1. It has made the prison more bureaucratic, following written rules and policies.
2. It has allowed prisoners greater access to the courts.
3. It has made the public more aware of prison conditions.
4. It has given prisoners more of a political attitude.
5. It has weakened the authority of prison officials.
6. It has advanced the cause of professionalism in corrections by setting standards.

Court intervention has also made corrections much more costly. Most of the initial budget increases in prisons and jails went to hire new staff, especially in those institutions that had relied heavily on inmate trusties as workers and guards. Capital expenditures were also necessary to renovate old facilities and build new housing to alleviate overcrowding, a frequent circumstance in the totality of conditions cases. Rehabilitation programs, medical care, and mental health treatment were costly new additions in many states. Then, as prison and jail populations really exploded after 1980, correctional systems were obliged to build new institutions to house the new inmates, instead of just cramming then into existing facilities as they would have done in the past. Corrections became a higher priority, because it was the subject of expensive and often embarrassing litigation.

Jails and prisons were obliged to find new ways to deal with prisoner complaints, so that every minor issue did not end up the subject of a federal court lawsuit. Discipline and complaint procedures were formalized. Prisoners were given rule books explaining their rights in custody, classifying disciplinary infractions as major and minor, and providing channels for complaints. Institutions established **grievance procedures** for inmates to follow. Several prison systems established the position of **ombudsman**, based on a long-established position in Scandinavian countries, to receive, investigate, and act on complaints--sometimes from staff as well as inmates. This puts the institution in the posture of being self-critical, which is a major step in actually trying to learn from your mistakes rather than just cover them over.

Most correctional administrators who were active in the period of the most intensive court intervention, from about 1970 through the mid-1980s, would agree that this was a difficult time for them. They were often caught between opposing forces--prisoners seeking their "rights," politicians who for the most part could not have cared less, and federal courts trying to define constitutional conditions. How do they view the effects of intervention, long after the fact? Although they may find fault with the details of some of the consent decrees, most agree that the prisoners' rights movement speeded up the process of change and brought positive results, making correctional management if not easier then more professional.

## Probation and Parole

When we think of "prisoners' rights" as applicable to persons confined in jails and prisons, we should remember that the term also applies to persons on probation and parole. A sentence to probation, in lieu of imprisonment, or release on parole, after serving a portion of a sentence in confinement, both require supervision, both impose conditions on the convicted person, and both involve a reduced-rights status in comparison to the rights enjoyed by law-abiding citizens.

In *Griffin v. Wisconsin* (1987), the U.S. Supreme Court ruled that a probation officer's warrantless search of a probationer's home was legal. In a related search and seizure case involving an offender on parole, *Pennsylvania Board of Probation and Parole v. Scott* (1998), the Supreme Court ruled that the **exclusionary rule**, which bars improperly obtained evidence in criminal proceedings, does not apply to parole revocation hearings.

The parolee's basic rights in revocation hearings were established in the landmark case of *Morrissey v. Brewer* (1972). The Supreme Court ruled that parole revocation represents a "grievous loss" of liberty to the parolee, to which the parolee is entitled to due process. In revocation hearings, the parolee is entitled to several protections--written notice of the violations, disclosure of the evidence against him, opportunity to be heard in person and to present witnesses, the right to cross-examine adverse witnesses, a neutral hearing body such as a traditional parole board, and a written statement of the reasons for revoking parole.

The following year, the Supreme Court applied these same six due process rights to probationers in *Gagnon v. Scarpelli* (1973). Probationers were entitled to a hearing, the Court ruled, but not to have an attorney represent them. Both *Morrissey* and *Scarpelli* clarified what had previously been highly variable revocation and often informal proceedings leading to the revocation of parole and probation.

## The Politics of "Modified Hands Off:" AEDPA and PRLA

Although both prisoners and jail and prison officials would agree that prisoners' rights litigation resulted in positive changes in corrections in the last decades of the twentieth century, they would differ on the continuing need for such litigation. Inmates often prefer to see *more* litigation--to challenge the legal system, to give them something to do while serving time, and to call outside attention to their problems. Correctional officials would like to see *less* litigation--to reduce the numbers of **frivolous lawsuits** (defined as those of a trivial nature or lacking in factual merit), to devote time to more important concerns, and to recognize that reasonable improvements have been made.

The public and political perceptions that inmates have won enough rights, that much litigation is frivolous, and that federal judges have been too intrusive into state affairs have led to important legislative changes in recent years. In 1996, the U.S. Congress passed two major pieces of legislation, the **Anti-Terrorism and Effective Death Penalty Act (AEDPA)** and the **Prison Litigation Reform Act (PLRA)**, both aimed at prisoners' rights litigation in the federal courts. AEDPA had several features intended to limit the number of *habeas corpus* petitions filed in U.S. district courts, including time limits and restrictions on filing second or successive *habeas corpus* petitions. The political intent of AEDPA was to speed up the processing of *habeas corpus* petitions, specifically reducing the time spent processing death penalty cases.

The PLRA was much more significant to prisoners' rights issues in general, because of the much higher volume of Section 1983 lawsuits, almost three times as many (42,000 to 15,000) as *habeas corpus* petitions in 1995. The PLRA reduced the intervention authority of federal judges, set time limits for any orders they might impose, and gave state prison officials a greater voice in court. It also limited prisoners' opportunities to file civil rights lawsuits, which has caused the numbers of such suits filed by prisoners to fall off sharply since the law took effect.

## Prison Litigation Today

In a 1995 article titled "The Supreme Court and Prisoners' Rights," Jack Call divided the history of prisoners' rights into three periods: the hands-off era (before 1964), the rights era (1964-1978), and the deference era (1979-present). In the hands-off era, prisoners had minimal legal standing. The courts took the abstention approach, saying that it was up to the executive and legislative branches of government to provide for the care of prisoners. The federal courts viewed prisoners as the domain of the states and rarely intervened in these cases. The **rights era** reflected a dramatic reversal of the hands-off approach. The Warren Court's due process revolution applied the Fourteenth Amendment and the Civil Rights Statute (Section 1983) to create national standards applicable to all prisoners. But the time of expanding rights quickly ran its course.

The official origin of the **deference era** is traced to *Bell v. Wolfish* (1979), a lawsuit filed over conditions in the new federal Metropolitan Correctional Center in New York City. Reasoning that the federal courts had become too enmeshed in prison operations, Chief Justice William Rehnquist wrote in the majority opinion rejecting the inmates' legal claims: ". . . the inquiry of federal courts into prison management must be limited to the issue of whether a particular system violates any prohibition of the Constitution or, in the case of a federal prison, a statute. The wide range of `judgment calls' that meet constitutional and statutory requirements are confided to officials outside of the Judicial Branch of Government."

Rehnquist's call for **judicial deference** to corrections and legislative officials was made in 1979. Long before Congress enacted AEDPA and the PLRA to restrict prisoners' access to the federal courts, Supreme Court decisions had made it clear that prisoners' rights went only so far--that in a federal system the states retain primary authority for the confinement of prisoners. The core of cases defining judicial deference would include the following:

*Gregg v. Georgia* (1976). State death penalty statutes that contain sufficient safeguards against arbitrary and capricious imposition are constitutional, thus reinstating the death penalty.

*Rhodes v. Chapman* (1981). Double celling of prisoners does not, in itself, constitute cruel and unusual punishment, which tolerates overcrowding.

*Turner v. Safley* (1987). A prison regulation that impinges on inmates' constitutional rights is valid if it is reasonably related to legitimate penological interests.

*Wilson v. Seiter* (1991). In conditions of confinement cases under Section 1983, "deliberate indifference" means a guilty state of mind on the part of prison officials.

*Lewis v. Casey* (1996). The constitutional right of court access is violated only if a prisoner's attempt to pursue a legal claim is hindered by prison officials.

*Turner v. Safley* provided the philosophical doctrine for deference in 1987. Its creation of the "legitimate penological interests" rule allows judges to defer to corrections officials provided officials can explain the reasons for their actions and policies. When prison policies and prisoner rights are in conflict, *Turner* applies the **reasonable relationship** test. All prison authorities have to do is prove that a prison regulation is reasonably related to a legitimate penological interest in order for that regulation to be valid even if a constitutional right is infringed.

The courts are not listening to prisoners as much as they once were, and federal courts are not intervening on behalf of prisoners as often as they once did. Recent research suggests that the filing of *habeas corpus* petitions continues to roughly parallel the numbers of state prisoners, while Section 1983 filings have dropped by almost half in the aftermath of PLRA. The amount of damages paid inmates in federal courts is down as well.

For now, it is more difficult for prisoners to get their cases into federal courts and keep them there. Prisons and jails have more discretion in managing prisoners, and many state corrections departments have established mechanisms--grievance procedures, mediators, and ombudsmen--for resolving complaints about prison conditions short of litigation.

Some prisoners--captives of their own adversarial mentality--either have not noticed or do not care. They remain committed to challenging the corrections system through the courts. Some have turned more often to state courts, thinking that state judges may be more sympathetic (more "liberal") than federal judges in the current political environment. Prisoners often fail to understand that their own excesses from the prisoners' rights era, which led them to file not only important suits but too many trivial suits as "**recreational litigation,**" when combined with the more conservative turn of the federal courts, have undermined support for any further extension of prisoners' rights. Even the litigation experts who have supported reform have suggested that prisoners need to be more "judicious" in attacking the legal system. Otherwise they run the risk of further alienating the public, the political officials, and most important, the judges whose support is essential if they wish to get a fair hearing in court.

## Collateral Consequences of a Criminal Conviction

One of the traditions left over from civil death is the felon's loss of civil rights, even after discharge from prison or supervision and carrying over beyond the end of his sentence. These civil rights, such as voting, holding public office, marital and parental rights, serving on a jury, and possessing firearms, are often lost to the convicted felon until he goes through the formal procedure to get them restored. The **ex-offender**, often labeled an **ex-con** if he or she has been imprisoned, must also comply with administrative and legal restrictions, such as registration or notification of authorities, and employment licensing; he must also deal with the social stigma of being a felon.

These are the **collateral consequences** of a felony conviction. Jeremy Travis, former director of the National Institute of Justice, called these consequences **invisible punishments** in that they pose legal barriers harmful to the economic, political, and social well-being of their communities, black communities in particular. The list of **civil disabilities** is a long one. Most of us would not quarrel too loudly with the restrictions on firearms possession by convicted felons, the single right that is most likely to be taken away and least likely to be given back. Keeping guns from felons is not such a bad public policy. But voting is almost as widely prohibited. Forty-eight states prohibit voting during imprisonment, 33 during parole, and 29 during probation. Seven states permanently bar felons from voting (unless pardoned by the governor or meeting other specific authorizations), while seven others have crime-specific bars or waiting periods.

131

Realistically, many ex-felons probably could not care less about some of the common civil rights they have lost--holding public office, serving on juries, or even voting. But housing, job training, temporary assistance, particularly if they have children, and employment--these are critical to avoiding returning to criminal activities. What they must have, first and foremost, is a job. Ex-felons face employment restrictions, including occupational disability statutes that bar them from licenses in certain trades and professions. And how would you deal with this question on an employment application: "Have you ever been convicted of a felony?"

The consequences to ex-felons are also consequences to their dependents. More than 10 million American children have a parent who has been in prison. A recent report, *Every Door Closed: Barriers Facing Parents with Criminal Records*, explored in detail the impact of criminal records on families. It identified six major areas of family life adversely affected by a criminal record--employment, welfare benefits, subsidized housing, loss of child custody, student loans, and immigration status. The report's executive summary suggests that these barriers, singly and in combination, tear families apart, create unemployment and homelessness, and guarantee failure, thereby harming parents and children, families, and communities. These barriers (most of all to stable employment needed to earn a living) are intended to reduce crime and enhance community security, yet their effect is just the opposite: they make it more difficult for ex-offenders to take care of their children and avoid criminal activity. And what will happen to the children of the parents to whom "every door is closed?"

## Criminal Registration

The offender's criminal record does not go away by itself at the expiration of the sentence; generally the offender must pursue legal action at his own initiative to clear his record. The most sweeping--and least available--method of wiping out a record is through what is called **annulment**. The National Council on Crime and Delinquency, in its Model Act for Annulment of Conviction of Crime, states that the effect of an annulment is to restore all lost civil rights and to cancel the record of conviction and disposition. The responsibility for annulment would lie with the court that convicted the offender. The judge would issue the annulment order to assist in rehabilitation, when it was consistent with the public welfare.

The trend in the United States is toward gathering more information on criminals, not erasing it. Centralized data banks are often used as sources of information in those states that require **registration of criminals**. Registration of certain classes of criminals, particularly sex offenders, is becoming more common in the United States today. In Europe, where citizens were often required to carry identity papers, former prisoners were once given a **yellow card**--like Jean Valjean in *Les Miserables*--showing that they had been in custody previously.

Sex offender registries have existed since California started one in 1947, but they really took off nationally in the 1990s. The Jacob Wetterling Crimes Against Children and Sexually Violent Offender Registration Act (The Jacob Wetterling Act), passed by Congress in 1994, required criminals who commit sex crimes against children or any violent sex offense against adults to register for a period of 10 years from the date of their release from custody or supervision. All 50 states now have sex offender registration laws.

**Megan's Law**, named after seven-year-old Megan Kanka, who had been abducted and murdered by a convicted sex offender in New Jersey, was passed in 1996. States were required to notify citizens of sex offenders in their communities through a variety of methods--Internet postings, including photos (used in 34 states by 2003), media releases, flyers distributed by offenders or public officials through the mail, and public meetings. Virtually all states have adopted some form of **community notification laws** based upon combinations of these methods.

The Pam Lychner Sexual Offender Tracking and Identification Act of 1996 amended the Jacob Wetterling Act by establishing a **national sex offender database**, maintained by the FBI. This national tracking system gives law enforcement authorities access to sex offender registration data from all participating states. It contained information on about 400,000 registered sex offenders in 2003.

Several objections to the broad scope of sex offender registration have been made:
　　　　1. It is permanent, lasting a lifetime, no matter how long it has been since the person last committed a sex crime.
　　　　2. Although the intent of the statutes is to protect children and others from sexual predators, all sex offenders who commit listed crimes are required to register. This would include many non-violent offenders, family offenders, and adults who have had sex with minors.
　　　　3. Registration is not based on risk. It feeds a kind of "witch hunt" mentality about sex offenders that is

not supported by research. Most sex offenses, especially against children, do not involve strangers, and recidivism rates for sex offenders are generally no higher and, in recent, detailed Justice Department statistics, lower than for other categories of criminals.

4. Registration stigmatizes criminals as another civil disability added to the other collateral consequences. Convicted sex offenders end up the "lowest of the low" among the criminal caste in American society.

## Civil Commitment

For some sex offenders, the end of the criminal sentence holds an even greater peril than registration--**civil commitment** for treatment as a **sexually violent predator (SVP)**. Washington passed the first of the "sexual predator" acts in 1990. Similar acts were adopted in several other states during the next decade. Kansas's Sexual Predator Act empowered the state's attorney general to bring civil commitment actions against individuals who are within 90 days of release from criminal confinement and who are deemed, through a review process, to be at high risk to re-offend. Through a civil commitment process, these individuals can be committed to a Sexual Predator Treatment Program (SPTP) for treatment until it is determined by treatment staff and the court that they no longer represent a high risk to re-offend.

The U.S. Supreme Court, in *Kansas v. Hendricks* (1997) upheld the law by a 5-4 vote. The majority opinion indicated that constitutional protections apply primarily to criminal, not civil, law. The Court said the Kansas law was not about retribution or deterrence, reasoning that "the confinement's duration is instead linked to the state purposes of the commitment, namely to hold the person until his mental abnormality no longer causes him to be a threat to others." This ruling seemed to make clear that SVP programs could legitimately hold people in restraint of their freedom only if the programs were willing and able to offer treatment aimed at reducing sex offenders' risk for re-offense and so afford them an opportunity to return to the community.

Some legal practitioners and medical professionals have expressed serious concern about these statutes and the treatment process they mandate:
1. The decision broadly redefines sexual criminal behavior as a mental illness for the purpose of allowing continued preventive detention--an unacceptable **medicalization of deviance**.
2. The legislature's main purpose is preventive detention and not treatment.
3. The criminal conviction assumes voluntary behavior, but the mental disorder assumes that the offender cannot control his behavior, warranting commitment and long-term treatment.
4. Treating sex offenders as "patients" in maximum-security mental health facilities will divert funds from other severely mentally ill patients.
5. This is a matter to be addressed by criminal sentencing and not the use, or misuse, of psychiatry.

## Restoring Rights

The traditional and most available way for an offender to get lost civil rights restored is through the **executive clemency** process, under the authority of the governor or president. What the offender needs is a **pardon**. In some states certain classes of offenders whose terms have expired may be entitled to so-called automatic pardons, where no discretionary board action is needed. In other states, offenders must petition the state pardon board and appear in person to ask for a pardon--either full or conditional--to get those rights restored. Even if a pardon is granted to the ex-offender, restoring the lost civil rights, under most state laws the offender still has a criminal record. To get rid of the record, the ex-offender must get an **expungement** order signed by the court in which the offender was sentenced. This order would result in the destruction of the criminal history record related to the instant case. Both manual and computer files at all levels--local, state, and federal--should be purged of all information related to the defendant's involvement in the case. A similar process, called **erasure of record**, is used for juvenile court records, which by law are supposed to be sealed and not mixed with or carried over to the offender's adult criminal records.

Ex-offenders are no longer civilly dead, but it still is not easy to make a fresh start. Many offenders released from prison want to go straight and avoid further run-ins with the law. Half of them may end up back in prison, but this statistic also means that half don't. Ex-offenders have families and friends; they need a place to live, a job, and productive ways to spend their time. It is not easy to leave prison, particularly if you have been away several years, and jump right back into mainstream society--not as an ex-con.

# Self Test

## Multiple Choice

1. The hands-off doctrine was finally abandoned during what decade?
   - a. the 1790s
   - b. the 1850s
   - c. the 1930s
   - d. the 1960s
   - e. the 1980s

2. The first important freedom of religion cases from the 1960s dealt with which one of these religious groups?
   - a. Quakers
   - b. Pentecostals
   - c. Wiccans
   - d. Black Muslims
   - e. Seventh Day Adventists

3. An important standard of prison medical care was established in the Texas case of *Estelle v. Gamble* in 1976; this standard was:
   - a. imminent danger
   - b. civil death
   - c. constructive contamination
   - d. benign neglect
   - e. deliberate indifference

4. The concept of collateral consequences generally has to do with:
   - a. lack of participation in prison rehabilitation programs
   - b. loss of civil rights upon conviction of a crime
   - c. harassment by the police because of a criminal record
   - d. lack of education and family support among ex-offenders
   - e. the friends the ex-offender is not supposed to see after his release

5. The term for a judicial proceeding that cancels out the ex-offender's arrest and conviction on a particular charge is:
   - a. allocution
   - b. annulment
   - c. autonomy
   - d. aggravation
   - e. amalgamation

6. *Glover v. Johnson* is said to provide for _____ treatment for women prisoners.
   - a. punitive
   - b. special needs
   - c. exceptional
   - d. preferential
   - e. parity

7. Four of the following rights are among those commonly denied ex-offenders; which one is NOT?
   - a. the right to hold public office
   - b. the right to appointed counsel if indigent
   - c. the right to vote
   - d. the right to serve on a jury
   - e. the right to possess a firearm

8. *Wolff v. McDonnell* is the landmark case in regard to:
   - a. the death penalty
   - b. probation and parole revocation
   - c. free speech in prison
   - d. prison disciplinary procedures
   - e. sex offender registration

9. This term, meaning "you have the body," is used in a writ ordering the prisoner to be brought into court for judicial review of the circumstances of imprisonment.
   - a. *habeas corpus*
   - b. *in loco parentis*
   - c. *ipso facto*
   - d. *memento mori*
   - e. *corpus juris*

10. *Turner v. Safley* is viewed as a key decision in the _____ era, having established the "legitimate penological interests" doctrine.

    a. liberty                                  d. activist
    b. deference                              e. discretionary
    c. reintegration

## True or False

_____ 11. Most prisons maintain a full staff of attorneys to help prisoners with their legal needs.

_____ 12. The courts have generally ruled that all prisoners except those in lockdown are entitled to unrestricted and unsupervised access to visitors.

_____ 13. State prisoners have always had access to the federal courts through the "freedom of petition" clause in the First Amendment to the Bill of Rights.

_____ 14. Any convicted felon, whether in custody or not, faces the loss of his civil rights as provided under state law.

_____ 15. The attorney general is the legal official who gives the order for an expungement to take place.

_____ 16. The offenders targeted most frequently by recent registration laws are drug dealers.

_____ 17. The ombudsman is an official within the system whose job it is to accept and investigate complaints by those within the system.

_____ 18. The Arkansas case of *Holt v. Sarver* is important as reaffirming the hands off doctrine.

_____ 19. The Prison Litigation Reform Act has had the effect of reducing prisoner lawsuits in federal courts.

_____ 20. Prisoners in custody have no right to refuse medical treatment.

## Fill In the Blanks

21. Either full or conditional, the act that restores lost civil rights is called a(n) _____.

22. Prison officials called the Black Muslims a political or radical group; the courts said they were a _____ group.

23. The justification for prison officials to open and inspect mail is that they are looking for _____.

24. The civil right that is almost universally denied to convicted felons is _____.

25. Either annulment or expungement would have to be authorized by the _____.

26. The focus of a Section 1983 lawsuit is on the inmate's _____.

27. The common law concept that a convicted felon forfeited all legal rights upon conviction was known as _____.

28. Recent civil commitment statutes have concentrated on offenders who are identified as _____.

29. The incorporation of the Bill of Rights to apply to the states was accomplished through the _____ Amendment.

30. If prisoners and prison officials reached agreement to settle a class action lawsuit over prison conditions, they would sign what is known as a(n) _____.

## Discussion

31. What was the legal status of a convicted felon under common law?

32. What do *habeas corpus* and Section 1983 mean to a prison litigant?

33. What alternatives do prisons provide in trying to resolve prisoner complaints without filing lawsuits?

34. Why is there any such thing as collateral consequences attached to a felony conviction?

35. A federal law is passed restoring all lost civil rights to ex-offenders immediately upon discharge from imprisonment. Is this good or bad? Explain.

36. Contrast the hands off, rights, and deference eras.

37. Why has the attitude of the federal courts toward prisoner lawsuits changed in recent years?

## CHAPTER THIRTEEN

# Rehabilitation

For the prison generation that fell between "hard labor" and "get tough on crime," rehabilitation was an important concept, representing a perspective that said one purpose of imprisonment was to promote positive change in the prisoner during confinement. Officially abandoned during the 1970s, it remains part of the prison landscape even in today's more punitive era. It may even be making a comeback in American corrections in the early twenty-first century. After reading this chapter, you should be familiar with:

1. The origins of rehabilitation in prison.
2. The post-World War II rehabilitation era.
3. The decline of rehabilitation in the 1970s.
4. Common forms of rehabilitation programs in prison, including education, vocational training, and therapy programs.
5. Issues in the provision of rehabilitation programs in prison.
6. Measuring rehabilitation through recidivism.
7. The rise of rehabilitation in recent years.

## Key Terms

rehabilitation
desistance
habilitation
reformation
reformatory
rehabilitation era
scientific penology
Elmira System
medical model
Robert Martinson
nothing works
silver bullet
forced rehabilitation
crimogenic environment
balanced model
recidivism
recidivists
rearrest
reconviction
reimprisonment
reimprisonment for a new felony
creaming
model program
exportability
treatment effects
policy effects
planned intervention
black box
prisonization
Austin MacCormick
Correctional Education Association
individually prescribed instruction
educational release
Project Newgate
anti-education bias
certified training
Windham School District

treatment modalities
psychotherapy
psychoanalysis
client-centered therapy
behavior modification
operant conditioning
aversive conditioning
brainwashing
sensory deprivation
stress assessment
chemotherapy
aversion therapy
neurosurgery
group therapy
transactional analysis
reality therapy
therapeutic community
community of peers
reintegration
principles of ineffective intervention
punishing smarter
principles of effectiveness
nondirective therapy
moral development
moral discussion approach
cognitive therapy
rational-emotive behavior therapy
cognitive-behavior therapy
SMART Recovery
empowerment
faith-based programs
InnerChange Freedom Initiative (IFI)
factories with fences
Prison Industry Enhancement (PIE)
  Certification Program
workability skills
whole person approach

therapy
psychological therapy
psyche
social therapy

Project Metamorphosis
Parallel Universe
criminal specialists

## The Birth of Rehabilitation

**Rehabilitation** is an often-used word in corrections. While it may be used generically to mean "something that makes a prisoner a better person," it has a more narrow definition as well--as specific programs applied within the prison setting (or outside) intended to bring about the end of criminal behavior, called **desistance**, meaning to cease or stop. This can be expressed in a kind of formula: prisoner classification times appropriate programming times positive participation equals probability of desistance. The aim of the prison is to get the prisoner into the right program, keep him or her there until the program is successfully completed, and then turn the prisoner out to test the commitment to non-criminal behavior.

Speakers at correctional conferences on rehabilitation are fond of referring to the dictionary definition of rehabilitation: "to restore to a previous condition." They then point out what we should know about prisoners by this point. They are undereducated, badly skilled, substance abusing, anti-social misfits who would not be making major contributions to society even if they were not behind bars. What these folks need is not to be restored to a previous condition, it is to be raised up to a position they have not previously attained in life. They need transformation, or **habilitation**, before they could hope to qualify for rehabilitation.

Pessimism--or reality--aside, what do we know about the association of rehabilitation with imprisonment? Rehabilitation is a relatively new concept in imprisonment, born of the increasing influence of social work and the behavioral sciences in corrections during the first half of the twentieth century. Rehabilitation was not a word to be found in the arguments about the place of the prison in nineteenth century American society. Whether in the Pennsylvania penance model or in the Auburn hard labor model, the emphasis was on **reformation**--either spiritual or social or both. The 1870 National Prison Congress adopted as its first principle: "Reformation, not vindictive suffering, as the purpose of penal treatment of prisoners."

Zebulon Brockway's new institution, the **reformatory**, which opened in 1876 in Elmira, New York, is often cited at the birthplace of prison rehabilitation in America. Brockway combined into one package many of the reform ideas of the time--the indeterminate sentence, basic classification, industrial training, religious and educational instruction, individualization of treatment, and parole. The reformatories for men and women that developed over the next half century applied these practices to the select few--mostly young, non-habitual offenders--while most ordinary criminals were sent to prisons to do hard labor. Not until the Big House was dead did rehabilitation began to be viewed as being applicable to the general prison population.

## The Rehabilitation Era

The **rehabilitation era** in American corrections is associated with the two decades from the mid-1950s to the mid-1970s, though in some places the beginnings would be earlier and the ends later, and in other places-- particularly in several Southern states and in local jails--rehabilitation never took hold as a primary purpose of imprisonment. Several circumstances would coalesce to promote widespread interest in rehabilitation by the middle of the twentieth century. First was the growth of **scientific penology** as a movement. Penology, the study of the punishment of crime, developed in the early to mid-twentieth century, when criminologists, social scientists, social workers, and prison administrators applied theories from the emerging fields of sociology, psychology, psychiatry, and management to study crime and punishment, and to attempt to create a more beneficial prison environment.

Brockway's **Elmira System** was a prominent early example of rudimentary classification, programs, and individualized release based on good behavior. Prison systems set up classification centers--later known as reception and diagnostic centers--to assess the needs of incoming prisoners. Prisoners began to be broken down into different custody levels--maximum, medium, and minimum. Specialized institutions, already in use for women and juveniles, began to be used for drug addicts and the mentally ill. These changes were accompanied by the rapid decline of prison labor, which turned the nature of prison life upside down between 1930 and 1945. The absence of work and other purposeful activities, resulting in inmate idleness, was blamed for the prolonged period of prison riots and unrest that took place across the country in the early 1950s.

John Conrad has pointed out that wardens in this era had three choices--put prisoners to work (which was less of an option in industrial prisons), offer them opportunities to improve themselves, or let idleness prevail. Many wardens wanted programs to keep prisoners constructively occupied, and rehabilitation enjoyed widespread support for a time. Some systems went much farther than others. The federal system under the direction of James Bennett went farthest of all in its adoption of the **medical model** of rehabilitation, which viewed criminality as analogous to a physical disease. The offender was perceived as a person with social, intellectual, or emotional deficiencies who should be diagnosed carefully and his deficiencies clinically defined. He would then be treated and prepared for return to society. In the federal system and the few states that chose to devote resources to the medical model, the promise was for even more programs and a customized treatment plan fitted to the individual prisoner.

## The Death of Rehabilitation

The decline of rehabilitation is most often tied to one specific historical event--the publication of an article by **Robert Martinson**, "What Works--Questions and Answers about Prison Reform," in the journal *The Public Interest* in 1974. In his introduction to the article, Martinson gave this summary: "With few and isolated exceptions, the rehabilitative efforts that have been reported so far have had no appreciable effect on recidivism." Or as it was widely reported: "What works? **Nothing works**." Martinson and his colleagues Douglas Lipton and Judith Wilks released a longer report, *The Effectiveness of Correctional Treatment*, in 1975, concluding "The field of corrections has not as yet found satisfactory ways to reduce recidivism by significant amounts," which was a way of saying that penologists had not found anything that worked perfectly well--a **silver bullet** that killed criminal behavior.

Other researchers questioned rehabilitation for other reasons. As crime rates rose, some "get tough on crime" advocates wanted to do away with any efforts that smacked of being nice to criminals. Conservative scholars argued that retribution and incapacitation were more appropriate objectives of punishment. Norval Morris and other reformers contended that **forced rehabilitation** was an inherently coercive game that could not be played fairly; they objected to sentence length--through release on parole--being tied to participation in rehabilitation. Psychologists in particular objected to the influence of the prison environment upon rehabilitation, suggesting that the **crimogenic environment** of the prison caused more new crimes than rehabilitation could prevent. The complete dominance of security over rehabilitation supported this argument. Prisoners often agreed that rehabilitation was manipulative and subjective.

The Federal Bureau of Prisons officially gave up its medical model in 1975, announcing its replacement by the **balanced model** in which retribution, deterrence, incapacitation, and rehabilitation were all considered possible objectives that might apply to different inmates. In the 1980s, a decade dominated by a conservative crime control ideology at the national level, rehabilitation faded in importance.

Some observers pointed out that it was the *ideal* of rehabilitation--or the emphasis on rehabilitation as a purpose of imprisonment--that had died; rehabilitative *programs* were still alive in most prisons. Prison officials did not rush to abolish traditional rehabilitative programs--education, vocational training, counseling--within their institutions. Prison officials want to facilitate change, and programs give prisoners something to do, something positive in an otherwise stale environment. Even when rehabilitation was dead as an ideology, the percentages of inmates participating in programs remained steady or increased.

## Recidivism and Rehabilitation

How does one measure the success or failure of people who have been through rehabilitation? We tend to focus on the repetition of criminal behavior, resulting in arrest, reincarceration, or a new conviction. The term is **recidivism**, which the dictionary defines as "repeated or habitual relapse, as into crime." Four different measures have often been used to identify **recidivists**:

      1. **Rearrest**, being taken into custody for a new offense.
      2. **Reconviction**, getting a new felony or misdemeanor conviction.
      3. **Reimprisonment**, returning to prison with a new sentence or as a technical violator of the terms of release under the old sentence.

4. **Reimprisonment for a new felony**, the most narrow definition of all, because it would involve the fewest number of prisoners.

Minnesota looked closely at recidivism among the 9,000 offenders released from prison or sentenced to probation in 1992. Their study found that 59 percent of prisoners were *rearrested* in Minnesota for new felonies or gross misdemeanors in the three years following their release, and an additional five percent were rearrested in another state. Forty-five percent of released prisoners were *reconvicted* of felonies or gross misdemeanors within three years. Forty percent of prisoners were *reimprisoned* within three years--28 percent for new crimes and the remainder for 'technical violations' of their prison release conditions. Many studies of recidivism use the first three years after release as the most critical study period, when reoffending rates are highest, but recidivism does not end after three years: it lasts for a lifetime.

When scholars tried to evaluate the effectiveness of various rehabilitation programs, they encountered many obstacles. Different studies used different measures of success, depending on how far into the system the failures went. Some focused on re-arrest, some on return to custody, even without new convictions, and some on new convictions. The percentages change significantly depending on the standards used. It is also difficult to compare experimental groups and control groups in determining effectiveness. Many prison programs pick volunteers or desirable candidates from a larger field of applicants--a process known as **creaming**, meaning to pick the cream of the crop--which enhances the likelihood of success from the start.

One of the things researchers were interested in was the concept of a **model program** that could be easily reproduced and exported to other settings. In examining similar programs, or programs that claimed to be applying the same type of treatment modality, such as behavior modification, observers noted that few "pure" programs following ideal models could be found. Rather, programs tended to be hybrid models combining different approaches and these modified to fix the circumstances of particular settings--meaning they had to be adaptable to the prison routine. This also hampers the idea of **exportabililty**, transplanting a successful model to a different setting.

Robert Martinson compared **treatment effects** to **policy effects**. Treatment effects were the *bona fide* results of treatment programs, objectively measured. Policy effects had more to do with interpretation of the results. If the people in charge of the program wanted people to succeed--perhaps because they were more humanitarian in their beliefs or because they needed to be successful to get their funding renewed--they could ignore minor violations and call outcomes successful even though a different evaluator might call them failures. Some programs achieved such remarkable successes that their results were clearly biased and unreliable.

Recidivism is not a universal language spoken by all people involved in prison administration and rehabilitation. It is not an absolute--black or white--but more a matter of degree in which success and failure are not always easy to measure.

## Rehabilitation in Prison

If rehabilitation is broadly defined as any program that makes people better or reduces criminal behavior, then several kinds of activities--religion, recreation, self-help groups, prison work assignments, and others--can be said to be rehabilitative in nature. The National Research Council's 1979 report, *The Rehabilitation of Criminal Offenders: Problems and Prospects*, called rehabilitation a **planned intervention** to reduce criminal activity, a definition that would be more appropriate to the traditional prison-sponsored programs emphasizing education, vocational training, and therapy of different types.

But what is it that actually promotes change in criminals? The results of rehabilitative interventions take place in the human mind and the human heart, where science cannot peer. We can never be sure whether change took place *because* of the interventions, or *despite* the interventions, or whether the interventions were merely part of a larger pattern of change that took place over a longer period of time, in and out of prison. Joycelyn Pollock has called this the **black box** of prison. She compares the prison experience to a "black box" that the researcher cannot look inside. She suggests that we can never identify which elements of the prison experience contributed to the results: "It may be that treatment programs provide positive elements to a course of changing one's life, but the negative aspects of imprisonment--**prisonization** (the socialization to the prisoner subculture), violence, attacks on self-esteem, loss of family support--may override any treatment effects."

## Prison Rehabilitation: Education

Prison officials have long recognized that prisoners as a group are undereducated. As early as the 1820s, prisons in New York and Kentucky offered brief classes teaching prisoners to read and write. In 1847, New York passed a law requiring the appointment of a full-time teacher in each of its state prisons. Teachers were common staff members in the first reformatories of the late 1800s.

In 1930, **Austin MacCormick**, called the father of modern correctional education, founded the **Correctional Education Association** (now an affiliate of the American Correctional Association). He established the *Journal of Correctional Education* in 1937. MacCormick was an advocate of **individually prescribed instruction** (IPI) in correctional settings, which meant that each prisoner should have his or her own plan of education and that much instruction was intended to be one-on-one as opposed to group- or congregate-based.

As the twenty-first century begins, prisoners remain poorly educated, and prison educational programs are abundant. Caroline Wolf Harlow reported in 2003 that a comprehensive national survey of prisoners completed in 1997 showed that 75 percent of state prisoner inmates, 59 percent of federal prison inmates, and 69 percent of local jail inmates had not completed high school. Most state and federal inmates do take some classes--most commonly working toward the GED test--while in custody, though research does not indicate that getting a GED has much impact on recidivism. As a substitute diploma for high school dropouts, it is often viewed not as a mark of attainment but of educational inferiority.

The few prisoners with college degrees have much lower recidivism rates, which at one time promoted the increased availability of college education for prisoners--either inside the walls or through **educational release** furloughs that allowed prisoners to attend class on college campuses. **Project Newgate**, a federally funded program, established college campuses within the walls of several prisons in the 1970s. Federal Pell Grants for prisoners were availabe until they were killed by passage of the Violent Crime Control Act of 1994.

These options became politically unpopular during the crime control campaigns of the 1990s, when state and federal funding were cut back. Internal support among wardens and administrators is often lacking as well. Thom Gehring has argued that many institutional staff seem to have an **anti-education bias** against college programs (and a bias in favor of training in manual trades) for inmates.

## Prison Rehabilitation: Vocational Training

Vocational training in American prisons was originally reserved for young criminals while adult prisoners labored at real work. Progressive prisons begin to offer skilled training for inmates after World War II. Vocational training was greatly expanded in the 1960s and 1970s during the rehabilitation era in corrections. Prison administrators and staff tend to be more supportive of work training for inmates than they are of college education, so these programs remain more pervasive in American prisons than higher education programs. In the 1990s, about a third of inmates reported receiving some type of vocational training since entering prison, but this training was not often ongoing. In a given year, fewer than 10 percent of prisoners participate in any kind of vocational training in or out of prison.

Vocational training in prison can be divided into two types--generic and certified. Generic includes job-based work assignments under the direction of staff members who are not certified instructors; they are staff members--correctional officers or civilians--who supervise inmates on the job. **Certified training**, on the other hand, is provided by vocational/technical instructors who could be teaching the same skill to free world students. The courses are the same as would be offered in a vocational or technical school outside of prison. They have structure, content, and exams, and the prisoners who complete them receive certificates.

Long recognized as one of the national leaders in providing vocational education to inmates, Texas created the **Windham School District**--the first correctional school district in the nation--in 1969. It provides educational, vocational, and life skills programs for incarcerated offenders. Over 20,000 Texas inmates were enrolled in one of three types of certificate programs in 1998:
    1. Secondary level vocational programs providing occupational training and industrial certification in 40 trade areas.
    2. Apprenticeship training programs in 32 crafts.

3. Post-secondary vocational programs in 19 course areas; courses result in the awarding of 20 semester hours of college credit upon satisfactory completion.

Vocational training in prison is slanted heavily toward skilled trades, such as carpentry, welding, upholstery, air conditioning, electrical work, auto repair, plumbing, data processing, printing, groundskeeping, and culinary arts. Women's training programs are often more limited than men's (though this has changed in several states as women's prisons have gotten bigger). The most common programs for women include office skills, culinary arts, garment production, the hospitality industry, and cosmetology. Programs to train women--and men--prisoners in sales, supervisory, management, health care, and service occupations are pretty slim. The assumption is that these jobs are beyond the skill levels (and outside the interests) of most prisoners.

## Prison Rehabilitation: Therapy

When some people think of rehabilitation in prison, they think specifically of **therapy**, a treatment process intended to cure the prisoner of criminal behavior. Such programs do go on in prison, but they are not as plentiful or as important as outsiders might think. Therapy is narrow and limited to the most disordered or the lucky few who fall into the slots available. If prisoners do get into a formal therapy program while they are incarcerated, it is most likely because they have been identified as falling into one of two groups of special needs offenders-- substance abusers or the mentally ill. Sex offenders have also received much more attention as a special treatment category over the past decade or so.

Therapy programs in prison have often been classified as two types--**psychological therapy**, which deals with the mental state or **psyche** of one individual person, especially in regard to motivation; and **social therapy**, which concentrates on the relationship between the individual and the people around him. Different therapists, typically with backgrounds in psychology and sociology, have devised **treatment modalities** for the application of their ideas to human subjects in the world at large. Some therapists then take these modalities and apply them to men and women in prison. They recognize the problems with both the clientele and the environment, and some therapists refuse to treat criminals so long as they remain in the prison setting.

**Psychotherapy** is one option not heavily used in corrections. Most people probably associate Sigmund Freud's **psychoanalysis** (literally the analysis of the psyche) with this form of intervention. It is "talk therapy" and involves one-on-one counseling over an extended period of time. Prisons do not put ordinary inmates into long-term individualized treatment. The M.D.s and Ph.D.s who work in prison are mostly concerned with diagnosis and treatment plans that will be carried out by others, such as social workers or counselors, and much more often in a group rather than an individual approach.

Another form of therapy that is individual but more humanistic in its approach is **client-centered therapy**, sometimes referred to as Rogerian therapy in applying the principles of Carl Rogers. In this approach, the therapist--who is supposed to be warm, friendly, understanding, and nonjudgmental--is a guide as the patient seeks self-understanding, not easy to do do among other prisoners in a secure environment. **Behavior modification**, in which Edward Thorndike and B.F. Skinner are central figures, emphasizes behavior or conditioning rather than attitudes or self-enlightenment. Its objective is to produce desirable behavior through the strict application of punishments and rewards. One version of this would be **operant conditioning**, which uses highly structured routine, rigorous monitoring, token economies, and earned privileges as rewards.

Another version of behavior modification is **aversive conditioning**, which is not favored in Western prisons because of its association, in extreme forms, with **brainwashing**. Jessica Mitford, in her chapter "Clockwork Orange" (referring to the title of the Anthony Burgess novel and Stanley Kubrick film about "resocializing criminals") in *Kind and Usual Punishment: The Prison Business* (1974), describes the control techniques being applied in some American prisons at the time:
    1. **Sensory deprivation**. Confinement in sterile "adjustment centers" with no activities for long periods of time.
    2. **Stress assessment**. Complete lack of privacy, often combined with sleep deprivation, to promote conflict and see how much the prisoner can stand without losing his temper.
    3. **Chemotherapy**. The use of drugs to control behavior.
    4. **Aversion therapy**. The use of physical pain and fear, through such techniques as electric shock and drug injection, to modify behavior.
    5. **Neurosurgery**. Brain surgery to reduce aggressiveness.

Aversive conditioning programs were generally ruled unconstitutional in the courts by around the mid-1970s and went out of fashion with the demise of the rehabilitation model. Some programs of this sort, using drugs and negative stimuli, have been resurrected in recent years for the specific treatment of sex offenders, but not for the general treatment of violent or habitual criminals.

Of the various types of social therapies, **group therapy** is the most commonly employed in the most varying forms. It begins with a group--perhaps eight to 12 persons--and a facilitator trained to guide group discussions. The members of the group can be crime-specific or diverse--drug abusers, for instance, or residents of a particular dormitory. Group therapy is recommended in corrections for several reasons. It is more cost-effective than individual treatment. The therapist does not have to be trained to the doctoral level. It is very flexible in its content and adaptable to the environment. It also benefits from peer feedback: convicts like to think that they are better judges of the true character of other criminals than non-criminals may be.

Three other forms of social therapy are prevalent:
1. **Transactional analysis**. Eric Berne and his colleagues developed a form of therapy based upon communication patterns, particularly our self-images as we think others see us, and life scripts, why people are consistent in their behavior, especially in repeating the same mistakes.
2. **Reality therapy**. Based on the work of William Glasser in California, reality therapy focuses on behavior rather than motivation: "What are you doing," not "Why are you doing that?" It emphasizes three Rs important to good conduct, in prison or on the street: reality, responsibility, and right and wrong.
3. **Therapeutic communities**. The therapeutic community is a treatment group sharing a common affliction and living together in a close-knit, family-like environment somewhat insulated from outside influences. According to Douglas Lipton the America model uses a "**community of peers**'" and role models as change agents rather than professional clinicians and trained correctional officers, and it is less democratic in operation and more hierarchical in structure. The U.S. model also is less psychiatric (and less medical) in origin, emerging from a recovered client self-help background. American TCs generally subscribe to a self-help, social learning model. The American TC is particularly associated with substance-abusing offenders.

## Questions about Rehabilitation

In the 1970s, criticisms of the prison environment and the inferiority of prison programs led to an emphasis on **reintegration** as an alternative to prison-based rehabilitation. Reintegration was community-based; it kept offenders out of prison, avoiding the negative effects of imprisonment, and it allowed criminals to take part in a more diverse set of programs (at least in theory) than what they would find in prison. But then researchers began to note that the community-based interventions were no more effective and sometimes even less effective (because they tended to be focused on younger offenders who have higher recidivism rates) than imprisonment. And then finally the crime control decade of the 1980s arrived, and the shift from non-secure alternatives to secure custody began in earnest. Both rehabilitation and reintegration went out of fashion.

Scholars continued to study rehabilitation, however, focusing not so much on broad policy initiatives but on specific features of individual programs that appeared to be successful. Paul Gendreau, a Canadian psychology professor, has long been among the adherents of practical rehabilitation programs. Gendreau has emphasized the positive influence of directing intensive services to high-risk offenders, the matching of offenders and intervention, the importance of disrupting criminal networks and providing relapse prevention, and the value of advocacy and brokerage services. He has identified **principles of ineffective intervention**, which include traditional psychodynamic therapies, non-directive relationship-oriented therapies, radical non-intervention (leaving the criminal alone), traditional medical model approaches, the use of intensive services with low-risk offenders, and clinical approaches that encourage externalizing blame to parents and others, venting anger or ignoring the impact of their crimes on the victims.

Gendreau has also been among the critics of the so-called **punishing smarter** strategies, which he says are no more effective long-term than traditional interventions. These new or faddish interventions include boot camps, electronic monitoring, longer periods of incarceration, urinalysis, humiliation, and shock incarceration. Many of these options are politically popular and more likely to receive scarce state or federal funding, but Gendreau's findings, supported by other research, illustrate the frustration of many observers that programs receive political support more for the appearance than the reality of working.

Kaye McLaren, policy and research analyst with the New Zealand Department of Justice, has identified several

**principles of effectiveness** associated with successful correctional interventions--a social learning approach; clear, consistent rules and sanctions; practical problem-solving skills; use of ex-offenders as positive role models; staff focus on strengthening pro-social and noncriminal behavior rather than stopping antisocial and criminal behavior; use of offender groups to reinforce pro-social and noncriminal behavior; emphasis on relapse prevention and self-efficacy; and matching individual offenders with specific interventions. She emphasizes that in putting offenders in programs it is a case of one size doesn't fit all. She recommended three approaches to offender placement: "Put offenders in programs that address problems they actually have, put offenders with more severe problems into more intensive programs, and choose programs that fit what's known about the most effective way to impact a given problem."

## The "New" Rehabilitation

How have prison rehabilitation programs changed over the past generation, from the rejection of the rehabilitation ideology during the 1970s to the resurrection of rehabilitation in the first years of the twenty-first century? We want to briefly touch on five major features of the "new" rehabilitation--substance abuse treatment, thinking patterns, faith-based programs, work, and the whole person concept.

We have already looked at the alcohol and drug abuse histories of men and women prisoners, and the nature of programs used to treat them in prison, in chapters nine and eleven. Many states are taking a close look at expanding substance abuse treatment within prisons, acknowledging that untreated substance abusers have very high failure rates when discharged from prison; generic treatment programs have fared little better.

Delaware uses a substance abuse rehabilitation program that follows three stages. In the first, about a hundred prisoners are pulled together into a separate housing unit away from the rest of the inmate population. Once there, they undergo three kinds of therapy--behavioral, cognitive, and emotional. Six months of work release at an outreach center follow. In phase three, participants are involved in a six-month aftercare program. The recidivism rate for these inmates (measured by arrests within 18 months) was less than half that of general population releasees. Many other states are considering intensive substance abuse treatment as ultimately being cheaper than the effects of crimes committed by those not receiving treatment.

Therapy in prison has traditionally been **nondirective** in nature; that is, it deals with people's problems and feelings and sense of self-worth. Recent therapy has been more cognitive in nature. It tends to focus more on how people think, and how thinking controls behavior or actions. One influential theory is Lawrence Kohlberg's **moral development** theory. Kohlberg believed that people progress in their moral reasoning--in their bases for ethical behavior--through a series of six stages. Using what Kohlberg called the **moral discussion approach**, prisoners are confronted with complicated moral situations that they have to discuss in class with other prisoners. The objectives is to make them think about how their conduct affects other people.

Another contemporary treatment approach is **cognitive therapy**, which assumes that faulty thought processes and beliefs create problem behaviors and emotions. The most influential cognitive therapists in programs treating criminals are Albert Ellis and Aaron Beck. Ellis's **rational-emotive behavior therapy** follows what he calls an A-B-C approach to defeating negative or irrational beliefs: (A) an activating event, usually a negative stimulus of some kind; (B) the belief system, which is the person's interpretation of the experience; (C) the emotional consequence, which leads to problem behaviors. Beck's approach is even more geared toward real experiences, as opposed to just talk or self-expression, to help people avoid the behaviors that come from their destructive cognitions. His approach is often called **cognitive-behavior therapy**.

**SMART Recovery** has attracted attention in its application of cognitive therapy to prisoners. This non-profit program is often cited as an alternative to the religion-based twelve-step approaches of Alcoholics Anonymous and Narcotics Anonymous, both prison self-help staples. SMART (which stands for Self Management and Recovery Training) defines its purpose as supporting individuals abstaining from addictive behavior by teaching how to change self-defeating thinking, emotions, and actions, and to work toward long-term satisfactions and quality of life. SMART is more structured, directive, and technological than AA; it emphasizes **empowerment** and problem-solving where AA emphasizes powerlessness and the need to believe in a higher power.

At the opposite pole from SMART's admittedly secular approach are the **faith-based** programs developing in several states, most notably Texas. In 1997, the **InnerChange Freedom Initiative (IFI)** was given about half the beds of the Texas's Carol Vance prison to operate as a Christian prison. The concept is to operate a prison as a Christian community. The inmates are volunteers, but not everyone agrees that this is a good concept, especially because public tax dollars are being used to fund the operation. Prison ministries are more active in working inside prisons than they have been since the early days of the penitentiary, and more states are looking at setting up faith-based housing units--looking at them as another type of therapeutic community.

When prisoners get out, no matter what their thinking patterns or religious beliefs, the first thing they need is a job. When money runs out, and friends and relatives get tired of footing the bill, ex-convicts find it easier to reenter the underground economy--crime. Prisons do little to improve employability or work skills of inmates. As Chief Justice of the U.S. Supreme Court in the 1980s, Warren Burger proposed that prison be turned into **"factories with fences"** providing prisoners with education, vocational training, and work skills necessary to make a living after release. Since then the percentage of prisoners working has actually declined, overwhelmed by the tremendous increase in prison population.

Prison labor is not a popular subject–opposed by labor unions who see job losses, prison activists who see exploitation, and victims's rights groups and politicians who raise public safety issues. The principal current means for expanding employment opportunities for prisoners is the **Prison Industry Enhancement (PIE) Certification Program** that was created by the Justice System Improvement Act of 1979. The program is designed to place inmates in a realistic work environment, pay them the prevailing local wage for similar work, and enable them to acquire marketable skills to increase their potential for successful rehabilitation and meaningful employment on release. PIE programs are small, employing a total of 4,650 workers in 2003.

If real work is out, prisons can still teach **workability skills** relating to seeking and finding employment after release. These skills are often taught as part of a **whole person approach** intended to address multiple needs in a prisoner approaching release. The concept is to make the last six months or so before release a period of intensive programming, aiming for the type of transformation that would bring about habilitation. The whole person approach attempts to remake the criminal by attacking his or her problems on several fronts simultaneously. Louisiana tried this approach with **Project Metamorphosis** from 1997 to 2001. The goal was to reduce recidivism by increasing vocational, cognitive, and employability skills and post-release employment and wage rates. Recidivism rates were lower than for general population inmates, but when federal funding expired the program was discontinued.

Missouri has conducted a similar but more enduring whole person program called **Parallel Universe**. Its premise is that life inside prison would resemble life outside prison, so inmates can acquire the values, habits, and skills needed to function as productive, law-abiding citizens upon their release. As a corrections-based reentry program, Parallel Universe inmates work, go to class, participate in treatment, and make their own decisions to a degree not common in prison. Reconviction rates have dropped sharply since the program was established, and it is now required for all inmates leaving prison in Missouri.

## The Latest on Recidivism

With or without rehabilitation, recidivism remains (or should remain) an important component of crime control policy. Do we know more about recidivism than when Martin wrote "nothing works" three decades ago? The most recent national survey on recidivism is Patrick Langan and David Levin's "Recidivism of Prisoners Released in 1994," a Bureau of Justice Statistics Special Report published in June 2002. Tracking 272,000 felons released from prison in 1994, Langan and Levin used four measures to calculate recidivism rates:

    1. Rearrest. An estimated 67.5 percent of the released prisoners were rearrested for a new crime (either a felony or serious misdemeanor) within three years.

    2. Reconviction. A total of 46.9 percent were reconvicted in state or federal court for a new crime (felony or misdemeanor).

    3. Resentence. Over a quarter--25.4 percent--were back in prison as a result of another prison sentence.

    4. Return to prison with or without a new sentence. A total of 51.8 percent were back in prison because of a new sentence or because of a violation of conditional release--such as by rearrest, failing a drug test, or absconding on parole. More were returned to prison for release violations--26.4 percent--than for new sentences.

For each of the four measures, men had recidivism rates about 10 percentage points higher than women, blacks had recidivism rates five to 10 points higher than whites, and non-Hispanics had rates about five points higher than Hispanics. Recidivism rates vary sharply with age. Over 80 percent of those under age 18 were rearrested, compared to 45.3 percent of those 45 or older. Other studies have shown that this steady decline continues from middle age into old age, making age at release the single best predictor of recidivism.

The crime is important also. Released property offenders had the highest recidivism rates. An estimated 73.8 percent of property offenders were rearrested within three years, compared to 66.7 percent of drug offenders, 62.2 percent of public order offenders, and 61.7 percent of violent offenders. Rapists and other sexual assault felons were considered **criminal specialists**, meaning that they were statistically more likely to be rearrested for the same offense, but murderers, public order offenders, and drug offenders were much less specialized.

Most felony prisoners are not one-time offenders. The 272,000 released prisoners had an average of 15 arrests each before their current prison term, and 2.75 arrests each on average within three years of release. Prisoners with 15 or more prior arrests had an 82.1 percent rearrest rate, while those with just one prior arrest (who are very likely to be violent offenders) had a 40.6 rearrest rate. Those who had been in prison two or more times had a rearrest rate about 10 points higher (73.5 percent to 63.8 percent) than those serving their first prison sentence. Langan and Levin reported a clear pattern--the longer the prior record, the greater the likelihood that the recidivating prisoner will commit another crime soon after release.

Louisiana prison journalist Douglas Dennis has pointed out that the higher recidivism rates of the 1990s were due to tougher supervision of parolees on the street and higher rates of return after new arrests and technical violations. He also observed that murderers and sex criminals are the best release risks, and that failure often comes early--the ex-con's first year out is the toughest, and most critical to success, with two-thirds of all arrests occurring during the first year. Citing the released prisoners disadvantages and social stigma, Dennis suggests that most people view an ex-con as toxic waste--and want nothing to do with him or her.

The state of Florida completed its own detailed study of recidivism based on 18 different factors relating to the prisoner's demographics, criminal history, and record in custody (but not rehabilitation programs completed). The study found that for both males and females, the two most influential factors on both reoffending and reimprisonment are prior recidivism and age at release. Among the factors that raised both reoffending and reimprisonment rates for males and females were more disciplinary reports, prior recidivism, burglary as the crime of conviction, more property crime convictions, and more drug crime convictions. Among the factors that lowered both reoffending and reimprisonment for males and females were older age at release, Hispanic ethnicity, lower custody level, more time in prison, higher educational level, homicide as the worst crime, and a sex offense or lewdness as the worst crime. The study did not evaluate the effects of prison rehabilitation programs or other post-release circumstances often emphasized today--substance abuse history, family support, and financial assistance.

# Self Test

## Multiple Choice

1. An inmate participating in the PIE program would basically be:
   a. taking a baking class
   b. a trusty working in the kitchen
   c. doing real work in prison for a private employer
   d. taking part in a college education furlough program
   e. undergoing psychological evaluation

2. SMART Recovery is a cognitive therapy program that has developed as an alternative to:
   a. neurosurgery
   b. brainwashing
   c. administrative segregation
   d. Alcoholics Anonymous
   e. therapeutic community

3. The researcher most closely associated with the "nothing works" idea in rehabilitation is:
   a. Carl Rogers
   b. Robert Martinson
   c. Donald Clemmer
   d. Albert Einstein
   e. Edwin Sutherland

4. Louisiana's Project Metamorphosis is an example of a program taking a _____ approach.
   a. nondirective
   b. moral imperative
   c. crimongenic
   d. stress assessment
   e. whole person

5. Which one of these groups of released offenders is likely to have the lowest recidivism rate?
   a. murderers
   b. car thieves
   c. burglars
   d. drug dealers
   e. check forgers

6. The goal of rehabilitation is to bring about the end of criminal behavior, which is called:
   a. pacification
   b. reconfiguration
   c. desistance
   d. obsolescence
   e. ambivalence

7. Former Supreme Court Chief Justice Warren Burger proposed that prisons be turned into:
   a. hell on earth
   b. out patient clinics
   c. higher education centers
   d. treatment labs
   e. factories with fences

8. Which one of the following is least likely to happen to a convicted felon released from prison?
   a. being questioned by the police
   b. reconviction
   c. reimprisonment for a new felony
   d. rearrest
   e. reimprisonment

9. If you were a child molester and I showed you pictures of half-naked children while giving you a series of severe electrical shocks, you would be getting a form of treatment known as _____ therapy.
   a. pleasure
   b. aversion
   c. holistic
   d. repulsion
   e. brain wave

10. The institution credited as the birthplace of practices that would eventually grow into rehabilitation was:
    a. the jail
    b. the women's prison
    c. the reformatory
    d. the prison farm
    e. the work release center

**True or False**

_____ 11. Recidivism rates are highest within the first year after the felon's release from prison.

_____ 12. More prisoners are enrolled in vocational training than college courses.

_____ 13. Norval Morris argued that forced rehabilitation would work if the prison were absolutely ruthless in its punishment of failure.

_____ 14. When the rehabilitation era ended, most prisons immediately abandoned the programs they had been offering.

_____ 15. If "treatment effects" are the objective results, then "policy effects" are the more subjective results.

_____ 16. Completing the GED has been shown to greatly reduce recidivism rates.

_____ 17. Faith-based programs that group inmates in special housing have been struck down by the courts as violating the separation of church and state.

_____ 18. Sensory deprivation would be commonplace in supermax housing units.

_____ 19. Female prisoners generally have access to more diverse job training than male prisoners do.

_____ 20. Most released felons who return to prison within three years are sent back for parole violations rather than for new sentences.

## Fill In the Blanks

21. Joycelyn Pollock suggests that the prison experience is a kind of _____ in which it is difficult to relate causes to results.

22. Austin MacCormick is most particularly associated with _____ programs in prison.

23. The most individualized and comprehensive form of rehabilitation was known as the _____ model.

24. The _____ era is said to have dominated some prison systems from the mid-1950s to the mid-1970s.

25. Prison is often said to have a _____ environment that causes more crimes than it prevents.

26. The National Research Council defined rehabilitation as a(n) _____ to reduce criminal activity.

27. The most prevalent form of social therapy in prison is _____.

28. Sigmund Freud's individualized form of therapy known as _____ is not much used in the contemporary prison setting.

29. The American form of therapeutic community emphasizes the influence of a(n) _____ to reinforce conforming behavior.

30. The approach known as _____ therapy assumes that faulty thought processes and bad decisions create criminal behavior.

## Discussion

31. For what reasons did rehabilitation go into decline in the late 1970s?

32. What are the traditional forms of rehabilitation that have been offered in prison?

33. Discuss the methods that might be used if you were attempting to brainwash prisoners.

34. What are the different ways to measure recidivism? Which do you think is most correct?

35. Describe the important new options in rehabilitation that have developed within the past decade or so. Which do you believe is most promising?

36. If we have moved from "nothing works" to "something works," what is it that we now think works in rehabilitation programming?

37. In terms of background, describe the prisoner most likely to succeed upon release from custody--and the prisoner most likely to fail.

CHAPTER FOURTEEN

# Parole and Release from Prison

This chapter considers parole and other ways to leave prison and reenter society. Parole was not a part of the original penitentiary, but over time it became a universal practice. The rise and fall of parole have had major effects on imprisonment over the past half century. After reading this chapter, you should be familiar with:

1. Parole from the inmate's perspective.
2. Parole and other options to get out of prison.
3. The development of parole as a practice.
4. The "old" parole board and process.
5. Parole and mandatory release today.
6. The parole officer and parole work.
7. Life as a parolee today.
8. The effectiveness of parole.

## Key Terms

executive clemency
pardon board
pardon
amnesty
reprieve
commutation
emergency release
shock probation
medical parole
discretionary parole
conditional release
indeterminate sentence
good-time release
mandatory parole
truth-in-sentencing standard
expiration of sentence
supervised release
indentured servitude
Alexander Maconochie
Norfolk Island
mark system
ticket of leave
English Penal Servitude Act
Sir Walter Crofton
Irish System
parole
good time
conditional pardon
Zebulon Brockway
Elmira Reformatory
parole board
marked men
parole hearing
parole plan
flopped
new parole
Board of Prison Terms

U.S. Sentencing Commission
risk assessment
parole officer
volunteer parole officer
case management
caseload
casework
law enforcement
social work
aftercare
parole conditions
standard parole conditions
special parole conditions
drug testing
law violation
technical violation
detainer
discretion
new penology
danger management
waste management
risk management
parole revocation
*Morrissey v. Brewer*
due process hearing
revocation hearing
absconder
revolving door
Proposition 36
reinvent parole
Project RIO
prisoner reintegration
reentry courts
personal responsibility model
neighborhood parole
offender reentry model

## On Parole

Jean Sanders was one of the more than 600,000 men and women released from prison in 2001, about a quarter of them on discretionary parole, meaning they were released through the authority of a parole board. Sanders had a 12-page criminal history in New York--including four prison terms--as a drug dealer, car thief, and addict. But this time he was determined to stay out of prison. As profiled by Amanda Ripley for a *Time* cover story, Sanders had a tough year on the street. Living in a homeless shelter because his family did not trust him, he could not find steady work. He smoked crack and was put back in drug treatment after a brief jail stay. After the 9/11 attacks on the World Trade Center, he was depressed and almost gave up; then he got a job as a gas station attendant, and his prospects began to look up. By New Years Day 2002, he had been out of prison for a year, his longest stretch of freedom in 15 years. Half of all parolees are back in prison within three years after release; Jean Sanders had barely made it through the highest-risk period without joining them. How would he deal with the risks of the next two years on parole?

## Leaving Prison

About 3,200 inmates died in prison in 2001 (most of them of natural causes) and about twice that number "escaped," the great majority as walkaways from work release or furlough programs who are soon recaptured. But most prisoners do not die or escape to leave prison; most earn their release by lawful means.

For a long time under common law, one common way out of prison was through the king's pardon, which today is a form of **executive clemency**. Clemency authority now resides in the offices of the President of the United States and the governors of the states. Through a legally defined process, often involving preliminary screening done by political appointees serving as a **pardon board**, an executive may intervene in the legal process in several different ways:

    1. **Pardon**, originally used to set aside wrongful convictions; it is now more often used to restore lost civil disqualifications, such as the right to vote or own firearms.

    2. **Amnesty**, which is a blanket freedom from criminal prosecution given to a group of offenders, such as those Americans who fled the country to avoid serving in the military during the Vietnam War.

    3. **Reprieve**, which is a stay, usually short term, from the imposition of a sentence.

    4. **Commutation**, which is the shortening of a sentence by executive order. Commutations remain important to sentenced offenders serving life sentences and other very long prison terms. A commutation of sentence can be to time served or it can restore parole eligibility--in either case it is an early out.

In the present era of "get tough on criminals," many governors are reluctant to use their clemency powers for fear of being called soft on crime. This executive intervention from outside the judicial system, once so common, has become rare. No politician wants to be haunted later by his opponent's criticism that he was too nice to criminals.

A few prisoners do benefit from court intervention to set aside convictions. Sometimes the state or federal court during the appeal or in post-conviction proceedings will simply overturn the conviction and order the offender discharged. More often, the offender is sent back for a new trial. If the criminal has already done a lot of time, or if the retrial case against him is weak, the prosecutor may elect to discharge him without a trial, or allow him to plead to a charge for time served, which results in his release from custody.

When severe prison overcrowding was a commonplace problem in the 1990s, prisoners in several states benefitted from so-called **emergency release** provisions adopted by state legislatures. In Texas, for example, when prison occupancy rates climbed above 95 percent, officials had the authority to provide early parole to inmates approaching their release dates. As prison populations have leveled off the past few years and new prison construction caught up with the need for beds, the use of this measure--which rates about the same popularity as executive clemency--has declined sharply.

Several thousand offenders serving **shock probation** terms will be released from prison to probation, under the authority of a judge rather than a parole board, after serving a short prison term, typically in the range of three to six months. This is one of the practices that has developed within the past three or four decades to make probation tougher. Only about nine states in the Midwest and South, led by Indiana with 3,000-plus inmates, use this practice for more than 1,000 prisoners a year.

Some unlucky prisoners are released at the end of one sentence only to be immediately picked up by authorities from another jurisdiction--state or federal--and transferred to another institution to serve another prison term. Defendants convicted of crimes in more than one jurisdiction are placed under detainer if the new jurisdiction wants them when they get done with the present sentence. This prevents them from being discharged from custody; detainers are also used to keep probation and parole violators in jail until a revocation hearing is held.

Another small group of unlucky prisoners qualify for release each year on what is called **medical parole**, or in some states a medical pardon. These are generally terminally ill prisoners--verified as such by medical staff--who are released to go home because they are about to die or because they are suffering from severe, debilitating illnesses that make them a minimal criminal threat.

All of the release options considered so far amount to no more than about 10 to 15 percent of the total releases in a given year. The three most prevalent forms of release--discretionary parole, mandatory parole, and expiration of sentence--account for the balance, approximately 85 to 90 percent of all discharges from prison annually.

**Discretionary parole** occurs through the action of a parole board. A prisoner becomes eligible for parole review after serving a specified portion of his or her sentence. If the board grants parole, the prisoner is discharged on **conditional release** to serve the remainder of the sentence in the community under supervision. Into the 1970s, discretionary parole was by far the most common means of leaving prison, with more than 70 percent of all prison releases each year occurring through parole board action. But reaction against the **indeterminate sentence**, which left it up to parole authorities to determine how long the prisoner served, led to the abolition of discretionary parole in 16 states by the year 2000, and restrictions on parole eligibility for certain violent and sex offenders in numerous other states.

The decline of the indeterminate sentence has seen the rise of the determinate sentence. In place of the parole board is a technician sitting with a calculator in a records office, tabulating **good time release** or what has come to be called **mandatory parole**, or mandatory release. This release date involves a simple mathematical computation--full term less good time credits earned equals release date. The prisoner is still on conditional release, and he or she can be returned to prison to serve more of the sentence if parole is revoked.

Supervision of mandatory parolees varies widely from state to state--from the same level of supervision as other parolees, to lower supervision, to no supervision at all. On either discretionary parole or mandatory parole, the former prisoner is still serving the sentence until the sentence expires. Good-time standards vary by crime, by class of offender (which in prison terminology refers to how many prior felonies someone has, not socioeconomics), and by state; by the year 2000, 30 states and the federal government had adopted the federal **truth-in-sentencing standard** of 85 percent for serious violent felonies. This standard requires the criminal to serve 85 perce. of the sentence to reach the mandatory parole date. A criminal serving 10 years for robbery who kept all of his good-time credits would earn his release after eight-and-a-half years.

The third common release option is **expiration of sentence**. This would apply to prisoners who are ineligible for good time or who lose their good time credits and serve their full term--every day of it. This was the original plan of imprisonment but it eventually became uncommon; now changing laws have again made this exit more common--nationwide almost as common now as discretionary parole. A criminal whose sentence has expired is not under supervision and has no conditions to abide by, unless he happens to be in the category of federal criminals sentenced to **supervised release**. In the federal courts, a prisoner is given a prison sentence and a good-time release date (all federal prisoners since 1987 have been under the 85 percent good-time rule); he or she is also given a specified length of time, such as 12 months or 18 months, of supervised release after discharge from custody. This is equivalent to the period of mandatory parole supervision in the states.

Into the early 1980s, most prisoners were released on discretionary parole. Twenty years later, the greatest number of prisoners were being released on mandatory parole at the good-time dates, and an increasing number of prisoners were being held to expiration of sentence. The big change was the sharp decline in the number of inmates granted discretionary parole; indeed, in the one-third of the states that had eliminated parole by the year 2000, the numbers had been reduced to a veritable dribble in comparison to 20 or 30 years earlier. Parole had undergone a sudden fall from prominence to disfavor.

151

## The Origins of Parole

Parole was so prominent in the rehabilitation era that many corrections officials and the great majority of prisoners probably assumed it had always been around, working in the past pretty much as it did in present day. In fact, parole in America was only about a century old in the 1970s, having been officially created by a New York statute in 1876. Parole and its delivery mechanism, the indeterminate sentence, were first put into practice at Zebulon Brockway's new Elmira Reformatory in July 1876. It antecedents came from the British prison system beginning with **indentured servitude**, which was practiced extensively in English courts of the 1600s and 1700s. The labor of convicted felons and debtors was contracted to landowners and businessmen in the American colonies for periods of servitude, typically seven to fourteen years.

The work of **Alexander Maconochie**, the former British naval officer who in 1840 became superintendent of the **Norfolk Island** penal colony east of Australia, was particularly influential in laying the philosophical foundation for parole. Maconochie's basic concept was that punishment should be by "task, not time." He developed the **mark system**, based on credits earned for hard work and good behavior, to replace the existing system of punishment by time served. Prisoners would buy their way out of custody and back to the Australian mainland with the marks they earned, passing through a series of stages--from solitary confinement to several levels of individual labor to group labor to discharge from custody through a **ticket of leave**. Maconochie's reforms were not popular with hardliners. He was recalled to England after three years and his methods were abandoned.

After the British parliament passed the **English Penal Servitude Act** in 1853, transportation to Australia was restricted, and prisons began to become overcrowded, leading to early release of inmates and an apparent increase in the crime rate. Under the direction of **Sir Walter Crofton**, the Irish prison system took a different approach incorporating Maconochie's principles. Crofton used a four-stage prison management system. The prisoner moved from solitary confinement to release on a ticket of leave by earning marks. Police were given the responsibility of supervising parolees, often delegating supervision to volunteer friends who stayed close to the criminal after release from custody.

The orderly progression of Crofton's **Irish System** was reported to have a greater crime reduction effect than England's unstructured and unsupervised ticket of leave distribution system, and it attracted many supporters in Europe and America. Americans had been talking about the practice of **parole** since Dr. Samuel Gridley Howe, a prison activist and ardent abolitionist of the day, began using the term in Boston in the 1840s. He based it on a French practice, *parole d'honneur*, or word of honor, a method of release from custody similar to release on recognizance today.

Two other practices in American prisons were also important antecedents of parole. The first, **good time**, was approved by legislative act in New York in 1817. Its purpose was the same as good time today: The criminal's sentence was shortened as a reward for good behavior in custody. Good time was generally adopted as an administrative control device providing an incentive for good conduct in prison in other state prisons during the remainder of the 1800s. The second practice was the **conditional pardon**, which was in use in a number of states in the 1800s. In this era, pardons were often used to set convicts free from imprisonment. The conditional pardon was a bit more complicated. It granted freedom but set conditions. The criminal could be returned to custody if he or she violated these conditions, much like what would happen on parole today.

**Zebulon Brockway** was an experienced prison manager when he came to New York to open the **Elmira Reformatory**. He wanted the criminals to be absolutely within his control, and the indeterminate sentence approved by the New York legislature in 1876 gave him authority to release any inmate after a year in custody. The men released, with a place to live and a job, were on parole for at least six months. They had to report on the first day of the month to a volunteer called a guardian and provide an account of their situation and conduct. Written reports, signed by the parolee's employer and guardian, had to be sent in to the reformatory each month.

Within 50 years, all states except three--Florida, Mississippi, and Virginia--had adopted parole in some form. In 1907, New York became the first state to adopt all the components of a modern parole system: the indeterminate sentence, a system for granting release, post-release supervision, and specific criteria for parole revocation. Parole was still considered a limited concept, applicable not to all prisoners but just to those on a reform track. Prisoners were divided into two classes--parolable and not, and the real convicts in the penitentiary were in the not group. Not until the 1930s would the majority of American convicts find that they were parole eligible, making the encounter with the parole board the crucial event in securing release from prison.

## "Old" Parole in Twentieth Century America

Parole was originally an ill-defined practice. All it meant was that the warden had the authority to turn some prisoners loose early. Someone was usually made responsible for the parolee--such as the local sheriff in Idaho and Louisiana--but no one was directly supervising the parolee in most states in the early years. Volunteers--as individuals and as a part of charitable organizations--were an important part of early parole, more important in most locales than full-time officers. In their early years, parole officers were more often housed in prisons and managed files, while the volunteers interacted face-to-face with the former prisoners in the community.

Old parole emphasized the authority of the prison warden, acting either alone or with the advice of other board members or prison officials, in selecting inmates to be released from prison early. Parole was decided within each prison for its own population, and inmates once paroled were responsible to the prison that released them--and to which they would be returned if revoked.

Over time, a gradual shift of responsibility took place; parole authority was transferred from the individual institution to an independent **parole board** within the department of corrections or another state agency, or reporting directly to the governor. Parole was seen as being closely linked to executive clemency under the governor's authority. Many states combined the two functions in one board that often had additional responsibilities for administering parole supervision, managing good time, and overseeing probation supervision as well. Texas created a combined Board of Pardons and Paroles in 1929 that still exists today; its dual functions were to recommend prisoners for parole to the governor and to make clemency recommendations as well.

As the responsibilities of these boards increased, two other expectations changed. Boards were expected to be less "political" and more professional in their approach, and their work should appear to be "scientific," as if they were following a methodology more precise than human intuition. They should be experts, making expert decisions. As the parole board gained decision making authority, the prison--which knew the inmate far better than the board did--lost any say in determining suitability for release. The professional parole board made its decisions based on two primary criteria--the contents of the inmate's file and the inmate's performance at the parole hearing.

The American Parole Association had adopted a "Declaration of Principles" in 1933 outlining the principles that would be used in determining the time at which a particular offender should be released from prison: "Has the institution accomplished all that it can for him; is the offender's state of mind and attitude toward his own difficulties and problems such that further residence will be harmful or beneficial; does a suitable environment await him on the outside; can the beneficial effect already accomplished be retained if he is held longer to allow a more suitable environment to be developed?" This put the parole board in the position of predicting the prisoner's behavior based on its interpretation of his state of mind, particularly whether he would be better off in prison or out.

New Jersey's parole system, which tied current criminological thought to institutional performance, was much admired in the 1930s. It used a system of classification, reclassification meetings every six months, transfer to the appropriate institution and training to prepare for release that was very individualized for its day. Parole decisions were made by a full-time board that worked closely with the classification committee (with strong medical and behavioral science representation) at each institution. When approved for release, the parolee was assigned to a full-time, professional parole officer in the community; different levels of supervision and special placements were possible. This system, which incorporated many aspects of the medical model that would be emphasized a generation later, was the most progressive of its day.

By the time of World War II, parole had spread across America and, though it ranged in practice from minimalist to fully-formed, it had become the most common means of release from prison. Prisoners were learning how to play the parole game, because it was the quickest way out of prison, but many of them hated it, for many different reasons, particularly the arbitrariness of the selection process and the element of supervision after release. Parolees recognized that they were the center of attention while on parole--that to the public and law enforcement authorities they were **marked men**. When a sensational crime was committed, the police always went after "the usual suspects," many of them parolees who would be questioned and released. If a parolee was the one responsible for a terrible crime, the whole parole system was attacked.

Convicts knew that the parole board, whether staffed by unpaid amateurs or by professional experts, held the key to their future. The **parole hearing** would typically involve a direct meeting with several members of the board. One of the parole board members was usually assigned the prisoner's file. He led the way in discussing the case, asking about the crime and the experience of imprisonment. "Why did you do this?" "What is your problem?" "How have you changed?" "What are your plans?" The board placed prime importance on the inmate's response to these questions, which made these few minutes really critical to the prisoner's hope of release--like being questioned by St. Peter to determine suitability to enter heaven.

In many states, to avoid emotional confrontations, the inmate was not informed of the board's decision at the end of the hearing. He would return to his cell and wait for the letter of formal notification. If it said "approved," it gave a release date, often contingent upon having both a place to live and a job--the **parole plan**, it was called. If it said "denied," that was all it said; sometimes it gave a date to apply again. Inmates called this being **flopped**. It meant try again later, though it did not provide guidance about what you should do differently next time. Get a program? Be more respectful? Or just lie more earnestly? You had a year to figure it out.

Most convicts would figure it out, or the board would figure they had done enough time and vote to let them go. By the 1960s, the prisoner who served his full term was becoming a rare bird. There were too many options to get out of prison early, and most prisoners found at least one of them, parole most frequently. Parole boards exercised general authority over virtually all inmates, and through the mid-1970s about three-quarters of all inmates discharged from prison each year left on discretionary parole. Then in the 1980s, rehabilitation went south and very nearly took parole with it.

## New Parole and Mandatory Release

The movement to abolish old parole began in the 1970s. It came without much warning. Suddenly it seemed that virtually everyone--the public, politicians, criminologists, convicts, prison officials--had terrible things to say about parole. The only people saying anything good were the people actually doing parole work, and their remarks often sounded defensive, like they were trying to justify their work and place in the system.

Maine was the first state to abolish parole in 1975. It was followed by California in 1976, Indiana in 1977, Illinois in 1978, and New Mexico in 1979. Over the next two decades they would be joined by a dozen other states and the federal government. The most notable feature of the **new parole** was that it no longer existed in a third of the states by the end of the century; in the remaining states, its form was much changed. The parole tide had flowed in strong at the beginning of the century, and at the end it had ebbed just as strongly.

Joan Petersilia has summarized the criticisms of indeterminate sentencing and parole as falling into three major categories--its ineffectiveness in reducing recidivism, its arbitrary and unjust nature, and the uncontrolled discretion in release decisions. Parole also had to confront the crime control politics of this era as well; whatever else it might do, parole let criminals out of prison early, and many of them returned to criminal behavior.

Release on parole in America began a major transformation in the late 1970s that continued through the remainder of the century. This transformation, focusing at this point on the role of the parole board, had four major legal and political causes:
1. The outright replacement of discretionary parole by mandatory parole in a third of the states.
2. Restrictions on the authority of the parole board to release offenders convicted of certain crimes, particularly violent crimes covered by truth-in-sentencing provisions.
3. Raised restrictions on eligibility, based on the proportion of the sentence served required for first review and the portion served by second-time or habitual offenders.
4. Political conservatism among appointed parole board members in most states.

In California, for example, what used to be the Adult Authority, with wide parole discretion, is now the **Board of Prison Terms** (BPT). Its once-broad discretionary release authority (subject to the governor's approval) is now restricted to lifers; all other criminals are released on mandatory parole at their good-time dates. At the federal level, the Comprehensive Crime Control Act of 1984 created the **U.S. Sentencing Commission**, which sets the sentencing guidelines judges use to fix sentences. The U.S. Parole Commission was abolished, and parole was phased out of the federal system in 1997. Parole has been replaced by supervised release, an added-on period of supervision when the federal prisoner is discharged at his 85 percent good-time discharge date.

Of the states that have not abolished parole, most have adopted truth-in-sentencing provisions applicable to violent crimes. To get parole or good-time release in these states, offenders must serve 85 percent of their sentences, the same standard used in the federal system. State adoption of this standard was tied to receiving federal funds for jail and prison construction and other anti-crime activities.

In the approximately 15 states that remain outside the "abolish parole" and "truth in sentencing" movements, other legal changes have changed eligibility dates and made some offenders serve more time before getting a hearing. Parole boards have amended their own rules about hearings and rehearings after denial. More than half the states allowing discretionary parole use some type of **risk assessment** instrument to assist in making parole decisions. These instruments, which quantify risk factors in the offender's background and predict the risk of recidivism, have been around since the 1930s, but they have been used more frequently of late--first, because they are more accurate than old "hunch" methods, and second, because they make the selection process appear to be more objective. The instruments used today generally quantify important variables such as criminal history, drug abuse history, unemployment, and so on; the higher the score, the greater the risk.

The composite result of these changes has been to make getting released on parole more difficult. The impact on imprisonment has not been as severe as some people anticipated. The average length of prison term actually served has increased by about five or six months over the past two decades, and the average length of time on parole has increased by about four months, meaning that a typical criminal would be under the control of the corrections system for almost a year longer than he would have been in the 1980s. Parole release options have been cut back and made less discretionary during this period of transformation; the same forces have affected the work of the field officers who make up the other part of the parole system.

## The Parole Officer and Parole Work

The parole board determines who will be released and when; the **parole officer** supervises the offender once he or she has been released from imprisonment. While discretionary parole release has been sharply curtailed over the past generation, parole supervision has been intensified, particularly in regard to its surveillance component. Just as new parole is very different from old parole, the work of the twenty-first century parole officer is much different from the work of the officer of a century ago or even 20 years ago.

Parole officers were originally tied to the institutions from which parolees were released. They managed the paper work and assisted prisoners with getting a job and a place to stay--and they set up the contacts with the **volunteer parole officers** who provided the direct assistance in the community. If the parolee failed, which in the early days meant getting arrested and put back in jail, or losing his job and source of income, then the parole officer oversaw his return to prison, which was carried out by law enforcement authorities. The parole officer's job for a long time was more **case management** than provision of direct services.

By the mid-1900s, the parole officer no longer worked for the prison; he worked for the parole board, and his job had become more focused on supervision of parolees. The key measure of workload was the **caseload**--the number of active files the officer was responsible for. The **casework** approach, borrowed from the social services, viewed the parolee as a client whom the parole officer was trying to assist with various social needs.

The literature of parole work often makes the contrast between the two functions of rehabilitation (or helping) and surveillance. Veteran parole officers used different terminology: They say **law enforcement** has replaced **social work**, and many of them do not approve of the trend. Marc Mauer of the Sentencing Project defines the traditional role as more of a balance--"half cop, half social worker." But the old timers are on the way out, replaced by a new wave of parole officers who never worked under the old models--when parole officers were more autonomous and less rule-oriented.

The parole officer of today is a state civil service employee. Parole is managed as a part of the state corrections bureaucracy in about 40 of the 50 states; the older model, in which the parole officer worked directly for the parole board, still holds in about 10 states. In about half the states, the same officer or agent is supervising both probationers--released under the authority of a local trial court judge--and parolees--released by the parole board or by the prison on good time. Probation is a mixed bag, felons and misdemeanants sometimes monitored by the same officer and sometimes by different officers depending on how governments organize these responsibilities. Probationers outnumber parolees about five to one in 2002 (almost 4,000,000 to 750,000), so if an officer is supervising both probationers and parolees, he or she is likely to have more probationers than parolees, and also to have other functions, such as presentence investigation reports, that accompany probation. Juvenile parole, correctly titled **aftercare**, is a separate function performed ordinarily by juvenile probation officers.

By 2000, the number of parole officers stood at about 7,000, while the number of combined probation/parole officers stood at over 18,000. Figuring caseloads is more complicated, because of the long-term trend to merge probation and parole caseloads in the same officer, but for parole alone the average for a regular caseload was about 73; for probation and parole combined, it was higher, about 94. With caseloads in the 70 to 100 range, a parole officer would see the parolees in his caseload perhaps twice a month--maybe once in the office and once on the street.

The movement toward stricter supervision has meant in part tighter enforcement of **parole conditions** the parolee must agree to follow when he leaves prison. Going back to the days of the Irish System, parolees have had such conditions to follow to remain free, but the conditions have tended to get longer and more complicated recently. The **standard parole conditions** would contain several key elements--obey the law, report as required, no guns or drugs, obtain approval before leaving the state or changing jobs or employment, pay required supervision fees. **Special parole conditions** are specific to the individual. Typical special conditions include abstaining from alcohol, participating in random drug and alcohol monitoring, avoiding contact with their victims or with children, refraining from associations with people involved in criminal activity, attending substance abuse treatment, attending mental health counseling, and abiding by a curfew. The most frequently imposed special condition nationwide is **drug testing**.

Parolees can be returned to prison in either of two common ways. One is an arrest or a conviction for a new crime; this is called a **law violation**--like an armed robber arrested for a string of new robberies. The other is for violating any of the other conditions of parole; this is called a **technical violation**--like failing to report or moving without permission. For either type of violation, you would be placed under a **detainer** (a legal order preventing you from being released) until a revocation hearing was held.

The enforcement of technical violations is up to the **discretion** of the parole officer--partly a matter of individual belief and choice, and partly guided by organizational policy and practice. A generation ago, when parolees were returned to prison, it was likely to be as a result of a criminal law violation. Today more parolees are returned as technical violators than as law violators; the majority of the 200,000-plus parolees sent back to prison each year are returned for not following the rules--particularly those dealing with drug use, maintaining contact with the PO, and employment--rather than for serious criminal behavior.

Joan Petersilia has pointed out that newly hired parole officers often embrace the "surveillance" rather than the "rehabilitation" model of parole, along with the quasipolicing role that parole has taken on in some locales. A veteran Illinois parole officer put it this way: "The philosophy of the parole unit has changed. Now they all have cars, guns, bullet-proof vests and badges." Parole officers used to try to help parolees succeed; now they look for ways to put them behind bars.

Malcolm Feeley and Jonathan Simon in 1992 defined what they call the **new penology** as the emerging strategy of corrections, including parole work. Their analysis suggests that corrections is dominated by a systems-analysis approach to the task they call **danger management**, which focuses on the old "dangerous class" of criminals who make up the urban underclass--a segment of the population abandoned to poverty and despair. Whereas the old parole officer focused on individual redemption and rehabilitation, with the goal of making the criminal "normal" enough to lead a productive life, the parole officer of the new penology sees not individuals but a class that cannot be helped. The goal of parole within the corrections system becomes that of "herding a specific population that cannot be disaggregated and transformed but only maintained--a kind of waste management function."

Jonathan Simon's social history of parole, *Poor Discipline: Parole and the Social Control of the Underclass, 1890-1990*, carries the concept of **waste management** a step farther. The "toxic waste" containment sites would be the underclass communities where those under the control of community corrections would be required to live. Parole officers and others in front-line penal jobs would not try to change people or relate to them as individuals; they would define their mission as managing risk and minimizing damage to the larger society.

Feeley and Simon present the new penology as an ideology, not as a set of procedures formally adopted to carry out public policy. It is clear, however, that parole management has adopted several important features of **risk management** in recent years, including greater use of statistical probabilities, detailed risk/needs assessments

156

of individual offenders, emphasizing documentation, records keeping, and data input into computerized databases, caseloads structured by perceived risk, using such designations as regular, intensive, electronic, and special, designation of targeted groups of offenders for concentrated supervision (which in recent years has emphasized sex offenders first and foremost) and use of formal monitoring criteria that can be counted and documented--urine tests, meetings attended, appointments kept, forms submitted on time.

The **parole revocation** process, like field supervision, has undergone considerable change from the old days. The old parole officer just went to the jail, picked the errant parolee up, and took him back to prison; or in the very old days just signed for the parolee when the local sheriff returned him to prison custody. Since 1972, parole revocation has been governed by the standards of **Morrissey v. Brewer**. The U.S. Supreme Court ruled in this case that Morrissey, a parolee from the Iowa State Penitentiary, was entitled to a **due process hearing** as part of revocation; the parolee was extended six basic due process rights--written notice, disclosure of evidence, opportunity to be heard in person, right to confront and cross-examine adverse witnesses, a "neutral and detached" hearing body, and a written statement by the factfinders of the reasons for their decision.

Many jurisdictions set up a two-stage revocation proceeding. A hearing officer, usually a senior parole officer or supervisor, holds a probable cause hearing to determine if the violation occurred. The parole board then holds the **revocation hearing**, at which it decides whether to revoke or reinstate parole.

Parole officers develop their own styles and management strategies for working with offenders, as numerous research studies indicate. Some are "by the book," some are laid back, some are more detailed manipulators, others are more remote. One parolee described the relationship between parolees and parole officers as "ranging from the difficult to the impossible." His explanation was that it would be difficult at best, because one figure was trying to impose control and the other was trying to resist it and live his own life without interference; it would be impossible when two personalities were in such conflict that they could not get along at all.

## Life as a Parolee

What are parolees like, and what kinds of lives do they live? Their basic situation is defined by two circumstances: They are convicted felons, and they have been in prison. On December 31, 2002, over three-quarters of a million (753,141) adult men and women were on parole, an all-time high. Five big parole systems--California, Texas, Pennsylvania, the federal system, and New York--dominate the statistics, containing 453,000 parolees, over 60 percent of the national total.

Regardless of race, ethnicity, or gender, parolees share the same problems upon release. A 1997 California report provided this background of the state's parolees--85 percent were chronic substance abusers; 10 percent were homeless, but this figure was higher in cities, as high as 30 to 50 percent in San Francisco and Los Angeles; 70 to 90 percent were unemployed; 50 percent were functionally illiterate, reading below a sixth grade level and unable to complete job forms or compete in the job market; and 18 percent had some sort of psychiatric problem.

When parole officers were asked to identify the most important aspect of reentry for improving parolees' chances for success, their top three choices were steady or continuous employment (34 percent), staying off drugs and alcohol (21 percent), and a support system--family, friends, or church (20 percent). For both men and women on parole, these are critical needs, for women needs complicated by two important variables: the stigma of being a "woman ex-con," with its connotation of being even lower than a man ex-con; and their children.

Patricia O'Brien's *Making It in the "Free World"* (2001) followed 18 women as they left prison and returned home. These women identified several key aspects to making the transition from prison--identifying sources of support prior to leaving prison; addressing issues of abuse and addiction; training for employment at living wages; and the positive support of other ex-inmates, helping professionals, and potential employers.

British criminologist Stephen Farrell has written about the relationship between the criminal and the parole officer in *Rethinking What Works with Offenders: Probation, Social Context and Desistance from Crime* (2002). Farrell suggests that the road to going straight is hardly straight at all. Offenders and officers disagree about the obstacles to be overcome and how to overcome them. In successful outcomes, they are overcome, but solutions imposed were more ad hoc rather than focused or sustained, and the important factors were generally outside the control of either party. Farrell wrote: "The two factors most favorably reported--by both probationers and offenders--were employment status and family formation. In the end, obstacles were generally, successfully overcome when probationers, rather than officers, initiated actions that led to improved employment and family situations." If family connections and economic support are most important to success on parole, we should keep in mind that most criminals released on parole have neither.

## The Effectiveness of Parole

Parole is still on shaky ground in the criminal justice system, and statistics on its effectiveness seem to support those arguing for abolition. From the early 1980s to the mid-1990s, the success rate of parole (discharges without revocation) declined from about 70 percent to about 45 percent, where it has remained since. About as many parolees are returned to prison as are successfully discharged, and about 10 percent at any given time are **absconders**, meaning they have disappeared and cannot be found.

Parolees are flooding the prison system. About a third of all admissions to prison in recent years are parole violators. John DiIulio, calling parole a **revolving door**, has pointed out that in 1991 nearly half of all state prisoners had committed their latest crimes while out on probation or parole. The general odds on a parolee being back in prison within three years of release are slightly better than 50/50.

A recent analysis of California's prisons calls its approach to ex-convicts one of "take-all-prisoners." Over half the inmates in California prisons are parole violators, most of them reincarcerated for technical violations. In 2001, about 125,000 new prisoners entered California prisons, compared to about 150,000 parole violators, most of them in and out (and often in and out again) within a few months. For many years, the great majority of California parolees were being returned to prison for failing drug tests, more than for all other reasons combined. This was part of the rationale for passage of **Proposition 36**, approved by voter referendum in November 2000; one provision calls for drug treatment for most routine parole violators in lieu of being returned to prison.

## Parole: Abolish or Reinvent?

The loss of faith in parole in the nineties brought about declining use of discretionary parole. As the prison system increased in size during the 1990s, the number of parolees remained virtually stable. Critics called for the abolition of parole, a trend was evident for several years. But after this time of soul searching, what emerged was a call to **reinvent parole** rather than abolishing it altogether.

Even parole's critics began to notice some good things about it. For one thing, rehabilitation--a more focused form of rehabilitation--is enjoying a comeback. Certain aspects of the new rehabilitation--drug treatment and job training--are highly compatible with parole. For the past two years, California has put many of its parole violators who would have been revoked for using drugs into intensive treatment. This could be done in prison, but most prison systems are in no way prepared to offer more than rudimentary relapse prevention programs that most convicts either disregard or cannot get into.

Texas established **Project RIO** (for Reintegration of Offenders) in 1985 to provide job placement services to parolees. By 1999, Project RIO had grown to 62 field offices providing pre-release employment assistance, assessment, job placement after release, and followup. Working with about 15,000 parolees a year, Project RIO had reduced recidivism rates at all levels of risk--high, average, and low--well below the rates for ex-offenders not participating in the project.

The role of the parole officer on the street is being reemphasized. Parole supervision is increasingly seen as being effective--whatever its limitations--in both of its primary aspects, helping and surveillance. The parole officer can be an important source of information and referral assistance for parolees; if the parole officer does not perform this role, who would? Likewise, conditional parole release requires someone to monitor compliance with provisions of release--work, residency, treatment, and so on.

As states increasingly grapple with the high cost of imprisonment, they look for options to keep more criminals in the community. Discretionary parole, which costs on average about $2,000 annually per offender as opposed to more than $20,000 to keep an offender in prison, is often cited as part of this movement.

Parole's supporters argue that parole's declining success rate--or, conversely, its sharply higher failure rate--is not the product of a "crime wave" among parolees. The high failure rate is due not to an increase in law violations by parolees, but to an increase in technical violations, which are discretionary with the parole officer. Nationwide (excluding California) about four in ten parolees will be returned to prison within three years after release. About half have new convictions; the other half are revoked for technical violations. There is no real evidence to suggest that today's parolees are any more mean-spirited or criminally active than those of 30 or 40 years ago; what is different is that surveillance has been stepped up, and enforcement of non-criminal violations is much more likely to result in revocation now than it was then. In other words, we have created the failure of parole by enforcing the rules as stringently as they could always have been applied.

Joan Petersilia's *When Prisoners Come Home: Parole and Prisoner Reentry* (2003) is a comprehensive argument for the reinvention of parole. It suggests that administrators should embrace the mission of **prisoner reintegration**, which would focus attention on better preparing the prisoner for release. Parole should be planned and monitored rather than being left up to haphazard occurrences.

**Reentry courts**, charged with overseeing a prisoner's reintegration into society, are already in use in a few places. The judge, already responsible for probation, would monitor parole also. The concept is to keep minor criminal violations and most technical violations at the local level--more support services, graduated sanctions, local jail time if needed--instead of immediately returning the parolee to prison.

Martin Horn has suggested that many parolees want to go straight and can make it "if they are literate, civil, and can stay off drugs, remain sober, and get a job." His proposal for reinventing parole is called the **personal responsibility** model. A released prisoner would be given the equivalent of a parole services voucher. For a fixed period of time--say, two years--he can use the voucher to seek education, job training, drug treatment, or other services from state-selected providers. If he wants to help himself, he can. If not, he's on his own.

Joan Petersilia describes **neighborhood parole** as a model of community engagement similar to community policing. Its key components include strengthening parole's linkages with law enforcement and the community, offering a "full-service" model of parole, and attempting to change the offenders' lives through personal, family, and neighborhood interventions.

The "offender in community" concept is equally important to Joseph Lehman and his colleagues in Washington, who have proposed an **offender reentry model** taking what they call a "victim-, family-, and harm-centered perspective" built upon three considerations--reparative (or restorative) justice, relationships between the offender and his family, and responsibility of the offender, the community, and the criminal justice system to carry out specific roles. This proposal would change parole at its core from "offender-centered"--punitive and rehabilitative--to "community-centered"--collaborative, reparative, and preventive. In many respects, this approach to offender reentry is the most ambitious, because it proposes to do the most *outside* the conventional criminal justice system. Given current attitudes on punishment, it may also be the most difficult to accomplish.

# Self Test

**Multiple Choice**

1. *Morrissey v. Brewer* is a landmark case most directly related to which subject?
   - a. parole revocation
   - b. use of parole guidelines
   - c. denial of parole
   - d. appointment of parole board members
   - e. forced community service by parolees

2. The federal system no longer uses parole but it substitutes a period of monitoring after discharge called:
   - a. surveillance
   - b. community control
   - c. guardianship
   - d. supervised release
   - e. extreme caution

3. Feeley and Simon's new penology defines the purpose of corrections as:
   - a. selective habilitation
   - b. social justice
   - c. danger management
   - d. spiritual renewal
   - e. crisis intervention

4. If a prisoner has been "flopped," what has happened to him?
   a. He has been convicted of a crime that makes him parole ineligible.
   b. While out on parole, he has been charged with a new felony offense.
   c. He has been denied parole.
   d. After he was approved for parole, the parole board moved back his release date.
   e. He has been changed from a good to a bad parole officer.

5. If you were sitting in a state prison cell serving a long term for armed robbery, which one of the following would have the most practical application to your efforts to get out of prison?
   a. pardon
   b. amnesty
   c. commutation
   d. reprieve
   e. indictment

6. In California, which has had a very high rate of returns to prison for parole violations, the largest number of parolees are returned for:
   a. committing new felonies
   b. refusing to work
   c. drug use
   d. leaving the state without permission
   e. failing to report to their parole officers

7. Alexander Maconochie used this method to determine when a convict had earned enough credits to be released from custody:
   a. hedonistic calculus
   b. mark system
   c. checks and balances
   d. intermediate sanction
   e. behavioral accounting

8. In the United States, parole was first used at the:
   a. Eastern State Penitentiary
   b. Sing Sing Prison
   c. Alderson Women's Prison
   d. Elmira Reformatory
   e. New York House of Refuge

9. The most important (and usually first on the list) of the standard parole conditions is:
   a. support your dependents
   b. abide by curfew
   c. avoid criminal associates
   d. avoid alcohol use
   e. obey the law

10. The term for Sir Walter Crofton's influential four-stage prison management model through which prisoners moved from solitary confinement to release on a ticket of leave was the:
    a. Australian System
    b. Crown Model
    c. Irish System
    d. Continental Plan
    e. Four-Stage System

**True or False**

_____ 11. The executive clemency power was traditionally exercised by the judge who imposed the sentence on the offender.

_____ 12. Parole was first used in Rome to apply to the status of foreigners who could not be trusted because they were not Roman citizens.

_____ 13. If you are a convict and the parole board declines to release you, you have to file a petition with the state supreme court to get that decision overturned.

_____ 14. In most states parole board members are appointed to office by the governor.

_____ 15. When a parolee is released from prison, he is still serving the sentence originally imposed on him.

_____ 16. Amnesty would usually be granted to a group or class of offenders who are all guilty of committing the same offense.

_____ 17. In the early years of parole in America, supervision of parolees was performed mostly by volunteers.

_____ 18. The states do not allow the same officer to supervise both parolees and probationers.

_____ 19. California has recently tried to reduce its stream of parolees flowing into prison by giving them drug treatment before they are revoked.

_____ 20. Most prisoners are released today at expiration of sentence, meaning that they are not subject to supervision after release.

**Fill In the Blanks**

21. Parole supervision is said to be a combination of the two functions of helping and _____.

22. The official with the most control over the makeup of parole boards in the states is the _____.

23. If the governor granted you a(n) _____, your criminal guilt would be wiped out and all your civil rights restored.

24. In 1817 New York became the first state to adopt the practice of _____, which was used to provide an incentive for good behavior in prison.

25. A parole violation that is not a criminal act is called a _____ violation.

26. Texas's Project RIO facilitates reentry by providing _____ services to parolees.

27. Discharge at your good-time release date is most commonly called _____.

28. Joan Petersilia has suggested that prison administrators, instead of just trying to keep prisoners safe and secure, ought to be more concerned with _____.

29. Ex-convicts on parole have referred to themselves as _____, meaning that they know others are watching them as criminal threats.

30. California's Board of Prison Terms, the replacement for the Adult Authority, now has parole authority only for those inmates who are _____.

**Discussion**

31. Distinguish among the main forms of executive clemency.

32. From the convict's point of view, criticize the parole board.

33. What concepts important to Maconochie and Crofton laid the philosophical foundation of parole?

34. What should the parole board pay attention to, when deciding whom to release?

35. Is there a functional conflict in the parole officer's mission?

36. Imagine that you are a parolee. What are the most difficult aspects of your life?

37. Your state is one of the ones that has abolished parole. What arguments can you make that it ought to be revived?

38. What are some of the specific suggestions grouped under the heading of reinventing parole?

# CHAPTER FIFTEEN

# Probation and Community Corrections

This chapter considers those forms of correctional supervision that take place outside secure confinement in jails and prisons. These alternatives, founded on probation and the suspended sentence, supervise more than twice as many offenders as are held in secure confinement. Probation is the principal option to imprisonment, but increasingly other intermediate sanctions are being used to fill the gap between prison and probation, which has led to the vast expansion of formal community corrections alternatives over the past 30 years. After reading this chapter, you should be familiar with:

    1. The history of the suspended sentence and probation in America.
    2. Probation work and administration.
    3. Probation as a sentence and a process.
    4. The profile of probation clients.
    5. Questions about the effectiveness of probation.
    6. The range of controls provided by intermediate sanctions.
    7. The options available under community corrections.
    8. The pros and cons of intermediate sanctions and community corrections.
    9. The future of probation and community corrections.

## Key Terms

bricks-and-mortar solution
selective incapacitation
chronic offenders
front-end solutions
suspended sentence
right of sanctuary
benefit of clergy
judicial reprieve
filing of cases
surcease
John Augustus
probation
probation officer
recognizance
juvenile probation
mentor
caseload
pre-sentence investigation report (PSI)
line probation officer
casework
risk/needs assessment
crisis management
intensive supervised probation (ISP)
surveillance
team approach
specialist
generalist
federal probation
principles of good supervision
felony probation
statutory restrictions
standard conditions
punitive conditions
treatment conditions
probation revocation

enhancement programs
desistance
tourniquet sentencing
risk management
restitution
restitution orders
day fine
punishment units
community service
community work orders
furlough
house arrest
home detention
electronic monitoring
electronic parole
halfway house
community residential treatment centers
day reporting center
day attendance center
drug court
shock probation
shock incarceration
boot camp
diversion
community-based diversion
police-based diversion
detoxification center
court-based diversion
pretrial intervention program
Federal Prisoner Rehabilitation Act
work release
community residential center
nonprofit organization
prerelease guidance center
partial incarceration

detainer
*Gagnon v. Scarpelli*
split sentence
credit for time served
absconded
real punishment
more resources
greater accountability
reinventing probation
Reinventing Probation Council
American Probation and Parole Association (APPA)
fortress probation
broken windows probation
proactive community supervision
what works model
reintegration era
intermediate sanctions
community corrections

least restrictive alternative
NIMBY
anything-but-prison theory
net widening
proportionality
sanction stacking
acceptable penal content
shame
community correctional center
halfway-out
halfway-in
reintegration center
integrated contract model
social justice model
accountability
community corrections acts
change agent
risk-control tools

## Corrections Outside Institutions

In the past 200 years, imprisonment has become the normal sanction for serious criminality. Before the 1800s, whatever punishment was applied to criminals, it was done *in* the community, not out of it. Criminals were beaten, executed, humiliated, fined, or otherwise punished while they remained in the community--indeed, often with the community observing the punishment. Even after prisons began to be used to punish serious criminals, the rates of imprisonment were low, well below 100 per 100,000 throughout the 1800s, in contrast to combined jail and prison rates averaging five to seven times that at the beginning of the 21st century. Criminals come from the community, and 96 of every 100 will eventually return there as they leave prison. One in every 20 adults--an estimated ten million people--have at least one felony conviction. With only 1,300,000 of them in prison at present, that means the other 87 percent are out there around you. Criminals remain a part of society, no matter where they are.

The question about community corrections--nonsecure supervision--thus becomes one of degree: how much of the criminal population should be managed in the community, and how much of it should be kept behind bars? There are vast differences in how the federal government and the states answer this question, several states incarcerating more than half of their felons, while on the low end other states lock up no more than 10 to 15 percent of serious criminals. Why would states differ so much in their use of imprisonment?

Since the 1980s, the United States has pursued a **bricks-and-mortar solution** to increasing correctional supervision, building new prisons and jails to increase the number of custodial beds from fewer than 500,000 to more than 2,000,000 in 20 years--this in an era when the crime rate has experienced an overall decline. Some criminologists and corrections experts define the proper role of the prison as **selective incapacitation**--protecting the public not equally from all criminals but from those high-rate and violent criminals who pose the greatest threat to public safety. These **chronic offenders** should be confined in prison, while other offenders could be supervised under less severe (and less expensive) sanctions in non-secure settings. What are the **front-end solutions**--the ways of dealing with criminals outside jail and prison--to America's punishment dilemma?

## The History of the Suspended Sentence and Probation

Probation, the chief alternative to imprisonment, is considered a modern sentence, but it has its roots in earlier forms of withholding punishment--what we often refer to as the **suspended sentence**. The **right of sanctuary**, under Hebrew law, set aside holy places for offenders to seek protection from secular laws; this practice continued under the Catholic Church. **Benefit of clergy** similarly allowed religious officials to avoid punishment in the criminal courts, which also allowed them to avoid the stigma of a criminal conviction and retain their church duties after a period of penance. English courts also recognized the practice of **judicial reprieve**, a delay in sentencing after conviction. Sometimes this delay became permanent, and the criminal never had a sentence imposed. American courts used a similar practice called **filing of cases** or recognizance. Judges sometimes withheld punishment for deserving offenders. The traditional European model of **surcease** withheld punishment if the offender committed no new crime during the period of suspension.

Imprisonment, in the Enlightenment argument, was supposed to eliminate these options and make punishment more certain to achieve deterrence. In the American courts of the early 1800s, the intent was that a serious or repeat criminal would spend time in prison. But almost at once court officials began to look for ways *not* to punish certain offenders they believed did not deserve imprisonment.

The origins of modern probation in America are often traced to the work of **John Augustus**, a Boston shoe manufacturer and civic reformer of the 1840s and 1850s. When Augustus took custody of a drunk coming up for sentencing in the Boston police court in August 1841, it began an 18-year career as a volunteer assisting the court. He would eventually be identified as the father of American probation. Augustus was the first person to use the term **probation**--which derives from the Latin term *probatio*, meaning "a period of proving or trial." He developed the ideas of the presentence investigation, supervision conditions, social casework, reports to the courts, and revocation of probation. Augustus would clean up his probationers and help them find a job and a place to live. He could not personally supervise more than a hundred criminals a year, so he recruited other volunteers as **probation officers** to work one-on-one with offenders for short periods of time.

Boston's judges, such as Judge Peter Oxenbridge Thacher, supported Augustus's efforts. Long before Augustus appeared in court, Judge Thacher had practiced **recognizance**, a form of release from custody--with or without the posting of money bail--sometimes permanently releasing offenders on recognizance never to return to court to have a sentence imposed. He did this informally at first, and then in 1836 Massachusetts passed a law formally recognizing recognizance. Massachusetts also passed the first probation statute--for juveniles--in 1878. Several other states followed, and the rise of the juvenile court in the early twentieth century promoted the continued expansion of formal probation services.

**Juvenile probation** spread more quickly than adult probation, but in both courts the concept of probation as the principal alternative to imprisonment gradually gained widespread legal acceptance. Probation began informally in many jurisdictions, often making use of volunteers who reported directly to local judges. The volunteers were often successful civic figures or religious activists who saw their role more as helping or serving as a **mentor** or father-figure than a paid supervisor with a checklist in hand. When probation became a formal governmental function, police were often asked to supervise probationers.

## Probation Administration and the Work of the Probation Officer

As it developed under the general authority of the trial judge, the means for carrying out probation varied widely in practice. No standard model of probation administration developed. It can be a state or local function, in the executive or judicial branches of government, supervising both felons and misdemeanants, adults and juveniles, and probationers and parolees mixed together--or these functions can be diversely separated.

Probation was originally very decentralized under the control of local courts, but over time the trend has been toward centralization of adult and juvenile probation at the state level--most often as a division of the state department of corrections. Texas and California have county probation offices under judicial control. Colorado places both adult and juvenile probation under the control of the state judiciary. Louisiana has adult and juvenile probation divisions in separate state-level corrections and juvenile departments.

Probation administered by a local government unit is said to be smaller, more flexible, and better able to respond to the unique problems of the local community; it can also work more closely with local government and make better use of existing resources. But local probation offices often suffer from the same types of problems as local police organizations, including inconsistent standards, inadequate funding, lack of training, and inconsistent policies and procedures. Juvenile probation is generally perceived as working better under decentralized control; thus it is more likely to be operated at the local level than is adult probation, which in most states is provided by agents who work directly for the state (though operating out of offices at regional and local levels).

For the probation officer in a typical state, county, or city probation office, the key term is **caseload**, referring to the number of clients supervised by the probation officer. Think of a caseload as number of files to be managed. For those states in which probation officers are supervising only probationers (including all felons and misdemanants), the official average caseload per officer in the year 2000 was 133; where probation officers were also supervising parolees, official caseloads were lower, averaging 98 per officer.

Supervising a caseload is only a part, in many offices a small part, of a much larger function. The PO does **pre-sentence investigation reports (PSIs)** for the court; the information in these reports often makes up the basis of the offender's permanent file, used in later cases and in parole- and clemency-related matters. The officer spends time in jail, in court, in sentencing hearings and in probation revocation proceedings. Probation officers complete paperwork to transfer offenders from one jurisdiction to another, and they must complete reams of forms to bureaucratically manage the clients of today.

At least 72,000 people were working for county, state, and federal probation and parole agencies in 2001. Slightly more than half of these were **line probation officers** providing direct supervision of criminals. The rest were management and supervisory staff, clerical workers (necessary to process the high volume of paper work), and support staff, such as technicians, treatment specialists, trainers, custodians, and others.

The issue of reducing caseload size to an ideal number--somewhere between 15 and 50--has been argued for a long time. The intended benefit would be to give POs more time to spend with their clients, more than a few minutes once or twice a month. But in experiments when caseload size was reduced, the two most notable results were, first, the officers spent a lot more time getting their paper work right, and, second, revocation rates went up because when the officers supervised their clients more closely they caught them doing wrong more often.

Arizona is one of the few states making a long-term commitment to holding down caseload size. By state law felony probation caseloads cannot exceed 60 offenders to one probation officer. State funding is allocated to maintain that level of service. As a result, probation departments in Arizona are nationally recognized to be among the best, providing their offender with both strict surveillance and needed treatment services.

If caseload is important as a measure of workload, a related term, **casework**, also has a history in probation work. Casework applies to an approach or methodology, typically a treatment-oriented model associated with the medical model in corrections. While juvenile probation officers were more inclined to see themselves as social workers with a rehabilitative mission, adult probation has moved away from the casework model in recent years as the emphasis on surveillance and crime control has increased.

Caseload management has been affected by two important trends--structure and specialization. Probation work is caught up in the effort to provide greater accountability based on outcomes. Many probation agencies use some type of **risk/needs assessment** instrument in determining how to manage their clients most effectively. Risk/needs assessment is based on those variables in a criminal's background that are known to be related to recidivism--such elements as age, criminal history, substance abuse, employment history and income, family life, education, and so on--to determine relative risk. Caseloads are then structured by level of supervision, based on frequency of contact, from minimal to medium to maximum to intensive, from fewer than one required contact per month to 10 or more.

A generation ago all probationers were supervised in general caseloads with the same general level of supervision. It was then left up to the officer, using his or her discretion in an approach often described as **crisis management**, to decide how many times a month clients would be seen. Many people you might see once a month or not at all, but when they were in trouble, you tried to deal with the crisis as an immediate concern. Structuring caseload supervision formalizes what was once an informal practice.

Georgia developed the practice of **intensive supervised probation (ISP or IPS)** in the early 1970s. Faced with severe overcrowding in its prison system, Georgia developed a model in which non-violent felons who would ordinarily have gone to prison were placed under ISP. Georgia's IPS was characterized by caseloads limited to 25 probationers supervised by two officers (or caseloads of 40, with three officers) who worked staggered hours. One officer specialized in rehabilitative programming and court liaison, and the other specialized in surveillance. Supervision standards included five contacts per week during initial stages, curfews enforced by frequent home visits, employment verification, unscheduled drug screening, and alcohol breath tests. This model was considered effective in controlling crime by emphasizing **surveillance** while simultaneously demonstrating a significant cost savings--about $6,000 per offender. It also broke down the generalist model of probation into a specialized model based on function and type of caseload or level of supervision.

Probation at the federal level and in many state and local jurisdictions has subsequently employed a **team** approach--a model in which probation officers specialize in performing one part of the process or in supervising one particular type of client. One officer might only do presentence investigations, for example, or handle revocation hearings. Another might only supervise intensive probationers or DWI offenders. These officers are often referred to as **specialists**, as opposed to traditional **generalists** who would supervise a mixed cased of randomly-assigned probationers without regard to crime or treatment needs.

**Federal probation** is often used as a model of what probation might become at the state level, if it had more resources and an expanded role. The U.S. Probation and Pretrial Services System, a part of the federal judiciary, was created in 1925. Federal probation officers have three core responsibilities:

1. Investigation. Officers investigate defendants and offenders for the court by gathering and verifying information about them.
2. Report preparation. Officers prepare pretrial and presentence investigation reports for the court.
3. Supervision. Officers supervise defendants in pretrial, probationary, and supervised release status.

Federal probation differs from typical state or local probation in several respects. First, the pretrial services officers pick up defendants at the point of arrest, rather than upon conviction or after sentencing, as is more often true in state and local systems. This provides for more information and greater continuity of supervision. Second, the supervision caseloads are small, averaging about 40 to 50 per officer throughout the system; this is lower than any state system. Third, the relative permanence of court staff--judges, probation officers, clerks, and other officials--promotes a very close working relationship and a team-oriented perspective on probation work. Federal probation work is highly bureaucratic in that the work is prescribed in detail in guidelines, manuals, policies, and procedures. The *Supervision of Federal Offenders* manual defines these major **principles of good supervision**--individualized, proportional, purposeful, multidimensional, proactive in implementation, and responsive to changes.

## Probation As a Sentence and a Process

In the early years of the penitentiary, probation for convicted felons was the exception. Now **felony probation** is an accepted practice. In many jurisdictions, more felons get probation, either directly or after a short jail term, than go straight to prison. Not all offenders are eligible for probation. Many states use **statutory restrictions** to deny probation to certain violent criminals and to repeat offenders. Offenders placed on probation are subject to required conditions that fall into one of three realms:

1. **Standard conditions** imposed on all probationers, including such requirements as reporting to the probation office, keeping contact information current, remaining employed, and not leaving the jurisdiction without permission.
2. **Punitive conditions** established to reflect the seriousness of the offense and increase the painfulness of probation. Examples are fines, community service, victim restitution, house arrest, and drug testing.
3. **Treatment conditions** imposed to force probationers to deal with significant problems or needs, such as substance abuse, family counseling, or vocational training.

Violation of any general or special conditions can lead to **probation revocation**. This generally occurs in a two-step proceeding. The probation violator is held in jail under a **detainer** that prevents him or her from bonding out until a hearing is held. A hearing officer will first hold a probable cause hearing to determine that the violation--a new crime or technical violation--occurred. Then the sentencing judge to whom the probationer is responsible is required by the Supreme Court decision of *Gagnon v. Scarpelli* to hold a due process hearing before revoking probationary status. Being rearrested for a new felony offense is highly likely to result in revocation in most jurisdictions, while misdemeanor arrests and technical violations allow the court more discretion to impose greater restrictions or treatment requirements to deal with the behavior.

## The Probationer: A Profile

How are people on probation different from people in prison? The most notable difference to keep in mind is that virtually all men and women serving prison terms are convicted felons, while about half of all probationers are misdemeanants under supervision for drunk driving, drugs, and assaults, among other misdemeanor crimes (many of which began as felony charges). In a 1995 national survey, probationers differed in profile from prisoners in other key aspects: women made up about 21 percent of probationers, more than twice as high as their jail and prison percentages; whites made up about 62 percent of probationers, with blacks, Hispanics, and others making up the balance; probationers were more likely to be married and to have completed high school; and probationers were also younger than prisoners, meaning they were earlier in their criminal careers.

The majority of probationers surveyed in this report were on probation for one of five offenses--driving while intoxicated (17 percent), larceny/theft (10 percent), drug possession (10 percent), drug trafficking (10 percent), and assault (9 percent). By 2003, the number of people on probation for drugs had increased sharply, as had the number of theft offenders.

By year end 2002, almost four million people were on probation, equally divided between felons and misdemeanants. The majority (60 percent) of adults on probation in 2002 were sentenced directly to that status. The rest were given either a suspended sentence (31 percent) or a **split sentence** (9 percent) involving jail or prison time followed by probation. The split sentence is most common for people held in jail until they plead guilty; they get **credit for time served** and are then discharged to probation. Most people on probation, get strings attached--additional conditions tacked on to probation supervision. The most common of these in 1995 were supervision fees (61.0 percent), fines (55.8 percent), court costs (54.5 percent), mandatory drug testing (32.5 percent), and restitution to victim (30.3 percent). Treatment, community service, and education programs were also common.

The length of time spent on probation varies sharply according to whether one was convicted of a misdemeanor or a felony--it can be from 90 days to five years. About one in five probationers (or more for felony probationers) faces a disciplinary hearing, most commonly because he or she has **absconded**--disappeared or failed to maintain contact. Probationers also get rearrested, fail to pay fines, fail to complete treatment, and test positive for drugs. Over the past decade, the success rate for probationers has been very consistent--about 60 to 62 percent described as "successful completions," which means they were discharged from probation on time or early. About 15 to 20 percent are incarcerated, while about the same numbers end up in the absconded and other unsuccessful categories. What this means is that at present about three of every five people put on probation complete it without being revoked or otherwise failing to comply with supervision.

Joan Petersilia has observed that there are two stories to be told in terms of probation recidivism rates. Rates are low for the half of the population that is placed on probation for a misdemeanor; data suggest that three-quarters of them successfully complete their supervision, in part because they are not monitored as strictly and get more slack from the courts because felons take bed space priority. For *felons* placed on probation, recidivism rates are higher, particularly in jurisdictions that use probation extensively, where offenders are serious to begin with, and supervision is minimal. In crowded times, felons get locked up, while misdemeanants get another chance.

## The Effectiveness of Probation

Probation has had its ups and downs over the past three decades. The rehabilitation and reintegration era of the 1960s and 1970s emphasized probation as the preferred option to imprisonment. But by the middle of the crime control decade of the 1980s this began to change. Probation fell out of favor for three main reasons. First, it was not perceived as a **real punishment**, either by criminals or by the public. Second, it was not controlling enough. Third, it was ineffective in changing behavior.

Probation officials and scholars supporting probation offered several waves of responses. The first followed the traditional **more resources** argument. To keep an offender in prison costs about 20 to 25 times as much as keeping him under probation supervision--$60 per day versus two to three dollars per day--and probation always gets cut first when money is short. Supervision and services could be enhanced with more resources, leading into the second wave of responses, often called the **greater accountability** model, that reflected an effort to make probation more "scientific." By using behavioral models, technology, and statistics, probation managers could require probation officers to manage their caseloads more diligently and keep up with their criminals better.

A third wave began to build in the latter part of the 1990s; this wave, which seeks not only to change probation management but also to redefine its philosophy, is most often called **reinventing probation**. The leading advocate of reinventing probation is John J. DiIulio, Jr, who has argued that probation and parole fail to protect the public by failing to adequately supervise offenders and apply sanctions to violators. Probation thus becomes a kind of do-nothing status, playing no real part in society's efforts to control crime.

DiIulio is a member of the **Reinventing Probation Council**, most of whose members are probation managers who are associated with the National Association of Probation Executives (NAPE) of the **American Probation and Parole Association (APPA)**, an organization that traces its origins to 1907. The council's August 1999 report, "'Broken Windows' Probation: The Next Step in Fighting Crime," acknowledges that "probation isn't working." It criticizes the **"fortress probation"** approach, which brings offenders to the probation office for brief contacts rather than taking the probation officer out into the community, and offers a model of **broken windows probation**--placing public safety first, emphasizing enforcement, and working in the community. Broken windows is seen as combining elements of community policing and private business management to take probation officers out of the office and into the community, where they will work with police and community organizations to supervise offenders more closely. The goal is to break down the old bureaucracy and replace it with a new, decentralized, but tightly managed strike force of probation monitors.

Faye Taxman and James Byrne have responded with a treatment-based strategy they call **proactive community supervision** probation; their approach is sometimes also referred to as the **what works model**, referring to Robert Martinson's 1974 rehabilitation essay. The emphasis of the proactive supervision model is on offender change, not merely surveillance and control. Broken windows is said to be community-centered and enforcement oriented, while what works is said to be offender-centered and treatment oriented. As many states look for ways to reduce their prison populations, probation officials will have to determine what principles should be emphasized in developing intermediate sanctions--surveillance and control, or treatment and rehabilitation? Or can these seemingly contrasting perspectives be reconciled in practice?

## Intermediate Sanctions

For many years the courts faced a simple "either/or" choice in sentencing convicted felons--either non-secure probation, allowing offenders to roam free under minimal supervision, or secure imprisonment, which isolated offenders from society. Since the **reintegration era** began in the 1970s, a range of **intermediate sanctions** has been developed to impose more controls and restrictions over offenders. Most such sanctions are considered a part of **community corrections**, keeping offenders at home or in a community-based residential facility. But some involve placement in custody for short periods, in combination with other periods of supervision in the community. Intermediate sanctions can provide more individualized controls matched to the offender's behavior; these sanctions also make probation more punitive by imposing greater costs on the offender's liberty. They are sometimes referred to as **enhancement programs**, because they enhance both the treatment options for the offender and the control options for the state. Their objective is to achieve the goal we have previously discussed, **desistance**, which is defined as the system's effort to get the offender to cease criminal behavior.

James Byrne has represented common sentencing options on a continuum or scale of controls, from least to most punitive--restitution, day fine, community service, active probation, intensive probation, house arrest, residential community corrections, split sentence, jail, and prison. The idea of a scale of options fits the scheme of **tourniquet sentencing**, tightening controls over the offender until desistance occurs. The corrections system is put in the business of **risk management**, which has to do with assessing risk and providing structured controls appropriate to the degree of risk the offender is believed to represent.

**Restitution** is at the low end of this scale. Restitution, which is akin to the old practice of *wergeld*, is accomplished through **restitution orders** that require the offender to repay the victim for economic losses; it is used more often in property crimes but can be used in violent crimes where injury also results.

Next on the scale is the **day fine**, which has been used in European countries for many years. Instead of a flat fine, such as $500 for DWI that all offenders pay, the fine is expressed as a part of the offender's income. Each crime is worth so many **punishment units**. The judge sets a number of units for the crime, and these units are multiplied by a standard percentage of the offender's income (such as 1/1000th of his annual income) to come up with a specific financial obligation. The premise, difficult to apply in practice, is that of equalizing economic impact.

**Community service** or **community work orders** are next up on Byrne's scale. Offenders are ordered to put in so many hours of time devoted to some public service or charitable work. Sometimes the work is skill-related, as a doctor who might provide free medical care; more often it involves social services, such as visiting a nursing home, or manual labor, such as picking up trash in a park. The idea is that the community work is more productive and more morally effective than being locked up or being let off with a fine or a suspended sentence.

Standard probation remains an option, though with typical caseloads of greater than 100, it provides minimal supervision. As we have already noted, many jurisdictions now structure probation supervision from administrative to low to regular to intermediate to high, with the highest level termed intensive supervised probation, or ISP, which has spread nationwide since Georgia's experiment in the 1980s.

Other intermediate sanctions center on confinement at home. This practice is related to the **furloughs** many states once used to allow inmates short visits home, often during the holidays, for family emergencies, or prior to release from custody. Furloughs have been less popular in recent years, primarily because political officials cannot take the heat when a criminal on furlough commits a new crime. Furloughs are still legally available in about half the states and the federal system, but they are infrequently used.

**House arrest**, or **home detention**, is an intermediate sanction now used in many states and local jurisdictions. It may be a part of probation or a sentence in itself, as it is in Florida's Community Control Program (FCCP). Home detention can be very restrictive, particularly when it is combined with **electronic monitoring** to impose even stricter controls over the offender's movements and whereabouts. The use of technological devices to monitor offenders was proposed in 1964 as **electronic parole**, but it has only come into general usage within the past decade. About one-third of offenders on house arrest nationwide are monitored through various types of electronic systems--some of which now have video and breath-testing capabilities. Global Positioning Satellite (GPS) technology has also begun to be used to monitor offenders sentenced to home detention. Success rates for electronic monitoring tend to be in the same range as routine probation, around 75% or higher.

If offenders cannot live at home, the next step up the scale is to place them in a non-secure residential facility. These facilities were typically called **halfway houses** when they became popular in the mental health field and spread to community corrections in the 1960s and 1970s. Their name came from their place--halfway between freedom and confinement. They were used both for offenders exiting the system, on pre-release, parole, or discharge, and for probationers who required stricter supervision. **Community residential treatment centers** today are almost always tied to employment, education, or treatment programs of some sort. Their emphasis is on making offenders productive and on providing intensive services that offenders cannot get as easily at home.

In some jurisdictions the latest twist on the halfway house is the **day reporting center** (called the **day attendance center** in Australia and in some other models). Offenders live at home, but they report to another site each day to report in and take part in specific programs, usually treatment-, education-, or vocation-focused. They then go home at night under curfew; with telephone checks or electronic monitoring added on, day reporting centers can be made nearly as restrictive as community residential centers.

Intermediate sanctions are usually tied to the community, as in recent **drug court** programs now proliferating in many urban areas, but there are variations that involve confinement in secure jails or prisons. Intermittent or weekend jail sentences and split sentences involving prison and probation are common in many jurisdictions. Accelerated or "shock" programs are another recent sanction combining time in secure custody with time under community supervision. The Ohio model of **shock probation**, established in 1965, uses a three- to four-month prison term followed by probation. The judge recalls the inmate from prison and sets the conditions for probation.

Georgia (1983) and Oklahoma (1984) were the first states to establish a different kind of shock program--**shock incarceration** or **boot camp**. People liked the *idea* of boot camp. It reminded them of the old-fashioned idea of sending a troubled young person off to the military to shape up. Dale Parent has observed that the original correctional boot camps resembled military basic training. They emphasized vigorous physical activity, drill and ceremony, verbal harassment, manual labor, and other activities to insure that participants had little, if any, free time. Strict rules governed all aspects of conduct and appearance. Correctional officers acted as drill instructors.

By 1995, state correctional agencies were operating 75 boot camps for adults and numerous boot camps were in operation in local jails, juvenile prisons, and private facilities. They had three main goals--reducing recidivism, reducing prison populations, and reducing costs (through shorter stays in prison). The long-term results have been mixed. Boot camps appear to have minimal effect on recidivism and not much effect on population. The number of camps in operation has declined, and many of the continuing programs have been redesigned to downplay the military format and upgrade treatment--especially for substance abuse--and job skills.

There are two major limitations to the boot camp approach. First, they are focused on younger offenders, who are often the least interested in changing. Their motivation is to get through the program quicker, and get right

169

back to the life they were leading before. Second, although they do satisfactorily in the artificial boot camp environment, it is too short to change their basic values, to which they revert as soon as they are released back into society. Boot camp for life (or until middle age) would be a better idea for them. Shock incarceration is said to be a new approach, yet its regimen is very similar to the first American reformatories of a century ago. Reformatories did not achieve remarkable success rates, and so far boot camps have not done so either.

## Diversion: Keeping the Offender Out of the System

Boot camps are at the high end of the scale of intermediate sanctions, closest to ordinary confinement. At the opposite end, before the offender acquires a record of criminal conviction, is another option called **diversion**. Diversion programs are said to be of three types: community-based, police-based, and court-based. **Community-based diversion**, which is more likely to be used with at-risk juveniles than with adults, sends the offender into an alternative treatment program prior to arrest and filing of charges.

**Police-based diversion** gives police authority to send certain types of offenders, such as those involved in incidents of domestic violence, into counseling or treatment programs. A prime example of the impact of this type of diversion is the practice of taking common drunks to hospital **detoxification centers**. The prevalence of "detox" has resulted in a sharp decline in the number of drunks put in jail and processed as criminals.

**Court-based diversion** programs have become the most common. They are based on the concept that the judge has the authority to dismiss criminal charges if the offender completes a specified program of rehabilitation or self-improvement within a mandated time period. The offender signs a contract with the court to complete the program; if he or she fails to do so, the original charges are reinstated. Many jurisdictions operate **pretrial intervention programs** under public or private authority to get the offender to "take charge" of his or her life before the case comes to trial instead of waiting until after conviction to start corrective action. The big incentive to the offender is avoiding the stigma of a criminal conviction. The "hottest" form of court-based diversion going in the United States today is the drug court movement. These treatment and monitoring oriented courts, operating under the direction of judges who want to work with drug offenders as a special purpose clientele, have been established in hundreds of local and state trial courts across the country.

## Community Corrections: Options

One of the most direct applications of community corrections alternatives is to aid offenders in making the transition from prison to the community as they approach the end of their sentence. The **Federal Prisoner Rehabilitation Act**, passed by Congress in 1965, provided several options--work release, furloughs, and community treatment centers--to assist in reintegration. Many state laws today do the same, though many of the statutes may exclude more offenders than they include.

**Work release** was first authorized at the state level in a 1913 Wisconsin statute allowing misdemeanor offenders to work at outside jobs while they spent their nights in jail. Practically all states have some felons on work release today. Work release is not only good for the offender, by helping him or her get back in touch with society and make some money; it also benefits society through taxes, welfare savings, and offenders bearing the costs of their incarceration while living in work release facilities.

The halfway house, which is now often called a **community residential center**, is probably used more today as a work release facility than for any other purpose. Originally used more to house parolees and homeless ex-offenders, the halfway house now holds primarily men and women still in custody but in prerelease or work release status. Halfway houses today may be publicly operated or privately operated either for profit or, more commonly, by **nonprofit organizations**--religious, charitable, civic, or purely correctional in nature. Most offer residential facilities housing anywhere from a dozen to several dozen residents, often in an old residence in an urban neighborhood, though some halfway houses may use old apartment buildings or even former motels.

Many states and the federal government operate a different type of facility called a **prerelease guidance center**, or prerelease center, for inmates at the very end of their sentence. It is usually located in larger metropolitan areas, and inmates from those areas are sent home a few weeks early to get counseling, find a job, and establish contact with their family again. If the state uses the furlough at all, as a form of **partial incarceration** reestablishing family and community ties, it can be attached to this center.

## Intermediate Sanctions and Community Corrections: Pros and Cons

Community corrections alternatives first began to be emphasized during the early days of the reintegration era of the 1970s. The arguments in favor of community corrections included:

1. Community corrections offered a normal, humane environment, as opposed to prison's artificial environment.
2. Responsibility was placed on the criminal.
3. It was cheaper than imprisonment.
4. Community corrections was the **least restrictive alternative**--less trouble for most offenders.
5. A much broader range of referrals and real-world programs was available.

But in the few years in which these programs were emphasized, several critical observations were commonly made:

1. The public was often apathetic or openly hostile to community-based programs, especially when residential programs put criminals into neighborhoods. The phrase **NIMBY** (not in my back yard) often came up when any type of residential facility was discussed.
2. Many programs were meagerly-funded, hand-to-mouth operations that provided only minimal services.
3. Because of their meager resources, many community-based programs suffered from the same failing as prison programs: they were single-purpose programs that could not meet the multiple needs of offenders.
4. Persistently high recidivism rates were a serious problem of community-based programs.
5. The cost differential in comparison to prison was often minimal; some halfway houses with more treatment staff actually cost more than imprisonment.
6. The lack of security was a problem, especially in regard to public concerns about the program. Each year the great majority of prison "escapes" are runaways or walkaways from open facilities of this type, many of them work release, prerelease, or treatment facilities.

Community corrections programs were often founded by well-meaning reformers who lacked any long-term commitment from politicians or correctional officials. Thus when politics took a hard right turn in the direction of crime control, it was easy to abandon community-based programs as haphazard and ineffective. "They just don't work," officials said, as they turned away from community corrections in favor of secure custody. But the emergence of intermediate sanctions in the 1990s has led to a resurgence of interest in community-based corrections, though this time the emphasis is placed more on public safety and victims' rights than on reintegration into the community and rehabilitation of the individual offender.

Andrew von Hirsch suggests that the new community corrections are founded on the **anything-but-prison theory**: "Intervention in the community is tolerable irrespective of its intrusiveness, this theory asserts, as long as the resulting sanction is less onerous than imprisonment." This view, that anyone who gets off with less than a jail or prison sentence (or more commonly a suspended jail or prison sentence assuming satisfactory completion of the community corrections alternative) is "getting a break," has several important consequences. First is **net widening**, which pulls minor offenders farther into the system and threatening them with confinement if they fail to comply with any intermediate sanctions that may be applied to them. Minor offenders who until recently would have simply been discharged with a fine and a suspended sentence are subjected to more rigorous penalties, with the possibility of incarceration hanging over their heads if they fail to comply.

Another consequence is the disregard of **proportionality**--the concept that the severity of punishment should reflect reflect the degree of blameworthiness of the criminal conduct. James Byrne has comment on the legal system's tendency to pile on intermediate sanctions, a practice he calls **sanction stacking**. The lesser criminal gets restitution, and a day fine, and community service, and day reporting, and a curfew, and a weekend in jail to start it out. Each of these is actually intended to be a stand-alone option, not part of a single, comprehensive intermediate sanction. The courts pile them on to put the criminal under a relatively heavy financial and liberty burden. To which some criminals say "Put me in prison," because it is less trouble than to stay on the street.

Von Hirsch suggests that the application of sanctions should be guided by the idea of **acceptable penal content**: the idea that a sanction should be devised so that its intended penal deprivations are those that can be administered in a manner that is clearly consistent with the offender's dignity. Many people take the view that **shame** ought to be a common part of intermediate sanctions, but von Hirsch suggests that we steer clear of punishments intended to make the person see himself or herself as a "moral pariah."

Von Hirsch gives us this cautionary warning: "With adequate ethical limits, community-based sanctions may become a means of creating a less inhumane and unjust penal system. Without adequate limits, however, they could become just another menace and extend the network of state intrusion into citizens' lives. We should not, to paraphrase David Rothman, decarcerate the prisons to make a prison of our society."

## Community Corrections in the Future

At the center of the movement toward community-based corrections is the **community correctional center**. This facility is an expanded or enhanced version of the current halfway house or community residential center, serving as the location for a wider variety of residential and non-residential programs for pretrial and sentenced offenders. Think of it as a department store with multiple floors: first floor, pretrial release; second floor, diversion; third floor, drug court; fourth floor, work release; fifth floor, day reporting; sixth floor, **"halfway-out"** prerelease inmates; seventh floor, **"halfway-in"** probationers in trouble; eighth floor, **reintegration centers** for closer monitoring of parolees in trouble for technical violations; ninth floor, electronic monitoring and house arrest.

Who would operate such a facility? The ideal candidate seems to be the local sheriff, who through the community correctional center would provide outreach options to the jail, while working closely with the local and state probation officers who would be the official monitors of behavior and treatment.

Richard Seiter has proposed the **integrated contract model** of offender management that would work well with the community correctional center. It would require the convicted felon to choose either punishment or reintegration. Some offenders would not get a choice--first-degree murderers, rapists, major drug dealers, third-time convicted felons, and firearms violators would go to prison to serve incapacitative sentences. If an eligible offender chose reintegration, he or she would be placed in a comprehensive reintegration plan that described the services to be provided, victim restitution, the least restrictive environment, and the treatment and management of the offender. A binding contract would be drawn up and signed by all parties requiring work toward defined goals within the contractual time period. Fail to live up to the contract and you would go to prison after all.

As the costs of imprisonment continue to rise and concern over the impact of imprisonment on large numbers of marginal offenders grows, the integrated contract and the community correctional center have a better chance to be put into practice. The **social justice model**, which Harry Allen and Clifford Simonsen see as a possible long-term end of corrections, suggests that community corrections is more just and fair to most offenders than imprisonment--and it is better for society in the long run.

As expenditures for corrections continue to increase, drawing money away from other governmental services, the key word becomes **accountability**. If community corrections can control offenders more cheaply, with better results, with less trouble, and without compromising public safety, it can probably draw increased popular and political support in the future. Allen and Simonsen have suggested that no more than 15 to 20 percent of convicted felons require imprisonment; the rest could be served by an expanded community corrections network.

More states have enacted **community corrections acts** to provide for a better organized network of intermediate sanctions and alternatives at the local level, which places more of a burden on state and local probation and parole officers to monitor the performance of the local programs. Instead of just doing investigations, writing reports, field supervision, and going to court, the probation and parole officer becomes the **change agent** responsible for managing the offender's movement among public and private organizations providing perhaps ten different control options with lesser adjustments attached to each. Using his or her **risk-control tools**--residence, day reporting, curfew, community service, drug testing, electronic monitoring, and so on--the probation and parole officer would manage the offender individually, tightening or loosening controls over time in response to the offender's behavior. This is the possible future of community corrections, but not all practitioners believe in it or want to make it real. The prison is a much simpler reality.

# Self Test

## Multiple Choice

1. Four of the following are commonly cited advantages of community corrections, in comparison to imprisonment; which one is NOT?
   a. The offender is more strictly controlled.
   b. The costs are less than the costs of imprisonment.
   c. The offender is made more responsible for himself.
   d. The effect of prisonization is reduced.
   e. Community ties are better promoted.

2. According to the integrated contract model, the convicted felon would choose either punishment or:
   a. freedom
   b. banishment
   c. community service
   d. state subsidy
   e. reintegration

3. Harry Allen and Clifford Simonsen have suggested that about what percentage of convicted offenders requires imprisonment?
   a. no more than 2
   b. about 5 to 7
   c. about 15 to 20
   d. exactly 33
   e. about 60 to 70

4. Probation is basically a contract between the offender and the:
   a. warden
   b. probation board
   c. district attorney
   d. judge
   e. victim

5. According to James Byrne, this term fits the circumstance when a judge piles on several intermediate sanctions instead of using them one at a time.
   a. brick-and-mortar punishment
   b. sanction stacking
   c. sentence swarming
   d. penalty heaping
   e. stonewalling

6. Where is probation best placed among these options?
   a. executive sanctions
   b. back-end solutions
   c. institutional refinements
   d. brick-and-mortar solutions
   e. front-end solutions

7. The idea of tourniquet sentencing basically means that if the behavior of an offender on probation begins to slip, the court will:
   a. revoke his probation and make him serve the full prison sentence
   b. try a different probation officer
   c. recommend mental health treatment
   d. impose stricter controls on the offender
   e. send the case to a more punitive judge

8. The European intermediate sanction recommended because it specifically adjusts for income inequality among offenders is the:
   a. enhancement
   b. split sentence
   c. community service
   d. day fine
   e. furlough

9. On James Byrne's scale of sentencing options, which of these provides the lowest level punishment?
   a. jail
   b. intensive probation
   c. restitution
   d. house arrest
   e. split sentence

10. Four of the following fit Georgia's model of intensive supervised probation; which one does NOT?
   a. a six-month boot camp first
   b. mandatory curfew
   c. unannounced alcohol and drug testing
   d. community service
   e. five face-to-face contacts each week

## True or False

_____ 11. The desirable legal outcome of a court-based diversion program is dismissal of charges against the defendant.

_____ 12. The integrated contract model would be used primarily with violent offenders who have been in prison a long time and need help readjusting to society.

_____ 13. The trend in probation services today is to emphasize the role of the probation officer as a therapist doing individual casework.

_____ 14. The courts have ruled that every convicted felon is legally eligible for probation.

_____ 15. Although its success rate has declined recently, probation still has more successful terminations than failures.

_____ 16. The broken windows model sees the probation officer as being more actively involved in enforcement on the street, as opposed to monitoring behavior from an office.

_____ 17. Under the more restrictive sentencing provisions currently being adopted, only misdemeanants and not felons are eligible for probation.

_____ 18. Most local jurisdictions now operate an integrated network of intermediate sanctions using the full range of sanctions on Byrne's scale.

_____ 19. Every offender on home detention is hooked up to some kind of electronic monitoring system.

_____ 20. The furlough was an early type of house arrest in which the offender lived at home while serving a felony sentence.

## Fill In the Blanks

21. If you were on probation and failed to keep in contact with your PO, you could be arrested and held in jail on a(n) _____ until your revocation hearing.

22. The two key features of active probation, in contrast to the suspended sentence, are conditions and _____.

23. The man called the "Father of Probation" in America for his work with the courts in Boston is _____.

24. *Gagnon v. Scarpelli* is still considered the landmark Supreme Court case dealing with the issue of _____.

25. Other than the time spent working with the probationers in his or her caseload, the generalist probation officer is likely to spend most of the remaining time performing the function of _____.

26. The call to abolish probation has been redirected to _____ probation instead.

27. The expanded, idealized model of the current halfway house, offering a diverse range of program options, would be known as the _____.

28. If an offender was violating curfew as part of a sanction to a day reporting center, the next sanction up the line that he might be moved to would be a(n) _____.

29. If you were protesting _____, you would probably argue that intermediate sanctions ought to be used less and straight probation ought to be used more.

30. A dentist convicted of a white-collar crime might be assigned to perform eight hours of work each week at a free dental clinic for the poor; this type of sanction is called _____.

## Discussion

31. How did probation develop in America?

32. What does a probation officer actually do?

33. What general and special conditions are typically applied to probationers?

34. Is probation a punishment? How can it be made more punitive?

35. Describe the elements of a typical intensive probation program.

36. What would seem to be the advantages of leaving the offender under intermediate sanctions living at home, as opposed to confining him in a secure jail or prison?

37. One of your neighbors comes by with a NIMBY petition when a halfway house for adolescent drug abusers is proposed for your neighborhood. What do you tell your neighbor?

38. Describe how the enhanced community correctional center of the future should operate.

# CHAPTER SIXTEEN

# Contrasting Philosophies:
# American and International Corrections Today

This chapter compares contemporary American corrections with the rest of the world. We will contrast the correctional philosophies and practices of the United States with those of other nations, discussing the influences that make us different. After taking a brief world tour of imprisonment, we will end with some thoughts on the recent past and the near future of American corrections. After reading this chapter, you should be familiar with:

1. The crime problem as a worldwide concern.
2. An overview of the corrections systems of seven major foreign nations: Canada, England, Germany, Russia, Saudi Arabia, China, and Japan.
3. How other nations view the use of imprisonment.
4. What the experience of imprisonment is like in other countries.
5. The reality and the ideology of American punishment.
6. How recent history has widened the gap between the U.S. and other nations.
7. The possibilities of the near future in American corrections.

## Key Terms

crime problem
international crime statistics
punishment scale
dual correctional system
Correctional Service of Canada
Corrections and Conditional Release Act (Canada)
core values
effective corrections
aboriginals
International Corrections and
  Prisons Association (ICPA)
National Prison Service
remand centers
dispersal prisons
young prisoner centers
borstal
Chief Inspector of Prisons
Prisons and Probation Ombudsman
Independent Monitoring Board
Prison Visitors
Home Office
racial politics
common sense connection
privatization
Prison Works
National Probation Service
Criminal Justice Act (England)
persistence principle
National Offender Management Service (NOMS)
contestability
guestworkers
progressive system
day fines
Prison Act of 1976 (Germany)
normalization
home leave
half-open release

thieves in law
Chechens
Russian Mafia
corrective labor colonies
prisoners' plague
Mutawa
Mubahith
bamboo gulag
administrative detention
reform through labor camps
laogai
public surveillance
shelter and investigation
Prison Law (China)
five rewards and five punishments
thought reform
yanda
Prison Law (Japan)
five principles
extraordinary leniency
volunteer probation officer
Naikan
Beijing Rules
welfare model
legalistic model
corporatist model
participatory model
benign-neglect approach
Amnesty International
Human Rights Watch
punitiveness
real crime
social dynamite
war on crime
enemy of the state
expressive justice
smart justice

Gulag

## Crime: A Worldwide Problem

When German prison warden Volker Bieschke toured six California prisons in 1999, he was most struck by the huge size of the institutions in comparison to German prisons. After spending their first year in a conventional secure facility, many German inmates qualify to transfer to small, community-based facilities that are more like our work release centers. Bierschke was skeptical about the physical environment of the prisons he saw and their control methods, but as he said, "My problems are not their problems."

With less than five percent of the world's population, the United States has 25 percent of the world's prisoners-- 2.25 million adults and juveniles behind bars at the end of 2003, out of a worldwide imprisoned population of just under nine million. One of every four prisoners in the world is behind bars in America. Do we have 25 percent of the world's crime to justify this level of imprisonment?

Many Americans believe that our crime rate is the highest in the world, and that our huge prison system in absolutely necessary as a crime control measure. Criminologists suggest otherwise, pointing out that crime has been an important domestic political issue not only in America but in other industrialized and developing nations since the late 1960s to early 1970s. The contemporary international **crime problem** is often broken down into several component parts of increasing criminality--traditional street crimes, especially property crimes; juvenile violence and public misconduct; political corruption and economic misconduct; female criminality, especially for nonviolent offenses; substance abuse; public fear of crime generating political attention; and political terrorism.

In comparing **international crime statistics**, we should recall the cautionary advice of Erika Fairchild and Harry Dammer, who warn us of the dangers of direct comparison--underreporting, nonstandard definitions, varying collection practices, and political manipulation of data. But looking cautiously at the data on crime incidence and victimization, we can get a sense that being a victim of crime is a pretty commonplace experience around the world today. In most countries, about two people in three could expect to be crime victims over a five-year period. Researchers suggest that victimization is generally lower in Asia and higher in Africa and Latin America, with Europe and the English-speaking New World countries somewhere in between. Most of the European countries have property crime rates higher than or comparable to our own.

The overall rates of violent crime are higher in the United States than in other Western countries, but we are not alone in our problem with criminal violence. Several of the former Soviet bloc countries, including Russia, had murder rates higher than ours in the 1990s, and numerous Latin American countries, led by Colombia and the Bahamas with their drug-related violence, had murder rates far higher than ours. When you look at the whole picture, the United States is far from the most crime-prone nation on earth. But many Americans would never accept this, or they would argue that the only reason it is so is because we have used such rigorous punishments recently. Where crime is concerned, we tend to think and act as if we are in a class by ourselves, with the result that our extreme devotion to the use of imprisonment has made that tendency a real public policy.

## World Imprisonment: An Overview

The table below shows the imprisonment response of the eight countries featured in this chapter.

### Imprisonment in Selected Countries

| Country | Year | National Population (in millions) | Prison/Jail Population | Imprisonment Rate (per 100,000) | Number of Institutions | Occupancy Level(%) | Ten-Year Rate Trend (per 100,000) |
|---|---|---|---|---|---|---|---|
| United States | 2002 | 290.0 | 2,033,331 | 701 | 5,059 | 106.4 | Up 196 |
| Canada | 2001 | 31.1 | 36,024 | 116 | 221 | 94.3 | Down 2 |
| England/Wales | 2004 | 52.8 | 75,324 | 143 | 138 | 112.7 | Up 37 |
| Germany | 2003 | 82.6 | 79,153 | 96 | 222 | 100.5 | Up 25 |
| Russia | 2003 | 145.0 | 846,967 | 584 | 1,013 | 90.7 | Up 97 |
| Saudi Arabia | 2002 | 21.6 | 23,720 | 110 | 30 | -- | Down 8[1] |
| China | 2003 | 1,304.2 | 1,549,000[1] | 119[1] | 689 | -- | Up 10[1] |

| Japan | 2002 | 127.6 | 69,502 | 54 | 189 | 106.5 | Up 11 |

[1]Sentenced prisoners only.

Source: International Centre for Prison Studies, 2004.

British researcher Roy Walmsley has pointed out, in regard to the computation of an international **punishment scale** based on numbers behind bars versus national populations, that countries with the highest prison populations may not necessarily be the most punitive. They may have the most serious crime to contend with, or they may be more effective in bringing to justice those who commit serious crime, or they may be more punitive in regard to certain crimes and less punitive in regard to others. Walmsley made these points about world imprisonment in 2001:

> The world prison population rate is approximately 140 per 100,000 citizens.
> About two-thirds of the nations of the world have rates of 150 per 100,000 or below.
> Ten countries have rates of at least 460 per 100,000, led by the United States and Russia. After these two countries come a group including Belarus, Kazakhstan, Kyrgyzstan, the Pacific Island of Guam, and four small states in the Caribbean--the Cayman Islands, the Bahamas, the U.S. Virgin Islands, and Belize.
> In the decade of the 1990s, prison populations increased steadily worldwide, with a median growth of about 40 percent over the decade. Prison growth was most notable in the Western Hemisphere, where in the five most populous countries--the U.S., Mexico, Argentina, Brazil, and Colombia--increases were between 60 and 85 percent.
> In the 118 countries (more than half the world's nations) for which consistent statistics for the entire decade were available, prison populations increased in 73 percent. This included 10 of 13 African countries, 25 of 33 countries in the Americas, 18 of 21 Asian countries, 27 of 42 European countries, and 6 of 9 countries in Oceania. Where declines occurred, they were generally smaller and marked by ups and downs in the rate from year to year. In only one country, Finland, was there a consistent downward trend throughout the entire decade.

## Canada

Although Canada has faced considerable internal political pressure to modify its imprisonment policies more in line with its southern neighbor, it has managed to maintain a stable prison population over the past decade, imprisoning more offenders than western European countries, but far fewer than the United States. Canada has a **dual correctional system** comparable to the federal/state split in the United States. Canada's provincial governments are responsible for probation and the confinement of short-term prisoners given sentences of less than two years. The federal government confines offenders given sentences longer than two years and manages parole. The split works out to about 60 percent (19,000) provincial and 40 percent (13,000) federal.

The federal corrections organization is the **Correctional Service of Canada** (CSC), operating under the control of the solicitor general, a position comparable to the American attorney general. For the past decade and more, the direction of Canadian federal corrections has been guided by the **Corrections and Conditional Release Act** (CCRA) of 1992. The corrections mission is guided by five **core values**--respect for dignity and human rights, the offender's potential to live as a law-abiding citizen, the role of staff in maintaining human relationships, sharing of ideas and experience, and openness, integrity, and accountability.

In the 1990s, Canadian corrections was dominated by the views of Commissioner Ole Ingstrup, who expressed his philosophy as "evidence-based corrections." His overall plan consisted of three main parts:

> 1. Holding down the prison population.
> 2. Preparing offenders for reintegration, and then reintegrating them under supervision.
> 3. As a philosophical approach, adopting restorative justice using three core models--victim-offender mediation, family group conferencing, and circles (derived from aboriginal practices).

CSC called the means to accomplish this plan **effective corrections**. One of its guiding principles was this statement: "Prison is the right place--the only place--for some offenders, but it is also the wrong place for others." Canadian corrections is much more focused on violent criminals; about 75 percent of federal prisoners in 1999 were convicted of crimes against persons. Although Canada is the world's second-leading nation in per capita drug arrests, it puts very few drug criminals in prison--fewer than 1,100 in 1999, or about eight percent of the prison population, in comparison to 250,000, or 21 percent, in the United States.

From the time the sentence begins, the plan is to return the offender to the community through a series of steps--unescorted temporary absence, day parole, full parole, statutory release (like mandatory parole), end of sentence. Canada's additional programming and services are expensive--the average cost to keep an inmate in a federal prison is over $50,000 (American) per year, more than twice the average cost of imprisonment in the U.S.

CSC has to contend with other problems, including the presence of large numbers of **aboriginals**, mostly First Nations (Indians) and Inuits, who find their way into the prison system; making up about two percent of the Canadian population, they make up 15 percent of federal prisoners. Another continuing battle of Canadian corrections officials is defending their costly, reintegration-centered corrections policies against those who want to see an "Americanized" approach.

So far the CSC has held the line against increasing imprisonment. It has funded the new **International Corrections and Prisons Association** to promote global correctional reform and exchange of "best practices." The key to Canadian corrections policy has been to convince the public that their community-based approach is a workable practice--that "effective corrections equals public safety."

## England

The view from the continent is that England's prison system is the "most troubled" in Western Europe; its continental critics view English prisons as captives of the old--architecture and tradition--and the new--conservative politics--creating a state of crisis that will be difficult to resolve.

The **National Prison Service** oversees the operation of all prisons in England and Wales--137 public and nine private prisons filled to 113 percent of capacity in April 2004, holding just over 75,000 male and female inmates. Its imprisonment rate of 143 per 100,000 is second only to Portugal in Western Europe. Scotland and Northern Ireland, though properly a part of the United Kingdom of Great Britain and Northern Ireland, each have their own separate correctional systems; the independent Scottish Prison Service is among the more highly regarded in Europe for its efforts to provide rehabilitative services to prisoners.

England classifies prisons into five types:
> **Remand centers**, also called local prisons, but comparable to larger American jails, that hold pre-trial and short-term inmates.
> Medium-term institutions holding inmates sentenced to terms of 18 months to four years.
> Long-term prisons housing inmates serving longer than four years.
> **Dispersal prisons**, housing high-security and dangerous inmates, including members of the Irish Republican Army and others considered terrorists.
> **Young prisoner centers**, secure prisons for young adults, comparable to American reformatories.

In the early 1900s, England developed an early model for youthful offender housing, the **borstal**, which became well-known around the world. The borstal was a small, campus-like facility, like a boarding school for criminals between 16 and 20. Borstals have lost favor and are being replaced by boot camps in the popular vernacular.

English prisons are regulated through mechanisms both internal and external. **HM Chief Inspector of Prisons** is independent of the Prison Service and reports directly to the Home Secretary on the treatment of prisoners and prison conditions. The **Prisons and Probation Ombudsman** is an independent point of appeal for prisoners and those supervised by the Probation Service. As an independent government official with authority to investigate complaints and recommend corrective action, the ombudsman has long been used by Scandinavian governments; lately it has spread throughout English government as well. The **Independent Monitoring Board** is a group of local political officials and private citizens. A separate board of 15 members monitors each prison in England and Wales. The IMBs were formerly known as Boards of Visitors, but the name was recently changed to avoid confusion with the **Prison Visitors**, a program set up to match private persons with prisoners who had no visitors. England has a strong tradition of private activist organizations supporting prisoners and prison reform, perhaps more so than any other country.

From the early 1980s through the first years of the twenty-first century, England's prison philosophy has been viewed as being remarkably similar to America's. The primary difference would obviously be that England has a national system under the direction of the **Home Office**, an important Cabinet-level office generally responsible for all public safety functions, thus making prison policies a matter of national political import.

179

Prime Minister Margaret Thatcher's Conservative government, in power from 1979 to 1993, was known for three dominant correctional politics--harsher punishments of street criminals, emphasizing **racial politics** targeting recent immigrants and dark-skinned minorities; a **common sense connection** between crime and punishment that overlooked the social context; and **privatization**, which was presented as a panacea to the problems facing the Prison Service--overcrowding, old buildings, high annual costs, resistance to reform, and a rigid prison guard culture reinforced by the powerful Prison Officers Association.

When the National Prison Service tried to reduce the use of imprisonment in favor of more community-based sanctions in the early 1990s, politicians attacked the bureaucracy's "soft on crime" approach. Home Secretary Michael Howard's **"Prison Works"** speech of 1993 articulated incapacitation and deterrence as the goals of increased use of imprisonment. He argued for an austere prison environment to protect society and "make many who are tempted to commit crimes think twice." After the Labour Party under Prime Minister Tony Blair took office in 1997, correctional policies did not change substantially for several years. Prison populations continued to increase steadily, and the old problems with overcrowding persisted. In 2001, the **National Probation Service** was created to provide more centralized management of what had previously been a function directed by local probation boards.

In 2003, Parliament passed the **Criminal Justice Act**, containing provisions for sentencing reforms that would back away from the punitive ideology established in the 1980s (although it did introduce the **persistence principle** allowing more severe punishment of habitual offenders). The Home Office ordered a comprehensive study of sentencing and report (now known as the Carter Report) that was completed in December 2003. Noting that sentencing has grown more severe and that prison populations were continuing to grow though crime had dropped steadily, the Carter Report gave many recommendations to reverse these trends--the use of day fines, a renewed focus on paying back to the community, more demanding community sentences, more extensive use of electronic monitoring, and more effective use of custody, including doing away with very short-term sentences.

At the national level in corrections, the Carter Report recommended that the Prison Service and the Probation Service be combined into a single **National Offender Management Service** (NOMS) within the Home Office. The concept is to establish a consolidated system focused on the "end-to-end management" of offenders throughout their sentence, with a clear responsibility for reducing re-offending two years after the end of the sentence. Because the Carter Report called for downsizing both prisons and probation through more use of fines, employee organizations had reservations about job security. They also had concerns about the report's emphasis on **contestability**, the contracting of public services to private and volunteer providers as competitive alternatives to public providers, which is generally opposed by the influential employee unions.

NOMS does offer two positive features that make many prison reformers in England and elsewhere happy. First, it provides centralized management over offenders with the specific goal of reducing reoffending. Second, the target is to reverse the long-term trend and make significant reductions in the size of the prison population. Even with the reduction hoped for under NOMS, England will still have the second highest rate of imprisonment in Western Europe, its prisons will still be old and overcrowded, and its concentration of poor people and dark-skinned minorities in prison will still trouble penal reformers.

### Germany

Among the major European countries, Germany has been considered the trendsetter in corrections in recent years. Germany is a federal republic similar in structure to the United States. It has a national government that makes laws to be carried out in the 16 lander, or states. No national prisons exist; each state operates an independent prison system, but under the control of the Ministry of Justice in the national government. The 222 German prisons held almost 80,000 men, women, and juveniles in custody at the end of 2003--an average of about 360 prisoners per institution. The incarceration rate has leveled off at just under 100 per 100,000. Of the total population in custody, 30 percent are foreign nationals, mostly young male **guestworkers** from foreign countries--Turkey, Eastern and Southern Europe, and Spain. About 21 percent of German prisoners are in remand status awaiting trial. German prisons, though commonly said to be "nice," are full--at 100.5 percent of capacity at year end 2003.

Germany had a typical European correctional system in the latter 1800s. When the German states were unified in 1871, the penal code provided severe punishments centering on confinement in big maximum security prisons and, by the 1920s, the **progressive system** based on English and Irish models that emphasized movement through different levels culminating in reintegration into society. The prison system was nationalized under Hitler's National Socialist government from 1933 to 1945. It became a huge system holding several million prisoners by late in World War II--Jews, foreign nationals, military prisoners of war, political dissidents, and even a few ordinary criminals.

At the end of World War II, the traditional state prison system was reestablished. In 1969, Germany adopted the First Penal Reform Law, importing the system of **day fines** already in use in Scandinavian countries. Over the next 30 years, the day fine would become the principal criminal punishment in Germany. It is used to resolve over 80 percent of all criminal and traffic cases in German courts, typically as a replacement for a short sentence to confinement. In 1968, the year before day fines were adopted, 184,000 sentences to prison were handed down; 20 years later, the number had shrunk to just 48,000. Imprisonment, which through the 1950s was being used as the disposition of choice in about 40 percent of criminal cases, was being used in fewer than 10 percent a generation later. So it has remained into the early years of the twenty-first century.

The German **Prison Act of 1976** set out a model of imprisonment that is still in effect today. This legislation stresses rehabilitation and reintegration as the primary purposes of imprisonment. It also defines the legal rights of prisoners as citizens, including visiting rights, home leave, medical care, and productive paid labor. Even before this law was adopted, visitors to German prisons described an emphasis on **normalization** of the prisoner's life--getting the prisoner back into society and better equipped than he was before. One 1976 visitor found a humane system in which 40 percent of prisoners worked in private industry. Each prisoner had his or her own room, and there were no cells with bars.

This environment persists nearly three decades later. German prisons are small and located in or near cities, making work, visiting, and home leave more accessible. Prisons in Germany look less like secure correctional institutions and more like factories or hospitals. Community contacts are an important part of the prison experience. Low custody prisoners get **home leave**--an average of two or three visits home each year. Married inmates get family visits in prison with their spouses and children. In the *freiganger*, or **half-open release** program, inmates who have served half their sentences go out to work or to school during the day and return to the prison at night. Inmates would be paroled after two-thirds of their sentences unless they were classified as a risk or unless they declined parole. All German prisoners are parole eligible. Most lifers would expect to be paroled after about eight to 12 years in prisons, and mandatory release for lifers occurs at 15 years.

Germany's approach to corrections is marked by several key features. First, the use of diversionary practices involving day fines. Second, the expanded use of probation for most other convicted criminals, in combination with avoiding very short sentences to confinement. Third, short prison terms focused on reintegration. Only about 10 percent of prisoners have sentences longer than five years; the average prisoner is in custody less than a year. Avoiding the influence of the American "tough-on-crime" model, Germany has maintained both the size and philosophy of its correctional system over a long period of time. If anything, German criminologists and prison officials are interested in *lowering*, not raising, incarceration rates, looking at the rates of their neighbors across the Baltic Sea.

## Russia

The prison system of twentieth century Russia is dominated by the history of the labor camps, the *Glavnoe Upravlenie Lagerei*, or Main Camp Administration, that existed in the Soviet Union from 1918 until 1986--almost the entire life of Communist Russia. The **Gulag** at its peak consisted of almost 500 camp complexes--thousands of individual camps--holding more than two-and-a-half million people--ordinary and political criminals, including Nobel Prize winning author Alexander Solzhenitsyn, who compiled the three-volume *The Gulag Archipelago* after his release from prison.

For most of the twentieth century, the prison system of Russia and the Soviet Union was the largest in the world. When Communism finally collapsed, Russian society was in chaos for several years. Crime rates soared. Organized crime, attributed to the old network of gangsters--including the "**thieves in law**" and the **Chechens** from the rebel state of Chechnya--and now known as the **Russian Mafia**, dominated the economy, sucking money from legitimate businesses and corrupting police and government officials. Violent crime--murders, rapes, robberies, and assaults--shot sky high; the murder rate was more than twice as high as in the United States. Alcoholism and drug abuse increased sharply.

The prison system was under great strain. Legal reforms took several years, culminating in the transfer of all institutions and agencies administering the punishment of criminals from the Interior Ministry to the Justice Ministry on August 31, 1998. To Russians this move meant a break with the past--with the law-and-order mentality and the camps--and a move toward legalism and decarceration.

The majority of Russian prisoners are held in **corrective labor colonies** of different regimes or custody levels-- general, reinforced, strict, and special (for dangerous recidivists and those formerly sentenced to death). There were also separate hospital colonies, protection colonies, colony settlements (open prisons without fences), two different levels of women's colonies, education labor colonies for minors 14 to 18, and reinforced colonies for juvenile recidivists. Normal correctional colonies were isolated institutions enclosed by barbed wire, fenced with alarm systems, and patrolled by armed guards and dogs. Fences divided the colonies into zones--work, housing, punishment, hospital, school, administrative. Men and women were kept separate. Different levels of internal treatment--light, general, and strict--were used within the camp, like trusty grades, according to behavior and length of stay. An average colony might hold 1,500 to 2,000 prisoners. Inmates typically slept in open dormitories holding 20 to 50 inmates, or in large locked cells of comparable capacity.

Two other types of facilities--cellular prisons and remand prisons--round out this system. Cellular prisons, holding only about one percent of the convicted criminals, are used to isolate particularly dangerous recidivists or long-term offenders. Prisoners are kept in small, multi-person cells, which they leave only for work, exercise, or visitation. This is the strictest possible regimen in Russian prisons. Remand prisons, known as "SIZOs," are jails, usually in urban areas, holding inmates up to time of sentencing. Inmates are not supposed to spend more than a year in remand, but this rule is often violated.

At the end of the twentieth century, the magnitude of Russia's prison problems made its system the worst on earth. Sentences were long, very similar to America--66 months officially on average, 37 months to release. Facilities, especially the remand prisons, were badly overcrowded. Money was tight, so prisons had little to spend on inmates--less than a dollar a day per inmate for food, no money for medicine or medical treatment, no programs whatsoever. Sickness was rampant. A third of the inmate population had a psychiatric disorder. About 11 percent of inmates, more than 100,000 men and women, were infected with the **"prisoners' plague,"** tuberculosis, about a third of these with the drug-resistant strains that derive from interrupted treatment. Four percent of prisoners were HIV-positive, much higher than in the U.S. Three percent had syphilis. Drug addicts were growing in number. Gangsters ran the inside of many prisons, exploiting other inmates, and violence was a daily occurrence.

Though many expected a violent uprising that would destroy the prison system, it did not happen, and gradually reforms began to take hold after prisons were transferred to the Justice Ministry. Medical treatment improved. Aggressive programs to separate and treat TB-infected inmates lowered the rate of infection by a third within five years. As the social order was restored, the crime rate began to fall. Fewer arrests were being made and more pre-trial inmates released from custody, which cut the population of remand prisons in half within five years. The number of sentenced prisoners was in decline also, and more prisoners were being moved from secure colonies into open colony settlements. In five years, Russian's overall incarceration rate had dropped from 688 per 100,000 to 584. The prison system was said to be stable, and Russian officials were happy to acknowledge they had lost a major battle: The United States had officially won the world war of imprisonment.

## Saudi Arabia

Imagine that you are arrested and locked up, but you are not told why. You are not allowed to make a telephone call or contact anyone outside the prison. Now imagine that your jailers begin torturing you. The only way to stop them is to sign a confession, which you eventually do. Then you are convicted on the basis of that "confession" after a secret trial. You had no lawyer and nor the opportunity to defend yourself. Finally, imagine you are living in a country where the punishment you might face after such summary justice could be death, amputation of a limb, or flogging. Welcome to Saudi Arabia, according to Amnesty International.

Saudi Arabia, as the oldest of the modern Islamic states, is often used as an example of Muslim penal philosophy. The most obvious feature of the Saudi prison system is its small size, which is a consequence of the very limited use of imprisonment under Shari'a law as practiced in Saudi Arabia. Saudi Arabia's incarceration rate in the year 2000 was 110 per 100,000. With an estimated national population of 21.6 million, just 23,720 were behind bars in 30 prisons. Only a third of these, 8,100, were sentenced prisoners. The balance, almost 16,000, were pre-trial detainees.

The official explanation for the low rate of imprisonment is twofold. First, because of the strict morality in Islamic society, the crime rate is low. Second, among the penalties provided under Shari'a law, imprisonment is considered a last resort; it is used primarily for recidivists after other measures--the corporal punishments prescribed in the Qur'an--have failed.

The Saudi crime rate is among the lowest in the world, which criminologists suggest is due not only to high moral standards but also to the lack of reporting of many criminal offenses, especially those occurring within the family and among friends. The possibility of severe penalties--flogging, amputation of hands and feet, and death by stoning or beheading--for criminal offenses, is a further inhibitor of crime reporting, as are the high standards of proof required under Islamic law. Adultery by a married person is a death penalty offense, for example, but conviction requires the testimony of four male witnesses or a confession.

A third of the people living in Saudi Arabia are foreigners, most of them there to work. Over half the prison population is foreign, and in most years a majority of the 80 or 100 people beheaded in public squares for capital crimes are also foreigners. The American embassy warns visitors on its web site about possession of alcoholic beverages, controlled drugs, and pornography, reporting that Americans have received 75 or more lashes for failing a blood alcohol test or a year in prison for alcohol-related offenses. The embassy describes the role of **Mutawa**, the morals police, who might arrest American men or women for appearing in public inappropriately dressed--or for being found in possession of contraband items, such as a Valentine card.

Once taken into custody, arrested persons, whether Saudis or foreigners, exist in a legal world very different from the West. The United Nations Committee against Torture, responding to a Saudi report in May 2002, noted the following problems with Saudi custodial practices: corporal punishment, including flogging and amputation of limbs; prolonged incommunicado detention, including lack of access to legal and medical assistance; minimal judicial supervision of pre-trial detention; lack of criminal sanctions for the crime of torture by officials; and prolonged pre-trial detention and denial of consular access to detained foreigners for extended periods. The committee also questioned the role of the religious police and the lack of procedures to investigate possible cases of torture--often torture carried out by the **Mubahith**, or political police, during pre-trial confinement.

English-speaking citizens of common law countries are confounded at the complete absence of procedural controls. Criminals, especially political suspects, are held in pre-trial confinement for years. If they survive detention, questioning, and sentencing, they may enter the Saudi prison system, which is under the authority of the Directorate-General of Prisons with the Ministry of the Interior. The Prison and Detention Regulations of May 28, 1978, indicate that the directorate-general supervises prisons for men 18 and over and prisons for women 30 and over. The Ministry of Labor and Social Affairs operates social surveillance centers for males under 18 and welfare institutions for young women under 30.

The adult prisons are said to be subject to the supervision of the judiciary, who are trained in Shari'a law, and the Public Investigation and Prosecution Department, comparable to the procurator's post-sentencing role in some legal systems. Prisoners are subject to psychological examination upon entry into the prison system, followed by classification according to gender, age, type of offense, duration of sentence and criminal record, state of health, and social circumstances and cultural circumstances (such as religious beliefs). In addition to secure custody, the regulations allow for other individualized sentences, including suspended sentences, pardon, release on probation, release on health grounds, and semi-liberty (work release). On the whole, the Saudi prison administration finds that its Prison and Detention Regulations "transcend" the U.N.'s Standard Minimum Rules for the Treatment of Prisoners, first adopted in 1955. In its view, Saudi prisons are highly focused, carefully monitored, and effectively performing their limited mission in the modern Islamic state.

## China

In prison circles, Chinese prisons are often referred to a **bamboo gulag**. The dual basis for this reference is, first, the political nature of imprisonment, and, second, the emphasis on full-time work as the pathway to reform in prison. The details of imprisonment in China remain foggy to outsiders. The People's Republic of China is a totalitarian Communist country, and, even as they encourage capitalist policies to develop China's vast economic potential, party leaders resist efforts to make government and social policies more transparent and open to debate. China still speaks with one voice--following a script written by the Communist Party.

At the end of 2003, China counted 689 prisons holding 1,549,000 sentenced prisoners. This is more sentenced prisoners than the United States, but remember that China has more four times as many people as the U.S.--1.3 billion to 295 million. The official imprisonment rate--viewed with skepticism by many outsiders--is 119 per 100,000, which is comparable to many Western nations.

In China, sentenced prisoners are held in institutions under the authority of the Ministry of Justice, while pre-trial detainees are under the control of the Ministry of Public Security, which is also responsible for policing. Five types of secure-custody institutions exist:
>    1. Detention houses (the *kanshou* houses or detention centers), which hold pre-trial and short-term sentenced inmates.
>    2. Juvenile reformatories (or reform houses), which house 14- to 18-year-olds who are considered more serious criminals.
>    3. Criminal detention houses (or reeducation through labor--*laojiao*--facilities), which hold those in the status of **administrative detention**. The status of *juyi*, or criminal detention, is an administrative determination without a trial; the offender is fined and placed in custody for an indeterminate period, commonly up to three or four years. His status is considered noncriminal, or administrative, even though he is locked up.
>    4. **Reform through labor camps** (commonly called *laogai*), which house criminals serving sentences of from one to 10 years.
>    5. Prisons, holding those serving sentences longer than 10 years, a life sentence, or a death sentence.

Noncustodial sanctions are also used. The principal one, similar to probation, is called *guanzhi*, also known as control or **public surveillance**. The offender continues to work and earn regular wages while reporting to the local public security office regularly. Other options include suspended sentences and fines. Minor criminals may also have some of their civil and property rights suspended, and they may be subject to censure or requirements that, under the direction of local committees--referred to as reconciliation and mediation committees--they renounce their crimes before gatherings of their neighbors or coworkers. From the 1960s through the 1990s, China used a practice called **shelter and investigation** to pick up, detain, and relocate unattached citizens-- unapproved migrants, transients, the unemployed, and in some cases political activists. They were managed under administrative policies and were subject to detention and relocation at the discretion of the police. This practice had reportedly been abandoned by the end of the century.

Chinese prisons draw their operating philosophy from old traditions filtered through Communist Party ideology. Confucianism, which flourished around 500 B.C., emphasized social harmony as best secured by moral education to bring out the good nature of all; this was achieved through informal social pressure from family and community. Legalism, which followed later in China, emphasized formal laws and strict punishments. Under the Communist doctrine of Mao Zedong (Chairman Mao), who led Communist China from 1949 to 1976, moral education and law were joined under the direction of the party. The basis of social control was through the committees in the neighborhoods and workplaces; prison was simply a stricter environment for control and education. Mao said that the prison should be run like a school, a factory, or a farm.

Prisoners, like other Chinese citizens, are obligated to work. The 1994 **Prison Law**, Article 69, states: "Any criminal with the labour capacity must participate in labour." About 85 percent of prisoners are working, some of them in manual labor jobs such as farming, clearing land, and building roads in rural areas, but many now working in industrial jobs in factories near cities. Western visitors to Chinese prisons are struck by the fact that virtually all prisoners are productively occupied. If they are not working, inmates are in class, in group recreation, or in counseling sessions called "political study," which is really about why their selfish criminal attitudes do not fit the social harmony of communism.

Chinese prisons are big, many of them averaging 2,000 to 3,000 inmates living in separate units. Inmates live in congregate cells typically housing 10 to 20 prisoners each. Visitors observe that Chinese prisoners have few creature comforts but that institutions are clean, well run, and completely free of violence and escape attempts. Discipline is maintained by the **five rewards and five punishments**. The rewards are praise, bonuses, recording merits in the official file, reduction of the sentence, and parole. The punishments are group criticism, an official warning, recording demerits, solitary confinement, and increasing the sentence.

Using work, peer pressure, and indoctrination techniques, prisons work to accomplish **thought reform**, which at one time was said by outsiders to be like brainwashing but is now viewed as being more akin to the cognitive training, addressing thinking patterns, that has become more prevalent in Western prisons. How effective is remolding behavior? Prison officials in the 1980s claimed very low recidivism rates, four or five percent, and, even today, when authorities acknowledge that crime and the prison population are increasing as China's economy grows, the official recidivism rate remains under 10 percent.

Although Chinese prisons are said to "work," in terms of the role they play in society, and have undergone substantial reforms in the past decade, since the enactment of the Prison Law, they continue to draw criticisms on several fronts. Forced labor by non-sentenced prisoners is one. The international sale of unmarked prison-made goods is another. The U.S. government has laws in effect to prevent items manufactured by prison labor from entering this country, but these laws have not been applied to exclude Chinese products.

China's prolific use of the death penalty is another problem. In most years, it may execute more criminals than the entire rest of the world added together. It launches large-scale anti-crime campaigns--called *yanda*, or "strike hard"--that often result in thousands of executions. What happens after the execution is also a matter of controversy. Many criminals are asked--or required--to sign consent forms allowing their organs to be donated after death. When the criminal is killed by a bullet to the head, medical staff are standing by not to save a life but to harvest the organs for transplantation. Kidneys, corneas, livers, hearts, lungs, the corpse is stripped of all usable parts, which are then distributed to recipients around the country, most notably in Beijing, Shanghai, and Hong Kong. Sometimes the organs are donated, and sometimes they are sold, with a kidney reportedly worth in the range of $30,000 to $40,000 dollars on the organ market.

## Japan

Japanese prisons much resemble Chinese prisons except that the system is much smaller. At year end 2002, the 72 Japanese prisons and 117 detention houses--all under the direction of the Correction Bureau in the Ministry of Justice--held 69,502 prisoners. With an estimated national population of 127.6 million, the incarceration rate is calculated at 54 per 100,000. Texas, in contrast, with a population of 22 million, held three times as many prisoners in custody, over 210,000, in 2002. Japanese imprisonment rates increased sharply in the 1990s as the country struggled with economic malaise and increasing crime.

The **Prison Law** of Japan, enacted in 1908, is still in effect today. It is long on granting authority to prison officials and short on the rights of prisoners. The prison approach is militaristic. Prisoners are subject to searches several times a day, beginning each day with a naked strip search in the cell. The rules are very detailed. Many prisons require prisoners to march in military unison from place to place. Talking in the workplace is forbidden, as is looking directly at another prisoner.

Prisoners work 40 to 44 hours per week; about two-thirds of all inmates worked in industrial production in 1994, mostly through contracts with private employers outside. Most of the remaining convicts work at the internal chores--cooking, cleaning, maintenance--necessary to maintain the prison. In some prisons, prisoners in the workplace begin the work day shouting out the **five principles** in unison–always be honest, sincerely repent, always be polite, keep a helpful attitude, and be thankful.

Japanese criminals are dealt with harshly until they reform themselves and conform to the interests of society, at which point they are treated with the **extraordinary leniency** that marks the Japanese legal system. Criminals who prove themselves deserving of leniency, by expressing sincere contrition and making amends for wrongs done, avoid imprisonment or get very short sentences. The Japanese legal system provides six main penalties:
1. Minor fines (less than 10,000 yen).
2. Penal detention (less than 30 days).
3. Fines (more than 10,000 yen).
4. Imprisonment without labor (rarely used).
5. Imprisonment with labor.
6. Death.
The death penalty is applied sparingly in Japan. A majority of the public approves of its use, and Japan continues to sentence a handful--perhaps five to 10--criminals to death for murder and maintain them in prison awaiting execution, but executions have become rare events. Some years no one is executed. When the death penalty is carried out, it is done by hanging.

Fines predominate, and suspended sentences without supervision are more common than probation. Imprisonment, mostly with labor but sometimes without, is reserved for those criminals not deserving leniency--

gangsters, gun and drug smugglers, foreigners (especially other Asians), Japanese burakumin (the native untouchable caste), and habitual offenders. Violent criminals may also be in this bunch, but they may not be in prison long if they are considered one-time offenders and have expressed real contrition. In most years, 80 to 90 percent of Japanese criminals sentenced to imprisonment receive sentences of fewer than three years in prison. It is not uncommon for criminals to get probation for robbery, rape, attempted murder, or even murder.

Japan has an expansive system of probation and parole under the Rehabilitation Bureau of the Ministry of Justice. The great majority of juvenile offenders (criminals under age 20) receive probation, as do many adults. The probation network in Japan emphasizes the work of **volunteer probation officers**, now numbering more than 50,000. Most of the volunteers are middle-aged and older private citizens who wish to work one-on-one with one or two younger offenders at a time.

Japanese prisons offer few educational, vocational, or recreational programs in comparison to American prisons, but they emphasize the role of the prison officer as a combined moral educator, lay counselor, security monitor, and reformer. Personal contacts between officers and prisoners are not forbidden. Officers are expected to act as surrogate fathers or brothers toward inmates.

Most Japanese prisons also practice **Naikan**, a form of therapy with philosophical roots in Buddhist spiritual practices. Used in Japanese prisons since the 1950s, Naikan begins with a week of intense (up to 16 hours a day) guided meditation in isolation. This immersion phase is focused on getting the prisoner to ask and answer a series of questions focusing on the important relationships in his life, especially the troubles the prisoner has caused these other people. Counseling continues on a weekly or less frequent basis as the prisoner continues to meditate and develop insight into living a constructive life in harmony with others.

The authoritative approach of Japanese prisons is a concern to many human rights organizations, who point out that "big brothers" are often abusive to "little brothers." This is happening with greater frequency, they maintain, as Japan's prisons have to cope with persistent overcrowding. The plain, dilapidated prisons, the five-and-a-half day work weeks, the meticulous enforcement of the rules, and the absolute monotony of the prison routine have reportedly led to more resistance by prisoners and more coercive responses by prison officers in recent years.

Prisons are orderly--there is no history of escapes, riots, or inmate violence--but the tight discipline used to maintain order invites abuses--long periods in solitary confinement kneeling or sitting in a fixed position, leather handcuffs and body belts that are kept on for days at a time, kicking and beating of unruly prisoners, and denial of medical treatment. Prisons are as secretive and autocratic as they were in the early part of the twentieth century in America before prisoners' rights had any widespread meaning.

## The Use and Purpose of Imprisonment

The prison is universal in modern society, but its use within a given country is highly individualized. Within each nation, the prison meets a certain purpose, but the purpose is defined within a social, political, and cultural context. Wealthy Western nations can devote more resources to maintaining nice jails and prisons, if they choose to. These countries often have nationalized corrections bureaucracies that oversee a network of specialized institutions. Less developed countries with lower standards of living often have low rates of imprisonment. Their justice systems are often localized, so that punishments are informal and occur outside the national system. They also cannot afford to maintain expensive prison systems applying rigorous international standards of confinement.

If we were to compare international imprisonment rates, one of the first things we would notice is that civil law countries often hold a greater percentage of their prisoners in remand status awaiting trial. This results from the civil law practice of holding accused persons in detention until trial while the thorough pretrial investigation is conducted. France is an example of such a nation. Until recently, a majority of its prisoners were pretrial detainees; the figure was down to about 38 percent in 2004, which is still about double the average rate of 20 percent or less that prevails in common law countries. The disproportionate number of pretrial detainees also appears in numerous other non-European countries whose legal systems are based on civil law, including most nations in Africa and Latin America. In these regions, the majority of all prisoners are awaiting trial.

We would notice also that Islamic countries often have lower imprisonment rates. Islamic law, which is most prevalent in Asian countries where imprisonment rates are lower regardless of the legal system, further limits the use of prison as punishment. Pretrial incarceration rates are often high in Islamic systems, but the relative informality of the legal system and the use of economic and corporal punishments tend to hold down the numbers of sentenced prisoners.

Countries experiencing prolonged periods of internal instability often see their imprisonment rates climb. This was surely noticeable in Russia, in many of its former components in Northern Europe, Central Asia, and Central Europe that were reborn from the former U.S.S.R., and in many of the Eastern European nations that had been under Soviet dominance for a good part of the twentieth century. Fifteen years after the collapse of the Soviet Union, the rates of imprisonment in the former Communist states remain on average two or three times as high as the rates in Western Europe. Russia seems to have a handle on controlling imprisonment at present, but its rates are five times the Western European average.

Finland, which in the 1960s had an imprisonment rate much higher than that of the United States, had reduced its rate to 52 per 100,000, the lowest in Western Europe, in 2002. It did so by deliberately implementing a series of policy changes in pursuit of one goal: To reduce imprisonment, either by diverting offenders to other forms of punishment or by reducing the time served in prison. In a given year, over 90 percent of Finland's convicted felons receive noncustodial sentences--day fines, probation, community service. Fewer than 10 percent receive prison sentences. Finland's imprisonment rate is slightly lower than its Scandinavian neighbors and its crime rate, which went up steadily during the reform period, leveled off in the early 1990s and has declined steadily since then. Punishment had little or no effect on the crime rate.

Marc Mauer of The Sentencing Project has often made this same point--that the use of imprisonment in America is not directly tied to the crime rate or, conversely, that changes in crime have not been the driving force in expanding the prison population over the past 30 years. Mauer indicates increased crime accounted for only 12 percent of the prison rise, while changes in sentencing policy--more direct sentences to prison, mandatory sentencing, truth in sentencing, three strikes and you're out laws, natural life sentences, and other changes leading to longer prison terms--accounted for the rest. The prison is used more because the justice system is far more punitive than in years past.

The use of prisons in a given country is determined by many conditions, as Baroness Vivien Stern of the International Centre for Prison Studies in London pointed out in 2003:

"Prison is an intensely cultural institution. The models of imprisonment in Western Europe and North America are imbued with Christian ideas of guilt, punishment and atonement. They are modelled on the monastery with individual rooms that are called cells. The Russian concept is of banishment and work. In the East, in China and Japan, the aim is to remould the person into conformity. In other parts of the world the whole idea of the prison as the main punishment for crime is an imposition, a colonial legacy, and still sits uneasily in the thinking of Africa or India. What is deemed right to take away from prisoners is cultural. What prisoners will see as legitimate deprivations and what they will not accept is also rooted in their ideas of right and wrong."

## Who Goes to Prison?

If we were to line up all the people behind bars in almost 200 nations worldwide, the first thing we would notice would be the overwhelming numbers of men--around the world only about six percent of prisoners are women. In countries where the percentage is higher--in the U.S. it was 8.5 percent of all jail and prison inmates in 2003-- this is mostly attributed to the involvement of females in drug and vice crimes.

The next thing we would likely notice is that minorities and foreigners always show up in disproportionate numbers behind bars. In England, the minorities are blacks--from the Caribbean and Africa--and dark-skinned Asians. In Western Europe, it is the young male guestworkers from Southern Europe, the Middle East, and North Africa and the transient foreigners who stand out. In some European countries, such as the ethnically homogeneous Switzerland and Luxembourg, two-thirds or more of all prisoners are foreigners. In Hungary, 40 percent of the prison population is made up of Gypsies--this nation's "usual suspects." In Australia the Aboriginal natives make up less than two percent of the population but 19 percent of prisoners. Canada has a similar experience with its First Nations peoples. Michael Tonry has pointed out members of minority groups are overrepresented among crime victims, arrestees, pretrial detainees, convicted offenders, and prisoners in every Western nation.

Finally, we would notice among those behind bars a very small number of juveniles, a practice in which the United States leads the world. The **Beijing Rules** (formally the United Nations Standard Minimum Rules for the Administration of Juvenile Justice, adopted in 1985) define juvenile status not by age, which varies widely from system to system, but by a legal process different from that applicable to an adult. These rules encourage dealing with juvenile criminal behavior outside of court except in the most serious of cases. They encourage noncustodial sanctions, and they forbid the application of the death penalty to persons under the age of 17, which in 2004 was allowed by law in 18 American states. Texas is the world's leading executioner of juveniles.

Philip Reichel has discussed four principal models of juvenile justice used in different countries.
     1. The **welfare model**, prevalent in many Western countries, centers on treatment and the delivery of social services outside the formal legal system.
     2. The **legalistic model**, which deals with the juvenile more formally under the strict control of the court.
     3. The **corporatist model**, of which England is a good example at present, which merges government officials and other public and private professionals into teams to manage juvenile justice at the local level.
     4. The **participatory model**, of which China is a good example, which tries to work with juveniles through local neighborhood committees outside the formal system.

Reichel also discusses the **benign-neglect approach** (adopted from James Hackler), which suggests that many underdeveloped countries, lacking a juvenile justice bureaucracy, deal with juveniles informally and do not lock them up. Although international studies suggest that juvenile crime rates peak out in the mid- to late-teen years, the preferred response is to practice leniency and await the maturing that comes with adulthood. The United States does this, but we practice rehabilitation within a secure institutional setting far more than other nations.

## The Prison Experience

One of the truisms of imprisonment, as applicable to other countries as it is to the United States, is that once you get past the condition of being locked up, the quality of prison life depends on the prison in which you are confined. The United Nations has adopted about two dozen standards pertinent to human rights and the administration of justice. The standards of the Basic Principles for the Treatment of Prisoners, for example, deal with such issues as avoiding discrimination, respect for human dignity, avoiding solitary confinement, paid work, access to health services, and reintegration into society. Needless to say, all nations regularly fall short of meeting the custodial standards set by these agreements. **Amnesty International** and **Human Rights Watch** both prepare annual reports highlighting specific problems with treatment of prisoners around the world.

Some nations--and their prisoners--have a lot more problems than others. The most pervasive problem worldwide is overcrowding. Only about one in five countries is below 90 percent of its maximum prison capacity--a level considered desirable for flexibility in housing prisoners safely. The majority of the world's prison system are above 100 percent capacity, several way above. Among the major countries--mostly in Africa and Asia--whose prison occupancy levels are more than 200 percent over capacity are Cameroon, Bangladesh, Zambia, Iran, Thailand, Kenya, Pakistan, and Rwanda; Honduras in Central America is also on this list.

Problems with hygiene, health care, food service, violence, stress, gangs, and abuse of inmates are common in overcrowded prisons. The prisons of Russia and Central Asia have high rates of MDR-TB. Many African prisons have very high rates of HIV/AIDS. British prisons suffered through riots attributed to overcrowding in the 1990s. Prison violence has been endemic in several overcrowded Latin American prison systems--Bolivia, Brazil, Peru, and Venezuela--for more than a decade. While American prisons are safer than the outside society, the Venezuelan prison murder rate is estimated to be more than 40 times the national average.

Corruption is a way of life in many of these systems. Congregate housing, easy access to weapons, including firearms, and low levels of staffing complicate prison life for ordinary inmates. Influential prisoners with money live well in these prisons, with private rooms, cell phones, family visits, and special meals. Other prisoners barely get by day to day, enduring a climate of fear, violence, sexual exploitation, and extreme deprivation that is completely contrary to the rights and dignities set forth in United Nations's agreements.

## Explaining Differences

American jails and prisons rank moderately low on the international scale of human rights abuses of prisoners. Our prisoners are relatively safe and adequately cared for in comparison to those of many other countries, and most American prisoners are no longer held in badly overcrowded facilities. But our correctional institutions do draw critical attention in regard to several human rights issues:

1. Overuse of solitary confinement, especially the conditions of prolonged isolation in supermax prisons.
2. Isolation of state and federal prisoners in rural institutions far from visitors, work, and treatment programs.
3. Imprisonment of drug addicts who are perceived elsewhere as a public health concern.
4. The traditional use of extralegal physical punishments of inmates by staff in several jail and prison systems.
5. Overcrowding and lack of activities and services in many local jails.
6. Overuse of secure custody for juveniles.
7. Continued use of the death penalty, which remains on the books in 38 states and at the federal level.
8. Overrepresentation of blacks and Hispanics behind bars.
9. And finally, and most noticeably, the extreme overuse of incarceration, making our custodial rates the highest in the world at more than 700 prisoners per 100,000 citizens. Once you take Russia and South Africa out of the mix, the United States locks up its citizens at a rate about five to eight times higher than other industrialized nations.

Why does America have such a high rate of imprisonment, especially in comparison to the other Western nations with whom we usually compare ourselves? We do have higher rates of violent crime and crimes committed with firearms than our Western neighbors, but violent criminality is only a minor part of the overall picture. In America, sentencing of all criminals has gotten a lot tougher over the last two decades.

At its heart of this change is the concept of **punitiveness**, defined as support for inflicting punishment. Research suggests that punitiveness is a cultural trait, an aspect of one society that can be compared to a corresponding society. Respondents in Asia and Africa are most punitive, those in North America and Latin America less so, and those in Western Europe much less so. Punitiveness is generally connected to the crime rate, except in Asia, which has generally lower crime rates. There is little connection between imprisonment preferences and personal victimization; punitiveness was not based on personal experience or contact with crime.

Punitiveness in practice is a combination of attitudes, crime rates, and government policies. Asians might be as punitive as Americans, but they have much lower crime rates to contend with. Africans might be as punitive, but their criminal justice systems are small, underfunded, and overworked; they ignore a lot of crime or punish less severely because their systems cannot afford to punish more harshly--and also because justice is still seen as more of a local concern, based upon old tribal or kinship networks, than a matter for national determination.

The Western Europeans and English-speaking industrialized nations who do face crime rates comparable to ours are not as punitive. They are more supportive of alternatives and short sentences. They do not have to live with the same perceived levels of violent crime that Americans do. They are also more constrained by the practice of criminal justice within a national framework.

The American criminal justice system is an odd hybrid--a nonsystem, it is often called--of local, state, and federal organizations. Most policies are made at the local level where politicians respond to citizens who not only think more punitively but also have more **real crime**--especially violent crime (though most of this happens to lower class people in cities)--to worry about. We think legalistically, emphasizing formal controls, and we are an affluent nation that can afford to maintain an expensive criminal justice system.

The number of people under correctional supervision--secure and nonsecure--has increased from one million in 1970 to almost seven million in 2004. Scholars who study social class in American history suggest that the big boost in imprisonment in the last 20 years of the twentieth century is the most recent incarnation of society's ongoing effort to control its dangerous classes. Scott Christianson has documented the concentration of immigrants and non-whites in jails and prisons throughout American history, suggesting that the class-based focus of confinement has found a permanent target in America's poor urban minorities.

It is black and Hispanic males (and more recently black females as well) in American cities who have born the brunt of the vast increase in correctional intervention over the past generation. This is particularly noticeable in the 16 Southern states, 12 of which have majority black prison populations, as do 10 other states outside the South. Other nations tend to do the same thing with the poor, and immigrants, and people of color, as we have seen, they just do not have as many of them to contend with as we do, nor are they generally perceived to be as physically threatening to the social order--**social dynamite**, in Steven Spitzer's definition of dangerous deviance.

189

One of the key elements in determining punitiveness is the contrast between homogeneity and heterogeneity. Nations made up of people who are very much alike--same ethnicity, religion, and values--tend to be much less punitive than nations made up of people who are very different from each other. It was no big surprise, in the 1990s, that the three leading countries in world imprisonment rates were the United States, Russia, and South Africa. Not only were Russia and South Africa going through major periods of social upheaval after changing governmental regimes, but both nations were also multicultural societies in which vastly different peoples were mixed together under extreme pressures. The criminal law and criminal punishments were used increasingly to impose formal order on these disorderly, conflict-ridden societies.

In the **war on crime** analogy that prevails in the United States, law-abiding people are "the good guys" and criminals are "the bad guys" in an ongoing civil war. Or, to carry the analogy forward into confinement, as Baroness Vivien Stern has suggested, the prisoner is seen not as a citizen but as the **enemy of the state**. Her position is that prisons are not places to hold people deemed to be enemies of the state. Rather, in a democratic society prison is a public service comparable to a school or hospital. The prison should have the objective of contributing to the public good. But many Americans would not agree with this position: The whole direction of American thought and public policy for a generation has been to see prisoners as the enemy. The political hyperbole and exaggerated punitiveness only make it more difficult for us to see them as fellow citizens in need of assistance, rather than evil adversaries to be feared, loathed, isolated, and controlled in perpetuity.

## American Corrections: The Recent Past and the Near Future

Where is American corrections headed in the near future? Our combined jail and imprisonment rates are five times higher than they were in the early 1970s; should we expect more of the same?

Most correctional policy in America is formed and implemented at the local and state level--rather than the federal level--and it is based far more on ideology or belief than upon fact or plan. This is the politics of **expressive justice**, as David Anderson has referred to policies based on how you feel rather than knowledge and reasoned thought. These policies have developed into a national model in response to what is often seen--incorrectly--as a constantly rising flood tide of crime in America since the 1960s. People have repeated the slogans so long they have become part of our way of thinking--a personal and often wrongheaded view of crime and criminals.

In some foreign countries, corrections policies are made at the national level based on research by criminologists. In the United States, national, state, and local politicians, led by or leading the public, individually and as members of various interest groups, decide on the policy first, then seek the research (or useful statistics) to support their position and establish policies. Criminologists, systems experts, and often practitioners are out of this loop.

It is striking, within the United States, how much imprisonment rates vary from state to state, the numbers a composite formed by policies based on the various internal conflicts--urban/rural, class, racial, religious, and cultural--that make up punitiveness. Imprisonment is said to be the reverse of prevention, and this is most noticeable in regard to children.

Each year the Annie E. Casey Foundation publishes the Kids Count Survey ranking the 50 states according to ten variables related to child well-being, including poverty, dropout rates, death rates, and other variables. Year after year, the states at the top of the list, in terms of being good places for children to live, are states with low rates of imprisonment; states with high imprisonment rates are worse places for children. Part of this is directly reflective of state policies: states ranking high on the Kids Count Survey spent larger percentages of the state budget on services to children than states ranking lower, while the lower ranking states spent more on imprisonment. This approach gives rise to a kind of "reverse welfare system" in America --spend nothing on children now, then spend $20,000 to $25,000 a year keeping criminals safe and secure in prison as adults.

Lately, there have been indications that several states would like to move in the direction of downsizing their prison systems. There is more talk of **smart justice**, a term that has come to mean more efficient use of resources, as in fewer prison beds, more community-based alternatives. The main motivation for this move appears to be the cost of imprisonment. As its share of state budgets increases, corrections has been consuming resources government would prefer to spend on other services--education, health, transportation, the environment.

The state that has held down the growth of its prison population most effectively over the past 25 years is North

Carolina. In 1980, North Carolina had the highest imprisonment rate in the country, 248 per 100,000. By 2001, this rate had increased by only about 35 percent, to 335, the second lowest in the South and well below the national average. Even some of the states ranking lower in overall imprisonment rates, such as Maine and Minnesota, had more than doubled their rates over this period. How did North Carolina control its prison population, even reducing its use of imprisonment after 1995? Research cites sentencing guidelines, treatment of drug offenders, shorter sentences for nonviolent criminals, and a depoliticized crime policy based on costs versus results.

It is not hard to find lists of what we as a nation could be doing differently. The American Bar Association set out its *Blueprint for Cost-Effective Pre-Trial Detention, Sentencing, and Corrections* in 2002. Roy Walmsley has outlined several critical measures to reduce jail and prison populations internationally--less use of pre-trial detention, quicker movement of cases to disposition, increasing the availability and use of alternatives to prison sentences, shorter prison sentences, increasing the use of early release, and using amnesties to correct existing inequities. Other international authorities have comparable lists focusing on reducing the use of imprisonment and emphasizing preventive and treatment measures. While these measures could return imprisonment rates to where they were a generation or two ago, it is far from certain that they are politically viable in the punitive environment of twenty-first century America.

# Self Test

## Multiple Choice

1. Four of the following would fit in the five principles of Japanese prisoners; which one would NOT?
   a. Always be honest.
   b. Keep a helpful attitude.
   c. Express your individuality.
   d. Sincerely repent.
   e. Be thankful.

2. What the United States calls a jail other countries generally call a _____ institution.
   a. transitional
   b. mental
   c. dispersal
   d. remand
   e. terminal

3. In the war on crime analogy, the criminal is viewed as a(n):
   a. victim of circumstance
   b. enemy of the state
   c. public health menace
   d. lost orphan
   e. illegal immigrant

4. The new combined prison and probation organization in England is known as:
   a. NOMS
   b. MOBS
   c. POPS
   d. COPP
   e. BONES

5. Which nation executes the most criminals each year?
   a. Russia
   b. the United States
   c. Germany
   d. China
   e. Japan

6. The nation which has recently had the worst problems with tuberculosis and HIV--AIDS in its prison population is:
   a. Russia
   b. England
   c. Japan
   d. China
   e. Germany

7. Naikan in Japan is basically a form of:
   a. martial arts
   b. family visitation
   c. recreation
   d. community service
   e. therapy

8. On his tour of California prisons, German prison warden Volker Bierschke said the most striking difference between German and American prisons was that American prisons:
   a. had more work for prisoners
   b. were much larger
   c. allowed more contact with society
   d. had much less security
   e. paid staff better salaries

9. If the United States has the highest incarceration rate, which country featured in this chapter has the lowest?
   a. China
   b. Germany
   c. Canada
   d. Japan
   e. England

10. Public surveillance in China is most like the American practice of:
    a. boot camp
    b. pretrial release
    c. probation
    d. furlough
    e. drug court

## True or False

_____ 11. Germany has abolished parole as being insensitive to crime victims.

_____ 12. Most Canadian federal prisoners are serving sentences for drug crimes.

_____ 13. Human rights groups report that Saudi Arabian police continue to resort to torture of prisoners in custody to get confessions.

_____ 14. "Smart justice" is a new campaign to imprison larger numbers of adolescents before they hit their peak crime years.

_____ 15. Japan is often accused of outside critics of allowing prisoners too many rights in confinement.

_____ 16. States that rank high in the Kids Count Survey generally have low rates of imprisonment.

_____ 17. Poor underdeveloped countries are most likely to practice the legalistic model of juvenile justice because it is the most simple.

_____ 18. Canada has deliberately increased its imprisonment rate to discourage American criminals from moving to Canada to operate.

_____ 19. The Western European countries generally deport rather than imprison foreign citizens who commit crimes on their soil.

_____ 20. Most countries around the world report a steady increase in imprisonment rates in the 1990s.

## Fill In the Blanks

21. The common term for the network of labor camps spread across the Communist Soviet Union was the _____.

22. English prisons rely on an official called a(n) _____ to investigate complaints by prisoners and recommend corrective action.

23. China's vigorous nationwide anti-crime campaigns are known by the term _____.

24. The nation that once emphasized the borstal as a sort of boarding school for adolescent delinquents was _____.

25. The German Prison Act of 1976 stressed the goals of rehabilitation and _____.

26. An ordinary felon serving a five-year sentence in China wold be sent to a *laogai* prison; the name means "reform through _____."

27. The most common punishment applied to German criminals is _____.

28. Contestability in England is the equivalent of _____ in the United States.

29. If you were in a prison cell and learned that several of your cellmates were Chechens who were said to belong to a Mafia, you would most likely be in the country of _____.

30. The Western European country that has pursued a policy of decarceration (reducing imprisonment) most diligently over the past 30 years is _____.

## Discussion

31. Is the "crime problem" a general international concern? Explain.

32. Describe the general trend in imprisonment worldwide over the past decade.

33. Explain Canada's "effective corrections" plan.

34. What are England's major prison problems at present, and what is the government trying to do to address these problems?

35. Compare the German prison experience to the American prison experience.

36. Why did Russian prisons get so bad in the 1990s?

37. Discuss the concept of prisoners' rights as it would apply in Saudi Arabia.

38. How does corrections in China fit into totalitarian political control of society?

39. Observers say that not many people go to prison in Japan but, for the ones who are imprisoned, prison conditions are tough. Explain the Japanese view of the place of imprisonment in society.

40. How does the experience of imprisonment vary from one country to another?

41. What do international observers find to criticize about the American corrections system?

42. Why is the American imprisonment rate the highest in the world?

43. What does the future of corrections in America look like to you?

# Answers to Chapter Self Tests

## Chapter 1: Early Punishments

| Multiple Choice | True or False | Fill In the Blanks |
|---|---|---|
| 1. b (p. 10) | 11. T (p. 14) | 21. Maison de Force (p. 18) |
| 2. c (p. 5) | 12. F (p. 12) | 22. transportation (p. 4) |
| 3. c (p. 15) | 13. T (p. 4) | 23. John Howard (p. 13) |
| 4. d (p. 16) | 14. T (p. 3) | 24. utilitarianism (p. 13) |
| 5. a (p. 12) | 15. F (p. 8) | 25. Enlightenment (p. 10) |
| 6. d (p. 4) | 16. T (p. 5) | 26. Shari'a (p. 10) |
| 7. b (p. 14) | 17. F (p. 6) | 27. stocks/pillory (p. 6) |
| 8. c (p. 18) | 18. F (p. 15) | 28. corporal (p. 2) |
| 9. c (p. 17) | 19. T (p. 13) | 29. socialist (p. 9) |
| 10. e (p. 14) | 20. F (p. 9) | 30. Penitentiary Act of 1779 (p. 14) |

## Chapter 2: The Penitentiary and the 1800s

| Multiple Choice | True or False | Fill In the Blanks |
|---|---|---|
| 1. d (p. 32) | 11. F (p. 32) | 21. silence (p. 27) |
| 2. a (p. 24) | 12. T (p. 23) | 22. Pennsylvania (p. 26) |
| 3. a (p. 37) | 13. F (p. 28) | 23. Auburn (p. 26) |
| 4. c (p. 31) | 14. T (p. 26) | 24. parole (p. 31) |
| 5. c (p. 26) | 15. F (p. 27) | 25. Alderson (p. 33) |
| 6. b (p. 28) | 16. F (p. 37) | 26. child saving (p. 35) |
| 7. b (p. 23) | 17. F (p. 34) | 27. reformatory (p. 37) |
| 8. e (p. 32) | 18. F (p. 32) | 28. penance (p. 22) |
| 9. b (p. 22) | 19. F (p. 35) | 29. prison farms (p. 36) |
| 10. c (p. 30) | 20. F (p. 39) | 30. reformation (p. 37) |

## Chapter 3: Twentieth Century Corrections Systems

| Multiple Choice | True or False | Fill In the Blanks |
|---|---|---|
| 1. c (p. 45) | 11. F (p. 53) | 21. the Great Depression (p. 47) |
| 2. e (p. 44) | 12. T (p. 46) | 22. work (p. 48) |
| 3. d (p. 47) | 13. F (p. 49) | 23. Sanford Bates (p. 47) |
| 4. c (p. 53) | 14. F (p. 47) | 24. icebox (p. 56) |
| 5. b (p. 51) | 15. F (p. 49) | 25. Prison (p. 51) |
| 6. b (p. 52) | 16. F (p. 57) | 26. recidivism (p. 53) |
| 7. a (p. 54) | 17. F (p. 50) | 27. women (p. 57) |
| 8. e (p. 55) | 18. F (p. 46) | 28. reformation (p. 51) |
| 9. c (p. 60) | 19. T (p. 56) | 29. balanced (p. 56) |
| 10. d (p. 45) | 20. T (p. 58) | 30. open (p. 58) |

## Chapter 4: Ideologies and Sentencing

| Multiple Choice | True or False | Fill In the Blanks |
|---|---|---|
| 1. e (p. 67) | 11. F (p. 79) | 21. selective incapacitation (p. 69) |
| 2. d (p. 78) | 12. T (p. 67) | 22. logical consequences (p. 69) |
| 3. e (p. 79) | 13. F (p. 66) | 23. reintegration (p. 68) |
| 4. c (p. 80) | 14. T (p. 74) | 24. good time (p. 77) |
| 5. b (p. 79) | 15. T (p. 78) | 25. disparity (or discrimination) (p. 79) |
| 6. d (p. 76) | 16. T (p. 76) | 26. judges (p. 77) |
| 7. a (p. 69) | 17. F (p. 69) | 27. guidelines (p. 81) |
| 8. c (p. 74) | 18. T (p. 80) | 28. parole (p. 77) |
| 9. e (p. 70) | 19. F (p. 72) | 29. misdemeanor (p. 71) |
| 10. d (p. 84) | 20. T (p. 74) | 30. prosecutor (p. 75) |

## Chapter 5: Jails

| Multiple Choice | True or False | Fill In the Blanks |
|---|---|---|
| 1. b (p. 102) | 11. F (p. 96) | 21. typhus (or gaol fever) (p. 95) |
| 2. a (p. 98) | 12. F (p. 97) | 22. community service (p. 114) |
| 3. d (p. 95) | 13. T (p. 102) | 23. Los Angeles (p. 107) |
| 4. e (p. 95) | 14. T (p. 98) | 24. sheriff's department (p. 106) |
| 5. a (p. 105) | 15. F (p. 102) | 25. community correctional center (p. 114) |
| 6. c (p. 99) | 16. F (p. 103) | 26. substance abuse (p. 101) |
| 7. e (p. 98) | 17. T (p. 101) | 27. mental health (p. 101) |
| 8. a (p. 102) | 18. F (p. 98) | 28. state prison (p. 99) |
| 9. c (p. 96) | 19. F (p. 98) | 29. SORT (p. 108) |
| 10. d (p. 101) | 20. F (p. 100) | 30. supervised pretrial release (p. 113) |

## Chapter 6: State and Federal Prisons

| Multiple Choice | True or False | Fill In the Blanks |
|---|---|---|
| 1. a (p. 122) | 11. F (p. 134) | 21. Texas (p. 127) |
| 2. c (p. 123) | 12. F (p. 139) | 22. maximum (p. 123) |
| 3. a (p. 123) | 13. F (p. 134) | 23. Philadelphia (p. 121) |
| 4. c (p. 134) | 14. T (p. 137) | 24. federal (p. 137) |
| 5. c (p. 137) | 15. T (p. 139) | 25. UNICOR (p. 136) |
| 6. e (p. 141) | 16. T (p. 122) | 26. high (p. 139) |
| 7. a (p. 133) | 17. F (p. 125) | 27. James V. Bennett (p. 136) |
| 8. d (p. 134) | 18. T (p. 121) | 28. Mexico (p. 141) |
| 9. b (p. 130) | 19. T (p. 124) | 29. military (p. 134-5) |
| 10. b (p. 125) | 20. F (p. 127) | 30. Oakdale (p. 138) |

## Chapter 7: Management and Custody

| Multiple Choice | True or False | Fill In the Blanks |
|---|---|---|
| 1. b (p. 164) | 11. F (p. 158) | 21. George Beto (p. 157) |
| 2. a (p. 159) | 12. F (p. 159) | 22. new (or incoming) (p. 159) |
| 3. a (p. 169) | 13. F (p. 157) | 23. overcrowding and gangs (p. 163) |
| 4. d (p. 170) | 14. F (p. 167) | 24. the count (p. 160) |
| 5. e (p. 167) | 15. T (p. 165) | 25. autocratic (p. 153 |
| 6. b (p. 159) | 16. F (p. 165) | 26. contraband (p. 160) |
| 7. e (p. 161) | 17. F (p. 161) | 27. CERT (p. 162) |
| 8. c (p. 166) | 18. T (p. 165) | 28. Thomas Mott Osborne (p. 154) |
| 9. a (p. 160) | 19. T (p. 168) | 29. MBWA (p. 151) |
| 10. c (p. 156) | 20. F (p. 162) | 30. open (p. 162) |

## Chapter 8: Corrections Policies and Issues

| Multiple Choice | True or False | Fill In the Blanks |
|---|---|---|
| 1. b (p. 190) | 11. F (p. 180) | 21. Certification (p. 179) |
| 2. a (p. 183) | 12. F (p. 183) | 22. Corrections Corporation of America (p. 195) |
| 3. d (p. 179) | 13. T (p. 185) | 23. less eligibility (p. 185) |
| 4. d (p. 179) | 14. F (p. 186) | 24. underclass (p. 182) |
| 5. c (p. 194) | 15. F (p. 177) | 25. three (p. 199) |
| 6. b (p. 193) | 16. F (p. 193) | 26. beyond rehabilitation (p. 202) |
| 7. c (p. 187) | 17. F (p. 187) | 27. convict leasing (p. 194) |
| 8. c (p. 183) | 18. F (p. 190) | 28. MDR (p. 183) |
| 9. e (p. 184) | 19. F (p. 193) | 29. front-end (p. 187) |
| 10. e (p. 187) | 20. F (p. 198) | 30. slaves of the state (p. 194) |

## Chapter 9: Male and Female Prisoners

| Multiple Choice | True or False | Fill In the Blanks |
|---|---|---|
| 1. b (p. 224) | 11. F (p. 228) | 21. drug (p. 226) |
| 2. e (p. 228) | 12. F (p. 226) | 22. 7 (p. 212) |
| 3. b (p. 224) | 13. T (p. 222) | 23. functionally illiterate (p. 213) |
| 4. a (p. 223) | 14. T (p. 210) | 24. murder (p. 210) |
| 5. b (p. 214) | 15. F (p. 224) | 25. hidden (p. 224) |
| 6. c (p. 219) | 16. F (p. 213) | 26. liberation (p. 226) |
| 7. d (p. 212) | 17. T (p. 232) | 27. parenting (p. 228) |
| 8. b (p. 210) | 18. F (p. 216) | 28. transinstitutionalization (p. 232) |
| 9. e (p. 216) | 19. F (p. 214) | 29. women (p. 224-5) |
| 10. d (p. 209) | 20. F (p. 232) | 30. cycle of violence (p. 216) |

## Chapter 10: Prison Life

| Multiple Choice | True or False | Fill In the Blanks |
|---|---|---|
| 1. e (p. 263) | 11. T (p. 255) | 21. vengeful equity (p. 259) |
| 2. b (p. 269) | 12. T (p. 261) | 22. state raised (p. 248) |
| 3. b (p. 242) | 13. F (p. 267) | 23. Rape (p. 267) |
| 4. a (p. 246) | 14. T (p. 271) | 24. Santa Fe (p. 263) |
| 5. c (p. 247) | 15. F (p. 242) | 25. furloughs (p. 267) |
| 6. a (p. 248) | 16. F (p. 265) | 26. argot (p. 242) |
| 7. a (p. 243) | 17. F (p. 269) | 27. deprivation (p. 246) |
| 8. b (p. 258) | 18. F (p. 263) | 28. security threat groups (p. 268) |
| 9. d (p. 249) | 19. T (p. 244) | 29. goon squad (p. 260) |
| 10. c (p. 247) | 20. T (p. 270) | 30. square (p. 248 and 256) |

## Chapter 11: Special Needs Prisoners

| Multiple Choice | True or False | Fill In the Blanks |
|---|---|---|
| 1. b (p. 285) | 11. F (p. 283) | 21. chancery court (p. 283) |
| 2. c (p. 283) | 12. F (p. 287) | 22. house of refuge (p. 289) |
| 3. c (p. 284) | 13. F (p. 284) | 23. Juvenile Justice and Delinquency Prevention (p. 287) |
| 4. a (p. 287) | 14. F (p. 297) | 24. mental hospital (p. 295) |
| 5. c (p. 294) | 15. F (p. 304) | 25. geriatric (p. 316) |
| 6. c (p. 297) | 16. F (p. 313) | 26. rehabilitation (p. 286) |
| 7. a (p. 307) | 17. T (p. 302) | 27. insane (p. 294) |
| 8. e (p. 295) | 18. F (p. 305) | 28. sex (p. 310) |
| 9. a (p. 304) | 19. F (p. 303) | 29. substance abuse (p. 299) |
| 10. e (p. 297) | 20. F (p. 287) | 30. sexually violent persons (p. 309) |

## Chapter 12: Prisoners' Rights

| Multiple Choice | True or False | Fill In the Blanks |
|---|---|---|
| 1. d (p. 326) | 11. F (p. 335) | 21. pardon (p. 364) |
| 2. d (p. 341) | 12. F (p. 343) | 22. religious (p. 341) |
| 3. e (p. 339) | 13. F (p. 335) | 23. contraband (p. 343) |
| 4. b (p. 357) | 14. T (p. 357) | 24. firearms possession (p. 358) |
| 5. b (p. 360) | 15. F (p. 364) | 25. judge (or courts) (p. 360 and 364) |
| 6. e (p. 346) | 16. F (p. 360) | 26. civil rights (p. 332) |
| 7. b (p. 357) | 17. T (p. 349) | 27. civil death (p. 325) |
| 8. d (p. 337) | 18. F (p. 330) | 28. sexually violent predators (SVPs) (p. 361) |
| 9. a (p. 327) | 19. T (p. 352) | 29. Fourteenth (p. 330) |
| 10. b (p. 353) | 20. F (p. 340) | 30. consent decree (p. 334) |

## Chapter 13: Rehabilitation

| Multiple Choice | True or False | Fill In the Blanks |
|---|---|---|
| 1. c (p. 398) | 11. T (p. 402) | 21. black box (p. 383) |
| 2. d (p. 396) | 12. T (p. 386) | 22. educational (p. 384) |
| 3. b (p. 377) | 13. F (p. 378) | 23. medical (p. 376) |
| 4. e (p. 398) | 14. F (p. 379) | 24. rehabilitation (p. 374) |
| 5. a (p. 401) | 15. T (p. 381) | 25. crimogenic (p. 378) |
| 6. c (p. 372) | 16. F (p. 385) | 26. planned intervention (p. 382) |
| 7. e (p. 397) | 17. F (p. 396) | 27. group therapy (p. 390) |
| 8. c (p. 380) | 18. T (p. 390) | 28. psychoanalysis (p. 388) |
| 9. b (p. 390) | 19. F (p. 387) | 29. community of peers (p. 391) |
| 10. c (p. 374) | 20. T (p. 400) | 30. cognitive (p. 396) |

## Chapter 14: Parole and Release from Prison

| Multiple Choice | True or False | Fill In the Blanks |
|---|---|---|
| 1. a (p. 437) | 11. F (p. 413) | 21. surveillance (or law enforcement) (p. 453) |
| 2. d (p. 416) | 12. F (p. 420) | 22. governor (p. 423) |
| 3. c (p. 428) | 13. F (p. 431) | 23. pardon (p. 413) |
| 4. c (p. 413) | 14. T (p. 426) | 24. good time (p. 421) |
| 5. c (p. 444) | 15. T (p. 415) | 25. technical (p. 434) |
| 6. b (p. 419) | 16. T (p. 413) | 26. employment (or job placement) (p. 445) |
| 7. c (p. 435) | 17. T (p. 422) | 27. mandatory parole (or mandatory release) (p. 415) |
| 8. d (p. 421) | 18. F (p. 433) | 28. prisoner reintegration (p. 447) |
| 9. e (p. 434) | 19. T (p. 444-5) | 29. marked men (p. 426) |
| 10. c (p. 420) | 20. F (p. 416-7) | 30. lifers (p. 430) |

## Chapter 15: Probation and Community Corrections

| Multiple Choice | True or False | Fill In the Blanks |
|---|---|---|
| 1. a (p. 489-90) | 11. T (p. 486) | 21. detainer (p. 472) |
| 2. e (p. 494) | 12. F (p. 494) | 22. supervision (p. 459) |
| 3. c (p. 495) | 13. F (p. 465) | 23. John Augustus (p. 460) |
| 4. d (p. 461) | 14. F (p. 470) | 24. probation revocation (p. 472) |
| 5. b (p. 492) | 15. T (p. 475) | 25. presentence investigation (p. 463) |
| 6. e (p. 459) | 16. T (p. 479) | 26. reinventing (p. 478) |
| 7. d (p. 482) | 17. F (p. 470) | 27. community correctional center (p. 494) |
| 8. d (p. 482) | 18. F (p. 495) | 28. community residential center (p. 488) |
| 9. c (p. 482) | 19. F (p. 484) | 29. net widening (p. 492) |
| 10. a (p. 466-7) | 20. F (p. 483-4) | 30. community service (p. 483) |

## Chapter 16: Contrasting Philosophies: American and International Corrections Today

| Multiple Choice | True or False | Fill In the Blanks |
|---|---|---|
| 1. c (p. 529) | 11. F (p. 517) | 21. Gulag (p. 518) |
| 2. d (p. 511) | 12. F (p. 509) | 22. ombudsman (p. 512) |
| 3. b (p. 543) | 13. T (p. 522-3) | 23. yanda (p. 527) |
| 4. a (p. 514) | 14. F (p. 547) | 24. England (p. 511) |
| 5. d (p. 527) | 15. F (p. 532) | 25. reintegration (p. 517) |
| 6. a (p. 520) | 16. T (p. 546-7) | 26. labor (p. 525) |
| 7. e (p. 531) | 17. F (p. 537) | 27. day fine (p. 516) |
| 8. b (p. 502) | 18. F (p. 508) | 28. privatization (p. 515) |
| 9. d (p. 506) | 19. F (p. 536) | 29. Russia (p. 519) |
| 10. c (p. 525) | 20. T (p. 506-7) | 30. Finland (p. 534) |